THE OUTER LIMITS

The first TV show to truly showcase startling visual effects, *The Outer Limits* was the creative seedbed for many of the people and techniques that later made *Star Wars* and *Star Trek* household words.

Now a recognized classic, the show combined a phenomenal range of talents, including makeup expert John Chambers *(Planet of the Apes)*, director Byron Haskin *(War of the Worlds)*, and a singular special effects conglomerate called Project Unlimited. Among its stars were Robert Duvall, Martin Sheen, Sally Kellerman, Chita Rivera and William Shatner.

This official guide tells the whole remarkable story, from the show's genesis, through the snags and successes of production, to the stormy end in 1965. Embellished with commentary by the program's prime movers, Leslie Stevens and Joseph Stefano, this unique overview provides the plotlines, credits and production background on each of the 49 episodes, as well as information on the show's spinoffs, from pilot films to bubblegum cards.

Comprehensive and irreplaceable, THE OUTER LIMITS is a rich, nostalgic memoir, an authoritative record, and an exciting journey back to the Golden Age when television and imagination were not strangers to each other...

THE OFFICIAL COMPANION

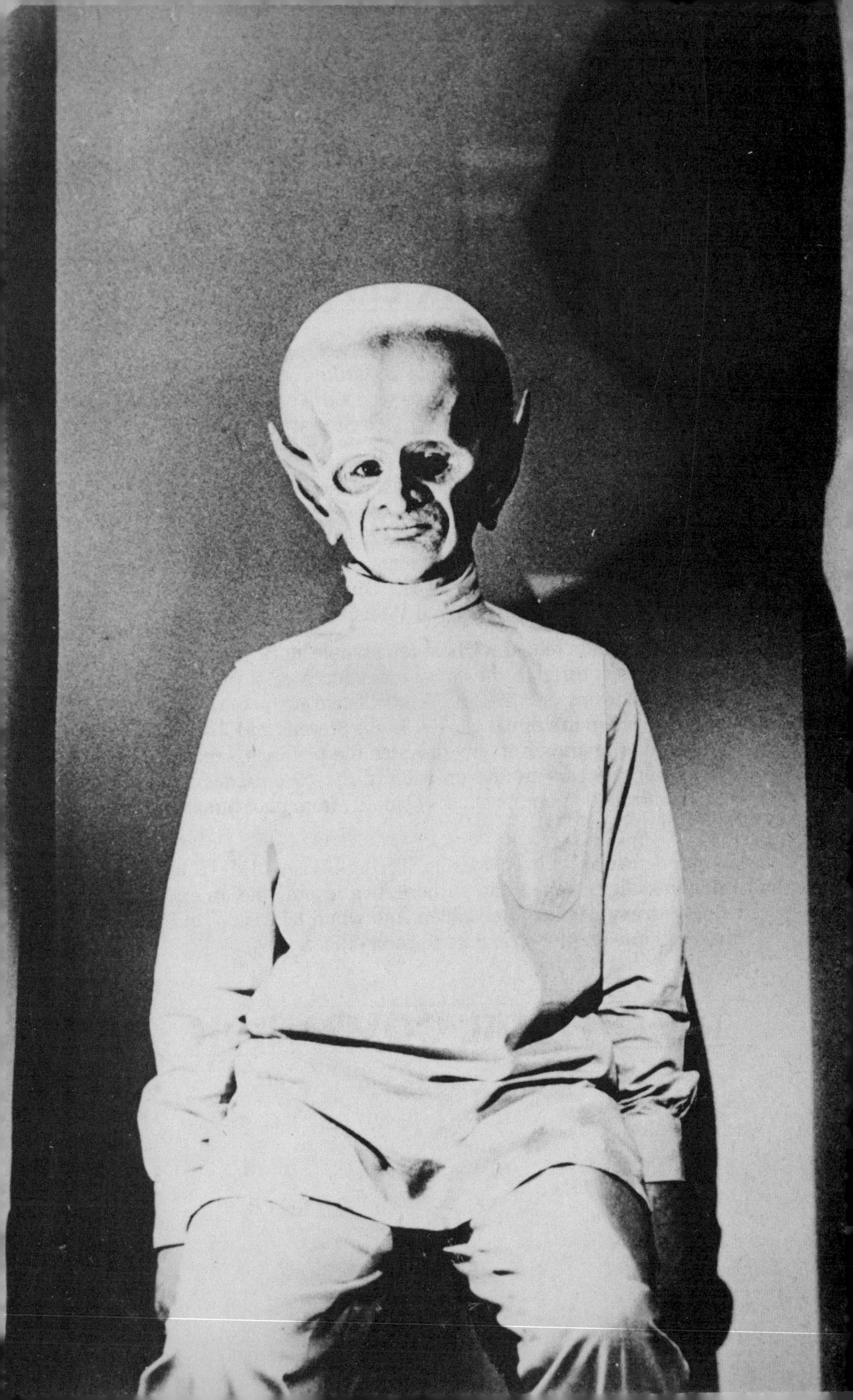

THE OUTER LIMITS

The Official Companion

David J. Schow and Jeffrey Frentzen

ACE SCIENCE FICTION BOOKS
NEW YORK

THE OUTER LIMITS:
THE OFFICIAL COMPANION

An Ace Science Fiction Book/published by arrangement with the authors

PRINTING HISTORY
Ace Science Fiction trade paperback edition/December 1986

Cover concept by David J. Schow.
Cover design by Gene Mydlowski.
Text design by Ernie Haim.

ISBN 0-441-37081-0

Ace Science Fiction Books are published by
The Berkley Publishing Group,
200 Madison Avenue, New York, New York 10016.
PRINTED IN THE UNITED STATES OF AMERICA

Acknowledgments

The book you now hold in your hands really has been *years* in the making, as they used to say in those old colossal/stupendous/gigantic movie extravaganzas. We did not intend it to be. But.

Applause, if you please, for our cast of thousands.

Above all, our deepest possible thanks go to Leslie Stevens and Joseph Stefano, who patiently endured repeated and often exhaustive delving into their pasts, and without whose kindness and assistance this book could not exist. Without their pioneering approach to television, you would be holding air right now, and we hope we've done their work some justice. Few words are comprehensive enough to convey the debt of gratitude we owe Murray Oken, formerly Western Division director of United Artists Television, who contributed selflessly to the project in its early stages. Special thanks, too, to Marilyn Stefano, who is a great hostess.

We must also thank the people who worked on *The Outer Limits* or with its creators, who accommodated many arcane questions and generously supplied information, referrals, photographs or other unique production materials from the program: Allan Balter, Claude Binyon, Jr., Orin Borsten, Ben Brady, John Brahm, Johnny Chambers, Wah Ming Chang, Francis Cockrell, Oliver Crawford, Robert Culp, Jim Danforth, Robert C. Dennis, Meyer Dolinsky, Richard Dorso, David Duncan, John Elizalde, Sidney Ellis, Harlan Ellison, John Erman, Roger A. Farris, Joanna Frank, James Goldstone, Conrad Hall, Byron Haskin (we miss you, Bunn), Robert Cleveland Johnson, Robert H. Justman, Lee H. Katzin, Milton Krims, Anthony Lawrence, Paul LeBaron, Seeleg Lester, Stephen Lord, Elaine Michea, Ib Melchior, David McCallum, Lou Morheim, Sam Neuman, John M. Nickolaus, Gerd Oswald, William P. Owens, Lindsley Parsons, Jr., B. Ritchie Payne, Kenneth Peach, Vic Perrin, Fred B. Phillips, John S. "Jack" Poplin, Dean Riesner, Ralph Rodine, Jerome Ross, Donald S. Sanford, Tom Selden, Jerry Sohl, Ellis St. Joseph, Harry Thomas, Gene Warren, Sr., Grace Lee Whitney, and Ben Wright.

We are also obliged to many people you may not know, who supplied data, entrusted us with rare or one-of-a-kind *Outer Limits* memorabilia (either from their personal collections or by digging them up with Egyptologist fervor), or otherwise helped the project along with their talents, encouragements and advice: T. E. D. Klein, Grant Christian, Dave Ayres, Douglas Barrett Anthony Jones, Forrest J. Ackerman, Robert Sabat, Jim and Elizabeth Trupin, the ever-patient Peggy Sniderman, Marc Scott Zicree, Gerald Hurley, Leo Leiber, Sandra Dodd, Terry Knipe, Shannon Parr and Cathi Milandin, Bob Reed, Gary Gerani, Bob Skotak, Gene Trindl, Paul Coltrin, Kevin Danzey,

Jim Rondeau, Terry Kepner, Abel P. Mills, Jeffrey Talbot, Harry West of KZAZ-TV, Ted Bohus, Susan Dalton of the University of Wisconsin, Tim Murphy, Jim Mathenia, James H. Burns, Marcus Nickerson, James M. Elrod, Andrew Sniderman, Dr. James A. Corrick, Curt Stubbs, Mark Kligman, Jon and Joan Rosen, Trini Ruiz, Randy Martin, Sharon Emily, Lea Braff, Mick Garris, Richard Curtis, Lea E. Harp, Jerry Neely, Dave Ichikawa, Jeff Weinstein, Brian Mathie, Karl Miller, Bill Warren, Darren Raley, Larry Rapchak, Mon Ayash, Joel Schulman and the jolly crew at Schulman Lab, John Windsor, John Javna, Gary Dumm, Nader Gabbai, Melissa Ann Singer, Ginjer Buchanan, John Rounds, Bob Martin and Dave Everitt (formerly of *Fangoria* magazine), Colleen Malone and Mark Hoist of MGM/United Artists, and the very demented folks at WERS-FM in Cambridge, and KXLU-FM in Los Angeles.

Finally, our thanks to the brigade of attorneys who helped us navigate choppy seas: Cynthia Webb and Richard Weltman, Herbert Nusbaum of MGM/UA, Thomas L. Scheussler, and David Siff.

Thank you all, ladies and gentlemen.

—DJS
JF

Dedicated to Connie Hall and Murray Oken

—JF

For Gisela Waltraud Hofmeister and George James Siebert. And, of course, for Murray.

—DJS

Contents

Introduction

There is nothing wrong with your television set...

As recited weekly by the omnipresent, yet never-glimpsed Control Voice, the opening narration for *The Outer Limits* has one of the highest recognition factors of any catch-phrase in the history of television. Today, the Control Voice seems familiar, like an old friend. In the early 1960s, it was new and decidedly odd. Here was a TV show "host" you could not see, and who might be a ghost, or a machine, or possibly an alien being. It was stuff that was not normal.

The central figures in the landscape of commercial TV at this time were a motley bunch. Our medical horizons were being defined by a pair of doctors named Kildare and Casey, the latter with the hopeful implications of his chalkboard infinity symbol. Legal fireball Perry Mason shared a caseload with *The Defenders* and a more vigorous, "now" gang who staffed a combination cop show/gavel opera called *Arrest and Trial.* Vic Morrow was still slugging it out with the Nazis on *Combat!* while *McHale's Navy* yucked it up in the Pacific Theatre. Sid Caesar and Joey Bishop were the kings of TV comedy. Fred Flintstone was in prime time. Variety shows toplined Ed Sullivan, Jackie Gleason, Danny Kaye, and a newcomer—a lanky, country-boy type named Jimmy Dean (in his pre-sausage days) abetted by one of the first Muppets, a ragged hound dog named Rowlf, whose canine contemporary, Lassie, was a biggie on Sunday nights as a lead-in to Walt Disney's program. The Clampett family was entrenched in their Beverly Hills manse, the fragile beauty of Inger Stevens graced *The Farmer's Daughter,* youth rebellion consisted of Fred MacMurray getting his best tie ruined by one of *My Three Sons,* and George C. Scott was in the midst of his acclaimed *East Side/West Side* series. Audiences were presumed to be singing along with Mitch Miller, dancing to Lawrence Welk, and being caught unawares by Allen Funt's obnoxiously intrusive *Candid Camera.* 1963 was the heyday of the western, and TV's most popular cowpokes included Matt Dillon and his deputy Chester, the whole Cartwright clan, the steer-punchers of *Rawhide* (including Clint Eastwood as the ramrod), and the pilgrims of *Wagon Train.*

The days of *Playhouse 90* had come to an end, and many anthology shows (shows without continuing week-to-week characters) had bitten the stage dust. In 1963, *Kraft Suspense Theatre* gave the format a last try, as did *Chrysler Theatre,* with host Bob Hope. *The Bell Telephone*

Hour was still around. Alfred Hitchcock had begun his ninth year of intoning "Good *Ev*ening" prior to the weekly mayhem on the program bearing his name. Suspense and the supernatural were a dead issue as far as *Thriller* (hosted by Boris Karloff) was concerned; that series had expired the previous year. Sporadic forays into science fiction were still being made by *The Twilight Zone*—generally very basic tales founded on the staples of science fiction literature, supplied with twist endings, scripted by the top fantasists of the period, and bracketed by the unforgettable presence of Rod Serling.

Apart from these shows, the history of science fiction on TV had been a dismal one indeed.

Tales of Tomorrow had touched on sf themes now and then, but its stilted, two-act format was reminiscent of a high school play. Ziv/UATV's *Men Into Space* was mostly concerned with the *Destination: Moon* angle, featuring rock-jawed space pioneers beset by meteor storms and depletions of precious fuel. When an anthology show made a stab at the genre, it usually followed this lead, as with a *Desilu Playhouse* segment, "Man in Orbit," which starred Lee Marvin as an astronaut. Science fiction was best served, it seemed, by the police-procedural approach used by Trueman Bradley for *Science Fiction Theatre,* which gave us dramas of chemical mixes and the laws of physics. The alternative was the rash of heavily militarized, proto-*Star Trek* space operas that had overrun the tube since 1949, and *Captain Video*. In his jetwash came *Tom Corbett, Space Cadet* (1950), *Space Patrol* (1951), *Rod Brown of the Rocket Rangers* and *Rocky Jones, Space Ranger* (both 1953), *Atom Squad* (1953), and *Commando Cody, Captain Z-RO* and *Jet Jackson, Flying Commando* (all 1955).

Although *The Outer Limits* could be considered a stepchild of Rod Serling's, a more direct conceptual antecedent can be found in the short-lived *Way Out* (1961), which was hosted by fantasy writer Roald Dahl. *Way Out* featured supernatural horror tales, frequently with downbeat endings, and outrageous monsters created by makeup artist Dick Smith—presaging the moody Gothic climate and bizarre beings that would become the backbone of *The Outer Limits*.

The earliest publicity for *The Outer Limits* did use the *Science Fiction Theatre* approach as a selling point:

> Each episode of *The Outer Limits* begins with a scientific fact. That fact is dramatized, illumined, projected into the Future and developed into a highly imaginative yet believable adventure... the swift developments in space, electronics, "miracle" medicine and atomics provide fresh stimuli for the creative dramatist, and bring "the unknown" more frighteningly close, more fascinatingly real.

Fortunately, the show shook off this dependency on textbook science early on, though its creator would remain intrigued by (and base most of his scripts on) hard science. *The Outer Limits'* initial promotion was actually less concerned with hewing to the boundaries of known technology than in providing the network brass with a template they could easily recognize, a past series to which *The Outer Limits* could favorably be compared. The brochures also promised the heady menu of "new worlds beyond reality; sights and sounds never before experienced; adventures of the innermost mind, the farthest galaxies, and all that lies between."

Twilight Zone's true province was fantasy, although it, too, is most often labeled science fiction. More importantly, it was a hit. "It was a prestigious show from the moment it went on the air," said John Erman, who worked as a casting director for both programs. "Rod was one of the most celebrated writers of his day; the show got good ratings and terrific acclaim." For the ABC network brass, then, comparison of *The Outer Limits* to Serling's show could only be beneficial. Once it secured a slot in prime time, *The Outer Limits* found its own way, but in retrospect the points of similarity shared by the two are intriguing to note.

By modern standards, both have two strikes against them by being black-and-white anthology shows, which means no color, and no continuing characters. *The Outer Limits'* third strike was that it comprised a TV syndication package of a scant forty-nine one-hour episodes. If it was "stripped" by local affiliates in syndication (that is, run daily on weekdays, or five times per week), it would barely provide two months of nonrepeating program material. Run once weekly, it could stretch to a year... almost.

Yet *The Outer Limits* and *The Twilight Zone* share a rare distinction among programs that have grown popular in syndication: They have been *in* syndication continuously ever since their network cancellations. Technically, neither show has been off the air since its inception. Apart from the rejuvenation of endless reruns, both shows have also gained the kind of immortality Joseph Heller unknowingly achieved when he coined the phrase *Catch-22*—a permanent place in the contemporary idiom.

Episodes from one series are frequently misremembered as being from the other. When the *Reader*, a Los Angeles tabloid, polled pedestrians as to their favorite TV reruns, they got the following recap from a young salesgirl:

> The old *Twilight Zone*s were scary even though they were in black and white. There was one episode I'll *never* forget... about a crazy scientist who creates a species of wild lizard people who use boomerangs with serrated edges. Then he puts two humans out into the swamp with them to see what will happen. The girl is always falling and twisting her leg. It's frightening, but I think they finally hack and slash their way out.

Well, not exactly. The plot described is that of an *Outer Limits* episode titled "Fun and Games"—slightly modified.

Outer Limits' most germane similarity to its half-hour predecessor was that it was blessed with extraordinarily innovative founders. The people in the key production positions were writers before becoming producers, and what Rod Serling was to *The Twilight Zone,* Leslie Stevens and Joseph Stefano were to *The Outer Limits*. Their series would blend science fiction and Gothic horror in literate teleplays, well-filmed *as* film, eschewing the prosaic techniques of TV and running contrary to the medium's entropic flow of dullness. The anthology format (held in such dread by the continuing-character orientation at the networks) lent itself uncommonly well to groundbreaking treatments of fantastic material. Themes so basic that they have since become the genre's cliches would be unveiled for the first time on TV. The show would be received as an alien element in the monochrome landscape of commercial TV, and its "numbers" would insist that it was not a success. More than two decades later, however, people are still watching it, and time has offered the acknowledgments of popularity and artistic success. In 1983 the series made the "Critic's Choice" section of *Video Review* after Stephen King, in his informal, book-length survey of the horror field, *Danse Macabre,* called it "the best program of its type ever to run on network TV."

For most viewers, the hallmarks of *The Outer Limits* were its more well-remembered monsters—the shimmering, mouthless Andromedan visitor of "The Galaxy Being," the antlike extraterrestrial bad boys who were "The Zanti Misfits," or the swollen-forebrained, pointy-eared superintellect of the far future presented in "The Sixth Finger"—as well as the Control Voice's cadenced invitation to venture *"from the inner mind to*... The Outer Limits." For the casual TV fan, this show was obviously not coming from the same place as *Bonanza* or *The Beverly Hillbillies*. To find out exactly where it did come from, we must delve into some unusual lives and the formation of one *very* unusual production company.

Consider this book a conduit back to a singular period in the TV timeline—the end of the so-called Golden Age, the genesis of televised science fiction and fantasy, and the inception of a series that has admirably withstood the harsh tests of time and video technology.

In the words of the Control Voice, you are about to participate in a great adventure.

PART ONE

The Awe and Mystery of the Universe

FADE IN: NEW YORK CITY–EARLY 1963

The Chairman of the Board of ABC Television takes his seat in the screening room along with the President of the network and representatives from a major film studio. They have assembled at the network headquarters to view yet another in a long string of pilot films—series hopefuls for the forthcoming TV season. Three producers have flown in from Los Angeles with this latest film, promising the executives "a drama of the Unusual, the Surprising, the Almost Incredible." The creator of the pilot, the man who thought it up, wrote it, and directed it, trades a look of cautious optimism with his two fellow producers, then smiles. Everyone in Hollywood has warned them that a science-fiction series just "won't go" with the brass. His expression says "well, we'll just see about that little rule," as the house lights DIM DOWN.

CLOSE-UP: THE PREVIEW SCREEN

As it is lit up with a weird, dreamy SINE-WAVE PATTERN, fluctuating hypnotically. An authoritative but gentle voice addresses the audience.

CONTROL VOICE
(commanding yet somehow comforting)

There is nothing wrong with your television set. Do not attempt to adjust the picture. We are controlling transmission. If we wish to make it louder, we will bring up the volume. If we wish to make it softer, we will tune it to a whisper. We will control the horizontal. We will control the vertical. We can roll the image; make it flutter. We can change the focus to a soft blur, or sharpen it to crystal clarity. For the next hour, sit quietly and we will control all that you see and hear. We repeat: There is nothing wrong with your television set. You are about to experience the awe and mystery which reaches from the inner mind to outer space. PLEASE STAND BY...

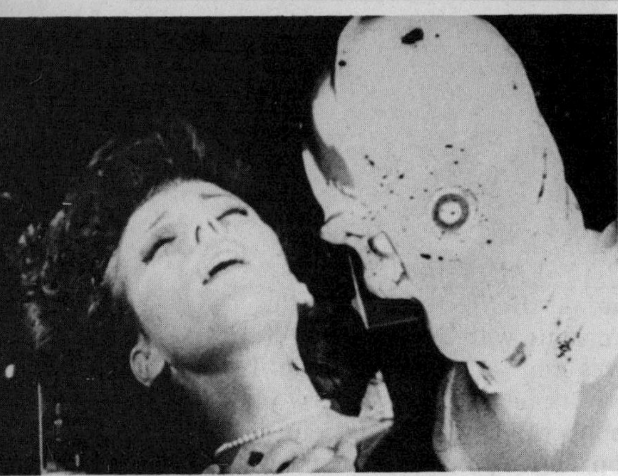

"The Galaxy Being" cauterizes a bullet wound sustained by Jacqueline Scott.

PLEASE STAND BY (pilot title) THE GALAXY BEING (premiere episode title)

Broadcast 16 September 1963
Written and Directed by Leslie Stevens
Assistant Director: Robert Justman
Director of Photography: John Nickolaus

CAST: Allan Maxwell (Cliff Robertson), Carol Maxwell (Jacqueline Scott), Andromedan Being (William O. Douglas, Jr. and Charles MacQuarry), Gene "Buddy" Maxwell (Lee Philips), Loreen (Allyson Ames), Caretaker Collins (Roy Sickner), State Trooper (James Frawley), National Guard Major (Bill Catching), Policeman (Allen Pinson). WITH: Polly Burson, May Boss, Don Harvey, Mavis Neal, William Stevens, Peter Madsen.

Cottage-industry inventor Allan Maxwell has built a high-powered transceiving device adjacent to his commercial radio station, and on it scans "three-dimensional static" that resolves into the image of an alien who hails from the Andromeda galaxy. Using a translating computer, Allan discovers that the Being is a tinkerer, much like himself, and they find time for a brief exchange of ideas before an unavoidable social commitment prompts Allan to leave temporarily. A snafu at the radio station during his absence causes his scanner to teleport the Being to Earth, where with its radioactive aura it kills a deejay, fries the station's caretaker, and wreaks havoc as it searches for Allan to help it. By the time Allan is able to conduct the creature back to his transmission shack, the police and National Guard have been called out. When a trigger-happy sheriff accidentally wounds Allan's wife, the Being cauterizes the wound with radiation and saves her life. Then it confronts its would-be destroyers with a show of force by wiping out the radio tower with a wave of its hand. "I warn you," it tells the crowd, "there are powers in the Universe beyond anything you know. There is much you have to learn. You must explore. You must reach out. Go to your homes—go and give thought to the mysteries of the Universe. I will leave you now... in peace." It reveals to Allan that since it has violated a law prohibiting contact with destructive societies (such as Earth), it will be destroyed by its own race. It cannot stay, and it cannot return home. Moving back into the workshop, it says, "End of transmission"... and then tunes itself out of existence by turning down the transmitter power.

> *The planet Earth is a speck of dust, remote and alone in the void. There are powers in the universe inscrutable and profound. Fear cannot save us. Rage cannot help us. We must see the stranger in a new light—the light of understanding. And to achieve this, we must begin to understand ourselves, and each other.*

Network executives are notoriously critical audiences, and this pilot film, with its dazzling alien, its visual/aural assault on the senses, its cosmic plot, and its offbeat Control Voice, might have been too much to digest in a single great gulp. No one in the screening room was more interested in finding out the reactions of the brass than the man who had conceived the whole project. To him, "Please Stand By" wasn't just science fiction and wasn't just another series pilot. This man was pitching a *philosophy.*

The Leslie Stevens Story

> One of the things that make me know *The Outer Limits* was ahead of its time was the restraint placed upon it by the network, by money, by time, keeping it from having its full shot. It's like something trying to peck its way out of an egg, only the shell is too hard. Let that shell crack open, and it will all begin to happen.
>
> —Leslie Stevens

Conversation with Leslie Clark Stevens III can be a spellbinding, disorienting thing. A keen-eyed, sharply cut, infectiously self-assured man, he speaks—or rather, he divulges information—in low, rhythmic, carefully-measured units, as though aware his mind is ramming ahead full-tilt, and conscious of the need to break his output up into digestible portions so his audience might assimilate it more easily. This process seems to amuse him. But on occasion he'll share the joke.

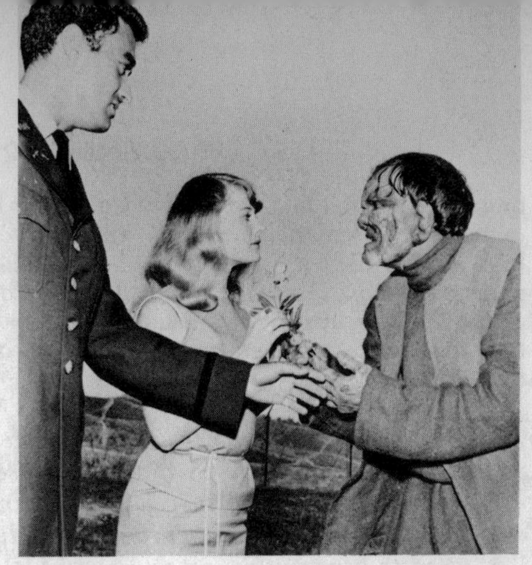

John Considine and Shirley Knight confront Martin Landau as "The Man Who Was Never Born."

"A funny thing happens with imaginative material," he says. "It has to have what I call the taproot into the awe and mystery of the universe, that overtone of truth behind appearances that shows up in all good science fiction. When you start to bullshit science fiction, it goes to pieces *sooo* fast! If you're into the absolute quintessence of the emerging new mythological age, read *Rhythms of Vision* by Blair. He ties together Mitchell, Atlantis, and all those books having to do with cosmic alignment, and the magnetic lines in the Earth, with people like Peter Tompkins—you know, the math that occurs in the Aztec pyramids—and then ties that with forms and resonances, with modern, heavy physics."

Stevens smiles a million-dollar smile. One is tempted to call it a Hollywood smile, the kind intended to melt the heart of a financial backer like sherbet in a microwave oven. "When you tie all that stuff together, you begin to see the dim outline of the Aquarian Age... and that's what *The Outer Limits* did at its best; that's what a good show has to do. If it doesn't tie into the emergence of a new awareness, a new age, then it's off target just enough to be a terrible off-putter."

Stevens, a typically robust Aquarius, was born February 3, 1924, at Walter Reed Hospital in Washington, DC, the only child of Nellie Stevens (nee Milliken) and Leslie Clark Stevens II. His father was a US Navy vice admiral, a graduate of MIT and inventor of the arresting gear used to land jets on aircraft carriers, a naval attaché to Moscow, and an author and artist whose own father, the original Leslie Clark Stevens, had been a Methodist clergyman and missionary.

Stevens describes his father as "very hard-science, but imaginative. He rewarded me with a weekly allowance at the rate of a penny a word for memorizing Shakespeare and the Bible." In 1934, as part of his schooling at Westminster Abbey, the eleven-year-old Leslie also attended performances of Shakespeare at the Old Vic. "As a result of this exposure and incentive," he says, "I decided one afternoon that I was a playwright. I had never written a play, nor *could* I write one."

At fifteen, while attending Western High School in Washington, DC, he entered one of his efforts, "The Mechanical Rat," in a contest sponsored by Orson Welles's Mercury Theatre, which was then touring the nation's capital doing *Henry IV, Part I*. "It was about robots," said Stevens. "It was sort of science fiction, even then! And the prize was to get to hang around with the Mercury Players." Stevens won the competition and immediately began showing up at rehearsals. "Orson started using me as his gofer; I guess he thought I was in the company. I'd get him coffee, a newspaper, stuff like that. And when they left Washington and went to Philadelphia, I just went with them!"

When Stevens' parents next heard from their son, it was by postcard. "They nearly fainted, because they didn't know what had happened to me at first. I told them I was safe, and they could reach me through the Chestnut Street Opera House. I meant that literally, because I was sleeping in a coil of rope up in the fly gallery." Stevens became a stand-in and assistant to lighting expert Jean Rosenthal. During performances, he would don a green doublet for a walk-on role as Hotspur's page. "Anything

"Now tell me: The seventy billion people of Earth—where did they hide?"
Robert Culp and Arline Martel from "Demon With a Glass Hand."

I could do to get an extra eight bucks was worth it. I ate well, because in the Boar's Head Tavern scenes they used real beer, loaves of bread, and cold vegetable soup, so the actors could actually eat something while they were performing. They'd leave all that after every show and I'd eat it every night."

After nearly a month the truant officers showed up to collect him. "But my parents made a deal with them," he recalls. "With their permission, I stayed out of school, provided I'd go to summer school later and graduate, which I finally did." Young Stevens toured with the company for nearly six months, and after graduating, wrote six plays for various summer stock groups.

In 1943 he enlisted in the US Army Air Corps and became an intelligence officer, spending the next three years stationed in Iceland, where he organized small stage entertainments to boost morale. He came out of the service a full captain in 1946, and spent the following year studying at the Yale School of Drama on his GI Bill benefits. Then he moved to New York and began a three-year stint with the American Theatre Wing, becoming a night clerk in a hotel to support himself while writing. At twenty-five he was a night-ward attendant in a psychiatric hospital, and at twenty-eight a copyboy for *Time* magazine. "I had the same job for the same people in both places," he would later remark to *TV Guide*. "They were all in little rooms, ready to jump out the windows, and I had to clean up after them and take them meals." During this time he also wrote eleven new plays, and some experimental ventures and musical revues with a new friend living in Greenwich Village, a songwriter named Joseph Stefano.

Inspired by the positive criticism he received from former teacher Joseph Anthony, himself an accomplished director and actor, Stevens set

Alien extras cavort behind the scenes of "A Feasibility Study."
(Courtesy Forrest J. Ackerman)

out to realize one of his dramas on a stage. The year was 1953 and the play was *Bullfight*. George Axelrod (then famous for *The Seven-Year Itch*), read and invested in the play; other backers followed suit and an equity bond was posted. When Stevens had a nut of $10,000, he mounted the production in the Theatre de Lys, a 299-seat venue in Greenwich Village.

"It's important to note that a Mexican tragedy about bullfighting with no bull involved a definite possibility of failure," Stevens noted wryly. Hurd Hatfield starred as Domingo, a highborn Castilian who falls from grace and destroys the lives of those around him, eventually causing the death of his younger brother (whom he sees as a better version of himself) in the bullring. The play premiered in January, 1954, and the enthusiastic reception afforded it by drama critics impelled it through fifty-six performances.

With his next play, Stevens stepped up to Broadway, as *Champagne Complex* ran for twenty-three nights at the Cort in Manhattan. The "complex" of the title refers to the leading lady's penchant for stripping down to her polka-dot underwear whenever she downs a glass or two of bubbly. Her straitlaced tycoon fiance calls in a "lay psychiatrist" to cure her, and she falls for the shrink after a few more sips and strips. Intended as frothy, double-entendre comedy, it was dismissed as slim and one-note by most critics. It did well enough, however, and kept Stevens in the public eye as a playwright.

Based on his experiences with anti-Communist exiles from the USSR, Stevens' father authored the 1953 bestseller, *Russian Assignment*. The senior Stevens was sometimes spotted by reporters, attending his son's plays. He died in 1956. "I still own his collection of H. G. Wells first editions," said Stevens. "Between us we had thousands of old pulps, *Amazing Stories*, and *Astounding*s."

Stevens' next play was his most ambitious yet, set in twelfth-century France and focusing on the *droit du seigneur,* a medieval custom giving the lord of a manor the right to sleep with the bride of any of his vassals on her wedding night. But *The Lovers* struck out, opening May 10th, 1956, at the Martin Beck Theatre and closing in four days. *Theatre Arts* found some good things to say about it: "[The] performances had an inherent dignity, and even an occasional loftiness, that Hollywood would do well to match when it undertakes this sort of thing, as it so often does." It did. *The Lovers* later became the foundation for the 1956 Charlton Heston epic, *The War Lord,* directed by Franklin Schaffner.

While *Champagne Complex* was still on the boards back East, Stevens broke into TV writing with a script for the prestigious *Four Star Playhouse*. "Award," starring Franchot Tone and Ida Lupino, was broadcast June 30, 1955. He then adapted the 1944 musical *Bloomer Girl* for a *Producers' Showcase* airing on May 28th, 1956. *Kraft Television Theatre* produced his teleplay, "The Duel," the following year, and then came *Playhouse 90*. Stevens' first script for this hallmark anthology series was

"Invitation to a Gunfighter," a hard, dark tale about a town that hires a gunslinger to assassinate an outlaw (it inspired the 1964 Yul Brynner film of the same title). Stevens' subsequent *Playhouse 90*s included "The Violent Heart" (an adaptation of the Daphne Du Maurier story), "The Second Man" (based on the Edward Grierson novel), "Charley's Aunt" and "Rumors of Evening." In "Portrait of a Murderer," Tab Hunter starred in Stevens' study of Donald Bashor, who was executed in 1957.

By 1958, Stevens had made Hollywood his home, sold his first movie script, and had his biggest success on Broadway. The film script was *The Left-Handed Gun*, based on a *Philco TV Playhouse* drama by Gore Vidal titled "The Death of Billy the Kid." A low budget precursor to the nihilist Westerns of the mid-1960s, the film was Arthur Penn's first feature as a director, and Paul Newman repeated the role he had played in the TV version. More of a psychological study than an oat opera, it incorporates realistic violence and an existentialist tone upon which Stevens, a proponent of the New Wave in European cinema, would later rely when filming his darkly disturbing film *Private Property*.

On Broadway, *Marriage-Go-Round* became the pivotal production of Stevens' play-writing career when it commenced a two-year run of 431 performances at the Plymouth Theatre, October 29, 1958. Charles Boyer played an anthropology professor who is visited by the daughter of an old Swedish colleague—a Nordic bombshell (Julie Newmar) bent on seducing him, so that she may bear a child of guaranteed brain power as well as physical superiority. While Stevens' return to the realm of adult comedy did not garner many critical plaudits, his slickly-conceived, risque fable was a tremendous hit with audiences.

Soon 20th Century–Fox was interested in a film version of *Marriage-Go-Round*, and Stevens was forming his own company, Daystar Productions, in partnership with one-time talent agent Stanley Colbert. Daystar's star client was actress Kate Manx—Stevens' second wife, after Ruth Ramsey, whom he'd wed during his salad days in New York and later divorced. While cementing TV and film deals with Fox, Stevens began work on his first independent feature, *Private Property*, while simultaneously preparing a new play about the cosmetics industry, *The Pink Jungle*, for Broadway. By 1959, at age thirty-five, he was pulling down $9,000 per week, and was firmly in his element in Hollywood's pervasive environment of deal-making and high stakes. But was the writing any good?

"There's nothing wrong with being a hack writer," Stevens told *Time* magazine. "I would point with pride to the inspired hacking of Shakespeare, Michelangelo—you can go through a big list. I am a firm believer in Hollywood's golden future, and thumb my nose at those who cry, 'Twilight in the Smog!'" From the moment his father had begun paying him to memorize the Bard, the connection between writing and money was well established in Stevens' consciousness, and he chased his goal

Leslie Stevens (R) discusses the script for his play *Marriage-Go-Round* with stars Charles Boyer and Claudette Colbert in 1958.

relentlessly. "The best artists I know suppress a smile when a member of the audience speaks of their talent or their 'gifts.' I write in longhand, and the pressure of the pencil through the years has created a ridge of callus on my fingers. Whenever I hear talk of talent, the callus seems to throb. But there is another gift—the ability to endure. And endurance and inner conviction, carefully chained to a writing desk, can be a powerful combination." Obligingly, *Time* would dub Stevens a "hot writer-tycoon" and a member of "the new breed; the curious combination of corporation executive and creative artist."

"He was dazzling," recalls John Erman, who linked up with Stevens at Fox. "He was like a blond Orson Welles. He was young, good looking, *very* sure of himself. He had had a terrific success in the theatre, and knew what he wanted and where he wanted to be—a man who was very secure in his craft. I was impressed with him."

Robert Justman, later to work for Daystar on *The Outer Limits,* said of Stevens, "He was quick to smile and had a good sense of humor. A very charming man, enthusiastic and omnivorously interested in everything. I think he was a sort of Renaissance Man. He was always planning, always trying to achieve successful ends, and he sometimes overreached himself. But you don't get anywhere without trying. He affected certain external characteristics. He always wore a black suit—he had a number of them."

"Leslie was an image maker," said Claude Binyon Jr., also soon to sign on with Daystar. "He was one of those guys with a black Lincoln Continental and eight pairs of sunglasses—all black—in the glove compartment, in case one pair got lost or broke or something. I think he wanted to be President of the United States."

True enough, Stevens rarely failed to impress those with whom he dealt in Hollywood. He was a doer, fast and competent, but also forward-thinking and revolutionary. No one knew quite what to expect of this offbeat and visionary young artist.

"Leslie was interested in various philosophies, and was very in charge of his emotions," said Justman. "I think he knew quite a bit about Zen and other Eastern-philosophical-religioso kinds of things. Because he looked so youthful, with his blond hair and fair skin and unblemished complexion, he seemed almost mysterious at times, as if he was ageless, or came from another time, perhaps from the future."

Tom Selden, a production assistant on *Outer Limits*, adds, "Or maybe Leslie just has a portrait in his closet that's very old. . . ."

Daystar Productions

> Basically, I'm a writer. I became a director to protect the writer, and I became a producer to protect both of them, and a company owner to protect them all. The artist is a serious danger in this business. Suddenly an artist will say, "I really *like* this. You guys are telling me to stop at 5:30 and wreck an entire sequence when everything is going great? This might go down in *history,* and you're asking me to save five grand?"
>
> —Leslie Stevens

Throughout his career, Stevens had grown to resent interference from the noncreative backers he calls "producer types"—the executives and money men who frequently dismissed him as a writer-for-hire, appropriated credit they did not earn, or handed down commercially-motivated edicts that hampered his artistic expression. Independent production was the solution and in 1959 the trade papers announced the formation of Daystar Productions.

"It's from Shakespeare," said Stevens. "The star that shines in the day is the sun. I wanted to use 'Solar' but that was already taken by some other company.* I'm a great believer in the 'solar channel,' the realization that the actual body of the sun itself is conscious—not sentient, but conscious. Now, that usually makes people say, 'Holy shit, what's he talking about, and why isn't he in a lunatic asylum?' There's so much to it that to cover it casually in a couple of sentences, won't do it justice. But it will whet your appetite... right?" The logo of the new firm was the sun, surrounded by five stars. Years later, Stevens put an "S" in the center of the sun.

Other "indie-prods" existed at the time, such as Quinn Martin Productions, which turned out *The Untouchables* on the Desilu Studios lot. "We called Daystar 'Hollywood's First Free-Independent' because everyone else, like Quinn, was studio-connected," said Stevens. "We wanted the distinction of not being tied to anyone."

The Stevens-Colbert combine's first production was a film titled *Private Property* (1959), also written and directed by Stevens, who bankrolled it out of his own pocket to the tune of $60,000, and shot most of it at the Hedges Place address he shared with Kate Manx, who starred. The total outlay for sets was $500—one month's rental on the empty home just above Stevens's own. Colbert paid rock-bottom wages to all participants, and overtime to no one. To save more money, they even put used bulbs in the lighting equipment. "On studio sets, it's like one big taxi meter, running all the time," said Stevens, who put both cast *and* crew through two weeks of rigorous rehearsals, then shot the film in ten days.

The story involves two Beat-speaking hoodlums, Duke (Corey Allen) and his impotent, slightly retarded pal Boots (Warren Oates), who victimize a housewife (Kate Manx) entirely at random. Duke's plan is to seduce her, then turn her over to Boots. Both men wind up dead on the bottom of the Stevens' swimming pool. "The seduction-by-proxy campaign inevitably makes one squirm a bit," reported *Newsweek*. "*Property* compels the attention in a way that is almost hypnotic." *Time* said that the film "carried the New Wave crashing into the heart of Hollywood," and the Catholic Church rated it *Condemned*. 20th Century–Fox was impressed by the boxoffice returns of over one million dollars on Stevens's shoestring investment, and quickly tried to interest Daystar in a five-picture deal budgeted at the same figure.

*It was Steve McQueen's Solar Productions.

"I wouldn't touch a big Hollywood picture with a barge pole," Stevens said at the time. "When millions are involved, you have to satisfy the bankers. I want to satisfy myself. I don't need money now; I want freedom—and in the movies you can only have freedom on a low budget." After completing a never-produced murder-on-the-backlot script, *Mask of Terror,* for Fox, Stevens entered into a coproduction deal with them for the film version of *Marriage-Go-Round,* which became one of Walter Lang's last features (he had directed *Tin Pan Alley* and *The King and I*). Julie Newmar reprised her Broadway role while James Mason and Susan Hayward took over the parts played on the stage by Charles Boyer and Claudette Colbert. Stevens had also planned to make a novelization of the story the first publication of Daystar Press, but had to put his literary aspirations on hold. "The disciplines of prose tend to hamper me," he said. "I'm an 'ear' person and I write dialogue and drama far better, I think." Stevens became an author in 1969 with the publication of *EST: The Steersman's Handbook*, under the byline L. Clark Stevens.

In 1962, James Mason coproduced and starred in Daystar's next film, *Hero's Island,* an adventure in which a recently freed indentured servant's family must battle pirates and colonial overseers on an island off the North Carolina coast in 1718. "It was way ahead of its time," said Stevens, "and a true art film, because who the hell would want to see a movie about indentured servants in 1962? It didn't mean anything." It was filmed on Santa Catalina Island, an hour by boat from LA.

Today, independent TV production companies are legion, but in 1962 the story was different. "Daystar was originally formed to make features," said Stevens. "But we discovered that each time we finished a film, we'd lose the whole crew because there was no way to employ them continuously between films. We moved into TV to hold on to the same group of reliable artists. We went to United Artists and said, 'Look, here's a full-fledged production company ready to do stuff. You have anything you want done?'" At UA he met Richard Dorso, a vice president in charge of developing new programming, and was handed a list of series concepts, with instructions to check off whatever ideas struck his fancy as possible Daystar fodder. "One of the items on that list was a thing called *Rodeo*. I checked it off, not realizing that that little mention on the list meant that United Artists would later *own* any show I *ever* did having *anything* to do with rodeo performing, because they had originally 'suggested' it."

"Rodeo, USA" was the pilot teleplay Stevens completed in December, 1961, and it sold a series, *Stoney Burke,* for the 1962–63 season, with UA as the co-owners. Jack Lord played the title character, a rider on the modern-day rodeo circuit, and among his semiregular sidekicks were Warren Oates and Bruce Dern. "The very fact that we turned out shows was staggering to the rest of the industry," notes Stevens. "How in the name of God could a company with no soundstages, no equipment, nothing, deliver first-run, full-production, glossy-gorgeous *stuff*, with photography and casts better than theirs?"

A big part of the answer was found in *Stoney Burke*'s production manager, Lindsley Parsons, Jr., a *Twilight Zone* alumnus who had signed onto "Rodeo, USA" as an assistant director. He had a knack for unearthing inexpensive locations and hammering together shooting stage rental deals on a day-to-day basis with Revue, Fox, and MGM. "*Stoney Burke* was allegedly shot all over the Midwest," said Parsons. "But we shot it mostly in the Santa Clarita Valley, using a bunch of livestock provided by a rodeo supplier who lived next to the Disney Ranch." When Daystar took on *The Outer Limits*, it was Parsons who negotiated a cut-rate deal for the use of the famous MGM backlots, and the soundstages at KTTV–Channel 11 on Sunset Boulevard in downtown Hollywood.

With the *Stoney Burke* deal set at ABC-TV and twenty-eight episodes in production, Daystar moved its headquarters, taking over all four floors of the old Crosby Building at 9028 Sunset Boulevard, strolling distance from such famous industry eateries as Scandia's and the Cock and Bull. Stevens wrote the first eight scripts ("and rewrote most of the others"), and, after bumping Parsons from Assistant Director to Production Manager, set about devising a flock of new series pilots, most of them *Stoney Burke* spin-offs. "The pilots were quality product for the price," said Parsons. "Leslie wanted to become a 'mini-major,' the Spelling-Goldberg of those days." Stevens was shooting for the sort of continuous, multiple-series reputation ultimately enjoyed by his old competitor, Quinn Martin.

Kincaid was begotten of the *Stoney Burke* episode of the same title, and starred Dick Clark and David Winters as youth counselors. It filmed at the Glendale YMCA and the backlot ranch sets at Columbia Studios. Done concurrently with *Kincaid* was *Border Patrol*, based on the "Point of Entry" episode of *Stoney Burke*. It starred William Smith, Cesare Danova, and Antoinette Bower.

Mark Vickers, Master of Weapons (alternately known as *Mr. Vickers*) was a Zen-flavored detective affair starring J. D. Cannon and Keigh Deigh. Spun off from "The Weapons Man" episode, its home location was to be Venice Beach's famous Windward Avenue.

The only pilot not of *Stoney Burke* origin (until another, titled *Stryker*, was done late in 1963) was *Mr. Kingston*, which dealt with espionage, drug-smuggling, and similar action-adventure situations aboard a globe-cruising luxury liner. Filmed aboard the *Dominion Monarch* in Seattle, the pilot starred Walter Pidgeon as the ship's captain, and Peter Graves as the first officer. In anticipation of the series, Stevens considered purchasing an ocean liner that was up for sale in Italy.

But the ship would not be needed. None of Daystar's new pilots found a buyer, and *Stoney Burke* was facing cancellation after only one season on the air. It was at this point Stevens formulated the concept for a science fiction show that would jump far beyond conventional TV fare—just the sort of show that could use fully the talents of the artists and technicians gathered together under the Daystar umbrella, and who were responsible for the high-quality level of the company's product. These were the professionals that Stevens had affectionately dubbed the Blue Ribbon Crew.

The Blue Ribbon Crew

"We were crusaders; we were nuts trying to do television better than anyone else," said Allan Balter, one of Daystar's nucleus of associate producers. "And Leslie wasn't just a producer. He was a guy who wanted to make the world a better place." This sentiment was echoed by nearly all the former employees of Stevens's quirky little independent. They all

Members of Daystar's "Blue Ribbon Crew" meet on the Samuel Goldwyn recording stage. (L-R:) John Elizalde (back turned), Roger Farris, Allan Balter, Ron Silverman, John Erman, Leslie Stevens, who is almost totally obscured by Dominic Frontiere, and (peeking in at edge of frame) Ralph Riskin. (Courtesy Roger A. Farris)

Composer Dominic Frontiere in 1957.

considered Daystar a wild and stimulating place to work, a unique, experimental atmosphere remembered with the sort of fondness reserved for family.

"We had a marvelous crew," said Elaine Michea, the company's Production Coordinator. "Leslie hired very good people, many of them young and just starting out in the industry. It was the same group, basically, throughout both *Stoney Burke* and *The Outer Limits*." Michea had joined Daystar after working for Philip Yordan's Security Pictures in the 1950s, as a production secretary on such films as *Inherit the Wind* and *Studs Lonigan*. "When we did *Marriage-Go-Round*, I was Leslie's secretary," she said. "We had a little office over at Fox." This phase of Daystar consisted of Stevens, Michea, an accountant named Gerry Fischer, and a hotshot young composer named Dominic Frontiere, who became Stevens's new partner in the company after the departure of Stanley Colbert.

Born in 1931 in New Haven, Connecticut, Dom Frontiere had by the age of four studied the violin, piano and accordion. At six he was entertaining regularly at a tavern in the Italian district of his hometown, and at twelve he played the first of four solo engagements at Carnegie Hall. An accordion virtuoso by the time he graduated high school, he replaced Dick Contino in Horace Heidt's Orchestra and toured throughout Europe, Africa, and the Orient. In 1952 he began to study composing under Mario Castelnuovo-Tedesco, conducting under Felix Slatkin, and arranging with Robert Van Eps. He had just turned twenty-one when composer-conductor Alfred Newman, then the music director of 20th Century–Fox, took notice of the ambitious young man and sponsored his education in the arts of music adaptation and arrangement. Within no time Frontiere—always a quick study—was arranging music for such films as *Meet Me in Las Vegas* (1956), *Ten Thousand Bedrooms* (1957) and *The Young Lions* (1958), as well as composing TV music for Ed Sullivan, Steve Allen, Jack Benny, Edgar Bergen, and Dean Martin. In early 1957 he also recorded his first album, *Dom Frontiere Plays the Classics*—all on the accordion. Jazz musician George Shearing noted, "Technically, 'Flight of the Bumblebee' is the high spot, but for an all-round display of taste, 'The Nutcracker Suite' stands out above the rest." The following year, Dominic Frontiere and his Orchestra recorded the album *Pagan Festival*, "An Exotic Love Ritual for Orchestra."

Frontiere had become friends with Stevens while providing the music for *Marriage-Go-Round* in 1960. Their temperaments cleaved neatly; both enjoyed playing the executive game from the inside, like a pair of mischievous kids stowing away aboard a stuffy, straitlaced yacht party. In addition to his passion for composing, Frontiere was also an extraordinarily keen deal maker. "He knows expenditures, and was very talented on the accounting end," says John Elizalde, Daystar's music supervisor. "His whole schtick was, 'I don't want to be a producer, I just want to make the music.' But I'm sure he enjoyed the day-to-day machinations of making Daystar go."

"Dom was into postproduction and music," said Elaine Michea. "And Gerry Fischer was a CPA who was an advisor to Leslie's financial world. I signed the checks and took care of the money." Stevens dealt with story material, with writers and directors, while Frontiere's baliwick was administrative. "Elaine put it all together so we could work," said Stevens. "She did payroll, timecards, bank stubs, and all of the office records, seemingly with ease. She knew the business at a level where she could say, 'Don't hire this person, he drinks too much.'"

Just below this top echelon was a group of titular associate producers that Stevens nicknamed "the Six Bright Young Men," beginning with Leon Chooluck, a Security Pictures veteran and former coworker of Michea's. He had worked on *Private Property, Stoney Burke* and most of the failed pilots. When *Outer Limits* came along, he switched positions with Lindsley Parsons and became production manager. Chooluck helped Michea recruit many of Daystar's "below-the-line" production personnel, and oversaw series production on location while Parsons conducted his negotiations away from the sets. Chooluck was privy to all phases of production from script meetings through shooting, organizing costs and making sure everyone was in the right place at the right time.

The next Bright Young Man was Ralph Riskin, formerly Frontiere's agent. New projects were his specialty, and he also worked on most of Daystar's pilots. Then came Bob Barbash, *Stoney Burke*'s story editor, and Ron Silverman, whose new Daystar title was Vice-President of Administration. He was a marketing and research man who had developed his own private polling system, ANTENA, to compete with the Nielsen ratings. Silverman had also been a writer for *Variety*. Allan Balter's am-

Dominic Frontiere conducts an *Outer Limits* recording session at the Goldwyn Studios. Music Coordinator Roger Farris, wearing sunglasses, is seated behind him.
(Courtesy Roger A. Farris)

bition was to write scripts and produce, he had been a publicity flack for 20th Century–Fox and served the same function at Daystar.

The sixth Bright Young Man, also from Fox, was John Erman. "I had been in an acting class with Jack Lord, who'd signed to star in *Stoney Burke* at the time I was running the casting department at Fox," recalled Erman. "Leslie invited me to be Daystar's casting director. I watched the *Stoney Burke* pilot, and while I thought there were some admirable things about it, I didn't think it was going to succeed. I told Leslie it would be foolhardy for me to leave Fox, where I was an executive with security and benefits. He asked if anything would change my mind, and I told him the *only* thing would be if he allowed me to direct. I had asked to direct episodic TV at Fox, but they were very happy with me right where I was. Leslie said, 'All right, I think you're someone I'd really like to have working with me, and if you'll come over to *Stoney Burke*, I'll let you direct an episode.' I told him he'd better let me direct two, because the first one would be rotten! And he agreed, in a foolhardy sort of way. The Six Bright Young Men really only had one role each. We *did* get the responsibility of associate producership, one out of every six shows. But being very covetous of his power, Leslie did most of that work himself. Our titles were more of an incentive to stretch ourselves."

The AP duties involved script conferences, working with directors and in postproduction. Apart from their principal functions (Erman in casting, Balter in publicity, and so on) each AP served another purpose, since Stevens enjoyed an environment of quick, sharp dreamers and conceptualizers. "One thing that struck me," said Erman, "was that Leslie, who was so obviously Aryan, had surrounded himself with all these aggressive, ambitious young Jewish men." Stevens soon had a chain-of-command chart distributed throughout the offices in the Daystar Building. "It was like a family tree," said Erman, "with Leslie at the top."

"If it was off the wall, Leslie was for it," says John Elizalde. "He instituted a night school at Daystar for learning foreign languages, in anticipation of getting work offers from outside the country. I figured what the hell—we were all there sixteen to twenty hours a day anyway, so why not consider it? Leslie had a dynastic bent, shall we say. He wanted to establish Daystar as the *ne plus ultra* of production houses."

Elizalde was just one of the below-the-line crew, that is, the personnel who transformed ideas into viable filmed product. "At Daystar there were the dreamers and the workers," says Lindsley Parsons. "We never really knew just what it was that the associate producers, or 'ass-prods,' did since we didn't have to go through them to get to Leslie, who would listen to *any* of us. Somehow, he enjoyed absorbing and using, in some small way, input from anyone. He'd take it from the craft servicemen. It was fun to work at Daystar because we had a tremendous amount of freedom." Parsons was brought in by Elaine Michea, along with makeup artist Fred Phillips, master set designer Jack Poplin, and propman "Rapid" Richard Rubin.

In retrospect, Daystar's camera crew is the most impressive ever assembled for TV, and it started with a fellow named Ted McCord. "Ted did *major* movies," said Stevens, "like *Treasure of the Sierra Madre, East of Eden, The Sound of Music,* all of Bette Davis's films including *Dark Victory,* and a lot of Joan Crawford's pictures. You just couldn't get any bigger." McCord shot *Private Property,* then fell ill after filming five *Stoney Burke*s. "On doctor's orders, he couldn't work," recalls Lindsley Parsons. "So he brought up his camera operator, a young man named Conrad Hall."

Stevens had already contracted John Nickolaus as director of pho-

Director of Photography Conrad Hall (L) and First Assistant Director Lee Katzin in the Daystar meeting rooms in 1963.

tography for *The Outer Limits* when *Stoney Burke* was cancelled. He personally worked out an arrangement whereby Hall would alternate *Outer Limits* episodes with Nickolaus, in order to keep Hall with Daystar. "Connie Hall could get so much out of so little," said Stevens. "Once, he was shooting someone on a balcony, through the branches of a willow tree. He tied a rope to the branches of the tree from below and had someone pull it very gently, giving the branches this wonderfully subtle motion. It cost fifteen cents more and made all the visual difference in the world. Another time, he lit an actress from the center of her forehead with a tiny light used for closeups. I asked him what he was doing that for, and he said, 'Wait till you see it on film!' The next day, we ran the rushes, and every time she blinked, these tiny little shadow lines of eyelash were thrown all the way down her face. Now, when you think of what you're getting for the extra two minutes, that's incredible."

"I was fairly new at the game, and had the chance to experiment a lot," said Hall. "Anything I ever heard about, dreamt about, or thought up—I tried everything in the book. *The Outer Limits* became a school for the development of my craft." When Hall later left TV to do movies, he began, like his mentor McCord, to collect Academy Award nominations. Among his notable films of the middle 1960s were *In Cold Blood* and *Cool Hand Luke*, and he won his first Oscar in 1969 for *Butch Cassidy and the Sundance Kid*.

Hall's camera operator was William Fraker, who went on to shoot *Bullitt* and *Rosemary's Baby* in the late '60s. "His nickname was Frakersawa," laughs Lindsley Parsons. Today, both Hall and Fraker sit at the top of their field. Even Dick Glouner, the man who loaded film into their cameras on *Outer Limits*, is now a cinematographer in his own right.

"I don't think Hall or Fraker would be cameramen today if it wasn't for Lloyd Garnell," said Jack Poplin, *Outer Limits'* art director. "Because he taught them a hell of a lot." Garnell was Daystar's gaffer—the man in charge of the lighting set-ups—and the inventor of the Garnell Light, a lightweight, portable spotlight of the sort used for Hall's eyelash shot. His nickname was "Goldie," and thus the term "goldie lites" for another type of spotlight he devised.

As the new Daystar Building filled up with equipment and personnel, it became a hivelike, all-inclusive postproduction facility as well as a meeting place and think tank. On the ground floor (which today houses the L.A. Cafe) was the production/accounting arm, and the offices of Gerry Fischer, now titled Vice President/Treasurer in charge of business operations, Elaine Michea, and her payroll man, Robert Johnson, a singer and announcer late of Seattle who was also a skilled CPA. Johnson eventually provided many of *Outer Limits'* monster voices a la carte, and by virtue of a strategically produced Screen Actors Guild card wound up with a small role in *Hero's Island*.

Jack Poplin was also quartered on the ground floor, along with Day-

The Outer Limits' foremost First AD (and later Production Manager), Robert Justman.
(Photo by J. S. Frentzen)

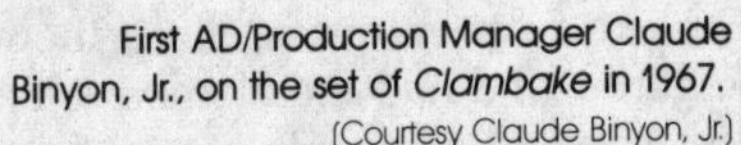

First AD/Production Manager Claude Binyon, Jr., on the set of *Clambake* in 1967.
(Courtesy Claude Binyon, Jr.)

star's gang of First Assistant Directors—Robert Justman, Lee Katzin, and latterly, Claude Binyon, Jr. Justman, who was to become *Outer Limits'* most versatile and valuable AD (and later, production manager) had worked on the 1952 Harry Horner film *Red Planet Mars*, and as AD on several episodes of *One Step Beyond*. He was recruited to Daystar by Leon Chooluck, who also brought in Katzin, another aspiring director, on the basis of film work they had done together in the 1950s. Katzin had worked his way up to the 1st AD position on *Stoney Burke*, and like John Erman, had been promised some *Outer Limits* shows as director by Stevens. Binyon arrived midway through *Outer Limits'* first season, and came from film and TV production work at Warner Brothers. His entrée was Lindsley Parsons, with whom he had ridden the same bus to military school in the 1940s.

"In TV, most ADs are not considered as creative people," said Justman. "*Outer Limits* was unusual in that there was a very free exchange of ideas. I felt that I had a creative contribution to make, and that if I could get some of my ideas accepted, that was a kind of 'overscale' payment."

A 1st AD functions on the set rather like a stage manager, yelling constantly and supervising all set-ups so that the director may walk in and begin immediately to direct without worrying why, for example, a truckload of fish monster suits is stalled somewhere near the Barham Boulevard off ramp instead of in the studio.

"The First ADs had a terrific amount of responsibility on *Outer*

Limits, coordinating all the various elements of special effects and production," Katzin said. "We were not all that privy to the initial concepts of the shows. In the beginning, Daystar was prepared four episodes in advance. We'd prepare a show for seven days, then run out onto the floor and film it. Since at that time there was no such thing as a location manager, we had to get locations, too."

So what else does an AD do? "The best he can... with limited resources," says Justman. Frequently the ADs would gather with Conrad Hall, Bill Fraker, and Jack Poplin at a bar near Daystar to, as Katzin put it, "discuss ways to do things on *Outer Limits* using a lot of imagination and very little money." The bar was called the Phone Booth. "As you faced south from Daystar, it was about ten points off the starboard bow," said Justman. "I went there with Katzin and the others once or twice. It was a place where scantily-clad young ladies would serve your drinks. That was a big thing, in those days."

Daystar's second floor housed Stevens's office plus an executive secretary, the Six Bright Young Men and support personnel. One of Stevens's assistants was Lloyd Haynes, later the star of the *Room* 222 series.

Dominic Frontiere's office was found on the third floor amidst a clattering aggregation of sound machines and film editing gear. On the top floor, film cutters Tony DiMarco, Richard Brockway, and Fred Baretta ran millions of feet of 35 millimeter *Outer Limits* film through a cluster of moviolas, at first under the supervision of Stevens, and later under the watchful eye of producer Joseph Stefano, who taught himself the craft of film editing in these upstairs rooms.

"I was also on the third floor," noted John Elizalde, whose chaotic arrangement of homemade signal generators, customized oscillators, and primordial synthesizers provided most of *Outer Limits'* weird sound effects. He was brought into Daystar by Richard Brockway (who had edited *Hero's Island),* and had worked previously with Frontiere at Quinn Martin Productions on a pair of pilots, *Skyfighters* and *The New Breed.* Besides sound effects and distorted alien voices, Elizalde did live taping of the Control Voice speeches done by Vic Perrin, and all the postproduction dubbing and looping of dialogue. He and assistant John Caper, Jr., also worked in Daystar's basement, where the music cutting equipment was installed, adding Frontiere's ethereal *Outer Limits* music to finished episodes. The music was either scored (using material Frontiere had composed and timed to fit specific parts of the show) or tracked (which involved editing music from the Frontiere library into a new form). It was also here that Elizalde added his sound effects to each new show, and he and Caper were assisted by Arthur Cornall, Jay Ashworth, Jack Wood, and a part-timer, Harold Smith.

Another of Daystar's early idea men was M. B. Paul, who was credited as the optical unit's director of photography. He was the on-set supervisor for shots that would include special optical effects, and owned and operated his own equipment rental house. Jack Poplin credits Paul with the invention of the Adlux Trans-Light Screen, an oversized backdrop, like a giant color slide, that was inserted into windows or other such openings on a live set and lit from behind to provide "instant background." Director Byron Haskin was soon to sign on as an uncredited "effects supervisor," but there was very little overlap with Paul's field.

Mechanical on-set effects such as wafting curtains, falling debris, or off-camera manipulation of props fell to Thol "Si" Simonsen and Pat Dinga. Daystar's costumers were Forrest "T Bone" Butler and Sabine Manela, who had joined the company as of *Hero's Island*. "They worked on some of the actual monster suits," noted Elaine Michea, "but always from designs provided by the special effects unit."

Construction and design of *Outer Limits'* unique aliens and creatures was entrusted, for the most part, to a group of independent contractors known as Project Unlimited (about whom more a bit later), and, on occasion, to makeup artists hired to assist Fred Phillips. "Projects" (as the company was alternately called) also provided optical effects which were turned over to one of three Hollywood labs specializing in combining effects with live-action footage: Butler–Glouner, Ray Mercer and Company, and Consolidated Film Industries, Inc.

The man who built the *Outer Limits* sets—Art Director Jack Poplin, in 1963.
(Courtesy Jack Poplin)

Jack Poplin's crackerjack construction crew—the men responsible for every Gothic interior, every spaceship cockpit, and every moonscape you see in *The Outer Limits*—included Chester Bayhi (a propman from Fox who became a set decorator on the *Mr. Kingston* pilot) and Tracey R. Bousman, "Dick Tracy" to his pals, who brought his experience at the Chouinard Art Institute to the *Outer Limits* pilot film. "We were like a club," said Poplin. "I'd break down a script and hand it to Dick, who would put it into working drawings, then we'd talk with Chet about how to dress it. From there, we'd wing it with a marvelous construction foreman we had, Lowell Thomas."

"Stop and think of all the control that was necessary to create an illusion for *The Outer Limits,*" says Lindsley Parsons. "We had to use a tremendous amount of ingenuity and innovation just to get the show done; we were a well-oiled machine without pretenses. Leslie sat down and ate with the crew. Anybody was approachable; if you had a better idea, we'd use it. Leslie was very much in favor of people improving themselves. He came up with an honor he bestowed on only two people that I know of, because I was the second. It was a Daystar Employee of the Year medallion, with the Daystar emblem in gold. Henry Maak [the key grip, or supervisor of the set-building crew] got it the first year."

"Daystar was a terrific group who all enjoyed what they were doing," said Lee Katzin. "We had a lot of fun, worked our collective asses off, and did some first-rate work."

It was time for Stevens to apply his Blue Ribbon Crew to a pilot venture less conventional than his failed tries at action-adventure formats. In his own words, he wanted to "stress, dwell on, and get *into* the awe and mystery of the universe; tap into other dimensions, other beings, and alien *stuff* that truly went to the outer limits of the imagination. Now, you can only do that for so long until you begin to hear, 'Uh—you're getting pretty far out, there. That may be interesting to a handful of people, but can you bring it back down to Earth so that the big numbers, the masses, will understand?'"

Melnick's Folly

Daniel Melnick was only twenty-six years old when he was made vice-president of programming at ABC in 1959. For Stevens, in 1962, talking with ABC meant talking with Melnick: "The very origin of *The Outer Limits* was a conversation between Dan and myself."

When Stevens talked with United Artists, he talked with Richard Dorso, the programming VP with whom he had developed *Stoney Burke* into a series. "I had a deal with Leslie as a producer under contract to UA," said Dorso. "And I said, Let's cook up a TV series about science fiction. Leslie was a talented, able producer, and I knew the idea could be sold to ABC." Dorso had similarly cooked up *The Fugitive* for Quinn Martin's group, and many other series. "Once Dan Melnick agreed it was something he wanted to see on the air, then we'd plan how to sell it to people like Goldenson and Moore." Leonard Goldenson was ABC's president and chairman of the board (he holds the latter post to this day).

Tom Moore, at one time a publicist for a cemetery, was Goldenson's executive VP, and would ascend to the network presidency by the end of 1963.

"Melnick said, 'Definitely, let's do it,'" recalls Stevens. "But he stressed that our concept had to be presented in 'exhibitor's terms.' ABC was very uneasy about any departure from conventional programming, so the only way I could really *sell* it to them was to stress that it was not far removed from a scare show. The one thing Dan urged me to do was to put a monster in every show, and put it on fast—within the first five minutes. Because ABC would regard the show as a monster show more than anything else."

"My responsibility," said Dorso, "was to see that the concept worked, and when it got to the public, that the show worked." Stevens credits Dorso as the man "who held the battery and the bulb together."

A deal for a pilot film was struck with Melnick, the third side of the Daystar/UA/ABC triangle. "He called the series Melnick's Folly," said Stevens. "By so doing, he disowned it in case it was a flop. But if it worked, then it became like the steamboat—it sails, therefore Melnick's Folly is a big success. Dan is very astute, and capable of handling himself in the Executive Wars." Melnick had shrewdly followed the Golden Rule of corporate thinking by covering his ass both ways. The pilot was titled *Please Stand By* at his suggestion. If it flew, he could claim a modest measure of credit, and if it died, he could safely say I-told-you-so to ABC.

But "triple-threats," writer/director/producers, were considered pushy by the networks, and Stevens' name had already acquired a bit of a stigma. The free-flowing setup at Daystar was not comprehensible to the rigidly compartmentalized bastille at ABC, and to top it off, Daystar's salvo of new pilots was a complete wash. Stevens was anxious to move on to still more new projects, including a series based on the short stories of Frank Merriwell, and a show on contemporary artworks called *American Masterpieces*. If *Please Stand By* was presented to ABC with Stevens appearing to grab too much of the credit, it might be jinxed before a single frame of it was seen. Stevens illuminated another hitch: "They felt that a show wasn't a success if it didn't run endlessly. So no matter how good *Stoney Burke* was, it had been cancelled, and they thought of me as not really coming through, and that might jeopardize selling *Please Stand By* to the sponsors."

Stevens's solution was to add new blood to the project in the form of a producer who had some name recognition in Hollywood as a very successful screenwriter. Someone who could line-produce the series if the pilot sold, leaving Stevens to pursue further new projects for Daystar.

Once he rolled the final page of *Please Stand By* out of his typewriter, Stevens phoned his old songwriting partner from the Greenwich Village days, Joseph Stefano.

Joseph Stefano at his parquet desk in the Villa di Stefano offices at KTTV. (Photo: Leon Chooluck; Courtesy Joseph Stefano)

Enter Joe Stefano

One of the most famous scenes in motion picture history was written on November 10, 1959, and the script presents it this way:

> MARY - EXTREME CLOSE UP
> As she turns in response to the feel and SOUND of the shower curtain being torn aside. A look of pure horror erupts in her face. A low terrible groan begins to rise up out of her throat. A hand comes into the shot. The hand holds an enormous bread knife. The flint of the blade shatters the screen to an almost total, silver blackness.
>
> THE SLASHING
> An impression of a knife slashing, as if tearing at the very screen, ripping the film. Over it the brief gulps of screaming. And then silence. And then the dreadful thump as Mary's body falls in the tub.

"I think I was probably five years old when I knew I had to be connected to the movies in some way," said Joseph Stefano, a compact man with a classically Roman profile and a remarkable fluidity of expression and emotion. "My mother and father took me to a movie with Greta Garbo and John Gilbert, and Garbo died at the end.* When we left, I

*It was *Love* (1927), a silent version of *Anna Karenina*, which Garbo redid as a talkie in 1936.

thought it was very sad because we'd never see her in another movie, and my parents explained that she didn't *really* die, she was just pretending she'd died, and that was the *movie*. And I thought, aha! Some kids pick up a baseball bat and that's it; I saw that movie, and that was it. After that I went to the movies continually; you could get me to do anything if there was a dime or quarter in it for the movies. There were about eight theatres within walking distance of my house, and they changed films every two days. You could go to a different movie every night of the week, which is almost what I did."

But Stefano's show business career was seeded even before that when at the age of three he won a theatre-sponsored Charleston contest against two dozen older contestants. Born Joseph William Stefano in South Philadelphia, Pennsylvania, on May 5th, 1922, he was the youngest of the Stefano clan. His father Dominic was a widowed tailor with three children who married a widow, Josephina, who also had three children. "She had three sons, and he had a son and two daughters, and after they married they had two more children—my brother Peter and myself. The others were much older; they were in college by the time I was three. It was like gluing together two families that did not get along, and it was a very strange pyramid to be on the bottom of. To me, they were *all* my family, but the two sets of children were enemies. Eventually my parents broke up. My mother got a house with her three sons, who were working by now, Peter, and myself. After a year or so, my father came back, but without his children—he broke up with them, so to speak. It was a very painful situation, losing people who were dear to you, people you weren't supposed to see anymore. It caused all that is good about me, and all that is bad. I escaped early into fantasy, into movies."

By age ten, Stefano was singing for radio audiences as part of the weekly children's hour, and song-and-dance heavily influenced his school years. Once he discovered "this thing called theatre," he began composing songs and writing lyrics.

The move to Philadelphia little theatre was inevitable, and Stefano did original musicals, writing the book (words), but not the music, mainly so he could be in the productions. "I never thought of myself as an actor," he said, "until a long time later, after I'd toured."

He turned twenty-one in 1943, and in order to "get the war out of the way," he tried to enlist in the Navy but was rejected because he had two punctured eardrums. Not knowing whether this would keep him clear of the draft-hungry Army as well, he spent the next six months at home, not working, waiting for his number to come up. An aunt of young Joe's had a piano, which he transported to his home and began to practice on, religiously. "I had a girlfriend who was teaching me," he said, "but mostly I just played by ear." Military service never materialized, and the following year Stefano went to New York to expand his performing experience and wound up going on the road for a full season as part of a touring company doing *The Student Prince,* and, in 1945–46, *The Merry Widow.* He also pulled down a living in New York doing nightclub revues. "I auditioned for a nightclub job, playing piano and singing. After the audition, Mervyn Nelson said to me, 'What're you wasting your time *singing* for? You've written some great stuff here; you should be a writer. Anybody can be a singer.' That really had a strange, powerful effect on me. I began to think in terms of writing a whole musical, book, songs, and all. I worked on a thing called *It's Your Move,* rewriting it about fifteen times. It finally got produced off-Broadway in 1946, at the Provincetown Playhouse. After that I proceeded to make a living by writing popular songs as well as the revues."

Stefano wrote hundreds of tunes—pop music and show music, with and without lyrics. "Just a *pile* of records," he smiles. "By 1952 I was making very good money. My first hit was a Karen Chandler tune called 'One Dream.' It was a hit mainly because of the song on the flip side, which I didn't write." A song titled "Heartbeat" was recorded by a British artist named Ruby Murray, and became a Number One hit in England for fifteen straight weeks. Other Stefano tunes were recorded by such artists as Sammy Davis Jr. and Eydie Gorme.

While living in Greenwich Village, Stefano first encountered Leslie Stevens, who was then still trying to crack Broadway as a playwright. "My roommate, Steve, was studying modern dance, and so was Leslie—he's always been interested in taking classes in everything, even if you were never going to use it. Steve mentioned that he had a roommate who wrote songs, and Leslie said he'd like to meet me, that maybe we could do a nightclub act or something."

Stevens conceived the idea of trying to do a musical soap opera for TV, a collaboration which would require an extremely fast production pace. "We tried it to see if we could do it," said Stefano. "We wrote about eight episodes, him doing one half-hour script per day, and me writing two new songs per day. He took the idea to the networks, but nothing

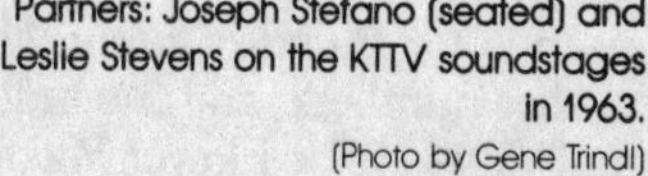

Partners: Joseph Stefano (seated) and Leslie Stevens on the KTTV soundstages in 1963.
(Photo by Gene Trindl)

ever came of it. Then we did a nightclub act for a girlfriend of his; he did the patter while I did the original score. We also did a musical version of *The Pickwick Papers*. He did the book and I did the music and lyrics. Nothing was ever done with that, either."

Meanwhile, Stefano's revue work got him gigs in Las Vegas and Paris, France, where he wrote material for the Folies Bergere. After a long period of no contact with Stevens, Stefano was asked to do *entr'acte* music for *Champagne Complex*. "It was a fun idea," said Stefano, "so I did it." He also introduced Stevens to his first wife, Ruth Ramsey, a friend of Stefano's from *The Merry Widow* touring company. "I lost track of Leslie when he went to Hollywood to do *Marriage-Go-Round*. The next time he heard of me, I was a screenwriter. That really threw him."

One January evening in 1953, Stefano received a call from a boyhood buddy visiting New York from Philadelphia on business. They arranged to meet at a local bar. "I went over to the jukebox to see if any of my records were on it," recalls Stefano. "This young girl came over to put a coin in and I said, 'Play *that* one,' and when she asked why I said, 'Because I wrote it!' The song was 'One Dream' and the girl's name was Marilyn. She was secretary of the New York Jazz Society, where these great artists would get together to jam. She liked my song and invited me to one of the sessions. We started seeing each other, and got married in December of '53." While Stevens became a much-married man, Joe and Marilyn have been together ever since 1953.

New York was also where Stefano first encountered psychiatric analysis, while still a songwriter. "I think analysis is probably why I began writing in the first place," he reflects. "As a writer, I'm fearless when it comes to material that is disturbing to me. I would credit to the analysis itself the release of inhibitions, of anything that might be repressed." While producing *The Outer Limits*, Stefano was also undergoing "hard-core Freudian analysis," which consisted of lying on a couch and free-associating for fifty minutes every morning, with a doctor who didn't say a word. "Then, having gone through fifty minutes of hell, I'd drive to KTTV and work on the show. It was a very lush period for me, creatively, and I wrote continually."

But what started him writing in the first place? The *satori* occurred in 1956, when Stefano was in the middle of a year-long break from songwriting.

"I was watching a *Studio One* or a *Robert Montgomery Presents*, and I said to Marilyn, 'I could write a play like that.' But I had never seen a screenplay before. I finally asked an actor friend of mine what one looked like, and he explained scenes, shot numbers, and the indentations for dialogue." Stefano's story, originally titled "The Flower Maker," featured characters loosely modeled on his parents. "It began essentially as a scenario—what would be called a treatment, today—and ended as a full script. I wrote it almost the way you'd do a stage play." After changing the title to *The Black Orchid*, he submitted the piece to a New York agent and friend with the improbable name of Daniel Hollywood, intending it for *Studio One*, an hour-long mystery-suspense series on the air since 1948. It could be said that Hollywood called right back, in both senses. He'd shown *The Black Orchid* to Carlo Ponti, whose most recent production had been the epic King Vidor *War and Peace*. Ponti wanted the property as a vehicle for his then-wife, Sophia Loren, and asked if Stefano could transform the teleplay to feature-length.

Filming was not to commence for a year, due to Loren's other commitments, and in the interim Stefano wrote "an American version of an Italian film" for Ponti's coproducer, Marcello Girosi, from a literal translation of the Italian screenplay. The film, *Fast and Sexy*, was shot both ways by Vittorio De Sica, and starred Gina Lollobrigida as a girl who returns to the Italian village of her birth a wealthy widow after her rich Brooklyn husband dies. Stefano spent two months of 1957 in Italy on the project, which he titled *Anna of Brooklyn*. "De Sica put a lot of stuff from my version into the Italian one," said Stefano. "I have a funny feeling that although I wouldn't understand it, since I don't speak Italian, that it would look more like my script than the American version. *Fast and Sexy* was an *awful* title!"

On the basis of the script Stefano wrote for *The Black Orchid*, 20th Century–Fox offered him a term contract to write two new screenplays per year for seven years. "It all happened so fast I didn't know where in hell I was," noted Stefano. "I was suddenly thrust into a position it takes most writers years to get to, and I never thought I'd realize my ambition to be connected with the movies by doing screenplays." When the Stefanos finally hauled stakes for California in 1958, Joe had only one other piece of writing in his folio—a treatment for a drama called *Made in Japan*, which his agent submitted to Herb Brodkin at CBS, for *Playhouse 90*.

Made in Japan is a powerful drama about honor, race hatred, innocence versus passion, and the conflict between what is right and what is legal. Set in post-Occupation Japan, it concerns a soldier of good Philadelphia socialite stock (Dean Stockwell) who falls in love with a Japanese girl (Norbu McCarthy) and decides to break it off because she is not his kind of people. His status allows him to slip through the cracks of the law when he inadvertently allows her to die. When he realizes he really *did* love her, his emotional self-destruction begins. *Made in Japan* is an excellent story of characters in crisis, and was awarded the prestigious Robert E. Sherwood Award, given by the Ford Foundation's Fund for the Republic to "a television program contributing to the understanding of freedom and justice." Stefano split the $5,000 prize with producer Brodkin and director Herbert Hirschman. "I was stunned when it won," he said. "Everybody thought *Judgement at Nuremberg* would take it that year."

Then *The Black Orchid* (1959) was directed by Martin Ritt, who had just done *The Long Hot Summer* (and would later direct *Hud* and *The Spy Who Came in from the Cold*). Costarring with Sophia Loren was Anthony Quinn as a man who falls in love with the widow of a gangster and fights to convince all their assorted children that a marriage would benefit everybody. "For a kid who saw *42nd Street* fifty times, it was thrilling to walk onto the Paramount lot," said Stefano. "The first time I walked onto a soundstage, the red light went on just as I got inside the door. They were shooting a tiny office set at the far end of the stage, and I couldn't see a thing. But I could *hear* Sophia Loren saying my words, and it was an unbelievable feeling." Shortly after the Stefanos arrived in Los Angeles, Marilyn gave birth to their only child, Dominic, and Joe began his contract work for Fox. "It was very different from what I'd expected. For one thing, I had no idea of the bullshit that goes on."

His first taste was a project called *A Machine for Chuparosa*, about a tiny Mexican village that gets a tractor for the first time. The producer could not decide whether to shoot the film in Mexico, Rio de Janeiro, Peru, or the Pyrenees, hopping from one to the next with Stefano in tow to do endless location rewrites. After a month wasted with no resolution, Stefano asked to be released from his contract. "I went to the front office at Fox and said, 'I know I've written a movie that's gotten great reviews (which *The Black Orchid* had, along with winning a Venice Film Festival Award for Sophia Loren's performance), but I need strength. I'm not ready to deal with this sort of thing.' My agent hit the ceiling and told me I'd probably never work at Fox again. Two weeks later I got a call from Fox."

He did a treatment for Jerry Wald, *The Lost Country,* which was to star Anthony Perkins as a teacher who falls in love with a young student. It fell into limbo and was rewritten two years later by Clifford Odets, eventually being filmed as *Wild in the Country* with Elvis Presley. But Stefano's early experiences at Fox taught him the value of turning down some assignments: "I learned how to say *no*. And to this day, I've never regretted not doing something to which I had originally said no. I can't think of a single exception."

He did say yes, however, to a variety of TV assignments. "Mainly, I did shows for friends of mine who had series. I saw the pilot for *Saints and Sinners* and I liked it, so I did a show called 'Source of Information' for (producer) Adrian Spies." It featured Scott Marlowe as an unscrupulous ne'er do well who steals a play written by series regular Nick Adams, and uses it to interest a hospitalized ex-movie queen in a comeback.

"Tony Curtis called and asked me to do a *Ford Startime,*" said Stefano of his next teleplay. "Universal wanted to do a new version of the Juggler legend—where the guy has nothing to give the Madonna as a gift, so he wants to juggle for her and the townspeople won't let him." The script was titled "The Young Juggler."

For *General Electric Theatre* Stefano did two half-hour dramas. The first was a fictionalization of his father's life, "The Committeeman," which starred Lee J. Cobb. The other, "Hitler's Secret," was based on a story written by Richard Oswald, the father of director Gerd Oswald, with whom Stefano was soon to work so closely on *The Outer Limits*.

He also wrote three segments of *The Detectives* and several episodes of *The Lloyd Bridges Show.* The first of these, "A Game for Alternate Mondays," starred Glynis Johns as a woman who habitually takes her daughter to a railroad station every other Monday, which is the only time a train comes through. Each time she tells the girl her father is coming home on the train. Bridges steps off the train one day and is drawn into their fantasy, allowing himself to "become" the father they have pretended will arrive—rather like a version of *Waiting for Godot* in which someone becomes Godot, just so he can show up at last and end the waiting.

By 1959, Stefano decided he wanted to make a feature with a "big" director, and after securing a new and stronger agent, Elliot Kastner, he gave him and fellow agent Ned Brown a list of ten preferred directors and said "Call me."

The first call was from Otto Preminger, the second, from William Wyler. Due to various creative conflicts Stefano had to regretfully say no to each of them. The third call was from Alfred Hitchcock, who had run into trouble with a low-budget script called *Psycho* when a first draft by another screenwriter proved inadequate. Hitchcock's agents set up an interview at Paramount, and while Hitchcock did not like *The Black Orchid,* he did hit it off with Stefano.*

"I'd almost turned *Psycho* down," said Stefano, "because I'd read the novel and didn't like it. But I had ideas about what I could do with the story. Hitchcock's eyes lit up when I said, '*If* the movie seems to be about this girl who we meet and get to know, who happens to stop at this motel and get murdered half an hour into the picture...' A lot of *Psycho*'s success has to do with your knowledge of movie conventions. It was a movie made for people who watch movies, particularly Hitchcock movies. If we had killed, say, Grace Kelly, the audience would expect it was a trick. Janet Leigh was at just the right level; you would accept the fact she had really died." With *Psycho,* Stefano drank deeply from the cup of dark Gothic wonders that was to color nearly all of his later work, particularly his *Outer Limits* episodes. The combination of the film by Hitchcock (who was steeped in a tradition of brooding, baroque images), the novel by Robert Bloch (who had made the Grand Guignol entirely his domain in literature), and the screenplay by Stefano make the movie version of *Psycho* the ultimate tale for a rainy night.

*Stefano's dealings with Hitchcock are recounted in detail in John Russell Taylor's *Hitch: The Life and Times of Alfred Hitchcock* (Pantheon, 1978). and Donald Spoto's *The Dark Side of Genius* (Little, Brown, 1983). He is quoted extensively in the sections of both books dealing with *Psycho* and *Marnie.*

"I agreed to do two more pictures with Hitch," said Stefano. "But I didn't want to do *The Birds* because I didn't like it." After *Psycho,* he spent several weeks writing a one hundred-page treatment based on the Winston Graham novel *Marnie,* at the time Grace Kelly was interested in playing the lead role of a kleptomaniac.

In 1962 Stefano wrote the pilot for the *Mr. Novak* series, and adapted the Max Erlich murder mystery *Last Train to Babylon* into what was to be Gary Cooper's last film, *The Naked Edge*. "I started on that script right before *Psycho* opened," he said, "just when the Writer's Guild went on strike. United Artists was the only studio I could legitimately work for, and they offered me the film. At the time, I was in the hospital, having a disc removed from my back. I got flowers from Hitchcock, with a card reading, 'Why didn't you have your operation in the cutting rooms?'"

When Hitchcock decided to proceed with *Marnie,* he called Stefano again. But Leslie Stevens had called first.

"Leslie was building himself a company," said Stefano. "He needed *Stoney Burke* to be renewed, and needed to have more than one show on the air. He was having a hard time."

"Joe started with us as a kind of figurehead," said Stevens. "He had a name and he was new blood, which was what we needed to sell *The Outer Limits* as a series. We hired him, and he came in a day or two before we started shooting the *Please Stand By* pilot."

The Stevens/Stefano partnership is announced to the industry-at-large in mid-1963.

"I was told Hitchcock was very upset because I wasn't available to do *Marnie,*" Stefano said. "It was insane. How can you get angry just because someone is busy? He said, 'Oh, Joseph is busy *producing* these days, and can't do *our* little project over here.'"

"Joe would be the first person to say that he hadn't produced his left shoe until the day we began shooting the pilot," said Stevens. "There wasn't much for him *to* do except stand there and watch us film it. He deserves all the praise in the world, because at the very first he had to stand there and bite his tongue instead of saying, 'Why don't you do *this,* Leslie?' or 'Why don't you stop fooling around?' I'm sure he wanted to produce then, but it wasn't his time. He was very professional with me by doing the thing we agreed to do, which was help to sell the pilot. When we went into production on the actual series, Joe came into his own as a producer."

"Each one of Joe's 'firsts' has been a gigantic success," Tom Selden, Stefano's personal assistant on *Outer Limits,* points out. "His first script sold as a movie screenplay, his first TV script won awards, and his first series was *The Outer Limits.*"

"I was hip to life, to people and situations," said Stefano. "I wasn't terribly naive. I didn't know much about being a producer. But with me, you never hire a producer; you hire Joe Stefano."

Please Stand By: The Pilot

> A pilot should be hard-hitting and noisy. If you get stuck with a quiet scene, have somebody in the room kick over an ashtray!
>
> —Daniel Melnick, to Leslie Stevens

Please Stand By typified Stevens's approach to science fiction: His plot was speculative and fantastic; his lead actor was a popular film star; his technical jargon was fast, wild-sounding and essentially credible, and his affection for hard science as a story springboard was obvious. His script was finished November 11, 1962, and the pilot was budgeted at $213,000. After a hectic two weeks of preproduction, film started rolling on December 3rd. Shooting took nine days at a closed-down radio station in Coldwater Canyon, and at MGM on Backlot #4's Andy Hardy Street

Cliff Robertson, the highest-paid actor ever to work on *The Outer Limits*, poses for a *Please Stand By* publicity shot while Daystar technicians fiddle around in the background.

and on Stage #3. The completed footage then vanished into the labyrinth of the Daystar Building, where it was edited, dubbed, and scored.

Dominic Frontiere claims that the opening title theme for *The Outer Limits,* beginning with the powerful musical "sting" that rivets the viewer's attention instantly, was composed at his desk in fifteen minutes. The music he did for the pilot is eerie, drifting and melodic, rich with strings—exactly the sort of thing Stevens needed to differentiate his film from the run-of-the-mill TV product. Large orchestras were rarely used in TV, and the forty-four musicians used by Frontiere lent the pilot a degree of class.

One of ABC's first questions to Stevens was, "Who's going to host it?" Most anthologies of the day featured on on-camera host, usually a celebrity, and every show even remotely associated with science fiction had had one. Stevens asked his new producer, Stefano, if he would like the job *a la* Rod Serling. Stefano declined. Then, during a meeting with ABC and UA executives, inspiration struck: "They cornered me on the topic of the host," said Stevens. "I heard myself say, 'You are a television set. Well, *turn off!* There'll be a little picture-dot, and then a voice would say there was nothing wrong with the set, then the picture would come back on out-of-focus, then, as we took control, it would roll and flutter. By then, we'd be in the outer limits.' It just came to me in a blind flash, in the middle of a conference, and I thought to myself, my god, that sounds good!"

The planet Earth is a speck of dust...

The major theme of *Please Stand By* was summed up by Stevens in the closing speech he wrote for the Control Voice. Its minor premise comes from the mouth of Allan Maxwell, when he attempts to justify to his skeptical wife Carol his modest efforts to investigate the unknown. An aggressively normal person who would rather not ponder such things,

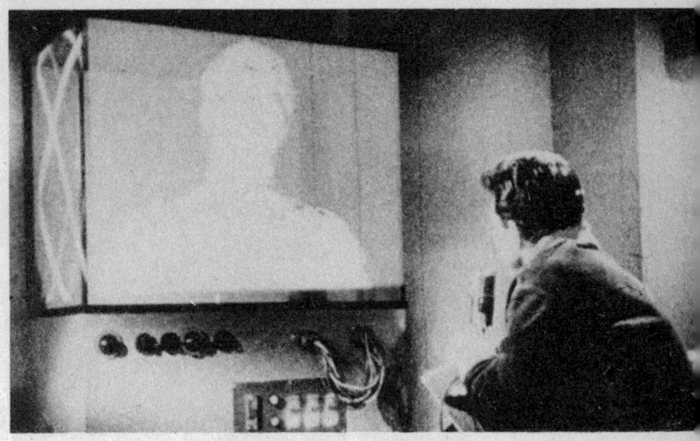

"Who are you?" Cliff Robertson makes first contact.

Carol says, "What makes you think you can discover anything? *Who* are you?" Allan's reply:

> Nobody. Nobody at all. But the secrets of the universe don't mind. They reveal themselves to nobodies who care. Isaac Newton was a nobody. Michael Faraday was a bookbinder's apprentice. . . . The big laboratories spend millions of dollars, Carol, and they work slowly and surely, and they get results. But not the big steps. Those come from the human mind, not from the laboratory. Call them inspiration, call them intuition, maybe blind luck. Maybe it's God, saying, "Now's the time."

Significantly, "Who are you?" is also the first question asked Allan by the alien, and the real answer is that he is the kind of solitary, science-smart misfit that is the core character for most of Leslie Stevens's *Outer Limits* scripts. One nice touch is that both Allan and the Being are scientific loners, kindred spirits whose contact is possible only because both of them are breaking rules to satisfy their curiosity—Allan is bleeding power away from the radio station that provides his livelihood, and the Being says he is "not allowed to use equipment for exploration."

Rather than a raygun-slinging octopus come to appropriate all of Earth's virgins, lightbulbs, and Dr. Pepper for the nefarious ends of its homeworld, here the alien visitor is benevolent, even passive. The destruction it causes is unintended, as is the panic it later prompts. It is here by accident, and only resorts to a show of force to get everybody to shut up and listen to it. This establishes one of *The Outer Limits'* archetypes: The humane, quizzical alien who interacts with humans who only hasten its death.

As far as the network was concerned, a radioactive extraterrestrial

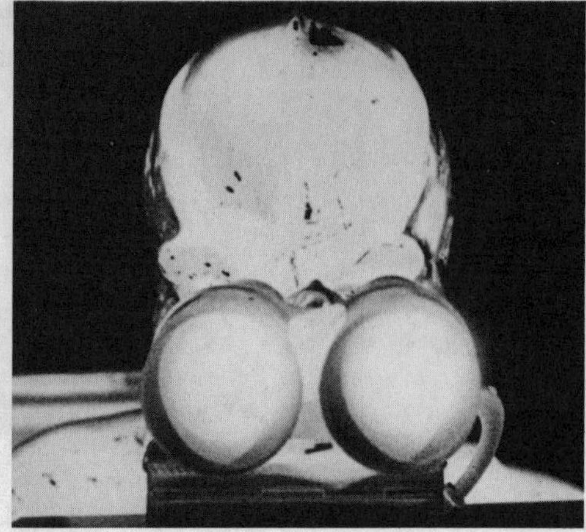

The Andromedan investigates a pair of binoculars in an antique shop.

was a monster regardless of his better qualities, and the first appearance of *Outer Limits*' first monster is a memorable one. Keeping in mind Dan Melnick's admonition to get the monster on-screen quickly, Stevens brings on the Being thirty seconds into the first reel, as a ghostly coruscation in the "solid static" pattern on Allan's 3D monitor. It resolves to recognizability nine minutes into the show proper, and a nice resonance is established by the fact that as Allan watches his screen, the TV viewing audience is watching him on *their* screens, just after being told their TV sets were beyond their control. In *Please Stand By*, a similar "loss" of control results in the transmission of the Being to Earth. Moral: Don't monkey around with the knobs while someone else is controlling all that you see and hear.

The story's conceptual antecedent is the Robert Wise film *The Day the Earth Stood Still* (1951), reduced in scope for TV. The character of the Being combines the civil pragmatism of Klaatu, the alien emissary, with the awesome physical presence of his police robot, Gort. While Klaatu arrives in a flying saucer, the Being, fittingly enough, crawls forth from a kind of TV screen, and tunes himself out at the end of the show. Both visitors deliver speeches laced with cosmic profundities after demonstrating their superior destructive power, and both films utilize easily identifiable science fiction trappings without succumbing to a conventional monster-run-amok plot.

One convention Stevens does exploit is the fear of the masses for technology. Carol Maxwell's fear of Allan's research has driven them apart, and her alienation from his work is made clear in what she says when she sees the static pattern on the monitor: "I don't like it. Don't ask me to appreciate it because I can't. It's cold. It sounds like sleet and snow, and it looks like electricity, frozen. I don't like it; I'm sorry." Fear of the unknown (and the machines that probe it) has made Allan an introspective oddball in the eyes of his family and coworkers. His transceiving rig does worse than make no money; it draws so much power that the radio station's signal is reduced to "a feeble beep," which causes Carol's dislike to tip over into active hostility: "You know we could lose our sponsors!" But Stevens demonstrates a love for the toys of technology, a willingness to embrace strange new devices in a society of neophobes like Carol. Allan's clearly impossible transceiver exists not because *Please Stand By* was any great proponent of 1960s science, but because Stevens understood that the essence of the science fiction form is speculation—not documentation. By keeping one foot firmly in the real world of marriage and bills and sponsors, and the other in fantasyland (Allan's shed), the story slides neatly into the realm of *what if* without bothering to explain the warp and woof of Alan's gadgetry. We are given a few credible tidbits about radio waves coming in "at twenty-one centimeters" from somewhere Out There.* To explain further would engulf the story in the octopoid justifications of "hard" science fiction—a digression that a hard-hitting, comprehensible and commercial pilot could not afford. Allan Maxwell could almost be Stevens himself, attempting to sell his unusual pilot to a network composed of mentalities like Carol and Gene Maxwell—people who sometimes need their horizons broadened directly and eye-wideningly. Stevens also uses the fear of technology as a breach point for his message that science and its devices require the same leery respect that a mariner accords the sea—the potentials for risk, danger, and death are balanced by the opportunities for uplift and discovery. For now, the abrupt announcement that nothing was wrong with the television set put the unsettled viewer right where Stevens wanted him or her.

The casting of Cliff Robertson as Allan was a coup for Daystar's John Erman, who secured the actor in the wake of his much-lauded portrayal of John F. Kennedy in *PT-109*. "He took forever to make up his mind," recalls Erman. "So we finally gave the part to Lee Philips. At the eleventh hour, Cliff calls with the news that he's decided to do the pilot, so I had to consult Leslie since Cliff was very big stuff in those days and his salary was $10,000, much more than Lee's. Leslie, being courageous and wanting a success, said to get Cliff, feeling he would add to the prestige of the show. Lee chose to play Allan's brother." Since the technological

*While the revelation that Allan is "scanning the hydrogen static coming in at a frequency of twenty-one centimeters" could be dismissed as colorful sci-fi gobbledygook, it is essentially valid. All stars contain hydrogen which, when ionized, emits radio waves at a natural wavelength of twenty-one centimeters. Reading these radio waves is one way astronomers can chart stars that are so far away they are invisible to conventional telescopes. A perfectly acceptable way for an alien to contact civilizations that do not suspect its existence is to use those radio waves as a carrier for a signal.

exposition in the script was relatively meaningless to Robertson as an actor, Stevens used cue cards and off-camera prompting to help him through the dialogue, eventually changing camera angles after every line or two, allowing the speeches to be pieced smoothly together in the editing room.

The show's other noteworthy performance was that of William O. Douglas, Jr., son of the Supreme Court Justice. Douglas's mime training under Marcel Marceau was applied to his portrayal of the Galaxy Being as well as several other creatures he played while under contract to Daystar during *Outer Limits'* first season. "The face is hidden and the voice is generally distorted," he noted in an interview. "So, if they are to be made anything but lunging hulks, characterization must be done with the body, or with a tilt of the head."

"We didn't want some lumbering stunt man in a monster suit," said Stevens. "Douglas added a touch of weirdness to the way he walked by using a praying mantis as his model; you can see how he looks and turns with his whole body. The creature perceives a world that is, to him, made of glass—he can't keep his balance, as though he's about to fall off this transparent place."

The Being costume itself was an innovative amalgam of costume, makeup sculpting, and optical effects, rare in an era when TV did most of its monsters in greasepaint. To get the Being to "glow and flicker like a man made out of blue light" (in the words of Gene Maxwell), a brown wetsuit was heavily coated in oil and glycerin, which reflected the brilliant stage lighting in endlessly shifting patterns. When the film of the Being was negative-reversed, the dark brown costume became glaring white. Because of this optical trickery, Douglas could play none of his scenes on the actual sets or with any of the other actors. He was composited with the normal footage in postproduction. To enhance the effects of radiation-light emanating from the Being, Stevens used a mobile acetyline torch rig in some shots, and an extremely bright spotlight called a "scissors arc" in others.

While this effect was inspired, the original design of the actual mask worn by Douglas was not. The Being's face was at first a wholly inadequate *papier-mâché* construction, and Elaine Michea at Daystar invited her makeup-artist friend, Fred Phillips, to take a diagnostic look at it. When Phillips said, "It stinks!" Stevens immediately asked him to fix it.

Phillips drove William Douglas to the Ellis Burman Studios (then in Laguna Beach) and made a life-mask of the actor's face in plaster. "Since I was working on another project at the time," said Phillips, "I asked Chuck Schram to complete the head. He made it after hours, behind everyone's backs at MGM." Schram was, at that time, working as an assistant to William Tuttle, *Twilight Zone*'s regular makeup artist. The new head was made of slip rubber and opened only in the back,

The Galaxy Being "wetsuit" as it looked during filming, prior to the negative-reversal effect.

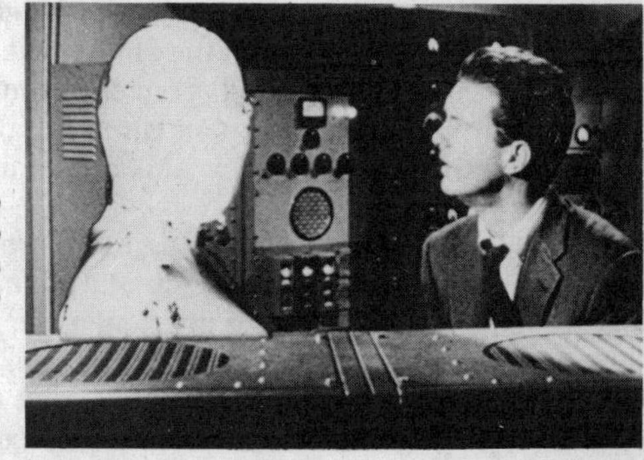

Cliff Robertson talks to the superimposed image of the alien; note how the Being's image "bleeds" slightly onto the top of the generator.

sealing off the face entirely. Douglas had to draw oxygen through a tube that fed into the mask from an air tank strapped to his chest inside the wetsuit. Large-pupiled eyes from an oversized statue of a crow were implanted into the mask's eyesockets to give the "tri-pupilled" look Stevens had requested. The new mask took three days to complete and was delivered the day before shooting commenced on the pilot. "It was a real rush job," said Phillips, who fitted Douglas into the contraption on the set. After seeing his work, Stevens gave Phillips most of the makeup duties on the pilot, and Phillips remained with the *Outer Limits* crew on a per-assignment basis through both seasons of the show.

The creation of the alien's distorted electronic voice set another standard for the soon-to-be series. "We used a single-side band transmitter and receiver so that the voice would sound strange, but retain a maximum of intelligibility," said John Elizalde. "You can not only modulate sounds, but you can transfer inflections and emotional qualities. We used this set-up all the time, and then would add filters or echoes or whatever to vary the voices." The technique Elizalde used had the unintended by-product of producing an actual radio transmission that radiated within a hundred yards of the Daystar Building—which means that, if you had chanced past around New Year's of 1962, you might have been able to catch Leslie Stevens's voice, reading the Galaxy Being's lines, on your car radio at two in the morning!

The chaotic "energy noise" of the Being's radioactive aura was produced by sticking a microphone next to a vacuum cleaner hose and "valving" the nozzle with the fingers. Elizalde even put the nozzle into his mouth to achieve weird sounds, and overlaid this with an MGM sound effects track from *The Time Machine*. "It was a tape called *Morlocks,*" Elizalde recalled. "It was a composite of elephants and lion roars and stuff. We needed sounds that were otherworldly, but sounded like someone putting out vast amounts of information. I used it as a basic track."

First AD Robert Justman scouted the shut-down FM station used for exterior shots nestled into the Hollywood hillside. "I used to listen to a show on that station called 'Concerto from Coldwater Canyon,'" said Justman. "It was quite cold, and we were up there in the middle of the night, firing blanks from a 50-caliber machine gun."

Awaiting Stevens, Stefano, and Frontiere in ABC's New York screening room were Leonard Goldenson and Thomas Moore. Daniel Melnick and Richard Dorso were also in attendance.

"They had been watching pilots all week," recalls Stefano. "I wasn't sure how they'd take this one. When I met them, something in the air gave me the idea that it had *already* been seen."

"I used to have a man travel with all of our pilots," said Dorso, who was there representing United Artists. "He'd sit in the back of the screening room and tell the projectionist to gradually build the sound volume, until, *blam!*, it hit at the climax. In slow spots, you'd distract the execs—everybody did it in those days. Today, they test shows in front of a live audience."

Accordingly, Stevens told the projectionist to crank up the sound during Act Four of *Please Stand By.* Having no ashtrays to boot over, Dorso did his best to distract Goldenson when he caught the Chairman of the Board straining to read his watch in the dark.

The differences between *Please Stand By* and "The Galaxy Being" (the title used for its broadcast as the premiere episode of *The Outer Limits)* versions of the pilot are primarily found in the sound mix. In *Please Stand By*, the background music is more subdued, muted, and Frontiere's end title theme is an expanded version never heard on TV. Allan's radio station, KXKVI, spins different dance tunes. The Being's "signature noise" includes an asthmatic, bellows huffing-puffing sound, as though it is having difficulty breathing in our atmosphere, or it is heard to "pump up" power preparatory to blowing something down with radiation.* The shock scenes, such as the discovery of the dead deejay's corpse, are edited to be more impactful. In order to speed the film to the first appearance of the alien, some expositional dialogue heard in the "Galaxy Being" version is cut. In *Please Stand By*, the extra, "bonus" dialogue includes an addendum to the Being's line, "I am danger to my galaxy... They will come for me... *destroy your planet*"—which sheds a slightly more malevolent light on his fellow Andromedans. When Carol sees the Being in the transmission shack, she comes completely unhinged, screaming and scrabbling around until Allan gives her a good shaking. The death-scream of ill-fated deejay Eddie Phillips, as well as the lusty shriek put out by Gene Maxwell's date, Loreen, at the sight of Eddie's charred corpse, were dropped from "The Galaxy Being."

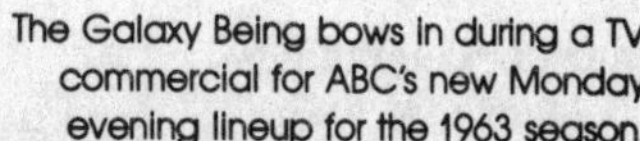

The Galaxy Being bows in during a TV commercial for ABC's new Monday evening lineup for the 1963 season.

The extra screaming and commotion did not necessarily sell the pilot to the execs, but it helped. After the screening, Stevens notes, "Dom and I were watching Tom Moore, and it was really kind of comedic. I stood there while Moore outstretched his hand and walked toward me... then went right by me and hugged Stefano! It was like a Chaplin movie; I stood there thinking he was going to hug *me*. But they were all tickled to death, congratulating Joe and telling him how marvelous his show was. That always floored us—the ones who really worked on the pilot. I was left holding a potato chip at the buffet table and thinking, *shut up, it's selling, that's what counts, don't say a word! Don't rock the boat!* The fact that it was going well was all that we really needed."

"Goldenson turned to me and said something that gave me the

*This noise, excised from "The Galaxy Being," was used later for the fish creatures in "Tourist Attraction."

impression he liked the idea of the monster," remembers Stefano. "Since I was well-known for *Psycho,* they tied that into horror, and when they saw this Galaxy Being on the screen, everybody was in sync. My whole idea of science fiction at the time *was* monsters anyway—y'know, *The Thing.*"

While Stefano left the screening feeling that *Please Stand By* was "too different; too intense" for the executives, Stevens was more optimistic: "Once we showed them the pilot, they knew they had something. They seemed kind of astonished by it. But it was hard-edged enough to sell itself."

Later in the day, Stefano received a phone call from Dorso in his hotel room. ABC wanted to buy the series.

A Villa di Stefano Production

> I'm sure that as a new producer, I must've done things that shocked people. Because I didn't know how to "be" a producer—all I knew was how to come up with a movie that I liked.
>
> —Joseph Stefano

Once ABC voted in favor of *Please Stand By*, a package deal was assembled by the William Morris Agency, which at the time represented *both* United Artists and Daystar. "They did two months of contract writing and *nothing* else," laments Stevens. "They took advantage of the goose with the pewter egg." To this day, as a result, William Morris takes 10 percent of *The Outer Limits'* earnings from syndication sales.

ABC was also keen on having Stefano. In fact, Daniel Melnick had sent feelers concerning TV projects Stefano's way about the time Stevens secured him for *Please Stand By.* In order to become a full partner with Stevens and UA, Stefano incorporated as Villa di Stefano Productions—the villa being the Beverly Hills home in which he still resides. His wife designed the company logo, deriving it from an architectural blueprint of the house. "My company was, in effect, renting me out to Daystar," said Stefano. "When I got the word that the show had sold, I thought, okay, we're in business."

Initially, Villa di Stefano's office was two blocks from Daystar, at 934 North La Cienega in West Hollywood. Harlan Ellison, who went there to pitch story ideas, recalls it as "an itty-bitty office somewhere near the Cock and Bull." It was actually on the floor right above Scandia's.

Villa di Stefano's main men (L–R): Tom Selden, Joseph Stefano, and Louis Morheim, near CBS Studios on Sunset Boulevard, just prior to the network premiere of *The Outer Limits.* (Courtesy Joseph Stefano)

Stefano had given Stevens a frank overview of the pilot while still in New York: "To me, it was like 1950s science fiction movies, which I never saw, never liked, and wasn't about to produce. I remember telling him that doing 'The Galaxy Being' every week was not my idea of what the show was about, and he said, 'Fine; do whatever you want—it's your show.' He was terribly angry when *Stoney Burke* did not get renewed, and the fact that ABC picked up *The Outer Limits* did not placate him, because he wanted several shows on the air all at once. As soon as it became obvious to Leslie that I knew what I was doing, he kind of backed off from *The Outer Limits* to pursue other new shows. I certainly didn't enter into it with any idea of pushing him out. The problem always was that you don't need two guys like me and Leslie to produce one show. And I think Danny Melnick, right off the bat, knew which of us was going to be making the shows that *he* wanted to see."

Stefano was introduced to the four floors of personnel at the Daystar Building. "I couldn't imagine what some of them were doing there," he recalls, bemused. "Leslie just said, 'Well . . . they're *bright*.' It was like Camelot. Leslie would hire people he just *liked*, whose actual jobs were a mystery to me. I was never sure what Allan Balter's job at Daystar was, for example. But Leslie loved to give jobs to people—he had these great, lavish gifts of love that he would suddenly decide you were going to be the victim of. One day he told me, 'I've got a man to do all of our script mimeographing. He's kind of expensive, but really worth it.' This man was a murderer who'd just gotten out of prison, was enormously overweight, and gay. And I said, 'Oh, Leslie, that's so wonderful of you; we're so *glad* to do this.' He loved being in the position to do people good, but it was never for me or for you. It was always for him, because it made him feel wonderful."

Stevens advised the Daystar crew that whatever Stefano requested must be done, and his time was not to be wasted with any problems, which were to be brought directly to Stevens or Frontiere instead. When

Stefano walked onto the *Please Stand By* set for the first time, he was surprised to find himself regarded with a mixture of awe and fear—the "image" Stevens had created for him as producer.

"Bob Justman said something during a meeting," said Stefano, "and I watched him, thinking, *he knows what he's talking about*. I said to him, 'Stick around, because I'm going to need you.' He looked at me like he couldn't believe it—this was *not* the Joe Stefano that Leslie had told the crew about. One day, after a meeting with Edgar Scherick (Melnick's replacement at ABC), he said, 'You're not intractable!' and I thought, oh my god, where did he get that idea? Leslie was protective of me, and wanted to make the show as comfortable as possible. For me, producing was a 'fools rush in' situation. I had no trouble with acclimation, and everybody seemed to be able to do anything I asked them to."

Stefano's education in the tasks of producership was furious and rapid. From the day regular production on *The Outer Limits* commenced, it absorbed all his time. When he wasn't writing or rewriting, he was meeting with writers, screening actors, or holed up in the editing rooms at Daystar, or in transit between studio sets and locations. "Once I started, I realized I *had* to be at the studio. I couldn't sit around the far end of Sunset Boulevard while the crew was working at KTTV or MGM." He moved Villa di Stefano to one of a cluster of "shabby little bungalows" on the KTTV lot next to the soundstages.

Marilyn Stefano assumed the role of interior decorator. Proudly, Stefano notes, "My office was one of the first in the business to be done entirely in antiques. We had a huge breakfront thing, a seventeenth-century armoire with big doors that we outfitted as a bar." Mixed among the required office appurtenances were small Mediterranean end tables and settees. Collector's pieces in baroque, gilt frames hung from the walls. Stefano's desk was an ornate affair of Italian parquet. "It was absurd, impractical," said Allan Balter. "Like some period villa." On the other hand, Stefano's assistant Tom Selden said, "The offices were gorgeous, really elegant. We had modern things, of course, accessible for story conferences and meetings, but Marilyn did a magnificent job."

The decoration scheme also illustrates another aspect of Stefano the producer, according to Leslie Stevens: "The first day Joe was in the office, he went to Frontiere and requested the antiques. Everyone else had the standard-issue Formica desks. Within a month, Joe got his way. He was a real *impresario;* the type to order lobster on the set while everybody else had mixed meats."

"I was real grand studio style, and they all loved it," said Stefano. "No actress ever appeared on a show of mine without finding flowers in her dressing room. Everyone with a speaking part received a personal telegram from me before they arrived. I treated my people like stars, and we later got a lot of actors because of that." Stefano also sent personal letters of congratulations to each writer who worked on the show, a week or so in advance of their air dates.

Billeted in the KTTV bungalow were Lou Morheim, *Outer Limits'* recently-engaged story editor, and Tom Selden, an ex-actor who Stefano recruited as an assistant after seeing a play he'd directed at the Angels Theatre, *Call Me By My Rightful Name*—which starred Robert Sampson and Sally Kellerman, two actors shortly to appear in *The Outer Limits*.* "There was a large reception area," recalls Selden, "where you'd find Barbara Williams, who was Joe's secretary and our coordinator. Lou Morheim's office was to the left, Joe's was straight ahead, behind Barbara, and my office was off to the right—that was where Joe did most of his writing. I functioned out of his office most of the time while he did rewrites locked up in mine." Selden joined Villa di Stefano in late June of 1963, while the "Architects of Fear" episode of *Outer Limits* was in postproduction.

Louis Morheim was the man who bought the Kurosawa film *The Seven Samurai* and packaged it, in a partnership with Yul Brynner, to produce *The Magnificent Seven*. With Fred Freiburger (a future producer of *Star Trek*), he cowrote *The Beast from 20,000 Fathoms* in 1953, adapting it from the Ray Bradbury story, "The Foghorn." Of *The Outer Limits*, Morheim said, "I was impressed by the pilot, and I smelled that these guys at Daystar were on the cutting edge of the future; they were not tired old hacks. Leslie Stevens asked me what my criteria would be for judging whether a script was good or bad, and I started to say, 'Well, I'm a student of Lajos Egri, and—' I never got past the 'and.' For Leslie, the duck just came down. He said, 'You've got the job.'"† That same week, Morheim had previewed the pilot for *Voyage to the Bottom of the Sea*, at the invitation of producer Irwin Allen. "I knew I could make a much better contribution, as a dramatist, to something like *The Outer Limits*," he said. "It was something I wanted to watch. I would never be an audience to something like *Voyage*."

Morheim and Stefano formed the powerful story-generating combine that became the heart of *The Outer Limits*. Morheim screened oral story submissions and rode shotgun on the useful ones through the first draft stage. "From the oral submission," he says, "we'd figure two weeks for a treatment or outline, and three more weeks for a first draft; for the balance of the writing, another two or three weeks. So with an organized,

*Selden's acting career included parts in *Daddy Long Legs*, *The Young Captives*, and *Conquest of Space*.

†Egri authored the fundamental text *The Art of Dramatic Writing*. As for the "duck," the reference is to the quiz show *You Bet Your Life*, in which a prop duck would drop down from the ceiling on a wire to accost host Groucho Marx with the Secret Word.

professional writer, we're talking two weeks for original material, and six weeks for a teleplay."

"Lou saw all the writers before I did," said Stefano. "At first, there was maybe one out of ten writers he thought ought to meet me; not much was coming around. When somebody had an idea he liked, it was rare that I didn't like it, because Lou knew exactly what I was looking for."

ABC, however, did not. They wanted a more concrete bottom line, a theme statement as to just what the hell the new series was supposed to be *about*. "They were constantly on our backs," says Stevens. "They wanted to know what we were going to do with the show, how we were going to 'control' it. They wanted something on paper as a guideline for everybody, hence, *The Canons of Please Stand By*."

The *Canons* were in the form of a "bible," or series format booklet, dutifully hammered out by Stefano for distribution to agents and prospective scriptwriters. "It was from Leslie's ideas," he said, "and based on the pilot." While it is clear that Stefano considered such an absolute, boiled-down summary to be superfluous, it is also obvious that he had a bit of fun stretching a handful of generalized concepts out to fifteen typed

Charles Schneeman's promotional painting for "The Galaxy Being"'s network premiere.

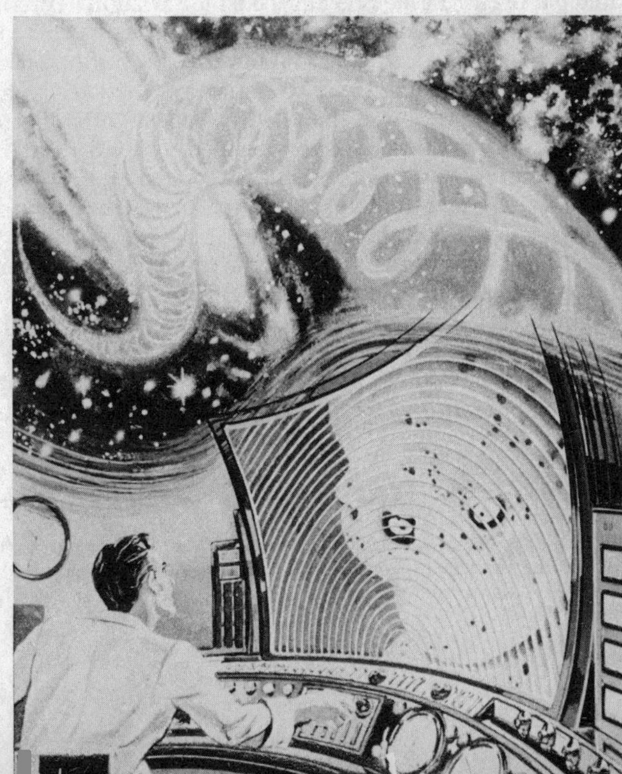

pages (see Appendix I). Prime among the ideas was the "hook" Daniel Melnick had insisted on, the one-per-week monster effect, which came to be called the "bear." Stefano explained in a magazine interview: "In the days of vaudeville, when things were going wrong and the audience was getting bored, out would come a comic in a bear outfit. Or a *trained* bear. That's what we do in each of our shows—we bring on the bear!"

Once ABC got their bible, they objected to *Please Stand By* as a title. It was still less than a year after the Cuban Missile Crisis, and they did not want the program's opening to be misconstrued as a bonafide emergency alert. Stevens took a cue from his Control Voice speech, briefly renaming his new show *Beyond Control*. "Nobody was really happy with that," said Stefano, who wrote his earlier scripts for the show under this mantle, which one reviewer suggested might make too ripe a target for derisive critics. Soon enough, Stevens hit upon *The Outer Limits* as a substitute, and retitled his pilot "The Galaxy Being," making the appropriate adjustments in the introductory Control Voice narration. The great adventure in which the TV viewer was about to participate now reached "*from the inner mind to* The Outer Limits." The tag speech of the original pilot had run:

> *We now return control of your television set to you, until next week at this same time, when the Control Voice takes over. Until then, Please Stand By.*

This was modified to: "*. . . when the Control Voice will take you to* The Outer Limits."

Of the Control Voice, Stevens says, "I originated the concept of the theme statement. I wrote it into the pilot and thought that at the end of each episode we could have some kind of brief nod to high-minded ideals." Regardless of who wrote the subsequent scripts for the show, Stefano wrote most of the Control Voice speeches, and his moralistic tone soon became another "thread" giving the show a week-to-week continuity. "Some of them are pretty outrageous," he said. "But the narration never said anything I didn't firmly believe in, and never without a certain amount of tongue-in-cheek. There's a lot more humor in *The Outer Limits* than anybody ever dreamed, simply because that's a part of me that must play."

In reediting "The Galaxy Being" for its network premiere, Stefano got his first taste of working on a moviola. "I learned how to cut film by watching footage on the machine. For example, there was a moment when the actress crosses into shadow, and you couldn't see her face. I said, 'Right there—start her dialogue, then cut to Cliff reacting, and we've gotten rid of three whole pages.' For me, seeing film in a moviola was like getting it back into the typewriter again—just an extension of writing."

A new credit sequence was done, with a slower succession of astronomical plates run behind the end credits. The final credit was a real mouthful: *A Villa di Stefano Production/In Association with Daystar Productions/United Artists Television.*

The most favorable reaction to the September 16, 1963 premiere broadcast of "The Galaxy Being" came from *The Hollywood Reporter:* "[Stevens has] allowed his imagination to run wild almost to the point of incredulity in the initial plot, but the production was mounted so handsomely with special effects, smoothly accelerating suspense, and acting played straight down the middle for human values rarely given more than fleeting development in shock themers, that this viewer's reaction was: 'It couldn't possibly happen... but I wouldn't bet *heavily* that it couldn't.'"

Production on regular series episodes for *The Outer Limits* began in May of 1963. The Villa di Stefano bungalow, like the Daystar Building, buzzed with activity. "Just getting scripts completed was a seven-days-a-week job," said Morheim. "It never stopped. I was always taking scripts home with me."

"We always had five shows going at once," said Tom Selden. "One being readied, one in preproduction, one shooting, one being edited, and one in final postproduction." A new *Outer Limits* was born almost once every seven days.

Stefano found himself creating scripts "in a whirlwind, overnight—I'd hand stuff to Lou the next morning. I found out that when you're totally in control, you can get as much as you want—you get it written the way you want it, you get the director you want, and you do it the way you want to do it. But... your wife doesn't see you, your little boy doesn't see you, and you become so exhausted that when the alarm goes off in the morning, you wonder if you're even capable of getting out of bed. When I found out ABC wanted this show, I realized that I'd have to do this every week, for twenty-four hours a day."

PART TWO

We Are Controlling Transmission

> It got on the edges, in the first fifteen weeks, of being a breakthrough show. We could all feel it. After it was over, we felt like it was an *okay* credit, and that was it. After five years, we saw it hadn't died, and it may have been an important show after all. In fifteen years' time there was a genuine feeling of, "Yes, there *was* something in there!" It was worth all of the care and love we'd put into it. So the feeling we got during the first few weeks came true in the long run.
>
> —Leslie Stevens

> Other shows being done then, things like *The Untouchables*, had a raw-nerved edge to them. People don't work that way anymore. It was kind of wild in those days. The so-called Golden Age of TV was just about over, and everybody was saying, "Let's get out there and just have a ball!" It was kind of like what I imagine they felt like during the heyday of Hollywood, with certain groups off in a corner somewhere, getting away with murder—little kook groups making the films they really wanted to make. And those are the films we're still watching today.
>
> —Joseph Stefano

The order in which the episodes of *The Outer Limits* were broadcast bears little relation to the order in which they were produced. "You're shooting a show every seven days," said Leslie Stevens, "and as soon as they're edited, you run rough cuts for the network. That was where people like Dan Melnick and Richard Dorso were really good—they'd pick what they thought were the best shows, the ones that should run first, of the ones we had finished."

When "The Galaxy Being" premiered, it also featured a clip of coming attractions, with the Control Voice saying, *"Experience the awe and mystery of the hidden world in these coming episodes of* The Outer Limits!" Footage from "The Borderland," "The Hundred Days of the Dragon," and "Architects of Fear" was shown.

Joe Stefano recalls an early piece of mail the company received just after the premiere: "It was from a woman who wrote: 'Your Control Voice didn't give us back control of our set at the end of the show. Our vertical has been in trouble ever since, and we think you should pay our TV repairman!'"

A shot from "The Borderland" in an ABC promotional slick.

THE BORDERLAND

Broadcast 16 December 1963
Written and directed by Leslie Stevens
Assistant Director: Robert Justman
Director of Photography: John Nickolaus

CAST: Ian Frazer (Mark Richman), Eva Frazer (Nina Foch), Mrs. Palmer (Gladys Cooper), Edgar Price (Alfred Ryder), Lincoln Russel (Phillip Abbott), Dwight Hartley (Barry Jones), Benson Sawyer (Gene Raymond), Dr. Sung (Noel DeSousa).

The mind of man has always longed to know what lies beyond the world we live in. Explorers have ventured into the depths and the heights. Of these explorers, some are scientists, some are mystics. Each is driven by a different purpose. The one thing they share in common is a wish to cross the borderlands that lie beyond the Outer Limits . . .

During a seance intended to make spiritual contact with the dead son of industrialist Hartley, attending physicists Ian and Eva Frazer expose the medium, Mrs. Palmer, as a fake. Then they offer the grieving man an alternate path to the afterlife, one without guarantees. Frazer's left hand was recently trapped in an electrical field during an experiment in polarity reversal, and the two perfect right hands he shows Hartley (one his normal right, the other the "reversed" left) convince the magnate to fund a larger-scale attempt to pry open the doorway to the alternate dimension, the "borderlands" Ian glimpsed . . . *if* an attempt to contact his dead son is included in the deal. Mrs. Palmer's vindictive henchman, Price, arrives to sabotage the equipment just as Ian steps onto his newly-constructed energy platform. Price is electrocuted, the breakers blow, and the power loss causes Ian to get stuck between dimensions. He calls his wife's name, unable to orient himself in the limbo realm, his voice echoing through the lab weirdly out of sync with his lip movements. Eva blacks out the city to draw enough power to pull him back, and when his re-reversed, now normal left hand reaches through the "ionic rain" obscuring the platform, she grabs it and hauls him out intact. Hartley chooses that moment to jump into the field, calling his son's name, and burns out and vanishes before the machines can be shut down.

There are worlds beyond the worlds within which the explorer must explore. But there is one power which seems to transcend space and time, life and death. It is a deeply human power which holds us safe and together when all other forces combine to tear us apart. We call it the power of love.

"Science fiction is a doorway that allows your imagination to freewheel," said Stevens. "Science is a carefully gridded and structured view of the mysterious, so that the rational mind has a firm grounding from which you can gaze into the inexplicable peculiarity of the universe—the fearsomely odd space-time reversals, black holes, and so on. There are actual mysteries that occur constantly, and to look at them rationally turns up extraordinary bends in math, like Hausdorf's Theorems—madness that is totally real. Cold, analytical logic that proves the sun can change places with a pea, and that you can put the sun in your pocket. Science fiction is a way to express these phenomena without becoming so technical that you lose everyone except a few technicians."

"The Borderland," Stevens's opening salvo for his brand-new science fiction series, crackles with highly technical dialogue, but the depth of his concept is lost amid the pyrotechnic flash of the Frazers' other-dimensional probing. The cast tries valiantly to make the drama work, but is perhaps overqualified to play second behind the thunder and fury of the special effects, and all the characters emerge as thin as paper. Wrapped up in his desire to produce an impressive followup to "The Galaxy Being," Stevens edited most of the character out of his teleplay in favor of the confusing, though extravagant, barrage of visuals.

Mark Richman exposes a phony wraith for Gene Reynolds (L) and Nina Foch.

Mark Richman (L) is visited by Joe Stefano on the "Borderland" set. Note Richman's two right hands.

Stevens enjoys dealing with characters of position and wealth, expressing a working knowledge of the power-brokering that transpires in the corridors of the elite, where the tuxedo can be seen as a uniform that confers high social status on the person who wears it. The beginning of "The Borderland" is overwhelmed by the trappings of affluence and upper-caste protocol—which are intended to divert our attention from the fact that the players are pretty dull and conventional. From Hartley and Sawyer we get the doubletalk of cool cash; from the scientists, a lot of important-sounding credits, such as Eva's demure acknowledgment that she holds "the Rensslaer Chair at Midlands University"... whatever that is. Without knowing who these characters are, we are supposed to be impressed with them, but they remain only thumbnail sketches. Ian, in particular, comes off as a bright-eyed fanatic and a bad risk. We don't know what drives him because Stevens cut from his script a speech by Eva that gives us a hint:

> EVA: He's being pulled along, in a straight line, almost as though some invisible force is pulling at him. We keep thinking he's abnormal, a genius compelled to march into the unknown. But he's more like a child, trying to find something he's lost.

Also omitted was an exchange between Eva and fellow researcher "Linc" Russel that sheds some light on what drives *her:*

> RUSSEL (smiles sadly): I used to think you were coldblooded.
>
> EVA: Because I helped him go into danger?

RUSSEL: No—because you're a mathematician. It's unusual for a woman. Austere.

EVA: And beautiful. He taught me how beautiful it can be.

RUSSEL: Oh yes, I know how he feels about mathematics. It's like music to him. He has a way of making ordinary things, like magnets, become mysterious and beautiful. And something else I know. You're not cold and you're not austere. You have mastered the sternest discipline for the simplest, feminine reason. You want to please him.

EVA: I love him.

RUSSEL: I wish I had what he has.

Once again, we have Stevens's solitary scientist, on a quest. This speech also lends some context to the closing narration by the Control Voice on the efficacy of love. But stripped of such background shading, the scientists in "The Borderland" *do* very little other than bustle around their lab in a mock-epic succession of rigorous, procedural tests, yelling such stuff as "Primaries, three-three-one, stroke, one-one, stroke, one, polarity minus-two!" This (plus a litany of countdowns) is intended to maintain a tone of technical veracity that is unnecessary by the last act, when the floodgate of special effects opens up full bore.

For all that, "The Borderland" is handsomely mounted and intelligently cast. The Midlands lab set is impressive, vast, and lit in a darkly sinister fashion. The "coil cell" platform is gloomy and ominous, and in Stevens's first draft included a "device resembling an electric chair;" it looks like a Tom Swiftian deathtrap that comes alive with the unsettling hiss of the ionic rain when running at full power. The fleeting glimpses of "borderlandscape" seen through the curtain of ions were paintings by renowned astronomical artist Chesley Bonestell. Jack Poplin's crew constructed the "magnetic coil" power pylons by winding spray-painted garden hose around cores; these props were to turn up in many other *Outer Limits* episodes as background hardware.

One curious note sounds when Mrs. Palmer, the spiritualist, attempts to stop Price from sabotaging Ian's experiment. The possibility that the Frazers just might legitimately contact another world captivates her, and while she is leaning toward the scientific, the scientists are

High-angle view of the "coil cell," featuring Jack Poplin's garden-hose "power pylons."

A brief glimpse of the other-dimensional "borderland."

hampered by unexpected visions: "I've got a feeling, Eva," Ian says. "I can see myself later, alive and well, with you." Eva responds, "I've got to say it, Ian—I see you *lost*." They both turn out to be right, while Hartley later says, "I feel it! I feel I shall reach my son!" Whether he does remains a mystery.

Mark Richman, a casting suggestion of Stefano's (he was in *The Black Orchid*), is a good choice for Ian Frazer. He wordlessly conveys the sweat and spirit needed to tackle the unknown, like some metaphysical Eagle Scout, or maybe just another Stevens surrogate, bucking the system.

"Leslie has a fantastic facility of ideas," said Stefano. "I couldn't begin to write the *Outer Limits* he wrote. I don't find his writing terribly deep—not shallow, but not resonant. He goes off on scientific flights of fancy that simply lose me as an audience, and he's more interested in what he's writing about than the characters he creates. They're puppets, and they tend to come out a little empty. His is just a very different style—different from what I was into, but just as good. In 'The Borderland,' even though I thought Leslie's ideas were great and the drama worked for me, Danny Melnick was very concerned about it, and during a meeting he asked me what I could do. I said, 'Honestly? Nothing. You want me to tell Leslie you don't like what you're seeing? Besides, how can you even tell? It isn't finished; the special effects aren't in yet.'"

Stevens did have a handle on the visual impact he desired for the episode: "They go inside-out, into a new realm. There was no LSD at that time, no expanding of consciousness. I wanted to get what was later called the psychedelic look, to blow everyone's mind." This effort caused a lot of grief, and after principal photography was completed, Stevens called in veteran director and visual effects expert Byron Haskin to lend a hand. "'The Borderland' was filled with moving, shimmering lights filmed at odd angles," said Haskin. "And you've got to know what an effect is going to look like in advance, so you can shoot to fit it. You can't go panning around an actor when the background is going to be double-exposed. We had to take the film apart reel by reel, frame by frame. We marked the many times the [ionic rain] effect was to be seen, and doing this one effect ultimately cost $14,000. Stevens saw the bill and cried."

Apart from the huge postproduction bill that was not appreciated by the money men, "The Borderland" had no "bear," as "The Galaxy Being" had. ABC was very uneasy with the finished product, and held it in inventory until the middle of the season before broadcasting it. "They were terrified we weren't going to do a good, solid, commercial monster show," said Stevens. "To them, the thread of *The Outer Limits* was merely to present monstrous ideas. I broke the rules a few times, rather badly, and got called for it. In 'The Borderland,' the 'bear' was not acceptable to them. And since that show was the first to be shot, I was *already* breaking regulations, in their eyes. They wanted me to get back over into my corner and give them something—killer bees, plants with spores, anything! There had to be a creature or menace that would hold the audience if they didn't like science fiction."

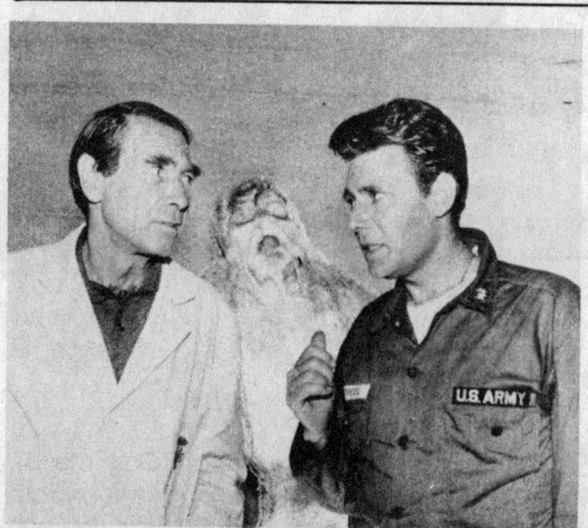

Gary Merrill, Chill Charlie and Harry Guardino.

THE HUMAN FACTOR

Broadcast 11 November 1963
Written by David Duncan
Directed by Abner Biberman
Assistant Director: Lee H. Katzin
Director of Photography: Conrad Hall

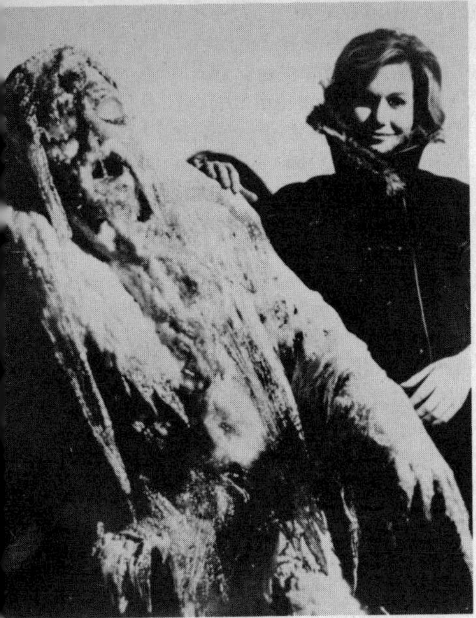

Chill Charlie mugs for publicity photographers, in the company of Sally Kellerman.

The Ghost of Private Gordon as he appeared in the episode.

CAST: Major Roger Brothers (Harry Guardino), Dr. James Hamilton (Gary Merrill), Col. William Campbell (Joe de Santis), Ingrid Larkin (Sally Kellerman), Major Harold Giles (Ivan Dixon), Dr. Soldini (Shirley O'Hara), Orderly (James B. Sikking), Peterson (John Newton), Sergeant (Art Alisi), Nurse (Jane Langley), Pvt. Gordon/Ice Ghost (William O. Douglas, Jr.), Sentry/Stunt Hamilton (Matty Jordan), Stunt Brothers (Dave Perna), Intercom Voice (Vic Perrin).

In Northern Greenland the mountains stand like a wall along Victoria Channel, whose straight course marks the line of the Great Baffin Fault. Until recently, not even the Eskimos ventured into this Arctic waste. But today, as in other lonely places in the world, the land is dominated by those instru-

ments of detection which stand as a grim reminder of man's fear of man. This is Point TABU, a name given this predominantly underground base by a young officer who explained that the letters in TABU stood for Total Abandonment of Better Understanding. Some two hundred men and a few women make this their permanent residence. Their task is to maintain a constant alert against enemy attack, and be prepared to respond to it, devastatingly...

In his lab at the remote base, psychiatrist Hamilton has devised a diagnostic apparatus that permits two minds to link and share thoughts. His newest patient is Major Brothers, whose most recent crazy behavior has been an attempt to blow up the nearby Hecla Isthmus using the base's atomic cartridge, a portable nuclear device. Earlier, Brothers had led an exploratory sortie to the Isthmus and allowed a trapped member of his party, Pvt. Gordon, to die there. Now he is haunted by the accusing spectre of the dead man, and believing it to be a "monster" intent on destroying the base, he wants to eliminate it first with the bomb. Hamilton wires Brothers up to his machine in order to lay bare Brothers's mental state. A tremor rocks the base, the machine shorts fizzlingly out, and Hamilton's mind regains consciousness in Brothers's body... and vice versa. Seeing another opportunity to get at the atomic cartridge, Brothers, as Hamilton, orders "Brothers" locked up. Hamilton's fiancée, Ingrid Larkin, gets wise to the exchange; having melded her mind with Hamilton's before the accident, she believes "Brothers'" wild tale of actually being Hamilton, and helps him to escape. They return to the lab where Brothers, determined to murder his old body and keep Hamilton's, bursts in and grapples with Hamilton. He shoots Hamilton—in the "Brothers" body—before getting knocked out. As the Brothers body dies, Hamilton manages to switch their minds back, and Brothers dies in his own body. When asked by Ingrid how he'll report the incident, the now-restored Hamilton says, "Only the truth—Major Brothers shot himself."

A weapon? No, only an instrument, neither good nor evil until men put it to use. And then, like so many of man's inventions, it can be used either to save lives or destroy them, to make men sane or to drive them mad, to increase human understanding or to betray it. But it will be men who make the choice. By itself the instrument is nothing, until you add the human factor.

The first produced *Outer Limits* not written by Leslie Stevens, "The Human Factor" outwardly has much to recommend it. It was the first episode to employ Conrad Hall's outre camera angles and moody, heavily-textured lighting effects, and features fine performances from its three leads in an ideally otherworldly setting. As in *The Thing* and the memorably weird TV movie *A Cold Night's Death,* a snowbound outpost isolated from the world at-large seems a perfect stage for eerie events. David

Duncan's script, however, is a depressingly conventional drama hinging on an old-hat sci-fi gimmick—in this case, a brain swap between a psychoanalyst and a psychotic. The teleplay is not sub-par or badly written; like Abner Biberman's direction, it is merely adequate.

Biberman, an ex–character actor (his most noteworthy bit part was in the Val Lewton/Jacques Tourneur film *The Leopard Man)* was a competent journeyman director who logged his six days on *The Outer Limits* and never worked on the show again. "Abner was a little out of his element with this stuff," said 1st AD Lee Katzin.

Similarly, "The Human Factor" was the only script done by David Duncan for *The Outer Limits*. At the time, Duncan's screenwriting credentials included *The Black Scorpion* (1957), *The Thing That Couldn't Die* and Jack Arnold's *Monster On the Campus* (both 1958), and George Pal's *The Time Machine*. "You may have noticed the blurry bit where the heroine attempts to get the keys to the cell," said Duncan of his story. "I had rewritten this scene at the request of Joe Stefano, who had said, 'Let's get some suspense into it, so she has difficulty getting the key.' The panel holding the keys was placed behind a switchboard operator, who thereby became its guardian. The excuse manufactured by the heroine so that she could approach the panel was that she pretended to forget the number of her own extension, and so had to look it up in the phone book, which was right next to the panel. While doing so, she pinches the keys. In the finished film, the key panel was ten feet behind the operator, and within easy reach of the heroine, so that all my dialogue—which had been retained—became meaningless. When I saw the film, I asked Stefano how come, and he said something like, 'You know, I thought that looked sort of strange myself, but no one else said anything, so I figured it must have some kind of subtle meaning, and I wasn't going to lay myself open by asking any questions!"

Duncan's script was heavily revised about a month after the original draft was submitted, in April of 1963. Most of the dialogue remained intact, and another doctor—Ingrid's romantic rival for Hamilton—was eliminated. Interestingly, Ingrid's line to Hamilton, "You don't need a woman or a wife," originally ended with, "but you might want a mistress" (at which the censors might have shaken their heads *no)*.

One very real drawback was that "The Human Factor" was basically a psychological suspense story that allowed little room, once again, for the "bear" ABC had been promised. "The Borderland" had already focused on a scientific menace rather than any kind of resident gargoyle, and to omit one from the very next show would not foster any faith between the producers and the network. Thus was born the entity known in the script as the Ice Creature, a.k.a. the Ghost of Private Gordon, an ice-encrusted hallucinatory product of Major Brothers's dementia. It fades in three brief times to point *j'accuse* at Brothers, and it was better than nothing.

The Outer Limits' unbilled special effects advisor, Byron Haskin, and Wah Chang of Project Unlimited designed a lifesized figure encased in translucent amber ice, with frozen stalactites hanging from its outstretched arm and a yellow bulb inside the head that caused the empty eyesockets to glow. Nicknamed "Chill Charlie" by Haskin, the statue never appears in the episode. In its stead is William O. Douglas, Jr., wearing a fatigue jacket sheeted in plastic icicles, his eyes blackened and corpselike. Chill Charlie was vanquished to the realm of UATV publicity photographs, where he can be seen in stills, posed next to Sally Kellerman or Harry Guardino, or as the "front man" for the wrapper used on the *Outer Limits* gum cards that were eventually produced. Though Douglas looks thoroughly grotesque in makeup, he simply isn't as creepy as Chill Charlie would have been.

"The Human Factor" marks Sally Kellerman's first TV role. "I'd seen her in Ibsen's *The Master Builder* in a theatre on La Cienega," recalls Stefano. "When I was introduced to her, I said, 'If I'm ever in a position to do anything about you and it hasn't already been done, I'm going to do it.' At the time she said sure, thanks a lot, that sort of thing. Then came a small part in 'The Human Factor,' and I got Sally for it. I told her it wasn't much, but it was a piece of film she could show anybody. Then I told Connie Hall, 'Don't give me any shit about how we're in Greenland; I want Dietrich, Garbo, right out of the Thirties!' Then I told the costumers to find a way to get her out of uniform and into something glamorous. Everyone thought she was my lady, but it wasn't anything. She was my Harry Cohn personification!"

Casting director John Erman had also directed Kellerman in little theatre. "Stefano saw, in her, his chance to do what Hitchcock had done with Ingrid Bergman," he said. Appropriately, the name of Kellerman's character is Ingrid. "Since I was dating Sally at the time, I remember very specific things—Stefano got her to diet, got her a new wardrobe, and finally decided to fashion a whole episode around her. That show, 'The Bellero Shield,' was the beginning of the new Sally Kellerman, and she was delighted and grateful, because she had just been kicking around, like so many of us." Based on her "piece of film" from "The Human Factor," Kellerman was quickly signed to the William Morris Agency.

Of "The Human Factor," *Daily Variety* was quick to cite "motivational haziness, loose ends and apparent contradictions," calling the episode a "lesser edition" of *The Outer Limits*. More to the point, it is unfortunately easy to say that "The Human Factor," but for its too-few bright spots, is as cold and barren as the Arctic tundra itself.

Henry Silva (L) as General Mercurio.

TOURIST ATTRACTION

Broadcast 23 December 1963
Written by Dean Riesner
Directed by Laslo Benedek
Assistant Director: Robert Justman
Director of Photography: John Nickolaus

CAST: John Dexter (Ralph Meeker), Lynn Arthur (Janet Blair), Tom Evans (Jerry Douglas), Prof. Arrivelo (Jay Novello), Gen. Juan Mercurio (Henry Silva), Reporter (Willard Sage), 2nd Reporter (Edward Colmens), Oswaldo [Major Domo] (Jon Silo), Capt. Fortunato [Mercurio's aide] (Francis Ravel), Skipper (Stuart Lancaster), Paco [Janitor] (Martin Garrelega), Mario (Henry Delgado), Butler (Marco Antonio), *Ichthyosaurus Mercurius* (Roger Stern). WITH: Noel de Sousa and Shelley Morrison.

In man's dark and troubled history, there are vestiges of strange gods. This stone statue was once such a god, a thousand years gone by, in the central mountains of Pan America. Today, new gods have emerged—the god of power, the god of money. The Republic of San Blas lies west of the Orinoco Basin and slightly north of the Equator. Its principal exports are coffee, copra, mahogany, mace, and saffron. In a hundred-odd years the reins of government have changed many times in blood and fire and death. The last of the revolutions was led by General Juan Mercurio, the most absolute and powerful ruler of them all. Only the Indians who live close to the old gods in the volcanic uplands are unimpressed. They have seen the coming of Conquistadors, with the power of their guns and flashing flags; the revolutionaries, with their zeal and willingness to die; the Americans, with the power of their

> *money and bulldozers, with their summer houseboats in the crater lake of Aripana, with their gadgets, and machines, and devices . . .*

In the coastal waters of San Blas, corporate mercenary John Dexter captures an enormous, prehistoric amphibian, one that resembles the ancient stone carvings of reptilian gods. His plans to ship the creature back to the U.S. for study are countered by Mercurio, a Castro-like dictator who promptly christens the find *Ichthyosaurus Mercurius*, disallows its removal from the country, and plans to exhibit it in his World's Fair to draw tourist trade. The amphibian is locked in a freezer under guard, but an accident allows it to thaw out and escape. It is quickly recaptured. Arrivelo, a professor at the local university, reveals that the creature used ultrasonic emissions to disintegrate the iron of the freezer door, and that the similar sounds it continues to broadcast may be a form of SOS to others of its kind. When Dexter tries to smuggle the creature out of San Blas, an army of the beasts rises from Lake Aripana to reclaim their comrade. The sight paralyzes Dexter with fright, and he is convinced to let the captive creature go free. The school of creatures then destroys Mercurio Dam with their ultrasonics, bringing an apocalyptic flood to San Blas. Mercurio's corpse is seen among the victims of the catastrophe. Dexter survives, and his newfound experience with fear and humility allows him to reach a reconciliation with his estranged mistress, Lynn Arthur.

> *The forces of nature will not submit to injustice. No man has the right, nor will the checks and balances of the universe permit him, to place his fellows under the harsh yoke of repression. Nor may he again place the forces of nature under the triple yoke of vanity, greed, and ambition. In the words of Shelley: "Here lies your tyrant, who would rule the world immortal."*

"'Tourist Attraction' was the closest we ever came to those kinds of schlocky sci-fi movies that overran the 1950s," said Joseph Stefano. Echoing him, writer Dean Riesner said, "The closest I ever came to science fiction is that I once went to a track meet with Ray Bradbury."

Stefano had expressed an interest in doing an *Outer Limits* with a political slant, and at the time public notice was very much on Dominican despot Raphael Trujillo, who had just died. Riesner took the Trujillo slant and merged it with his recent reading on John Lilly's famous research into dolphin intelligence, thus yielding the show's main attraction—the corps of dinosauric, skindiving sea monsters who use a sophisticated form of sonic communication, like dolphins, and were prehistoric in origin, like the coelacanth. What evolved was almost a line-for-line remake of the 1954 classic *Creature from the Black Lagoon,* even down to the tedious expositional dialogue that establishes the coelacanth as the present-day role model for the antediluvian amphibians.

"The material I'd written was mediocre," says Riesner. "I blame certain shortcomings the show had on the fact that I wrote in many special effects aspects that gave the production people difficulty." When Stevens reviewed the teleplay, he told Stefano it was too expensive to produce. Stefano rewrote the script to simplify it, and whereas the straightforward narrative set-up related by the Control Voice is Riesner's, the business of "old gods" and quotations from Shelley is pure Stefano. "They didn't have to change it too much to make it awful," Riesner maintains. Undaunted, Stefano asked Riesner to consider doing another episode, and the writer declined, responding, "I had no real interest in writing science fiction."

One way Stefano bridged broad gaps in the story was to bring on the Control Voice in the middle of the show, twice, to explain what was going on during underwater scenes:

> *Moving through the deep, protected only by a tank of air and a hunting spear, the scientist-explorer descends beyond the San Blas shelf. But all unknown to him, the observer is himself observed. Hidden in the sinuous rills of seaweed, sightless eyes, blind for centuries, stare out of the abyss. The legendary creature of the deeps, sensing through nerve receptors in its skin, becomes aware of the alien invader, man.*

And later, when the creatures gang up on Mercurio Dam:

> *Pressed and strained by constant drilling of ultrasonic beams, the concrete face of the dam cracks and faults. Ten million tons of pressure builds toward ultimate collapse...*

These editorial intrusions on the episode-in-progress were jarring and mostly superfluous, and the technique was not used again until Harlan Ellison wrote similar descriptive passages in *Outer Limits'* second season, for "Soldier."

"I didn't get too involved in that show," said Stevens. "Although I did insist the fish be true to form, and not have two legs or something. The script called for hundreds of these creatures, and we could only afford three."

The manufacture of the full-body amphibian suits was the largest single *Outer Limits* job handed to Project Unlimited, and Byron Haskin and Wah Chang collaborated on the design, which is froggish, toothy, and a bit wall-eyed. "We used these huge, industrial-sized baker's bowls to mix the latex, fifteen, twenty gallons at a time," recalls Projects team member Paul LeBaron. "There was a failed paint store on one side of the Projects address, and we rented it just to get enough room for the baker's oven we used to cure the suits. We built a shell around the oven, to make it even bigger. The mold for the suit weighed three hundred pounds. We had it on a block and fall, and everybody at Projects would have to gather around it just to lift it into the oven! We made all the suits from that mold, and once, while we were heaving it out, the darn thing slipped and nearly broke my leg. I got a contusion on my right thigh that swelled up like a balloon, and after about two weeks I had to have it operated on. They took out almost a cup of blood."

Once the suits were completed, Production Manager Lin Parsons loaded them into his station wagon and met the stunt crew at his home to test-dunk the costumes in his swimming pool. "We put in little bags of lead shot for negative buoyancy," he said. "And the hump on the back of the suit was for a scuba tank. I went into the water with the stunt men during the tests. It startled my neighbors a little bit!"

When the suits absorbed enough water to sink properly, a new problem arose. "They'd get waterlogged, like a sponge," said 1st AD Robert Justman. "So they became incredibly heavy, and hard to move around in." Another handicap was described by Wah Chang: "The time we had to put these costumes together was not sufficient to safeguard against certain factors—like the divers literally bursting through the suits after being submerged." Either the latex rubber ripped apart due to the added weight of the water, or the divers would become claustrophobic. Underwater cameraman and stunt regular Paul Stader initiated a hand-clapping gesture for the fish-men to use to indicate their need to surface. On one occasion the signal was misinterpreted as hammy self-applause for a successfully completed shot, and Stevens recalls watching rushes in which the monsters suddenly surface and tear their heads off, yelling, "Goddammit, I'm drowning!"

Typical of the fast shuffle suffered by the plot in favor of monster window-dressing is the scene where the captive *Ichthyosaurus Mercurius* is put on ice. There is no question that the beast will thaw out and go on the rampage, and that the "accidental" defrost is at the hands of a pair of drunken ethnic stereotypes brings the show in line with even Stefano's definition of schlock. The creature drags itself through the freezer door, top-heavy and wobbling, a scant menace hardly justifying the wholesale panic that ensues. There is a vague hint that the creature's ultrasonic buzzing somehow immobilizes human beings, but not enough of one to overcome the visual evidence that these sluggish monsters could easily be outdistanced by a brisk walking pace.

With the exception of Henry Silva's steely-eyed Mercurio, a tinpot tyrant brimming over with swagger and cunning, the performances are disposable. In the early scenes, Ralph Meeker's aloof delivery serves well the sort of corporate dispassion that makes Dexter little better than Mercurio, but his cynical asides are often so dry and quick that they speed past both the viewer and the other characters. Too quickly, Meeker seems simply bored with the whole affair, and since Janet Blair is twice as old as the Lynn Arthur character is supposed to be (in the script), the two form another *Outer Limits* Odd Couple, like Gary Merrill and Sally Kellerman in "The Human Factor."

This was the first of three *Outer Limits* assignments for Hungarian director Laslo Benedek, whose biggest successes had come a decade earlier with the Frederic March *Death of a Salesman* and *The Wild One*, with Marlon Brando. "Laslo was a very precise man who had done features for years," said Jack Poplin. "His first comment would always be, 'De scrip needs to be vorked on,' and since he was used to a feature pace, he'd get into corners. For this episode, we built the rear end of a yacht. Laslo was always shooting the wrong way; we'd have to keep scooting the backings around."

Much of the music heard in the episode is by Dominic Frontiere's old teacher and friend, Robert Van Eps. "Bobby is really a world-class orchestrator," noted John Elizalde, "and Dom brought him into *The Outer*

A horde of *Ichthyosaurus Mercurius* emerges from the backlot lake at MGM. (Courtesy Claude Binyon, Jr.)

Limits." Some Frontiere music was tracked into Act Four, and both composers received credit. Van Eps's music then went into the stock library for the show, to be heard in later episodes such as "Moonstone" and "The Mutant."

Dean Riesner later wrote the phenomenally successful TV miniseries *Rich Man, Poor Man*, and cowrote the Clint Eastwood vehicles *Dirty Harry* and *The Enforcer*. He has seen "Tourist Attraction" several times in syndication, and says, "I sit and watch it with dreaded fascination, wondering what the hell is going on."

"Leslie had told me to take care of all the 'artistic stuff,' and put my mark on *The Outer Limits*," said Joseph Stefano. "Then United Artists called us to New York, to ask why these shows were coming in $20,000, $30,000 overbudget. And I thought, aha, Leslie's letting me have whatever I want! If I wanted five actors, all of whom would get top-of-the-show billings, I'd get them—and there went the budget for the whole show. I did not know we could not do that, but afterward, I was in on all the budget meetings, paring down. I'd take one top-of-the-show actor and then get others who weren't as well known. I'd rule out scripts with special effects we couldn't afford. I could rewrite a three-set scene onto a single set and still get the writer's ideas across. We were getting about $120,000 per show, and my primary concern became bringing our budgets as close to that figure as I could, because anything over that was deficit financed. That $120,000 mark was where UA was waiting for us, with money they wouldn't get back until reruns. Leslie and I weren't paying for all the overages!"

"For *this* show, it was impossible to gauge costs on a set basis," said Stevens. "We broke costs down in order of importance—overhead, then sets, then casts, then effects and makeup." While Stefano was phasing into *The Outer Limits*, getting his sea-legs as a producer, "The Borderland" went far over budget, and the Chill Charlie fiasco helped do likewise for "The Human Factor." Early advertising for *The Outer Limits* touted "distinctive stories and distinguished stars"... and stars of distinction, like Cliff Robertson, Gary Merrill, Ralph Meeker, and Janet Blair, were usually expensive.

Then "Tourist Attraction" achieved the dubious distinction of being the most expensive *Outer Limits* episode yet produced, and as a result, in late June of 1963, Stevens's office filled up with accountants from UATV. "Their 'creative voice' was the veto power they could wield by turning off the financial spigot," Stevens said. "It was their job to jump on us, screaming, whenever we went the slightest bit over."

About the time "Tourist Attraction" was completed, another incident brought a UATV accountant to Stefano's office. "When we first began production on *The Outer Limits*, I asked for my check, and they sent me a check," said Stefano. "After I'd collected five or six checks, this young man from UATV came to see me, and said, 'We are very worried, Joe, because you have now collected your producer's fee on six shows, and you've only shot your third. And if something happened to you...' But what he meant was, *if you suddenly decided to fuck off to South America, we'd be in trouble!* Here was this man I'd never seen before, this *child,* sitting in my office telling me we'd have to work out some arrangement, and what if I'd collected on thirty-six shows and only finished twenty? He was *really* hot. I listened to his whole spiel, then said, 'What it comes down to is you're afraid I'm going to collect my money and walk away from my *own* show.' When he left, I called Leslie and told him I would not accept any more checks until each show went on the air. I just thought you got paid for thirty-six episodes—I didn't know you had to wait until they were finished! And then the calls started, from UATV, from ABC; they were all very worried because now I wasn't taking *any* money. They said, 'C'mon, Joe, this is ridiculous, everybody needs money, it's okay.' I just said nope. And that's why, long after we finished production, I was still collecting a check, every week."

Fresh from his flying classes, Stevens dropped by and asked if Joe wanted to ride in a helicopter. They went up with Stevens at the throttle, flying out from an airport in Santa Monica to buzz Stefano's Beverly Hills home. "Afterward, in the car, Leslie turned to me and said that everyone was very upset over what I was doing with the producer's fees," said Stefano. "They thought I was gearing up to leave the show in a snit. I told him not to worry, I wasn't angry, I wasn't going to leave the show. But I'd made my statement, and that was how it was going to be. It was fun sticking to my guns. I thought it was important to do that."

Stevens found one solution to the dire problem of budget overruns right in *The Outer Limits'* own backyard. At his request, Byron Haskin put on his director's hat and did the next show on the production roster, "Architects of Fear"—the first episode to come in *under* budget. This turnaround sent the accounting munchkins back to their cubicles, permitting Daystar, Stefano, and company to return to the business of doing weekly television.

Presenting Byron Haskin

The *Outer Limits* budgets were not tops, not adequate for the material, and under-average for the time. A lot of directors, including Stevens,went over; some shows cost twice their budgets, and others you had to wrestle them off the set to finish them. I had originally been contacted

> to work on *Outer Limits* by Leon Chooluck, and Stevens and I agreed that my association with the show would be in a nameless position, supervising the special effects. I didn't want credit as an associate producer—the "ass-prod" credit suggests a gofer, a guy who fetches coffee for the real producer. I worked as an advisor, and didn't want screen credit *except* as a director, because a "triple-threat" guy is always suspect in this business.
>
> —Byron Haskin

Once known as John Barrymore's favorite cameraman, and winner of an Academy Award for special effects as far back as 1938, Byron "Bunny" Haskin's career in the film industry is diverse and far-ranging. At the time he joined the Daystar team, he had been working in film for nearly half a century.

"I think *The Outer Limits* far surpasses those things that Rod Serling did," said Haskin. "*Twilight Zone* was off into other areas. In *The Outer Limits* there was a thread of spookiness, of the offbeat; the title itself was the dress-coat that held the series together—taking things to the outer limits of your credence, and your ability to absorb shock." An outspoken, amiable walrus of a man given to scatological wisecrackery, Haskin proved capable of tossing together creatures and camera tricks despite the constant shortages of time and money, and was adept at running interference with what he called the industry's "mogul types."

Born in 1889 in Portland, Oregon, Haskin spent three years as an art student at the University of California at Berkeley before enlisting as a Naval Aviation cadet during World War One. He later worked as a cartoonist for the *San Francisco Daily News*, and dabbled in advertising before signing on as a cameraman for *International Newsreel* and *Pathé News*. He migrated to Hollywood in 1919 and became an assistant cameraman to Lyman Broening, then an AD for Louis J. Selznick. By 1922 he was a first cameraman for Warners, after brief stints at the old Samuel Goldwyn and Metro companies. Among the directors he worked with during the 1920s were Allan Dwan (who did the Douglas Fairbanks *Robin Hood*), Malcolm St. Clair (who did the original version of *Gentle-*

"Bunny" Haskin, Hallowe'en, 1983.
(Photo by D. J. Schow)

men Prefer Blondes in 1928), the legendary Raoul Walsh, and Alan Crosland (director of *The Jazz Singer*), whose son would later become another of *The Outer Limits*' directors.

Haskin's first three features as director were all silent films for Warners, done in 1927: *Ginsberg the Great, Matinee Ladies,* and *Irish Hearts.* That year he also did *The Siren* for Columbia, and in the early 1930s he joined the special effects department at Warners, working in production, as a second unit cameraman/director, and as an effects photographer on such films as the 1935 *A Midsummer Night's Dream* (the James Cagney version, featuring a fifteen-year-old Mickey Rooney as Puck) and the classic *Captain Blood.* In 1937 he succeeded Fred Jackson as head of the special effects department at Warners, a post he held until the end of World War Two. Stage 5 at Warners became "Bunn's stage," and most of the special effects copyrights secured by the studio at this time were developed by Haskin and his crew, who in 1938 were awarded a "Class III Scientific/Technical Prize" from the Academy of Motion Picture Arts and Sciences for "pioneering the development, and for the first practical application to motion picture production, of the triple-headed background projector." Haskin was also an Oscar nominee for his work on *The Private Lives of Elizabeth and Essex* (1939), *The Sea Hawk* (1940), *The Sea Wolf* (1941), and *Desperate Journey* (1942).

Haskin resumed his directorial career in 1947 with *I Walk Alone,* starring Burt Lancaster and Kirk Douglas. After *Too Late for Tears* (1949) he made the Disney *Treasure Island* in England the same year. Then he linked up with fantasy film producer George Pal in the early 1950s. Pal had just done *Destination Moon* and *When Worlds Collide,* and his love for science fiction was well-matched with Haskin's expertise with optical trickery. Their first collaboration, *War of the Worlds* (1953), is probably the film for which Haskin is best remembered as a director, and it deservedly won an Oscar for its special effects.

Throughout the 1950s, Haskin directed a broad variety of pictures, including, for Pal, *The Naked Jungle* (1954), *Conquest of Space* (1955), which featured future *Outer Limits* co-worker Tom Selden in a small role, and *From Earth to the Moon* (1958). He also did a lot of Westerns and swashbucklers, including *Tarzan's Peril, Warpath, Silver City* (all 1951), *The Denver & Rio Grande* (1952), *His Majesty O'Keefe* (1953), *Long John Silver* (1954), *The First Texan* (1956), and *The Little Savage* (1959). Before retiring in 1968, he would do the noteworthy *Robinson Crusoe on Mars* (1964), one last film for Pal, *The Power* (1967), and lend technical assistance in 1966 to a science fiction TV pilot called *Star Trek.* His last film prior to linking up with Daystar was *Captain Sindbad,* completed in Europe in early 1963. Haskin had made the transition to TV work in 1957 on the *Meet McGraw* series, and he worked exclusively for *The Outer Limits* through mid-1964.

"My topmost post, if you could call it that, was organizing the design and construction of the monsters," he said. "I had a good rapport with the people at Project Unlimited, especially Wah Chang, who had a wry, weird sense of the strange." Chang, Haskin, and Projects cofounder Gene Warren round-tabled various *Outer Limits* "bears" during conferences with Daystar and Stefano's story department. "Stefano and I would talk over each story at those meetings, and I would sketch my ideas for monsters on a charcoal pad. After we oohed and aahhed them, we'd take them to Projects to see what could be made from them. I tried to keep the ones I designed down to the workable size of an average man. We didn't make any problem out of solving such things, we just did them one way or another—whatever the hell would fit the money."

After "rescuing" the special effects of "The Borderland," Haskin helped design Chill Charlie for "The Human Factor," intending to use it in conjunction with a special "transmission mirror"—an optical effects tool he had used on *Captain Sindbad,* and had shipped in from Europe to use on *The Outer Limits*. It was a budget-saving plan that backfired when Chill Charlie was abandoned. Then came "Tourist Attraction," of which Haskin said, "It starred this well-known singer dame, but it was *not* a musical. It went thousands of dollars over cost, took ten days to shoot, and was no damned good anyhow!"

Then came "Architects of Fear," a turning point for *The Outer Limits* in more ways than budgetary ones.

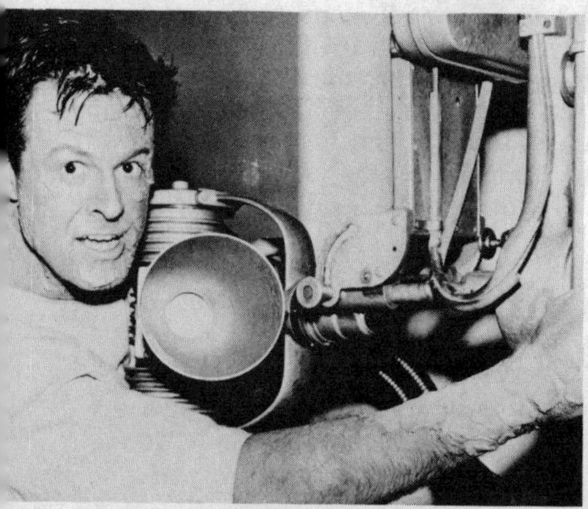

Robert Culp in mid-mutation: "I am Caliban—with a Ph.D.!"

THE ARCHITECTS OF FEAR

Broadcast 30 September 1963
Written by Meyer Dolinsky

Directed by Byron Haskin
Assistant Director: Lee H. Katzin
Director of Photography: Conrad Hall

CAST: Allen Leighton (Robert Culp), Yvette Leighton (Geraldine Brooks), Dr. Phillip Gainer (Leonard Stone), Dr. Herschel (Martin Wolfson), Dr. Paul Fredericks (Douglas Henderson), the Thetan [Allen as alien] (Janos Prohaska), Carl Ford (Lee Zimmer), Bert Bolsey (Hal Bokar), "Big Tom" (William Bush), Fred (Clay Tanner), and Ginger the dog.

Is this the day? Is this the beginning of the end? There is no time to wonder, no time to ask, "Why is it happening, why is it finally happening?" There is time only for fear, for the piercing pain of panic. Do we pray? Or do we merely run now, and pray later? Will there be a later? Or is this the day?

An idealistic coterie of scientists resolves to unify the warring nations of Earth by providing a common enemy to unite against, an extraterrestrial "scarecrow" that will land a spaceship while the UN is in session, and confront the General Assembly, laser pistol in hand. They draw lots, and physicist Allen Leighton is chosen to undergo a radical surgical procedure that will transform him into "a perfect inhabitant of the planet Theta." Allen's death is faked and the grueling series of transplants and modifications to his body proceeds. Unaware of the plot, his wife Yvette persists in believing he is not dead, and thanks to a vague psychic link they share, she "feels" sympathetic pains as Allen suffers on the operating table. Once the bizarre transformation is complete, Allen is launched into orbit as a weather satellite, but he comes down off course and makes a forced landing in the woods near the United Labs facility where the plan was hatched. Now a hideous, scaly, bird-footed, nitrogen-breathing monstrosity, Allen uses the laser to disintegrate a station wagon as a warning to a trio of hunters; they in turn put a bullet in his back as he makes a run for the lab. Yvette again feels her husband's pain, and hurries to United Labs, beating Allen's fellow scientists there. Before dying from its mortal wound, the creature demonstrates the "mark against evil"—a personal gesture Allen had shared with his wife—and Yvette realizes the horrifying truth.

Scarecrows and magic and other fatal fears do not bring people closer together. There is no magic substitute for soft caring and hard work, for self-respect and mutual love. If we can learn this from the mistake these frightened men made, then their mistake will not have been merely grotesque. It will have been at least a lesson—a lesson at last to be learned.

The Outer Limits' problems with budget hassles and lackluster scripts were both squashed for the first time by "Architects of Fear," a compelling episode that showcased many of the elements that became icons of the program's unique identity. Despite its obvious plot contrivances, the show

Robert Culp and Geraldine Brooks.

is frankly unforgettable, with convincing, straight-arrow performances and dead tough dialogue. It features what is probably the most ambitious monster suit ever attempted for TV, a creation that caused not only a deluge of fan mail, but an unexpected bout with home-town censorship. Ironically, the story starts with the "it's so crazy it might work" philosophy that traditionally crops up at the *end* of most science fiction B movies, and proceeds with uncondescending logic toward a climax that is believable in spite of all the outlandish elements that must mesh together.

Leslie Stevens notes, "I produced, or helped produce, the first few shows to help Joe get his feet under him, to let him get scripts ready, to start preproduction, and help him find his way around. Then, when it was his turn to *produce,* he came through full blast, with flying colors. The unit was able to hear him talk sensibly, with all kinds of taste and authority, and watch him get things done." Stefano wanted strongly to make shows that looked like short feature films instead of run-of-the-mill TV, and with "Architects of Fear" both he and *The Outer Limits* began to hit their stride. Production on the series had been grinding away for just over a month, and the script was the first story purchased by Lou Morheim. "I knew Meyer Dolinsky as the writer of a number of *Mr. Novak*s," said Morheim. "He was also a friend of mine who was part of a playwright's group I once conducted."

Dolinsky recalled his first meeting: "I threw out an idea that Lou just fell in love with—that the only way you'd stop war and really make this planet shape up would be to get somebody to scare the shit out of everyone. Love was not going to do it. Lou liked that, but Stefano decided our message couldn't be that grim. So we tossed a little love into the final scene, so it ended up that love *could* do it. Probably rightly." Dolinsky's teleplay is crisp and specific, the only omissions from his draft being Yvette's final scenes with the "normal" Allen. She plucks a grey hair from his head, joking, "He loves me..." Before she can get to *he loves me not*, he stops her, but by then she has noticed an irregularity in the skin of his forehead—the first outward manifestation of his biological mutation. She touches his scalp-line, drawing her finger down toward his eyes, and this is the genesis of the personal gesture they share. "The thing that worked best was the 'mark against evil,'" said Dolinsky. "I had restructured the old monster-on-the-loose idea, but that added a sensitivity not normally found in that sort of story."

Stefano wrote in the spectacular scene in which a trio of duck hunters is surprised by the first appearance of Allen in Thetan form. Byron Haskin added a dog. "Instead of having hundreds of people screaming and running from the monster, I used the dog as the first 'being' to encounter the Thetan," said Haskin. "Its reaction was more spontaneous, and therefore more real. A dog can't reason per se, and yet it was *scared*. An animal's reaction is honest, as opposed to an actor who reacts for money. It was a visual embellishment that made our monster more believably scary. I think all we did to spook the dog was kick it in the ass, which sent it howling."

The strengths of "Architects" are tied into human dilemmas: Allen's devotion to scientific ideals versus his genuinely sensitive relationship with Yvette; Gainer's tight-lipped, almost fanatic dedication versus his obvious concern for the ordeal Allen, his friend, must endure; the cadre of scientists, regular guys all, capable of the best intentions, yet victimized by screwups and poor insight. To try and unite the world, they destroy the already-perfect union of two people. Instead of bettering the world, they kill one of the small, good things left in it. Allen's transformation is an attempt by a group of technologically-advanced geniuses to redress the global nuclear threat made possible by their own scientific predecessors. They assume a massive responsibility for humankind, and then blow it. But even their hideous miscalculation is treated with a rare degree of compassion by the story.

What a Thetan might look like was a topic first round-tabled by Dolinsky. "There was a girl I was going out with who was seeing a doctor," he said. "She got a bunch of doctors together to give me the science of it. A lot was too technical to show up in the script, but we spent an evening throwing around the question, *What would you do to transform an ordinary human being into a projected figure from a planet with a different atmosphere?*" The teleplay describes the result:

> (Allen's) body is flatter, his skin made up of dark, oily scales. Infrared orbs are his eyes, his bald skull is flat with a bony grid structure on top for nitrogen processing and digestive gaseous expiration. His legs are bowed and foreshortened, and his arms

Janos Prohaska.

> have the same apelike appearance, with only three fingers; there is an extra knee joint for loping. There are no ears. Two small holes appear where once there was a nose. Two vertical slots replace a mouth from which is attached tubing leading to the nitrogen tank strapped around his middle.

Haskin brought in a Hungarian stuntman and acrobat named Janos Prohaska to portray the alien. Prohaska's specialties included playing apes in circuses and on TV (he later became the popular Cookie Bear on *The Andy Williams Show*), and building monster costumes that defied the man-in-a-suit look in his Santa Monica workshop. "When I first met Janos," said Haskin, "he came into my office, put a beer bottle on the table, and then stood on his head with his finger in the bottle, supporting himself. He could defy the law of gravity."

To realize the Thetan's backward-jointed, birdlike leg structure, Prohaska used taloned stilts that raised him nearly two feet off the ground. By gripping armatures inside the elbows of the Thetan costume, he could balance himself like a man leaning forward onto crutches. "Everybody at Projects worked on that costume," said Jim Danforth, "and I think Byron Haskin designed it." The enormous headpiece sculpted by Wah Chang included functional eyelids, pulsating veins, and a bellows-mouth all operated by a network of air cylinders. Prohaska was sealed into a rubberoid skin, canted plungingly forward on his stilts, his vision limited to what he could see out of the Thetan's "nose" while wearing a head four times the size of his own.

Lin Parsons recalled, "The suit arrived in pieces while we were shooting out on MGM Lot #3. We put the legs on Janos, then the torso, then the hands. Projects rushed in the head at absolutely the last minute. We slapped it on him and said, 'Do it!' And he started weaving around like a drunk! They'd used a lot of airplane dope in the head which hadn't quite dried, and so the minute he put it on he was gulping nothing but glue fumes!"

A Project Unlimited technician displays the unpainted Thetan headpiece.

"He managed a kind of loping walk, like a crow hopping along, that was effective behind bushes and in shadows," said Haskin. "But we couldn't get too much speed out of it. It was like a tree trunk with a whip on it from *Day of the Triffids*—clump!" Gene Warren, of Projects, noted, "Janos was crouched over all the time, and the odd leg position was very hard on him," and Lee Katzin, the 1st AD, said, "The heat inside the suit was unbelievable, and we had to stop a number of times just to let Janos breathe."

John Erman cast Robert Culp as Allen. "Culp was already a TV personality," said Erman, "and I was very impressed with him." Culp had starred as a Texas Ranger in the 1957–59 series *Trackdown*, and had just come from film roles in *PT-109* and *The Raiders*. He became *The Outer Limits'* most recognizable human face, and following his three star turns on the series, became better known as *I Spy*'s Kelly Robinson. In "Architects," he is very much the committed idealist, controlled, uncomplaining, resigned to his agreed-upon fate, yet guilt-ridden over his abandonment of Yvette for the "greater good" of the United Labs scheme.

"Culp's middle name should have been *Outer Limits*," said Haskin. "Because he's a weirdo, of sorts. He wanted to make up his own camera angles and use ideas that wouldn't have worked in a million years. I'd line up a shot that would get us through and make the budget requirement, and meanwhile Culp would be hanging off some part of the ceiling on a rope, telling me his idea of an entrance would be better. His line was always, 'This would be a great way to play it!' but I never fell for that. We had our explosive moments over such things, but we got along."

One such instance was a makeup whipped together in two hours, on the lab set, by Culp and Fred Phillips. "I had a 5:30 makeup call—four hours a day, for five days, just on makeup," said Culp. During these sessions he and Phillips hit upon the idea of showing an intermediate stage in Allen's literal alienization. "Phillips told me, 'We haven't any time at all, so let's go back to the original concept of Frankenstein.' He stuck a dixie cup over my nose and mouth, and built it up with cotton that was covered in latex, which burnt my skin." To this fleshy, scaly snout Phillips added surgical tubing, to provide a visual continuity between it and the Projects monster head. "It was not meant to appear for more than a few seconds," said Phillips.

"It was wasteful, and shot without my jurisdictive help," said Haskin. "I think it turned up in the final cut for about twelve frames of film." Just after Dr. Gainer tells Yvette, "You've got a baby to think about now," there comes a quick shot of Allen, beneath a sheet on the operating table, his head bandaged. He is hairless now, glistening and reptilian. If you blink, you'll miss the shot.

For the show's eventful last act, Projects executed shots of the Thetan space capsule against a starfield, circling prior to descent, and landing with animated retrorockets firing. Haskin claimed the "circling" shot was a rarity, since all through the 1950s model spaceships generally "flew" only in straight lines. The astonishingly quick disintegration of the hunters' station wagon was a startling effect, though simply achieved. It flares white, caves in and vaporizes in the blink of an eye, leaving a smoking residue on the ground. Projects man Ralph Rodine said, "We vanished things in a variety of ways on that series."

The "Architects" score was one of Dominic Frontiere's personal favorites, and incorporated eight different versions of a love theme, "Allen & Yvette." The marchlike music that rolls in full-blast as the Thetan crashes through the woods was titled "The Bug Bugs Out" by Frontiere's copyist, Roger Farris—the man responsible for translating the master score into individual sheets of music for each musician in the orchestra.

Some of *The Outer Limits' film noir* aspects were also tested in "Architects" by Conrad Hall. "There were TV technicians telling me things like I *had* to have a two-to-one lighting ratio, or people wouldn't be visible on TV," said Hall. "Well, people don't *have* to be visible all the time. Sometimes their outline is enough. When it's important to see their

Paul Pattee (R) tries to figure out what's holding up the completed Thetan costume, behind the Projects garage.

faces, you put light on them, or have them move into the light. We handled the show as if it was not an electronic medium, with certain technicalities required for reproduction. I made it look as if it was going to be seen on a motion picture screen, and what the 'experts' did not understand was that it was better! In every instance where they said, 'It won't look good on television,' they were wrong... because I'd seen it, and it looked great!" This reasoning makes it impossible for Hall to conceive of the program being done in color: "The *Outer Limits* look was very much a product of black-and-white photography."

During the broadcast of "Architects" on the last day of September, 1963, several of ABC's regional affiliates broadcast a black screen during the Thetan's appearance, since, in the judgement of more than one local station manager, the monster was too frightening to look at! The time-honored justification that it was "disturbing to young minds" was trotted out to support the decision to censor most of the show's final act, effectively blaming the tunnel vision of the affiliates on the kids in the audience. One such station was WEWS, Channel 5 in Cleveland, Ohio. The following day's edition of the *Cleveland Press* featured a photo of the Thetan alongside a column of viewer letters. Five out of six protested the action. In some parts of the country, the Thetan footage was tape-delayed until after the 11 o'clock news; in others, it was never shown at all.

One viewer called the WEWS censorship "reminiscent of something a police state would do." This moved Stefano to comment, "What do they think? That it isn't a police state already?"

Grace Lee Whitney blasts a "two-faced, no-good, blackhearted two-timer."

CONTROLLED EXPERIMENT

Broadcast 13 January 1964
Written and directed by Leslie Stevens
Assistant Director: Robert Justman
Director of Photography: John Nickolaus

CAST: Senior Solar System Inspector Phobos-One (Barry Morse), Accredited Earth Caretaker Diemos (Carrol O'Connor), Carla Duveen (Grace Lee Whitney), Bert Hamil (Robert Fortier), Arleen Schnable (Linda Hutchins), Voice of Martian Computer Control (Leslie Stevens).

Who has not seen the dark corners of great cities, whose small and shabby creatures wander without purpose in the secret corners of the night? Without purpose? There are those whose purpose reaches far beyond our wildest dreams...

Stuffy, prissy, by-the-book Inspector Phobos, a Martian administrator, arrives on Earth with instructions to assess the strange local custom of "murder" in terms of its threat potential to the galaxy at large. "It only happens here, on this weird little planet," he marvels to his Earth liaison, Diemos,* a friendly, if somewhat befogged, field man hermited away in his Earth Caretaker Post—a seedy pawnshop. Together this interstellar Odd Couple isolates a forthcoming incidence of murder—in which jilted sexpot Carla Duveen uses a pistol to blow away two-timing lothario Bert Hamil in the lobby of the Lux-Del Hotel—and uses a Martian "temporal condenser" to reverse time and replay the killing over and over, in fast and slow motion, even stopping the sequence altogether. Phobos is utterly befuddled by the illogical sequence of events that culminate in the shooting. When he tampers with the event by flicking Carla's bullet off trajectory, sparing Bert, Martian Computer Control sends a frantic alarm: "Fatal error!" They advise that in the new scheme of events, Bert and Carla will marry and produce a child that, because of Bert's miraculous escape from death, will think itself invincible, grow up to become a dictator and start an atomic war whose chain reactions will cause a galactic catastrophe. To save both Bert and the universe, Phobos then alters the events of the shooting so Bert is spared through a lucky accident. The lovers are reconciled and Phobos chooses to remain with Diemos on this quaint little world, that he might further sample such intriguing native diversions as coffee and cigarettes.

> *Who knows? Perhaps the alteration of one small event may someday bring the end of the world. But that someday is a long way off, and until then there is a good life to be lived in the here and now.*

No one believed Leslie Stevens when he proposed to complete an *Outer Limits* episode in four days... until he went ahead and did it. The skeleton of "Controlled Experiment" was typed up by Stevens on a New York to LA flight, and the show took four and a half shooting days to complete. At $100,000, it was the cheapest *Outer Limits* ever. Stevens dubbed this last-minute lifesaving technique the "bottle show"—as in pulling an episode right out of a bottle, like a genie.

"When they know you can do it, and do it fast, you become the fire department, to bail the show out of trouble," said Stevens. "And when you're really scared, you find yourself using every bit of your expertise to do a show that will be enormously inexpensive... and still be effective."

Constructed for three simple sets and five characters, the show is reminiscent of a filmed stage play, and cleverly stands precepts from other *Outer Limits* shows on their heads. Humankind's misinterpretation of benign alien intelligence is reversed here into the comical confusion Phobos experiences over the hows and whys of Earth people. Here is

*Both Martians are named for the respective Martian moons on which they were born. The actual spelling of "Diemos" is *Deimos;* Stevens' script uses the spelling *Diemos* throughout.

what happens when he examines some of Carla Duveen's money:

PHOBOS: *Annuit Coeptis Novus Ordo Seclorum*... what does that mean?
DIEMOS: It's a dead language. Latin. They use it to impress each other.
PHOBOS: What's this bird holding the vegetation?
DIEMOS: Nesting materials. Symbol of the home.
PHOBOS: And this brick pyramid?
DIEMOS: Also symbol of the home.
PHOBOS: But it's got one eye looking out of it.
DIEMOS: Symbol of the home *owner*.
PHOBOS: Who's the old lady?
DIEMOS: It's an old man.
PHOBOS: What does it all *mean*?
DIEMOS: Who knows?

Who knows? is also the question posed at the end by the Control Voice, which then puts forth the oddly inappropriate idea that the future doesn't matter, but the "here and now" does. This sentiment was atypical of both Stevens and *The Outer Limits*, with its party line of cosmic responsibility and the balances of justice, and soon the consequences of ignoring the future would be forcefully expressed in "The Man Who Was

Barry Morse (L) and Carrol O'Connor operate the Temporal Condenser.

Never Born." We are left with the impression that Phobos has doomed the galaxy merely to wallow in his newfound fondness for Earth. Technically, though, he hasn't, even though Bert will never find the cigarette case Phobos slips into his breast pocket to stop Carla's bullet—because Phobos steals it! The consequences are never meant to be deeply pondered, however, and the show is Stevens's attempt to have some fun inside *The Outer Limits* as well as save money.

As a simple comedy, the show is very good. Carrol O'Connor plays Diemos as a nonplussed, bemused tour guide to Barry Morse's Phobos, who maintains the no-nonsense, harried demeanor of a supervisor with too much to do... at least, until he gets his first taste of some of the more popular Earth vices. A scene in which Phobos gets "buzzed" on coffee while Diemos races to keep up with the labyrinthine coordinates rattled off by the Martian computer is done in a cascade of intercutting that is quite funny.*

Stevens wanted to shoot key scenes several ways, with normal-speed and fast-motion cameras, to permit repeated use of his lighting set-ups and allow a very fast shooting pace. "It was inventive," he said, "in terms of filling an entire show with half a show's worth of footage."

"Stevens wanted to reuse shots, and run the film forward and backward to save money," said Byron Haskin. "Once again, he didn't know ahead of time what the effects were going to look like, and Larry Butler ended up inserting an effect that looked like lightning, which disrupted the thing entirely." Whenever Phobos tinkers with time, the scene negative-reverses, then is obliterated by strobing flashes that white-out the TV screen—and kill the pace of the show. This effect alone (accompanied by the most grating sound effect John Elizalde could scare up on his equipment at Daystar) uses up a good two minutes or so of the episode's running time.

"We had a lot of fun making that episode," said 1st AD Robert Justman. "Robert Fortier was an extremely funny man who could walk backwards, miming his actions in reverse and keeping his eye dead-ahead while the other moved around him." In one scene, Fortier stands dead still while Morse bustles around him taking his temperature and affixing leads to his head. Later, aboard the elevator, he looks about to explode into laughter as Morse and O'Connor play their parts to the hilt, and as Phobos sneaks a cigarette the "frozen" Bert Hamil begins blinking furiously in the background. Grace Lee Whitney, soon to achieve a measure of notoriety as *Star Trek*'s Yeoman Janice Rand, noted that "Barry Morse

*Offworlders have really got to beware Earth's bad habits. In 1961, a *Twilight Zone* episode, "Will the Real Martian Please Stand Up?" featured John Hoyt as yet another Martian victim of Earth's caffeine-and-nicotine syndrome. After drinking 15 cups of coffee in a diner, he says, of cigarettes, "They're wonderful. We haven't got a *thing* like this on Mars."

and Carrol O'Connor got along famously on that show. Between takes, they'd sit right down to their chess game."

Originally the Martians were to have *"long, bony fingers with extra knuckle joints and serrated, insectile fingertips,"* since the show—once again—lacked an operative "monster." Since there was probably no time for Project Unlimited to dash out two pairs of funky alien gloves, Phobos and Diemos wear simple Earth-type rubber gloves while operating their temporal condenser. Diemos also dons Earth sunglasses while staring into the machine's "lightning" effect. Strangely, a weird-looking flying saucer is seen hovering over Earth in the opening shot of the episode. It contradicts Phobos' comments about his "instantaneous transmission" from Mars and serves no purpose... except, perhaps, to demonstrate the rule laid down by Robert Silverberg in the days he wrote pulp science fiction: When in doubt as to whether something is science fiction, throw in a robot or a spaceship. Since the physical appearance of the Martians is prosaic, someone opted for the UFO (which is not mentioned in Stevens's script), probably to soothe ABC—*Yes, this is science fiction. Here's a flying saucer. See?*

Another funny bit involves one of Diemos's threadbare pawnshop customers, Frank Brant. Not to put too fine a point on it, but the object Frank trundles in to hock is a rebuilt typewriter—another bit of wry editorializing by Stevens. "I remember the last *Stoney Burke* Leslie wrote very well," said Lee Katzin. "It was about taking horses to slaughter. He wrote it as a symbolic piece, to show what was happening to him at ABC."

Sidney Blackmer (L) and running mate Phillip Pine.

THE HUNDRED DAYS OF THE DRAGON

Broadcast 23 September 1963
Written by Allan Balter and Robert Mintz
Directed by Byron Haskin
Assistant Director: Lee H. Katzin
Director of Photography: Conrad Hall

CAST: William Lyons Selby (Sidney Blackmer), Theodore Pearson (Phillip Pine), Carol Selby Conner (Nancy Rennick), Ann Pearson (Joan Camden), Li Chin-Sung (Richard Loo), Dr. Bob Conner (Mark Roberts), Dr. Su-Lin (Aki Akeong), Major Ho Chi-Wong (Clarence Lung), Wen Lee (James Hong), Li Kwan (James Yagi), Frank Summers (Bert Remsen), Carter (Dennis McCarthy), Briggs (Richard Gittings), Bryan (Robert Brubaker), Oriental in hotel (Eugene Chan), FBI Agent Marshall (Henry Scott), Voice of Mr Schumacher (Vic Perrin), Voice of Election Returns Commentator (Leslie Stevens).

Somewhere south of the Mongolian border and north of the Tropic of Cancer, in that part of the world we call the Orient, a slumbering giant has shaken itself to wakefulness. Passed over in most histories as a nation forgotten by time, its close-packed millions, in the short span of twenty years, have been stirred to a fury by one man: Li Chin-Sung. A benevolent despot in his homeland, Sung stands as an irresponsible threat to peace in the eyes of the rest of the world. William Lyons Selby—candidate for the Presidency of the United States; predicted by every poll, survey and primary to be a certain winner in the forthcoming election...

Behind the Bamboo Curtain, a Chinese scientist demonstrates to monarch Li Chin-Sung a serum which makes human flesh pliable, putty-like and easily changed. A physical double for American presidential hopeful William Lyons Selby is injected with the drug, and after a metal template is pressed onto his face he assumes Selby's features. He has already perfected his impersonation using tapes of Selby's speeches, and meticulous research into his personal background. In the States, the real Selby is assassinated in his hotel room while on the campaign trail. The bogus Selby is elected and inaugurated as the new Chief Executive. Although the switch remains undetected, Selby's associates and family have noticed disquietingly small personal changes, and Vice President Ted Pearson questions his running mate's radical policy alterations—in particular, his inexplicably cordial relations with the Sung regime in China. By now, "Selby" and Sung have plotted to replace the entire executive staff with double agents, as well as key figures in labor, industry, and the media. Pearson's double attempts to kill him at his home, but is thwarted by the timely appearance of Selby's daughter and son-in-law, who have come to discuss their suspicions about the man who seems to be Selby. With the help of the Secret Service, Pearson uncovers the truth, and exposes the scheme by presenting his own *doppelganger* to the guests at a posh Washington reception. While everyone watches, Pearson demonstrates the drug on the phony Selby, angrily mutilating his face once it has become pliable. A nearby aide suggests that Pearson's first act as the new President should be to order the retaliatory bombing of China. Considering the devastating results of such a move, Pearson replies thoughtfully, "There will be no order."

> *For Theodore Pearson, not even so monstrous a crime as the assassination of William Lyons Selby justifies an act of war, because there is no war as we know it—only annihilation. A great American has been killed in the service of his country. Now it is the job of those who continue to serve to carry on guarding our freedom with dignity and unrelenting vigilance.*

"Political science fiction was no longer a fantasy after November 22nd, 1963," said Joseph Stefano. "We were talking about the assassination of a President two months before a real President was killed. That hadn't happened in my time—the world seemed to be coming apart at the seams, and I wasn't about to trust anybody."

The title of this episode derives from the so-called Hundred Days of Napoleon—the span of time between Napoleon's return to France from Elba, and his downfall at the Battle of Waterloo. Here, the Hundred Days represents the short but damaging period the bogus Selby spends in the Oval Office. "The Hundred Days of the Dragon" was a first script sale for the team of Allan Balter and Robert Mintz. Balter, one of Daystar's Six Bright Young Men, later became the story editor (and a frequent scriptwriter) for the longest running spy show on TV, *Mission: Impossible,* and his *Outer Limits* script is very much in the same vein. "Suppose you could change people's faces," Balter suggested to Mintz. "Whose face would you change?" A few years after *The Outer Limits,* Balter was getting a haircut and listening to his barber reminisce about his favorite episode of the series. "He told me, 'That's still one of the best things ever

Blackmer (as the bogus Selby) steps out with Nancy Rennick.

put on the air,' and enthusiastically recounted the plot. When I told him I had *written* that particular show, he could barely finish cutting my hair."

"Dragon" teems with subtle, double-edged dialogue that reflects the deception-of-appearance theme, and the political doubletalk is mirrored by the sinister, alternate meanings implicit in almost everything the Selby imposter says. He laughingly quotes Calvin Coolidge, after we have seen the real Selby quote Truman and Dewey. After blasting a rattlesnake with a shotgun during a hunting sortie with Pearson, he says, "I've had my fill of hunting," and we realize that this is the man who has just gunned down the real Selby, with a smile on his face. Yet his marksmanship plants seeds of doubt in Pearson, who knows that the real Selby couldn't shoot worth a damn. The hunting scene smacks of Teddy Roosevelt (in fact, Sidney Blackmer portrayed Roosevelt in the 1948 film *My Girl Tisa*), a form of historical shorthand that establishes the American cliche of the "perfect president"—the rugged outdoorsman as well as one who walks the corridors of power.

Perhaps aware of the story's similarities to the recent film *The Manchurian Candidate* (1962), director Byron Haskin concentrates on the culture-shock and science fiction aspects, hitting the viewer with both in the first minutes of the show. The lab of Dr. Su-Lin looks deceptively ordinary, with the calming, swaying shadows of vegetation from the "real" world showing through half-closed venetian blinds. In this calculatedly normal setting, we are first exposed to the fantastic proposition of Su-Lin's shape-changing drug. The steel cookie-cutter molds used to mash the subject's pliable skin into a new physiognomy are quite unbelievable, but the plot follows realistically from this departure point. The dead earnestness and tight, unemotional logic with which Li Chin-Sung's plot unfolds directly contrasts the campaign trail babble, fireside chat homilies, and happy platitudes spouted by the Selby contingent. In "Dragon," it is the Chinese malefactors who are the show's alien menace.

The casting of Sidney Blackmer reflected Stefano's interest in procuring "people who were not working much in movies or TV anymore; people with fabulous faces, types, and styles, like Blackmer, or Neil Hamilton, or George MacReady with his great *scar*." Blackmer gifts the phony Selby with a stiletto smirk and narrowed eyes that signal a black shift in his character when he is exposed at the reception; earlier, we see him open faced and whitely American... but this is also the Selby imposter, practicing.

The awfulness of manually rearranging a person's facial features was nicely realized using a Project Unlimited clay bust of Selby never shown full-face onscreen because, as Fred Phillips put it, "Somebody always had their fingers in it." The scene in which Pearson meets his own double face-to-face, and later, exhibits him to onlookers at the reception, are a pair of breathtakingly precise split screen shots, filmed in color for use with the "blue backing" special effects process. First AD Lee Katzin supplied crowds where there were none, for the SRO scenes of parades and rallies. "We had fun making twenty extras look like two hundred," he said. "We doubled them back and forth in front of the candidate, wearing different hats we'd stick on them off-camera. We'd 'busy' the shot with people in the foreground, then I'd ride on top of the camera, in front of the dolly, with two balloons I'd run past in front of the lens."

One brilliance of the script is that Ted Pearson opts not to push that Big Red Button, even with our worst political fears realized. Phillip Pine, who, like Blackmer, had specialized in acting the parts of gangsters and crooked politicos throughout his career, invests Pearson with intensity and conviction. "Dragon"'s casting slyly ignores the slim line separating criminals and politicians, and Pine counters this cliche by making Pearson honestly friendly and sympathetic—the true "ideal American."

The story's only real drawback is that it has dated so severely in the wake of John F. Kennedy's assassination. It is difficult, today, to swallow Selby's utter lack of real security, his apparently limitless public access, and his surfeit of free time. That an enemy agent could sneak right in through Pearson's back door without being detected, let alone ventilated by a legion of Secret Service goons (who are handily in evidence during the climax), seems outrageous in light of the current political climate.

"Dragon" was chosen as the next show to be broadcast following the premiere of "The Galaxy Being," and Leslie Stevens said of it, "I was delighted to see that go as an early show. It gave the series the impetus and power to get it started and make it do well from the very first."

Donald Pleasence aids Priscilla Morrill after psychokinetically shoving her off the ladder.

THE MAN WITH THE POWER

Broadcast 7 October 1963
Written by Jerome Ross
Directed by Laslo Benedek
Assistant Director: Lee H. Katzin
Director of Photography: Conrad Hall

CAST: Harold J. Finley (Donald Pleasence), Vera Finley (Priscilla Morrill), Dean Radcliffe (Edward C. Platt), Steve Crandon (Fred Bier), Dr. Sigmund Hindemann (John Marley), Dr. Keenan (Frank Maxwell), Dr. Henschell (Paul Lambert), Dr. Tremaine (James McCallion), Emily Radcliffe (Ann Loos), Finley's MD (Harry Ellerbee), First Tree Pruner (Saul Gross), 2nd Tree Pruner (Fred Crane), Secretary (Diane Strom), Detective (Paul Kent), Nurse (Jane Barclay), Surgeon (Pat O'Hara).

In the course of centuries, Man has devoured the Earth itself. The Machine Age has dried up the seas of oil. Industry has consumed the heartlands of coal. The Atomic Age has plundered the rare elements—uranium, cobalt, plutonium—leaving behind worthless deposits of lead and ashes. Starvation is at hand. Only here, in the void of space, is there a new source of atomic power. Above us, in the debris of the solar system, in the meteorites and asteroids, are the materials needed to drive the reactors. Yet in their distant, silent orbits, these chunks of matter are beyond the reach of Man, beyond the reach of human hands... but not beyond the reach of human minds. Driving along a country road in an ordinary car is a modest man: Harold J. Finley, quiet and profound...

A tree pruning truck blocks the road, and Finley, an unassertive, Milquetoast college instructor, is intimidated into detouring by a pair of snarling workmen. After he departs, a broiling grey cloud shot through with snapping arcs of electricity appears, discharging hot bolts that gasify the men.

Eager to participate in some small way in space research, Finley has devised a "link-gate" which, when implanted into his brain, allows him to focus ambient cosmic energy into a discrete beam. He successfully levitates a half-ton meteor fragment, and a group of scientists decide that if Finley can control the power, the link-gate can be implanted into an astronaut for the purpose of telekinetically directing mining operations in outer space. Unknown to Finley, his unconscious resentments and hostilities also influence the growing energy he commands. His nagging, overbearing wife, Vera, is jolted off a ladder, and later begs him to spare her after she is tossed around the living room. Finley's dictatorial boss, who opposes the link-gate research, is vaporized in his own bedroom by the crackling cloud. When Finley realizes that human emotions are ill-equipped to deal with so huge a force, he protests the link-gate operation scheduled for a young astronaut. The duty-bound doctors drug Finley and proceed anyway. The unconscious Finley nevertheless stops the surgery within seconds as the energy cloud wipes out a nurse and two of the attending surgeons. Overcome with regret, Finley says, "If I have such power, then I don't want to live"... and the cloud disintegrates him.

> *Deep beyond the kindest, gentlest soul may lurk violent thoughts, deadly wishes. Someday Man will learn to cope with the monsters of the mind. Then, and only then, when the human mind is truly in control of itself, can we begin to utilize the great and hidden powers of the universe.*

Leslie Stevens's creative input influenced several *Outer Limits* episodes not bearing his name as writer/director, much like Byron Haskin's uncredited participation in special effects. "I became very much a part of 'The Man With the Power,' for example," he said. The notion of the energy flux, "the cosmic substance of the universe," was his, as well as the premise of the show: "A simple little nobody gains power over the whole world."

The show also reflects strongly the pro-space thinking of the early 1960s, when NASA's Mercury program was the Right Stuff to trailblaze that final, starry frontier. When Finley meets astronaut Steve Crandon, the man due for link-gate implantation, his remarks are impassioned:

> FINLEY: You astronauts have brought a whole new vitality to bear on the business of living. There's been nothing like you since the old pioneering days. You make up for all the miseries and disappointments, the failures and kicks in the teeth that the rest of us have to bear. Just do me one favor—don't wait till you're my age to make your mark. Do it while you're young and strong and vigorous. Do it right now.

The physicists of the Space Agency are depicted as desperate men who see, in Finley, a means of justifying their government tenure. They're as honest with him as they have to be, and when he threatens the status of their project, they are more than willing to roll over him. Their attempt turns out to be the *last* time anybody supercedes Finley's wishes.

The central conflict is that of Finley with the monster produced by his own Id, and although a psychiatrist ducks into the episode periodically to belabor the obvious, Finley does not see the light until late in the third act, by which time his fate is apparent even to those viewers who missed *Forbidden Planet*. The climax is a predictable frenzy of destruction with the party line of the worst monster movies as a coda: Man Was Not Meant to Meddle With Such Things.

"Man With the Power" was Jerome Ross's only *Outer Limits* script, and according to him the fact he was working simultaneously on other TV scripts while writing it may account for its derivative nature. "My diary shows that revisions took about two days," Ross said. "The shooting script contained few alterations, and I recall finding it satisfactory."

Donald Pleasence effortlessly essays the beleagured Finley, a part that hardly taxes his abilities. He was contracted by John Erman after completing his role in George Stevens's dinosauric Biblical epic, *The Greatest Story Ever Told*. "One of my closest friends was an actor in that picture named John Considine," said Erman. "Through him, I met Gary Raymond, David McCallum, Donald Pleasence, Jill Haworth, and others. I saw them all socially, and realized it would be a coup to get them all to do *The Outer Limits* while they were still in America; it was a very serendipitous thing. I went with Donald down to the immigration office to explain why his visa needed a two-week extension." Pleasence breathes life into the role of Finley, the downtrodden little man who longs to go to the stars, but the supporting cast is more strident than involving.

Leslie Stevens helped brainstorm the memorable optical effect depicting the energy cloud. "I was real proud of myself," he said, "for coming up with the idea of shooting a little electrical spark, enlarging it, and superimposing it on a cloud of ink."

For the most part, Laslo Benedek's direction is speedless. "Laslo did a bunch of *Stoney Burke*s that were very good," said Lee Katzin. "But on *Outer Limits* he just didn't fare well."

One of Katzin's duties, as First Assistant Director, was to break down the shooting script into a shot-by-shot schedule that provided for the most efficient usage possible of crew, actors, locations and material in the time available for each episode. For the first fifteen *Outer Limits* shows, he alternated the AD slot with Robert Justman (just as John Nickolaus and Conrad Hall traded off as Director of Photography). Together the two men evolved a wisecracking style for the breakdown sheets that became very popular with the casts and crew. Here is a sample from Katzin's breakdown for "The Man With the Power":

> EXT. FINLEY HOUSE–DAY–6 Scs.–3 3/8 Pgs.–(13)
>
> DESCRIPTION: Vera is really a vera nasty woman–Her snubbery incites Harold's ire–and you know what *that* means–That Terribly Hostile Shape makes his/hers/its appearance and Vera makes like Mary Martin right into the petunias.

Katzin noted that one *Outer Limits* actor sent a breakdown sheet to *The New Yorker:* "They submitted it as Perelman humor with its brains kicked out. I just hoped that people would read the scripts as assiduously as Bobby and I had to."

After reviewing "The Man With the Power," *Time* magazine projected *The Outer Limits* as a "foldee," saying, "Science fiction has never shot much of a ray into television, and this year's try, *The Outer Limits*, is unlikely to start a new trend." After a recap of the plot more simple-minded and wrong than the script could ever be, *Time* concluded, "At the end, an announcer said, 'We now return control of your television set to you.' That was a mistake. They'll never get control of it again."

"A simple little nobody who gains power over the whole world." The grid-shaped scar from the "link-gate" implant is visible on Pleasence's forehead.

"The Man With the Power," the fourth *Outer Limits* show broadcast, is the last to make use of a pretitle prologue—in this case, Finley's encounter with the tree pruners. By the fifth week of broadcast, ABC decided a shrewder commercial strategy was to insert a clip of each episode ahead of the opening titles, to give audiences a titillating glimpse of that show's "bear" before they saw *anything* else. This was done in the next show to be broadcast, "The Sixth Finger," which also debuted a shortened version of the original Control Voice introduction. Throughout both seasons of *The Outer Limits,* the speech was trimmed to speed things along, and its most familiar incarnation is the version used from "The Sixth Finger" until the end of the first season:

> *There is nothing wrong with your television set. Do not attempt to adjust the picture. We are controlling transmission. We will control the horizontal. We will control the vertical. We can change the focus to a soft blur, or sharpen it to crystal clarity. For the next hour, sit quietly and we will control all that you see and hear. You are about to participate in a great adventure. You are about to experience the awe and mystery which reaches from the inner mind to* The Outer Limits.

Stefano's Story Factory

"I can't tell you how I *fought,* and how my agents fought," said Joseph Stefano. "They wanted me, as producer, to write six shows the first year. I said four, and wouldn't budge. But when the production schedule came up short, or we needed a show in a hurry to fill a gap, guess who got to sit down and write one? We initially sought out science fiction writers, and they were the *worst!* They didn't seem to have any concept of what film writing was about." Among the earliest visitors to the Villa di Stefano bungalow at KTTV were Arthur C. Clarke, Ray Bradbury, and *Twilight Zone*'s own Charles Beaumont. "I told Lou Morheim that we'd better forget these guys," Stefano continues. "We did pay for some scripts we didn't shoot, and we got other scripts from well-known writers that were just as unproduceable. So, at first, Leslie just said, 'I'll do one,' and I said, 'Okay, I'll do another one....'"

"Joe and I did not grow up reading science fiction pulps, as Stevens had," said Morheim. "We were quite willing to buy published science fiction material, but most of it was about the exploration of other planets, which couldn't be done for an hour show on a limited budget. Secondly, we discovered that most of these stories had no uniqueness. The characters and concepts were all interchangeable, and did not work on a dramatic level. Most of it got so preoccupied with gadgetry and visual conception that the material that moves an audience on an emotional level was missing. We wanted to say things that had both a dramatic and an intellectual impact, and we were looking for ways to open people's minds to alien things—alien philosophies, creatures, cultures."

Of Stefano's first four scripts for *The Outer Limits,* only two, "A Feasibility Study" and "Nightmare" (written as "Ebon Struck First") ever went before the cameras. Another, "The Cats," featured an alien infiltration plot in which invaders possess the bodies of household pets. Stefano dropped it even though it was completed. "It suddenly occurred to me that a child watching this show might have a cat of his own, and make too close an identification," he said. The remaining script, a two-part episode entitled "Small Wonder," was judged too potentially costly to film since it involved a man who is microminiaturized to enter a woman's brain to destroy her "hostility center." Next came a massive rewrite of a script by Richard Newman, "Little Mother of All the World"—also never filmed.*

"In an anthology show, the biggest fight is with story material; to keep it coming and have it at some level of quality," said Byron Haskin.

*For a plot summary of these never-filmed *Outer Limits* adventures, refer to Appendix III.

"We had a real pro team with Stefano and Morheim. Seventy-five percent of the success of any individual episode lay not in the story selection, but in the writing and development Stefano put into it. The quality and appeal that *Outer Limits* had was mainly in this spooky talent that Stefano had. He put it into *Psycho,* and Hitchcock never again reached that level of creepy horror. Stefano and *The Outer Limits* were made for each other."

The period between the program's network premiere and Christmas of 1963 is packed with scripts Stefano wrote in a hurry, or, frequently, rewrote from scratch. These were not hunt-and-peck line revisions, but massive front-to-back overhauls that often scrapped 90 percent of the original teleplay. "Since I've never liked rewriting," he said, "a script had to be pretty good for me to want to rewrite it, or else the story had to be one I just didn't want to lose." Very quickly, his "four scripts" grew to fourteen. Besides these (and excepting the four shows scripted by Stevens), almost every *Outer Limits* show by another writer contains at least two major scenes written by Stefano.

"When you're in that kind of crunch situation," he said, "You draw on things you wouldn't use if you had more time. I was digging *fast.* I'd call Lou in and say, 'I've got this idea for a story; what do you think?' He'd say, 'Wonderful,' and I'd write it. I'd usually get up around five A.M., see my son before he went to school, then head for the studio. We were shooting at KTTV and MGM, and from one to the other is a long drive. Tom Selden, my assistant, drove me while I sat in the car with a typewriter on my lap. I wasn't about to waste that travel time. Other times, I'd just lock myself in my office and not let anyone come near, and I'd do a script over the weekend so we'd have something to send over to mimeo on Monday morning."

"I stayed at Joe's house as much as I did my own apartment," said Selden. "I'd sleep on the couch in order to drive him to the studio the next morning, while he typed in the car. I figure the average workday for that year was sixteen or seventeen hours per day, seven days a week. Joe wrote 80 percent of that time, or whenever he did not absolutely have to be on the sets or in the cutting rooms."

When Stefano and Morheim concocted a storyline, it was usually Morheim who wrote a treatment and fed the idea to an outside writer, who would produce a script that Stefano could work with. "It was in Lou's contract that he absolutely did not do rewrites," said Stefano. "He would do teleplays strictly a la carte, with us hiring him separately as a writer." When he and Morheim shared story credit, Stefano left the teleplay credit to the original writer. When the Stefano rewrite was more massive, the writer usually received the story credit. "Unless the Writer's Guild insisted on it, I didn't take credit," Stefano said. "For that, you had to have written 75 percent of what was seen onscreen. I never really gave a damn about the credits; arbitration was automatic. The only shows I really cared about, credit-wise, were the ones I'd written from scratch.

Writing is so visceral that if you're working on someone *else's* gut, it's just not as much fun." He also deferred to Morheim in matters of science: "Sometimes I'd tell Lou we needed a basis in scientific fact for a story, and he'd supply it. I tended not to rely on it too strongly in the things I wrote. I was not unaware of the scientific aspect, and I certainly knew where in hell it ought to be in anything brought in by any other writer. But my only real criterion was if I believed what I saw, then my audiences would, too. My feeling was that if a story took place in a house in Beverly Hills, it's going to be scarier than if it's on some unknown planet. I saw in *Outer Limits* an opportunity to express the normal worries that a man with a wife and growing son in this country would have, and the censors didn't mind that, because whatever ideas were being expressed were all in the realm of fantasy, to them."

While Stefano feels that working under pressure "produces the best you can possibly do," some of the scripts on which he was able to lavish more time show off his talent as a scenarist. "Joe was one of the few screenwriters who did beautiful narrative," said Morheim. "He never just typed, *He exits*. He gave you the attitude, the look, the atmosphere of a scene, which made for very good reading. When a script that has that kind of literary feel comes from the producer of the show, everybody kind of polishes their shoes."

As producer, Stefano also learned how to cut costs in the typewriter: "If I couldn't afford to shoot something, I'd find another way as a writer to make it work, whereas the producer who does not write tends to think in terms of doing without, or cutting, which destroys the fabric." He kept a tight rein on dialogue in both his own scripts and the rewrites. "On *The Outer Limits,* I had a rule that no one could change any dialogue without my okay. If it was a minor thing, I'd say no and hang up the phone. If it was something serious, I'd talk with the actor, and sometimes change what was written. But usually I'd have it shot both ways." With a knowing grin, Stefano adds, "Actors quickly learn that when a producer says to shoot it both ways, that means the actor's way isn't going to wind up onscreen, y'know? I can't act. And most actors can't write. It annoys me when a producer lets an actor get away with something like that. Too many producers just stop caring when they get the okay from a network to do a show—they know the thing is going to be filmed, and already they're off to find their next property. There's very little on TV today where I get the feeling, wow, they really dug doing this! I get the feeling they *had* to do it; that they had a large mortgage to pay off. It seems to be done by executive groups now, rather than by one individual with some vision, some terrible urge, who somehow breaks through, and does what he must do. Which, even if it isn't great, has a vitality to it. If you make it with someone truly spectacular, it can ruin your sex life for a year. No one can turn you on like that again. That's kind of what happened for me with *The Outer Limits*."

Phyllis Love inside the sterilization tube, while a Luminoid teenager looks on.

A FEASIBILITY STUDY

Broadcast 13 April 1964
Written by Joseph Stefano
Working title: "The Feasibility Study"
Directed by Byron Haskin
Assistant Director: Robert Justman
Director of Photography: John Nickolaus

CAST: Dr. Simon Holm (Sam Wanamaker), Andrea Holm (Phyllis Love), Ralph Cashman (David Opatoshu), Rhea Cashman (Joyce Van Patten), Voice of the Authority (Ben Wright), The Authority (Robert Justman), Father Fontanna (Frank Puglia), Teenaged Luminoid (Glenn Gannon).

The planet Luminos: A minor planet, sultry and simmering. Incapacitated. Earth scientists have concluded that there could be no life on Luminos, that it is too close to its own sun, and that its inhabitants would be victimized by their own blighting atmosphere. But there is life on Luminos—life that should resemble ours, but doesn't. Desperate life, suffering a great and terrible need. The Luminoids have begun to search the universe in an effort to gratify that need. They seek a planet on which life is healthy, vibrant, strong, and mobile. They need such people to do their work, to labor and slave for them, to manufacture their splendored dreams. The Luminoids need slaves, and they have chosen the planet off which their slaves will be abducted. Not too many at first, a neighborhood-full, perhaps. A neighborhood like mine or yours. Those who will be abducted sleep in dreamy ignorance, unaware that they are about to become the subjects of a grotesque and sophisticated experiment . . . a feasibility study.

Residents of a six-block section of Midgard Drive in Beverly Hills awake one morning to find the air alive with a strange, particulate rain, the telephone lines filled with insectile nattering, and their neighborhood corralled by a barrier of choking fog. When Ralph Cashman drives into it he is confronted by a pitted, volcanic landscape and stalked by three rag-clad aliens who appear to be composed of a silvery, mineral-like matter. Realizing they're not on Earth anymore, he escapes to warn the others, and before the shocked eyes of his wife Rhea and neighbors Simon and Andrea Holm, he is whisked away by a teleportation beam. An intruder Simon finds watching them from a toolshed turns out to be a curious alien teenager, also blemished with the silver, rocklike eruptions, who forces Andrea to chauffeur him back into the mist-bank. Simon chases them on foot and discovers a "Contemplative Energy Plant," an arena-like think tank housing dozens of aliens, all frozen fast by the growths. An elderly alien, the Authority, explains that he has brought Simon's neighborhood to their planet, Luminos, and encased it in a sterile bubble of fog in order to test the Earthlings' hardiness as potential slave labor, since a "hot organism in the genes" has rendered the Luminoids "doomed and immobile." The Authority reasons that the "vain flesh-men" of Earth would prefer slavery to being infected by the touch of the Luminoids and becoming ugly, motionless rocks; enough test subjects from the abducted neighborhood should survive, therefore, to justify the theft of the remainder of Earth's population. Simon arranges a neighborhood meeting in a local church, and finds that Andrea has been infected by merely breathing the same air as the Luminoid teenager. Then Cashman stumbles in, in an advanced state of contagion. Simon proposes they all voluntarily infect themselves to save the rest of the Earth. All in the group join hands with Andrea and Cashman, thwarting the Luminoid plot. Back on Earth, the enormous crater where their neighborhood once was remains as a kind of mute monument to their self-sacrifice.

"Do not enter upon or cross this area. Do not touch or remove possibly radioactive dirt or rocks. If you have any knowledge concerning this disappearance, please contact your nearest police department." It could have happened to any neighborhood. Had those who lived in this one been less human, less brave, it would have happened to all the neighborhoods of the Earth. Feasibility study ended. Abduction of human race: Infeasible.

"Joe Stefano came in one day and said, 'We're going to uproot a whole city block this week!'" said Leslie Stevens. "We all went crosseyed because it sounded so impractical."

Written during the hiatus between ABC's purchase of "The Galaxy Being" and the start of episode-to-episode production, "A Feasibility Study" is, according to Stefano, "the most humanitarian script of the series, I feel, though some of the events and dialogue are heavy-handed and preachy." The show hews to the loose rules set down in the *Canons* by outwardly being a thinly-veiled antislavery diatribe. What it is really concerned with are vivid sketches of the human spirit: Andrea's independence, crusader instinct, and will to fight; Ralph Cashman's dogged escape back to the town area; Simon's last minute surge of bravery and conversion to crusader, which wins the approval of Andrea (who had planned to divorce him) and leads to the nonviolent act of rebellion that spares all of Earth. There is also the spirit of the Luminoids, determined and smugly superior. Stefano's writing is at its most arch and fanciful in the grand speeches given by the Luminoid Authority, who slaps down each of Simon's protests with a handy and reasoned rebuttal. "Since no single fraction of life-energy is wasted on meaningless movement," he explains, "all energy, all the mad, monstrous force of it is made available to the mind. Can you comprehend the scope and skill of minds that are never drained, never dulled? Minds like nuclear birds, soaring to the most splendored dreamings of the universe?"

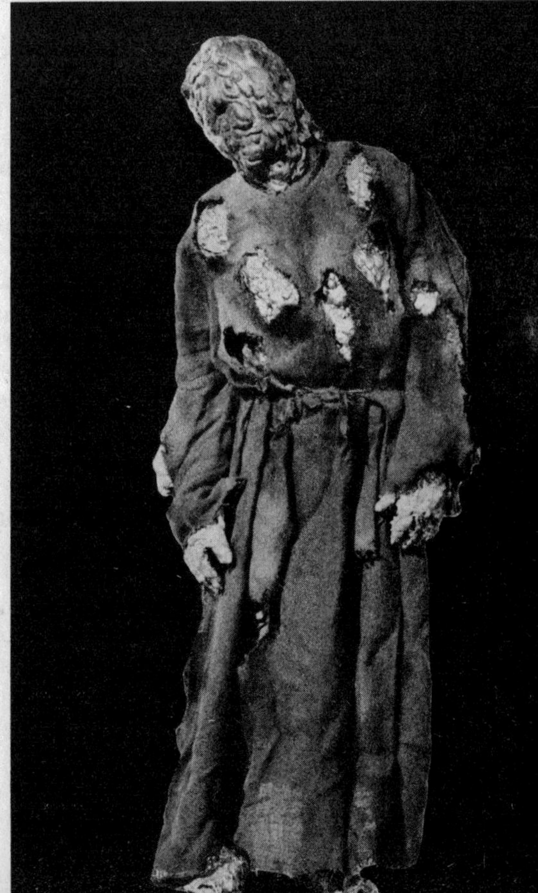

The head-to-toe Luminoid costume.
(Courtesy Jack Poplin)

The proper tone of administrative arrogance was provided for the Authority by the voice of Ben Wright, a British character actor soon to become better known for his portrayal of the head Nazi in *The Sound of Music*. "I rather imagine they wanted my British voice to contrast the American voices of the Earth people, to more clearly and easily differentiate them," said Wright. "I was originally to play the part, as well, but when they tried to fit me into the alien mask, they found my head was too big. Like most actors, I suppose."

So who was in the Luminoid suit? "That was me," said 1st AD Robert Justman. "Ben got paid for it, but it was me. It was one of those cases where I jumped into things on the set to expedite the production. I lip-synched his speech while he stood off-camera, reading it. I have this talent for miming speech while someone else is talking; I used to drive my wife crazy by repeating everything just as she said it."

In the interest of brevity, Stefano snipped some interesting insights from the Authority's lines. He notes that the Luminoid government passed an "Abduction Act" to legitimatize their interstellar kidnapping, and there is an added threat, besides contagion, that will prompt the new slaves to work:

> THE AUTHORITY: That veil of gas clouds you wandered through is little more than a deterrent, similar to those brick and mortar things you erect on Earth. But the humming you hear, *that* is what will keep you strong and useful. As anyone who has listened to a great, demonic speaker will tell you, sound waves can reach and subjugate the most recalcitrant organism.

The sci-fi "furniture" of the show—matter teleportation, disintegration rays, the goon squad of silent, lumbering monsters, and the cliche of extraterrestrial invasion—smacks of the supernatural in context, and the real excitement of the episode comes from the wall of Luminoid fog and the horrors that wait beyond it. For Ralph and Simon, penetration of the vapor takes on the nervous undertone of exploring a haunted house. The renegade Luminoid teenager plays the Gothic role of the Thing in the Attic ("I'll go away—if *you* will," he says in a creepy, distorted voice). The phones transmit only ghostly static (a speeded-up version of the Luminoid "crowd noise" heard later), and the Contemplative Energy Plant is a Dantean Hell, the opposite of the church in which Simon foolishly trusts to save him from his marital stubbornness. There's also a devil's deal of sorts: "You will be happy," says the Authority. "Your lives here will be comfortable and secure, and you will be free to worship and love and think as haphazardly as usual." It is the middle-class dream—guaranteed comfort, security and personal "freedom"—with enslavement as the price tag.

For the sake of credibility, Stefano substituted "Luminos" for Venus, the alien bastille of the original script. The Luminoid disability, described as a consuming growth of thick, black, glistening lichens, was changed to the metallic scabs and lava-like engulfment seen in the episode. Still other alterations came courtesy of ABC's Department of Standards and Practices—that is, the censors. "They were absolutely treacherous when it came to having children in jeopardy," said Stefano, whose first draft teleplay had the kids and pets of Midgard Drive as the first to succumb to the alien environment. Ralph Cashman's daughter Cynthia discovers her dad sprawled on the front walk, and witnesses the beam of light that atomizes him. "He poofed," she tells the adults. With the references to children removed, Midgard Drive was left conspicuously all-adult, and when Stefano condensed several minor characters into the principal ones, it seems that the Holms and the Cashmans are all alone until everyone gathers at the church for the denouement.

"There was enough thinking going on in *The Outer Limits* to worry people," said Stevens. "It was scary, because Congress was getting tough, and Minnow was calling TV a 'vast wasteland.'" ABC had gotten in hot water with the Federal Communications Commission the previous year for broadcasting William Inge's slightly racy play, *Bus Stop*. Oliver Treyz, the VP who had approved *Bus Stop,* was ousted and replaced with Tom Moore. The network censor assigned to *The Outer Limits* and other shows under Moore was Dorothy Brown.

"Dorothy Brown was the person standing between Stefano and the network people like Moore and Ben Brady," said Stevens. "The network is a triopoly—Programming tries to second-guess what the sponsors want, and Practices (or Network Continuity) can cut from a show whatever is necessary to please Programming. Brown's responsibility was not as a true censor, but to cover ABC's corporate behind. To make them look *awfully* good legally. To say, 'Sir, we *told* these producers, writers, and directors that they could not fire a gun and hit a man in this scene, and here's the memo that proves we told them, but they did not obey us. They just put it on the air that way. It's their fault because this memo proves to you how busily we're trying to regulate this show the way you want us to.'" Brown was on ABC's payroll, and her dictates were designed to keep the FCC at arm's length while the boys in Programming tried to squeeze around those edicts as covertly as possible. "The corporate way of doing things," says Stevens, "is to slam the accelerator to the floor and keep your foot on the brake. And you know what happens—you shake yourself to death!"

Director Byron Haskin summed up the censors and execs more pointedly: "They were bloated with self-importance, and threw down the most insane ukases of *do this, don't do that*. It isn't even the amusement business anymore, it's the world of advertising—and any relation to honest drama is purely coincidental."

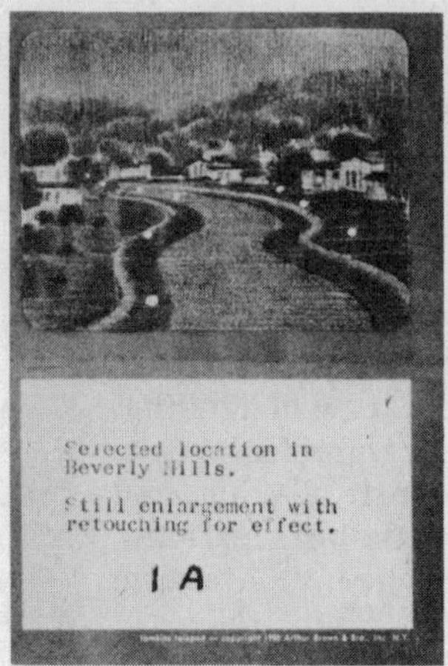
Selected location in Beverly Hills.
Still enlargement with retouching for effect.
1A

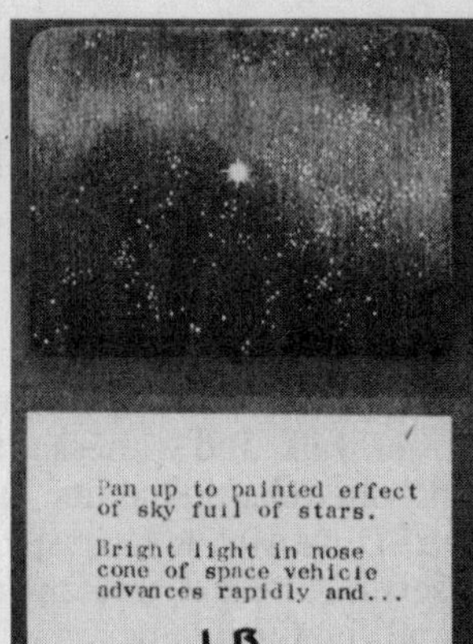
Pan up to painted effect of sky full of stars.
Bright light in nose cone of space vehicle advances rapidly and...
1B

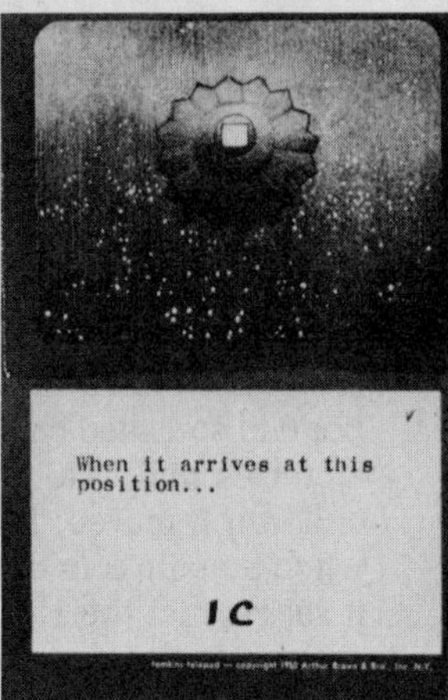
When it arrives at this position...
1C

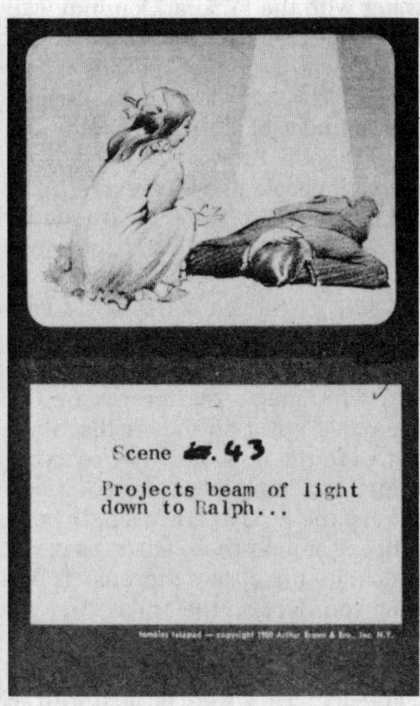
Scene .43
Projects beam of light down to Ralph...
tomkins telepad — copyright 1950 Arthur Brown & Bro., Inc. N.Y.

Byron Haskin's storyboard sketches depicting the disintegration of the six-block sample, the Luminoid's attack on Ralph Cashman, and Cashman's subsequent vanishment.

Brown's main objection to "A Feasibility Study" was its ending, which she interpreted as condoning mass suicide. "She saw the act of martyrdom as a negative gesture rather than a noble one," said Stefano. "But I probably proved my point when ABC saw the finished film, with everyone joining hands. It was very moving and inspirational, and that's when they approved it." This process took far longer than anyone reckoned, however, and the show was not aired until eight months after its completion.

Haskin directed the show two weeks after wrapping "Hundred Days of the Dragon." "It's not my favorite," he said. "From an effects standpoint, it was a little too ambitious for the series. The great power that controlled Luminos was a bunch of *rocks;* how can anybody generate suspense or excitement when the monsters look like still pictures?" The early acts, which take place mostly outdoors, are harshly lit and slightly overexposed, to lend them an eye-grating quality that aptly suggests the "hot" Luminoid atmosphere. When the Cashmans and Holms squint up into the sky, their features are obscured by haloes of blacklighting. Shooting through vaseline-smeared lenses and rippled glass helped to conceal the fact that the Contemplative Energy Plant is mostly a gypsum-and-plaster miniature set, in forced perspective, with live Luminoid extras filling up the foreground. Only a few feet behind them, off-camera grips manipulated foot-high photo cutouts of other Luminoids that appeared to be far away, dotted into the metallic hillside. Midgard Drive was MGM's backlot suburbia, where it proved impossible for Haskin to adequately present the wall of mist called for in the script. "We fucked around all day with one take that killed itself," he said. "Our smoke pots were at the mercy of gusting winds; our 'fog' floated aimlessly, everywhere." The barrier was provided in postproduction as an optical effect.

"A Feasibility Study" also gave Stefano a chance to fine-tune his film editing technique. "Tony DiMarco used to look at me with his mouth open most of the time, because I'd suggest things that sounded impossible," Stefano said. "In 'Feasibility,' we had an actress—Joyce Van Patten—who could not give a necessary reaction. I didn't know it until I saw dailies, and Byron said, 'She would not react the way we wanted.' Now, I didn't give a damn what the actress thought; I knew what I wanted my audience to think. I ran the film and ran it and ran it... and finally I ran it backwards, so that she appeared to recoil. I wasn't aware you could print film in reverse. And Tony said, 'You can only give her about three steps before it looks like she's walking backwards.' So I had him do it, to show me, and then I began to really see what could be done to a film in the editing stage."

In consideration of the censorship problem that kept the show in the can and on the shelf until nearly a year after he had turned in his teleplay for it, Stefano was asked if things might be done for TV today that were disallowed in 1963. "No," he said. "Maybe the other way around."

"I do remember cutting out all those squiggly monsters," recalled Jack Poplin. "My wife and I cut up a bunch of 8 × 10s and numbered them. Later I sent her a card with one of them glued onto it, saying, 'I was an all-American boy 'til I met you!'"

And Now... Gerd Oswald

> Gerd was one of my favorite directors—as you no doubt can tell.
>
> —Joseph Stefano

Born in Berlin, Germany, in 1916, Gerd Oswald was the son of Austrian producer-director Richard Oswald (formerly Orenstein), who directed the first film version of *Around the World in 80 Days* in 1919. Young Gerd appeared as a performer on the Berlin stage with Hedy Lamarr, and in several of his father's films, including *My Song Goes Round the World, Poor Like a Churchmouse,* and *Countess Maritza,* based on the operetta by Emmerlich Kalman.

"We got out of Germany by 1933, before things got rough with Hitler," Oswald recalls. "We moved back to Austria, where I'd spent a great deal of my youth, then got out of there just prior to the Onslaught. We spent a year each in England and France, and then I emigrated to the States, to Los Angeles, in November of 1938." He briefly transitioned through little theatre, as a producer. "I did a play called *Brainwashed,* which opened at the Trouper's Theatre, which is now the L.A. Stage Company. It was a leading experimental theatre at the time, and I met my first wife there. I was mostly stalling for time until I could get what I wanted, and within a year I'd become an assistant director. Throughout the early 1940s I did quite a few pictures, as an AD, between Monogram and Republic— *San Quentin, Silent Witness, Isle of Missing Men.* For the

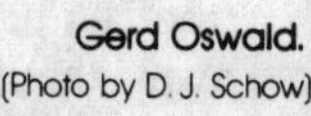
Gerd Oswald.
(Photo by D. J. Schow)

King Brothers I did *Hitler, the Beast of Berlin*." He also worked for the Producer's Releasing Company, and spent nearly ten years at Paramount before getting a break at 20th Century–Fox, where he worked as AD for Billy Wilder on *Sunset Boulevard*, George Stevens on *A Place in the Sun*, and Anatole Litvak on *Decision Before Dawn*. In 1951, Oswald was promoted to production manager, and by 1952 he was directing second unit assignments and studio tests.

"Everything I know now, I learned from assisting certain directors—what you should and should not do," he said. He worked with Lewis Milestone on the *ninth* remake of *Les Miserables*, and Joseph L. Mankiewicz on the four-star spy thriller *Five Fingers*. In 1953, after doing *White Witch Doctor*, Fox made Oswald an associate producer on Elia Kazan's *Man on a Tightrope* and Nunally Johnson's *Night People*. He moved up another rung, to full producer, for Fox's first European production in Cinemascope, *Oasis* (1954), and the following year did "an awful picture," *Untamed*, with Henry King.

More importantly, 1955 was the year Darryl F. Zanuck gave Oswald a long term directorial contract, and his first picture as director was done while on "loan-out" to United Artists. The film was *A Kiss Before Dying*, an adaptation of Ira Levin's best-selling first novel, starring Robert Wagner as a psychopathic killer.

Oswald did three more films for UA in 1956: *Crime of Passion* (another murder mystery starring Barbara Stanwyck), and a pair of Westerns, *The Brass Legend* and *Fury at Showdown*. In 1957 he directed *Valerie*, a post–Civil War drama, *Paris Holiday*, a Bob Hope comedy, and moved to Columbia to do *Screaming Mimi*, another mystery. At the 1958 Cannes Film Festival, Oswald was voted one of the ten most popular and promising new American directors, by his European peers.

He returned to Europe in 1959 to write, direct, and produce *The Day the Rains Came*, and in 1960 wrote and directed Stefan Zweig's *The Royal Game*, which was released by J. Arthur Rank as *Three Moves to Freedom*—and by Allied Artists, as *Brainwashed*. This story of a German aristocrat imprisoned by the Nazis won a prize for Outstanding Artistic Achievement from the Federal German Republic. Oswald was also one of the many directors who put in time on the overblown Darryl Zanuck war epic *The Longest Day*, directing the parachute assault on the French village of St. Mere-Eglise, which vignette featured Red Buttons. While living in Italy in early 1963, Oswald did a French-Italian thriller titled *Storm Over Ceylon*. "My father came to visit me while I was there," he said. "He got very ill and went to stay with my mother's family in Germany. When I took him to the airport, I knew it was the last time I'd see him. I came back to America, and when he passed away about a year later, it did not come as news to me. Since I had anticipated his death, I don't think it really affected my *Outer Limits* work, which I started soon after I returned."

A reedy, economically-statured man still working as a director as he enters his seventies, Oswald seems eager to jump into the thick of a question or problem in order to answer or resolve it as quickly and efficiently as possible. He is most often described by his fellow former Daystar workers as "journeyman" and "workmanlike," and looks back on the *Outer Limits* days with great fondness. "I was approached by Leslie Stevens to work on *Outer Limits* as one of the regulars," Oswald said. "He knew of my previous work, and showed me the pilot and series concept. By that time, they'd completed six or seven episodes, but I saw none of the sets or finished footage—merely some elaborate brochures Stevens had. Once I started working on the show, I never saw Stevens anymore; he was involved on other projects while Joe Stefano worked exclusively on *Outer Limits*. At the time I came into the fold, Joe was *the* producer, and I was fortunate enough to get his scripts. In a kind of mutual admiration set-up, I wound up doing every other one."

"I'd never heard of Gerd before *The Outer Limits*," said Stefano. "But he had a feel for Gothic drama and the Expressionist style of cinema. He could achieve a visual impact beyond the capabilities of a lot of American directors, and once I realized what I had, I set it up so he could do my scripts. That's one of the few chauvinistic things I ever did on the entire series." Oswald's technique also matched up with Conrad Hall's experimental camera style, and he often refers to the Stefano/Oswald/Hall creative threesome as the "troika."

Oswald directed nearly a full third of the *Outer Limits* catalogue—fourteen episodes pervaded by the dark, moody atmosphere he conjures up using sudden camera movements, odd angles, dense compositions, patterned splashes of background lighting, and a start-stop, "probing" aspect applied to the camera's point of view. "On every movie or TV show I ever did," he notes, "I called the shots on set-ups. All the camera blocking was mine, even the selection of lenses. A lot of our 'effects' were done in the camera. We used the old Caligari concept of fantasy, and talked a lot about creating an eerie mood in technical terms not necessarily requiring optical effects. I also worked very closely with Stefano during the editing stage. Most of the shows I did after that first one, 'Specimen: Unknown,' were by good writers—Stefano, Meyer Dolinsky, Robert Towne. Lou Morheim was also a very talented man."

Oswald commenced shooting "Specimen: Unknown" August 23, 1963, on Stage #4 at KTTV, while elsewhere Byron Haskin was steering "A Feasibility Study" through its final day of filming. Ironically, "Specimen: Unknown" would have *three* directors, due to production problems, but Oswald's *Outer Limits* work suffers little from this inauspicious debut; he was soon to demonstrate the power he could wring out of a six-day shooting schedule. Simply put, *The Outer Limits* would not have the unique look for which it is now famous, if Gerd Oswald had never come along.

Gail Kobe holds one of the lily-white invaders by its support tube (which, with luck, won't show up in the finished episode).

SPECIMEN: UNKNOWN

Broadcast 24 February 1964
Written by Stephen Lord. Additional material by Joseph Stefano. Prologue by Leslie Stevens
Directed by Gerd Oswald. Prologue directed by Robert H. Justman
Assistant Director: Lee H. Katzin
Director of Photography: Conrad Hall

CAST: Col. J. T. MacWilliams (Stephen McNally), Capt. Mike Doweling (Richard Jaeckal), Major Clark Benedict (Russell Johnson), Lt. Kenneth Gavin (Arthur Batanides), Lt. Gordon Halper (Peter Baldwin), Lt. Rupert Lawrence Howard (Dabney Coleman), Janet Doweling (Gail Kobe), Major Nathan Jennings (John Kellogg), Sergeant (Walt Davis), Project Adonis Intercom Voice (Robert Johnson).

For centuries, Man has looked to the skies and sought to uncover the mysteries of the universe. The telescope brought into focus the craters on the Moon and the canals on Mars, but it was limited, and Man's insistent hunger for knowledge and experience would not be satisfied until he broke the massive chains of gravity and set foot himself on a planet other than his own. Project Mercury was his first venture into space—a testament to his technical ingenuity and courage, a green light to a hundred other projects which would take him still further. This is Project Adonis, a laboratory orbiting a thousand miles above the Earth, a tiny, far-flung world connected only by radio and memory, and inhabited by a handful of men dedicated to removing the unknown for future space travelers. At ten minutes after six on January 8th,

Lieutenant Rupert Howard stumbled upon something clinging to the wall of the space-lock that appeared alive. He called them "space barnacles" for temporary identification. They were not...

When the mushroom-shaped "dormant spores" Howard removes from the hull of the Adonis space station are incubated, they quickly mature into white, poinsettia-like flowers, long-stemmed, with waxy petals, growing from pods that issue tentacled roots. The pod section suddenly showers Howard with fresh spores, and as he collects some for examination, the central petal lifts to expose the plant's stigma, which squirts a lethal white vapor into his face while emitting an unearthly screeching noise. Gagging, Howard stuffs the plant out a space-disposal hatch, but before he can get rid of all the samples he is overcome and killed by the gas.

The investigation into Howard's death is delayed by a change of shift in Adonis personnel. By the time anyone realizes the plants are responsible, they are already aboard a shuttle bound for Earth with the newly-relieved crew. When Capt. Doweling goes outside the craft to repair a damaged servomechanism, the other three occupants of the shuttle succumb to the gas as the plants multiply astonishingly fast, even penetrating the metal bulkheads with their stems. A plan to destroy the shuttle while still in orbit is scrubbed, and it crash-lands off course in a woodland area. By the time Project Adonis officers arrive, the plants have rooted by the thousands in Earth soil. A rainstorm sweeps through the area, and grim fears about the water nourishing the plants are allayed when it does quite the opposite—the plants screech, dissolve, and die when exposed to water. Doweling and all but one of the shuttle party are rescued and revived.

There are many things up there, evil and hungry, awesome and splendid. And gentle things, too. Merciful things like rain.

"'Specimen: Unknown' was a case where I was just in hysterics," said Leslie Stevens. "You get past being afraid and you laugh, and slide under your seat and have to be picked up. It was just a disaster; we got it together out of blind hope, really."

It's hard to believe that Stevens is talking about *Outer Limits*' highest-rated episode, but it might be said that "Specimen: Unknown"'s basic problem was that it was *short* on everything—short on plot, on running time, even short on death-dealing alien flowers.

"They wanted to present a menace from outer space and they didn't know what to develop it into," said scriptwriter Stephen Lord. "But it had to be something simple, that human beings regard without a second thought." Like other writers who had come to Villa di Stefano via the Hollywood method of the "cattle call," Lord knocked story seeds back and forth with Joseph Stefano and Lou Morheim until an idea took root. He soon turned in a first draft presenting alien plantlife as the menace-of-the-week. "The first act depicted two young lovers climbing around the hills in Malibu," said Lord. "They witness a flying saucer swooping across the horizon. Later, near the beach, they unknowingly come across the flowers and are the first victims." The saucer is seen to lay down a jetwash of spores that bloom instantly on contact with the ground, and emit the poisonous gas as a defense mechanism whenever anyone comes near them. "But it didn't work," added Lord. "Staying Earthbound wouldn't hold up for an hour-long show." He winged a variation on the idea in Stefano's office, setting the show's first half aboard an orbital space station, and added the punchline of rainwater killing the malignant plants. Excited by the twist, Stefano exclaimed, "Let's do it!"

"I got my 'legs' on *Outer Limits* by doing 'Specimen: Unknown,'" said Gerd Oswald. "It was a very weak story. The only interesting thing about it was the end—the rain destroying the plants like a word from God. I built the whole film up to that one moment; otherwise there wasn't much meat to it." Apparently, no one on the crew cared to acknowledge the just-released film *Day of the Triffids*, based on the popular John Wyndham novel about an invasion of lethal alien plants that are eventually destroyed by seawater.

Trouble—like the malignant plants—spread quickly.

"When I saw the first dailies," said Stevens, "they told me, 'Leslie, we cannot afford enough *flowers*.' I said that was too bad; they'd have to make more out of... something. So Dick Rubin, the prop man, made them out of Kleenex. Past the twenty or so flowers in the foreground, there they were, plain as day—Kleenex! And I thought, holy shit, this isn't going to work! And then we showed the flowers dealing death and it looked like they were squirting out talcum powder and popcorn. I was beside myself!"

When Oswald turned in his finished footage, Stefano's phone started ringing. "I got a call from Leslie, and he said that 'Specimen: Unknown' was too short, that it couldn't be used. To be five minutes short on a show was trauma, just horror time. Do you know how much film passes through a moviola in five minutes? Jesus, only the first *half* of the show! That was scary. I said, '*You* take care of it,' and Leslie took over."

"To have *that* show forty-five minutes long when it was supposed to fill an hour was adding the worst kind of insult to grievous injury," said Stevens. The shots of the Adonis space station (a model left over from the Ziv/UA TV series *Men Into Space*) were lengthened; the early portion of the episode cuts back to the station, floating in space, as often as possible. Agonizingly *slow* slow-motion was imparted to Mike Doweling's EVA to repair the shuttle, and the show gained a few more seconds. Finally, Stevens dashed out a prologue on his yellow legal pad and handed it over to 1st AD Robert Justman to get on film *fast*. Originally, the show opened with the burial in space of Rupert Howard, who had existed previously only in dialogue references by the other characters. The plants are not revealed as the antagonists until they kill a lab rabbit much later in the show—an element of suspense dispelled by the need for padding.

"We brought in an actor who was then very busy," said Stefano. "Dabney Coleman, whom we had used in other bit parts, and whom I liked." His scenes were filmed long after principal photography was complete, and none of the other actors in the show were available.

Justman recalls his directorial debut: "I did the whole prologue in one take, then did the cutaways (close-ups). There is a rather large shadow of a microphone hanging down into the opening shot. I cringed when I saw it. My big chance to direct at last... and there's the boom!"

Stefano rendered a long Control Voice speech that laboriously thumbnails the history of the space program, and even spells out the exact time and date of the prologue's action. The customary "teaser," the precredit excerpt showcasing the "bear," was in this case nearly three minutes long, but this helped the show reach an acceptable length. Just barely.

"Specimen: Unknown" is trapped in the idiom of the 1950s sci-fi flick to deprecating extremes, stressing hardware, phony pulp suspense (the shuttle's inevitable malfunction and Doweling's "perilous" EVA to fix it), technology-conscious cornball dialogue (MacWilliams says of Doweling's wife, "She's been sitting on the edge of her oscilloscope for *days*"), and a painfully preordained *deus ex machina* conclusion. The genre myth that the military is the sole group ideologically suited to be tinkering around in orbital labs "Up There" is perpetuated here for no reason other than its cliched expediency; it *sounds* terribly authentic when all the stalwart scientists have ranks in front of their names. Since the players are all interchangable Air Force joes, the performances, while competent, are all trapped inside uniforms. Arthur Batanides and Russell *(Attack of the Crab Monsters)* Johnson have fine, expressive faces, but no opportunity to express anything.

Project Unlimited supplied some 150 prop plants, some of which were rigged to "deal death" in the form of aerosol mist and spores (actually Puffed Wheat breakfast cereal). "The sculpt for those plants were done by a fellow named Johnny Neppolitano," recalled Jim Danforth. The crumpled, fullsized Adonis shuttle exterior was built by Jack Poplin's crew in the Tarzan Forest portion of MGM Backlot #3—in fact, shooting notes for the episode specify "extra foliage" to hide the World War II barges from the *Combat!* series, which were sitting in the lake just over the hillside from where the shuttle is augured nose-first into the ground. Writing in the April 4, 1964, *TV Guide*, Bob Stahl mentions, "In a rare spirit of cooperation, CBS's *Twilight Zone* has purchased a spaceship mockup created originally for ABC's *Outer Limits*." The mockup was painted black and used in *Twilight Zone*'s notorious Adam and Eve episode, "Probe 7, Over and Out." Stephen Lord added that, "To my knowledge, 'Specimen: Unknown' contained the first televised use of the word *shuttlecraft* in reference to a space vehicle."

Leslie Stevens only had two words in reference to the episode itself, and they were "desperation measures." Despite its literal shortcomings, it peaked the Nielsen ratings for *The Outer Limits*. "The thing I always found maddening was the network's inability to read their own lag in the ratings," said Stevens. "They're terribly misinterpreted all the time. Sometimes you get lucky; a documentary on army ants plays opposite your show, you get a good rating, and everything's okay. You'll notice that every new series is jammed with its best shows for the first five weeks or so, then you'll get a turkey. The audience usually forgives you for that first turkey, and it gets a good ratings because it *followed* a strong episode. But if you put on a strong show the next week, it'll get a far lower rating because everyone expected it to be lousy, because the previous show was the turkey."

"Specimen: Unknown"'s third director was Byron Haskin, who filmed the show's "pickups"—closeups and insert shots not requiring the principal actors, such as the shots of Rupert Howard's gloved hands prying spores off the Adonis hull, or close shots of the flowers doing their deadly stuff. A man named Rock Walker did "hand inserts" for the princely sum of $25.47 per day. Pickups were another of Haskin's routine chores on *Outer Limits;* he did them fast and without mishaps, using a crew of twenty. On the day pickups were done for "Specimen: Unknown," Haskin also completed all the insert shots for three other shows: "The Man With the Power," "A Feasibility Study," and "The Sixth Finger."

"Would you be willing to go back to an *ape*, Professor?" David McCallum freezes Edward Mulhare in his tracks with a pop quiz.

THE SIXTH FINGER

Broadcast 14 October 1963
Written by Ellis St. Joseph. Additional material by Joseph Stefano.
Directed by James Goldstone

Assistant Director: Robert Justman
Director of Photography: John Nickolaus

CAST: Gwyllm Griffiths (David McCallum), Prof. Mathers (Edward Mulhare), Cathy Evans (Jill Haworth), Gert "the Bread" Evans (Constance Cavendish), Wilt Morgan (Robert Doyle), Mrs. Ives (Nora Marlowe), Darwin the Monkey (Janos Prohaska), Constable's Deputy #1/Stunt (Chuck Hayward), #2 (George Pelling), Stunt Mathers (Al Wyatt).

Where are we going? Life, the timeless, mysterious gift, is still evolving. What wonders—or terrors—does evolution hold in store for us in the next ten thousand years? In a million? In six million? Perhaps the answer lies in this old house in this old and misty valley...

Guilt-ridden over his participation in an atomic bomb project, Prof. Mathers secludes himself in a bucolic Welsh mining town to seek a way to speed humankind's evolutionary progress beyond the capacity for war. Assisting him is Darwin, a superevolved chimpanzee that represents an early stage of Mathers's experimentation. Gwyllm Griffiths, brash, unwashed, but with ambitions beyond a lifetime of labor in the coal mines, applies as Mathers's guinea pig, eager to have his intellect thrust into the future. Through Mathers's "molecular approach to genetics," Gwyllm is advanced ten thousand years into his biologic future. He promptly reads Mathers's entire library in one night and becomes a virtuoso on the piano. His hairline recedes as his cranium expands, and he grows a sixth finger on each hand, for additional dexterity. Mathers realizes the evolutionary mechanism he has set into motion is now steamrolling along under its own impetus, and fearfully notes the psychological changes that accompany Gwyllm's growing brainpower. To him, Mathers soon looks "as monstrous as the Missing Link," and when his landlady, Mrs. Ives, spots Gwyllm she sees only an inhuman freak. Now telepathic, Gwyllm reads her intention to alert the townsfolk, and tells her heart to stop. To satisfy his old resentment for the town's "dirt and stupidity," he plans to obliterate it, and when Mathers feebly intercedes, Gwyllm knocks him unconscious with a kinetic potshot. He is about to deal likewise with a pair of deputies sent to intercept him when he suddenly evolves beyond the desire for vengeance. Returning to the lab, he mesmerizes his girlfriend Cathy into working Mathers's machinery so that he may evolve further, into a noncorporeal vortex of intelligence, but she snaps out of her trance in time to reverse the controls and bring the old, twentieth century Gwyllm—*her* Gwyllm—back.

An experiment too soon, too swift, and yet may we still hope to discover a method by which, in one generation, the whole human race could be rendered intelligent, beyond hatred, or revenge, or the desire for power? Is that not after all the ultimate goal of evolution?

"'The Sixth Finger' was the first, and possibly the only script I read through and immediately said *film it,"* said Joseph Stefano. "Now, you can't know what that means, when I felt the need to rewrite every script that came in."

Ellis St. Joseph's entrée to Villa di Stefano was a play he had written called *The Passage,* and he drew the seminal idea for "The Sixth Finger" from George Bernard Shaw's *Back to Methuselah:* "I wanted to depict Shaw's deadly serious feelings toward evolution, and extend them into my belief that man will evolve past the physical stage and into a creature of pure, formless intellect." St. Joseph framed these concepts in the Emlyn Williams play, *The Corn is Green,* whose protagonist, Morgan Evans, is a backward Welsh miner who craves an education. He falls under the guidance of a schoolteacher who ultimately sends him off to Oxford with a scholarship. The science fiction needs of *The Outer Limits* were served by recent developments in genetic research. St. Joseph contributed the idea of the additional finger. "This aspect of the story came from a personal incident," he said. "My grandmother gave birth to a child with a deformed sixth finger on one hand. It was immediately cut off. The boy died when only two months old."

St. Joseph's first draft impressed Stefano, who said, "I didn't touch a word of it." Some scenes and characters were dropped or condensed to save money, and five speaking parts were deleted—Bryn Evans, Gert the Bread's legless, wheelchair-bound, Bible-thumping husband; Wilks, the local constable; Robbart and Emlyn, two coal miners (the latter named for playwright Williams); and the fat Mr. Caradoc, owner of the mine. The beginning of Act Four, showing Gwyllm's vengeful rampage against the mine, was omitted. Originally, Gwyllm disposes of Wilks and his deputies, then proceeds to the mine, where a gatekeeper sees him coming, enveloped in a bituminous aura. Mr. Caradoc sets off the disaster whistle just as Gwyllm reduces him to smoldering ashes, then Gwyllm places a box of dynamite at the mouth of the mine and ignites the fuse with a burning glance. One of the trapped, terrified miners, Emlyn, attacks Gwyllm with a pickaxe and is flattened by a burst of kinetic force. Then Gwyllm suddenly becomes translucent—he has evolved beyond his need for vendetta (as he does after zapping Wilks's deputies off their motorcycles in the telecast version), and abandons the burning fuse to walk back to Mathers's lab. Robbart stamps out the fuse. Gwyllm later tells Cathy his ghostly translucence evidences another phase of his evolution: "I can now live by photosynthesis of pure light!"

Also deleted from St. Joseph's script was more of the scene in which Mathers tries to stop Gwyllm when he declares, "The whole town must be utterly destroyed. An example must be made."

MATHERS: You're wrong! We may seem stupid to you, primitive; we may have our shortcomings, but we are what you once were. It would be murder.

GWYLLM (smiles icily): Self-preservation.

MATHERS: Have pity...

GWYLLM: *Your* so-called civilization wiped out the savages that stood in its way! The man of the future must do the same with the man of today, before their brutality and ignorance can unleash universal destruction. Isn't that what you wanted, Professor?

MATHERS: Heaven help me; I hoped to *advance* humanity...

GWYLLM (deadly serious): You wanted an answer to the atom bomb. I am that answer.

MATHERS (desperately): Wait! For all your intelligence, you don't realize—you have passed the borderline that separates a human being from a biological monstrosity of all mind! *You no longer relate to humanity!*

Then Mathers pulls out his pistol, which does him no good.

The whittled-down version of the script was only forty pages long, and by the TV rule of thumb that one script page equals one minute of running time, something had to be done to fill "The Sixth Finger"'s gaps. "We had a meeting on the set," recalls director James Goldstone, "to determine what we could do that didn't disrupt the structure of the piece, and utilized things we already had at hand—we couldn't build new sets or introduce new actors, and it had to be the sort of thing that could run twenty seconds or two minutes, depending on how we wanted to play it. I don't recall who among us had the initial idea: What if Gwyllm discovered music? One of us went, 'Music! Aha—mathematics!'"

"I remember feeling a little bit responsible for suggesting that sequence," said David McCallum. "We came up with the idea of having Gwyllm play the piano in the night, having learned very fast. One scene had me looking through book after book; it was shot over my shoulder as I was turning pages, quite fast. And I found an edition of Bach preludes, flipped open to the music, and *paused,* just for a split second."

Stefano quickly wrote a five-page insert in which the music from Wilt Morgan's concertina matches with the first notes of Gwyllm's performance, during a dissolve to the house as Mathers is awakened by the piano.

"We sent a prop man to Wallich's Music City," said Goldstone, "to pick up the new Glenn Gould recording of the Bach preludes, which were performed faster than anyone had ever done them before. I'd heard them within the previous two days, on KFAC as I was driving to the studio. David picked the ones he thought he could master a little fingering for, and then mimed to the record." Since Goldstone wanted to begin the shot with Gwyllm's hands and tilt directly up to his face, no "cheating" using an off-camera pianist could be involved. McCallum's father was a

Gwyllm (David McCallum) advances 20,000 years...

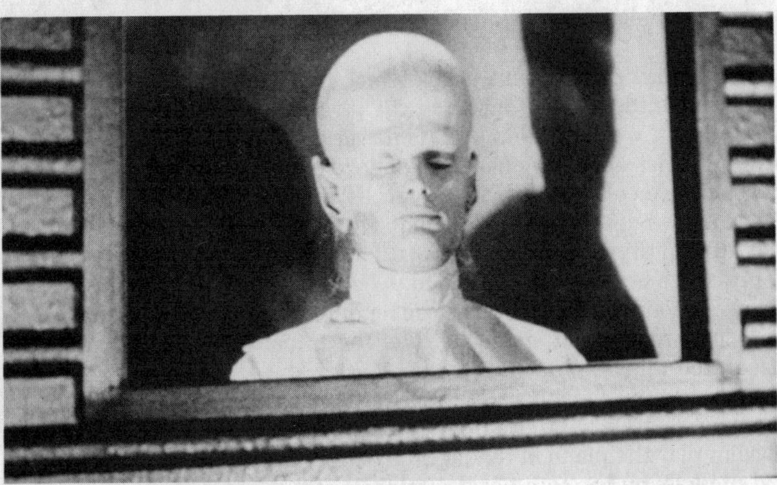

...one million years...

...backward to the protohuman...

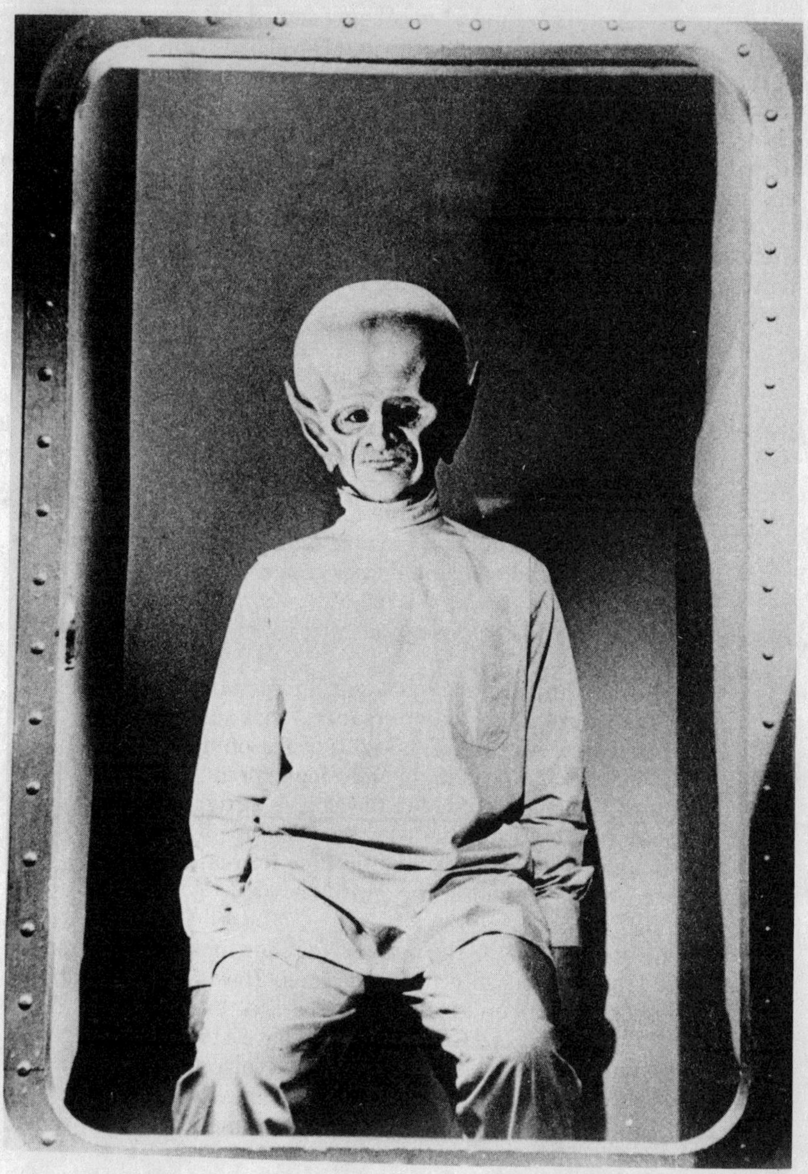

...and forward to the superhuman.

musician (as "The Sixth Finger" was being filmed, he was just starting a fifty-eight-city tour with Montevani), and David had spent several years at the Royal Academy of Music as an oboe player. "I took the recording home and learned enough of it to mime," McCallum said. "Joe Stefano wrote the dialogue where Gwyllm talks about it being a simple matter of mathematics and manual dexterity. But *you* try playing the piano with six fingers sometime—it's not all that easy!"*

Of Gwyllm's philosophical discourse with Mathers during this scene, Stefano said, "I tried to emulate Ellis St. Joseph's fine style." The blend between the work of both writers is seamless. Here, Gwyllm speaks Stefano's lines:

> GWYLLM: Amazing, isn't it, the things that endure the ravages of time and taste? This simple prelude, for instance. Bach will quite probably outlive us all.... Man produces little that is lasting—truly lasting. It's understandable. Fear, conformity, immorality; these are heavy burdens. Great drainers of creative energy. And when we are drained of creative energy we do not create. We procreate; we do not create.

And here, he speaks Ellis St. Joseph's:

> GWYLLM: The human race has a gift, Professor, a gift that sets it above all the other creatures that abound upon this planet: The gift of thought, of reasoning, of understanding. The highly-developed brain. But the human race has ceased to develop. It struggles for petty comfort and false security; there is no *time* for thought. Soon there will be no time for reasoning, and Man will lose sight of the truth!

Gwyllm's observations on the human condition make the piano scene one of *Outer Limits'* most captivating moments. "It was shot within hours of its conception, and it's an example of what is so exciting about film," said the lanky, mellow-voiced Goldstone. "You have a problem, and people of good will and creative spirit get together to solve that problem, and have an idea that becomes one of the best scenes in the show. This transcended intellectual point-making with a moment that was visual, and totally sensory. It was fun."

*The scene uses three different preludes. As it opens, Gwyllm plays the "Prelude and Fugue #2 in C Minor." Most of his conversation with Mathers is underscored by the "Prelude and Fugue #5 in D Major." When he says, "I shall stop soon, anyway," he begins the "Prelude and Fugue #1 in C Major." He does not quite finish any of the pieces.

"The Sixth Finger" would be much diminished without the powerful central presence of David McCallum, here making one of his earliest appearances on American TV prior to his worldwide, fast-lane success as *The Man From U.N.C.L.E.*'s Illya Kuryakin. He had crossed the Atlantic to play Judas Iscariot in *The Greatest Story Ever Told,* which is where John Erman found both McCallum and Jill Haworth, then only eighteen years old. "I originally offered the part of Gwyllm to Gary Raymond," said Erman. Raymond, late of *El Cid* and *Suddenly, Last Summer,* was another of Erman's friends from the cast of *Greatest Story.* "Gary thought it was a silly script, undignified for a professional. He told me, 'Oh, no, I can't do *this,* I'm a serious actor!' So David did it, and was wonderful. I've talked to Gary since then, and he always laughs and says, 'You know, I was a *fool* to have turned that part down!'" Raymond later became a regular on the *Rat Patrol* series.

St. Joseph met McCallum on the set one day. "He was terribly shy," St. Joseph remembers. "He came up and said, of the script, 'I hope I can do it justice.'" First AD Robert Justman adds: "David did a fantastic job. He had to go from a brash young miner to a being that was incredibly intelligent. As he went from stage to stage he changed the way he walked, the way he moved and phrased things. A most amazing interpretation."

The dangerous, critical-mass aspect of Gwyllm's literally swelling head is conveyed early, as he erupts into rage over his own ignorance: "What good is intelligence without knowledge? I'm hungry to know things. To learn everything that *is*. Fetch me books. Books about everything. All the books you have. I want to read them all!" In *The Corn is Green,* Morgan Evans voices a similar sentiment. "I want to get more clever still," he says, surveying a library. "To know what is *behind* all them books."

Gwyllm's physical evolution was the most elaborate prosthetic makeup job ever devised for *The Outer Limits*. John Chambers (who would win the first-ever Academy Award for makeup in 1968 for his revolutionary *Planet of the Apes* designs) made a life-mask of McCallum, then did concept sketches of the three evolutionary phases required. "I'd seen many movies that used appliances on the face, and there always seemed to be a *deadness,*" said McCallum. "I asked John to retain the mouth, the cheekbones, and my eyes, so I could go for expression." Chambers had the same idea. "I wanted to keep the basic thread of McCallum's

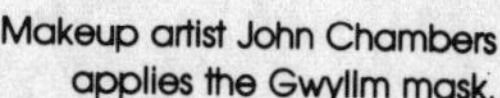
Makeup artist John Chambers applies the Gwyllm mask.

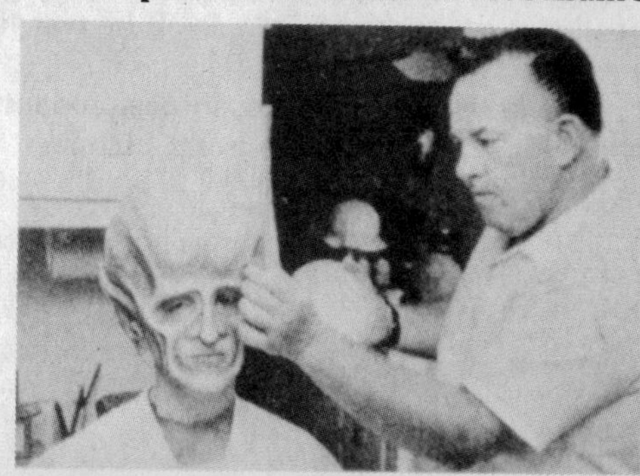

identity through each evolutionary stage," he said, "by adhering closely to his physiognomy. Keep the eyes, keep the mouth free. Don't lose sight of the man." His first sketch of Gwyllm's final phase incorporated grotesque, bulging eyeballs, which were eliminated. "Concepts often originate from what a graphic artist thinks will impress the producer, with little regard for feasibility of construction," Chambers added. He worked with the *Outer Limits* company for the first three days of shooting, until called away by a family emergency.

"John designed and made the appliances," said McCallum. "And Freddie Phillips put them on me." This took a patient three hours per day for each stage of Gwyllm's transformation. Even the large, final-stage mask (dubbed "Dr. Silvania" by Robert Justman) allowed McCallum a great deal of subtle facial animation, but because of its weight the actor could only keep it on for about four hours at a stretch. "If you stick a great big thing like that on your face and head," he said, "there's also a certain amount of claustrophobia." Phillips also improvised Gwyllm's brief regression to a Neanderthaloid stage when Cathy reverses the dial on Mathers's evolution machine. "I gave David an Abe Lincoln beard, stuck a quarter-apple into his mouth, and glued his lips together. They shot it that way." The bud of Gwyllm's sixth finger was also a quick on-the-set contrivance by Phillips, who adds, "It was made from spirit gum, cotton, and sealer in about twenty minutes. They wanted a finger and nobody had bothered to make one." A third makeup artist, Harry Thomas, was hired to assist Phillips during the six-day shoot.

The Welsh community backdrop was provided by English Towne Street on the MGM lot, and Mrs. Ives's boardinghouse was a Victorian mansion on Lot # 2 known as the Vinegar Tree House. The stock footage establishing the Welsh village was lifted from *How Green Was My Valley* (1941), and it was on these same hillsides, on the 20th Century–Fox lot, that a younger James Goldstone used to horseback ride at the time John Ford was filming that picture.

Janos Prohaska returned to *The Outer Limits* to play Darwin, using his own stage-tour chimp costume. "Janos was a delight," said Goldstone. "He had tremendous energy, and a sort of puckishness. With the suit on, he *became* an ape—a Hungarian ape, who'd peek up girls' dresses and say off-color things. Jill Haworth and the other women on the set were startled to find that this 'ape' was somewhat lascivious when his head was on, and when it was off he was just a craftsman with a thick accent, gasping for breath."*

Byron Haskin directed, in postproduction, all the shots of Gwyllm changing inside Mathers's "sonic chamber"—a long-winded session due

*Prohaska used the same costume in a much larger role in—believe it or don't—the 1967 film *Bikini Beach*.

Darwin the ape (Janos Prohaska) rehearses his lines.

In his Santa Monica workshop, Janos Prohaska sculpts one of many ape heads.

to all the makeup changes involved. McCallum describes this duty as "getting in the box"... and for a time there was some question as to what should come *out* of that box, at the conclusion of the episode. Dorothy Brown, the ABC censor, had objected to the Darwinism and promotion of evolution inherent in "The Sixth Finger." One of the earliest deletions from the script was a speech by Mathers on the taboo topic:

> MATHERS: In the short span of nine months, every human embryo passes through a million years of its previous evolution—from protoplasm to fish, to amphibian, to furry ape with a tail, to man. I'm experimenting with a means of continuing this process in the same lifetime...

This dialogue foreshadows the fate Ellis St. Joseph had in store for Gwyllm following his devolution:

134 <u>CLOSE SHOT—GLASS-DOORED CHAMBER</u>
Seen through the glass door, the half-human creature blurs, pulsates, reemerges as an ape; then, an amphibious reptile; then a sea-creature with gills, gasping on the floor; then the protoplasmic form of a jellyfish, clouding in death.
Dynamo's SOUND is suddenly silenced...

CUT SHARP TO:

135 <u>MEDIUM CLOSE SHOT—CONTROL BOARD</u>
as Mathers turns off the generator's switch. Behind him, Constable Wilks and the other armed men are hurriedly entering laboratory. Cathy has turned away, buried her face in her hands.

CONSTABLE
Where is he?

MATHERS
(gazing downward)
In there. He has gone back to the very origins of life...

AS CAMERA HOLDS on CLOSE-UP of the primeval substance:

FADE OUT.

THE END!

"That was unpopular with the production people," said St. Joseph. "So the way they ended it in the final version was less apocalyptic."

"There was also some discussion that Cathy should open the box and out would jump this sort of rhesus monkey," said McCallum, laughing. "For that we would've used a real monkey; that would be all that was left of Gwyllm, and he'd go leaping around the room. In the ending

Jill Haworth and David McCallum. "I brought him back. And he's glad. He touched me."

we did shoot, he comes back 'dead,' and discovers the tear on Cathy's face, which saves him—the classic *Matter of Life and Death* ending, you know, the tear on the rose. But at the time, I favored the idea of the monkey."

As McCallum was to discover, ABC's sensitivity to the topic of evolution was minutely focused: "I changed *one word* from the script, and it had to do directly with the religious aspect of the show." As written, Gwyllm's line was, "It is the goal of evolution; Man's final destiny is to become what he imagined in the beginning when he first learned the idea of the angels." McCallum continues: "I changed it to 'first *dreamed* the idea,' because it was as if Gwyllm was talking scientifically about angels, and I felt that was totally wrong. I was reprimanded by having to change it back, and if you listen, you'll notice that one line is dubbed in."

"We had all kinds of prolonged meetings in which the question of evolution was debated," said Lou Morheim. "Our position was that being able to evolve into the future was basic to science fiction, and to kill that would be to kill a whole body of science fiction material." Directing ABC's attention to a recent network broadcast of *Inherit the Wind* also helped. "In the end we prevailed. The new ending of 'The Sixth Finger' was probably more satisfactory to the audience, and the changes we were asked by ABC to make in the beginning were never made."

What evolved from all this was a stimulating and touching drama, one of the best shows *The Outer Limits* had to offer. "The main makeup, the big one, was just issued as a Hallowe'en mask," said McCallum. "They sent me one. After all these years, now I have my head back."

"Professor Andro" and Noelle, in her wedding whites.

THE MAN WHO WAS NEVER BORN

Broadcast 28 October 1963
Written by Anthony Lawrence
Directed by Leonard Horn
Assistant Director: Lee H. Katzin
Director of Photography: Conrad Hall

CAST: Andro (Martin Landau), Noelle Andresen (Shirley Knight), Bertram Cabot (John Considine), Capt. Joseph Reardon (Karl Held), Mrs. McCluskey (Maxine Stuart), Minister (Marlowe Jensen), Old Man [in unused footage] (Jack Raine).

> *Here, in the bright, clustered loneliness of the billion, billion stars, loneliness can be an exciting, voluntary thing, unlike the loneliness Man suffers on Earth. Here, deep in the starry nowhere, a man can be as one with space and time; preoccupied, yet not indifferent; anxious and yet at peace. His name is Joseph Reardon. He is, in this present year, thirty years old. This is the first time he has made this journey alone...*

While cruising in Earth orbit, astronaut Reardon penetrates a non-material barrier that shakes his ship and causes everything aboard to momentarily negative-reverse. He tries to raise his Project Control and gets only radio static. He immediately lands on a blistered, barren stretch of desert and is confronted by a gnarled, robe-clad mutant with a face like petrified lava. The creature addresses Reardon in English, says his name is Andro, that this is the planet Earth, and that the year is 2148—185 years after the date of Reardon's lift-off.

Andro explains that the wasteland Reardon sees is essentially the work of a single man—Bertram Cabot, Jr., who in the late twentieth century nurtured an alien bacterium that got out of control and caused the corruption of human DNA, mass sterility and global plague that resulted in Andro. Once they decide that Reardon passed through a "time convulsion" in space, the astronaut opts to return to the past, taking Andro with him as proof of the calamity in store for Earth's future. But the second trip through the warp kills Reardon, who fades to nothingness before Andro's eyes. His dying plea: "Find Cabot! Kill him if you have to!" Back in the Earth of 1963, Andro uses his power of hypnotic suggestion to conceal his true appearance. Others see him as a tall, haunted, vaguely European gentleman; his precise and poetical speech (learned from a vast library of literature that is all that remains of our culture in Andro's time) allows him to pose as a visiting academic. He meets and falls in love with Noelle Andresen, an occupant of the boarding house where he takes a room. Though drawn to the mysterious Professor Andro, Noelle is betrothed to an Army Lieutenant named Bertram Cabot—*not* the man Andro seeks, but his father-to-be. Andro realizes he must prevent their wedding and the birth of Bertram, Jr., but his attempt to shoot Cabot at the altar is foiled and he loses hypnotic control, appearing in his true form to the wedding throng and escaping in the ensuing panic. Noelle follows him back into the woods where Reardon's spaceship is concealed, proclaiming her newfound love for him, and insists that now she could never marry the violent Cabot, who pursues them with an impromptu posse. Andro and

Noelle escape in the ship and relocate the time warp. As they pass back through into 2148, Andro realizes his plan to change the world has succeeded—he immediately vanishes, having created a future world into which he was never born. Left in tears, totally alone, Noelle is stranded in the dark abyss of space.

> *It is said that if you move a single pebble on the beach, you set up a different pattern, and everything in the world is changed. It can also be said that love can change the future, if it is deep enough, true enough, and selfless enough. It can prevent a war, prohibit a plague, keep the whole world... whole.*

"I wanted to do a romantic fairytale," said screenwriter Anthony Lawrence of "The Man Who Was Never Born." "I wanted to touch people emotionally, with a kind of lyrical, poetic thing that not too many people were doing in TV." In this case the fairytale is *Beauty and the Beast*, and Joseph Stefano noted, "Leslie Stevens had this saying—'giving a story a haircut'—which meant altering a classic plot to fit your own devices." Lawrence's resultant teleplay is delicate and dreamlike, and lends the tale a resonance worthy of a vintage fable. Though it is the Möbius-strip twist of plot and the bravura performances that make this a perennial favorite among *Outer Limits* fans, it is also an ideal anthology script, a peak point for the series both musically and photographically, and a good story, well told—one dense with subtexts, and satisfying on many levels.

Andro is one of *The Outer Limits'* most tragic heroes. Like the series' more "humane" aliens, he is warm and sympathetic, but also imbued with a sad romanticism that cripples his outlook just as much as it makes him unique and poetical. The "safe and dear upholstered memories" of his 2148 library make him as much an inhabitant of the nineteenth century as the twenty-second; reared on *Anna Karenina* and "Mark Twain's whole meandering Mississippi," he finds himself a fairytale princess in Noelle, who is herself anachronistic and totally ill-suited for a lock-jawed war hound like Cabot. In a bit of dialogue cut from the original script, she tells Andro, "You don't seem like a professor. You're more like a prince—a cheated nobleman who has been imprisoned for a long time

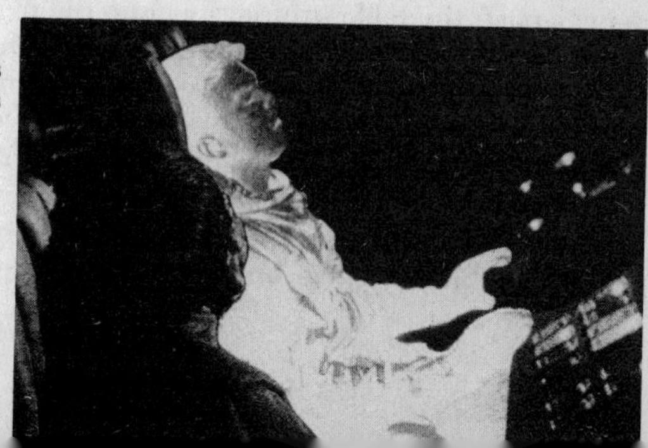

Martin Landau watches helplessly as Karl Held vanishes in space: "I'm not going to... make it *through*...!"

on a desert island somewhere." In another cut line, she tells him of her desire to become "a naturalist, a female Thoreau." Always clad in blinding white and frills, Noelle radiates purity like a searchlight at a world premiere, and once this princess meets her prince it is pretty clear she can dispense with her fiance altogether. "I don't love him," she muses. "I don't think I ever did." But in loving her, Andro speeds his own destruction, and to save the future Earth (a world that surely would have rejected him since he would still be a mutant, and a damned ugly one at that), he dooms them both. His nobly-motivated mission is actually a suicide run, since he has seen Reardon die on his second pass through the timewarp and has no reason to believe he will be spared the same fate. And even if there was some magical place, neither past nor future, to which these two could flee, their romance is ultimately unconsummatable. Bertram Cabot, Jr.'s plague has not only left Andro hideous, like the Beast, but sterile. These literally star-crossed lovers are allowed only a few moments to be together before oblivion enfolds them both.

The strongest theme in "The Man Who Was Never Born" deals with the power of illusions. The most contemporary piece of literature to which Andro refers is *The Great Gatsby,* in which Fitzgerald's Jay Gatsby lives a life that is a self-inflicted tall tale, or, as Andro says of his Professor face, "a suggestion." Gatsby's "greatness" is wrapped up in the fact that he dreams his dream-life so powerfully and completely; seeing things in terms of ideals, as he wants them to be, and not as they really are. Seduced by the literature of the past, Andro expects the reality of 1963 to be as refined as fiction, and after failing to stop the violent and abrasive Cabot, he opts to neutralize Noelle instead, since she, like him, has been chasing illusions most of her life. She dismisses her first glimpse of Andro's mutant form in the forest as a hallucination, and later, after his cover is blown at the wedding (where she stares right at him), she pointedly tells him, "I didn't see anything, except that you didn't want me to marry him." Noelle will *never* see anything but Professor Andro.

"The Man Who Was Never Born" was also *Outer Limits'* first sheer fantasy, if for no other reason than the broad impossibilities in story logic. Since Reardon's convenient disintegration is never explained, the sheer significance of Andro's death is undermined; the viewer expects him to vanish as a consequence of traversing the timewarp a second time, and not as a result of his rearrangement of history. Several fantastic coincidences push the table irretrievably into the realm of make-believe: that Andro could pilot Reardon's spaceship at all (think of flying one of those nice, familiar 737 jetliners all by your lonesome); that Andro, who says he has "memorized every detail of his life," would fail to instantly recognize Noelle as Cabot, Jr.'s mother; that Andro's lucky fall to Earth lands him practically in Noelle's backyard at not only the right place, but the right time for his purpose. But the fact that Andro overshoots his target year points up one small brilliance of the script: Bertram Cabot, Jr., is never seen, only spoken of in awed, hateful tones by Andro. He is another illusion, one Andro creates from history books, pursues, and never finds. He is the story's true Beast—monster, that is—and the real man who is never born.

The militant Cabot's illusion is Noelle, who abandons him to futilely clutch her wedding veil like some tangible leftover from a ghost. Lawrence says that the character of Cabot, for him, expressed a sense of rigidity and authority: "A kind of narrow, militaristic point of view. I don't think I was necessarily antimilitary, but I felt this was a good way to balance off Andro, who had an ugly exterior but a beautiful soul." Just as Cabot's illusion of wedded bliss with Noelle is shattered, so does Andro find a prosaic twentieth century that is not at all the antique shadow he expects. So much of what we see is his romantic fabrication of the type of world he *wishes* was his own—particularly the enchanted forest where he meets Noelle, his symbolic ideal, his Daisy Buchanan. Much of this intricate weave of illusions becomes clearer on repeat viewings of the episode.

Lawrence grew up reading Edgar Rice Burroughs, Ray Bradbury, and Jack London ("*The Star Rover* had a tremendous effect on me"), and favored the anthology format because, "You're not stuck with running characters, and you have a chance to do something a little more creative. There are very few people who have afforded me the luxury to write what I wanted, in the way I wanted to write it. Joe Stefano is one of them. He said, 'Go. Write it the way you *feel* it.'" With "Specimen: Unknown" and "Moonstone" in various stages of production, Stefano wanted to avoid doing too many overpriced shows set in outer space. Lawrence handed in his first draft, titled "Cry of the Unborn," in August of 1963. "Joe liked it," he said. "He said I had written something very much like his own writing, and I felt extremely complimented. He felt that to edge away from the technological themes would make a more interesting show, and not *just* because of the production costs. It was also right about this time that ABC started forcing him toward the monster-of-the-week. We gave the network what they wanted, and veered off in another direction at the same time."

Director Leonard Horn's excellent point-of-view camera takes us along for the ride, sneaking peeks at the real Andro while the hypnotized, blissfully unaware characters like Mrs. McCluskey (Noelle's landlady) have their

Martin Landau sees a face in the mirror at Mrs. McCluskey's boarding house.

backs turned. "You sound like an Englishman," she chirps, and the deformed mutant we see stumping up the steps behind her says, "Yes, I'm from London." After Andro's first confrontation with Cabot, Horn tilts from Martin Landau's perfectly human face to his gnarled and knobby hand, grasping the porch pillar—a subtly done and surprising visual touch that tells us all we need to know about Andro's hypnotic powers without tedious exposition.

First AD Lee Katzin recalled Horn as cinematically-oriented, emphasizing character, and a workhorse committed to long hours on the set.* "Lenny was really inventive," he said. "He and Conrad Hall played off each other's talents quite well."

"I wanted a romantic look to contrast the horror content," said Hall, "so I used a special filter originally designed for enlargers, to soften portraits." For the closeups, Hall draped netting, scrims, or sheer silk over the camera lens to diffuse the shot, giving it a filmy, dreamlike quality. The painstaking and time-consuming camera set-ups are evident throughout the show. One such shot is of Andro and Noelle, as they pause in the forest prior to their blastoff. "Tell me, Andro, what you really are," she says. A low, subjective angle gives us Martin Landau's head in dead silhouette, framed by bright foliage. As he responds, *"Ugly,"* his front teeth reflect a hard diamond of light.

The show's final shot is most striking: Noelle, alone in the spaceship cockpit, dwindles back and back into space until she becomes just another star in the firmament. Hall laid a great deal of camera track down inside KTTV's Stage #2, got the longest boom mike MGM had, and lit only the two cockpit seats, killing every other light onstage. Once the camera had pulled far enough away from Shirley Knight, she was replaced by a photo cutout that was shrunk optically.

*Horn died in 1975 at the age of 49.

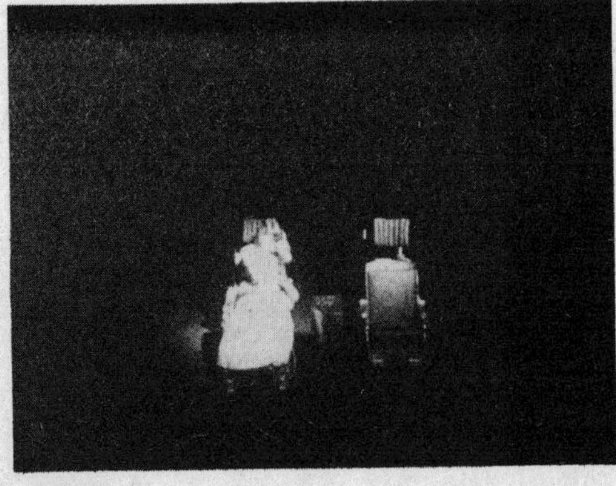

Shirley Knight fades out in Conrad Hall's ambitious closing shot.

The Andro mask supplied by Project Unlimited was so imperfect that most of the *Outer Limits* crew recalls its ill fit. "Martin Landau couldn't *breathe,*" said Jack Poplin. "It's too bad some of those things couldn't have been taped; there were some horrendous bloopers that went on." Fixing the mask fell to Fred Phillips. "It was another mask I didn't know anything about until they threw it at me," he said. "The strap that hooked around Landau's neck was not correct, the eyes did not work out, and the impression taken of his face was lousy to boot!" The appliance was corrected by Phillips and John Chambers, during Chambers's stint on "The Sixth Finger."

Landau was yet another alumnus of *The Greatest Story Ever Told* (he played Caiaphas, the High Priest), as was John Considine. While casting *Twilight Zone,* John Erman had gotten Landau for a show called "Mr. Denton on Doomsday" in 1959, and his friend Considine had just completed one, "The Thirty Fathom Grave," at MGM. Shirley Knight, already a two-time Oscar nominee in 1963, had taken an acting class taught by Landau in 1958, at which time Landau attended her first wedding, to Ben Perssons. "But that time," Landau told a newspaper interviewer, "I didn't pack a gun."

After the title was changed, Lawrence's script underwent minimal trimming.* One significant deletion was Andro's explanation that his psychic powers are another side-effect of the Cabot symbiote. The biggest change was the elimination of Lawrence's final scene, which was to *follow* the shot of Noelle, stranded in space. She awakes, as if from a dream, on a grassy knoll, and calls out for Andro, who is nowhere to be seen. Then she encounters a kindly, middle-aged man, piloting an air-car:

> MAN: Could I help you?
> NOELLE: (after a pause): What is this place?
> MAN: It is London. (smiles) That is, if you follow this road, you will come into the Old Town.
> NOELLE: And the time?
> MAN: The time?
> NOELLE: The year?
> MAN (a smile, then): Twenty-one-forty-eight. Are you lost?
> NOELLE (pauses): No. Just alone.

This scene was filmed on the MGM backlot, with Jack Raine as the future man, but was cut because it ran the show into overtime. Lee Katzin recalled the vehicle used was a hovercraft: "It was a futuristic-looking thing, but it sure didn't work terribly well." While the scene demonstrates that everything is indeed all right in the revised future, it suggests the cop-out that the whole drama was just a dream of Noelle's. Cutting it provided *The Outer*

*The altered title is frequently misremembered by both *Outer Limits* fans and crewpeople alike as *The Man Who Never Was*—the 1955 film about World War Two's famous Operation Mincemeat.

Limits with one of its most memorable downbeat endings (counterbalancing that of "The Sixth Finger," which had been revised to make it more upbeat), and Lawrence was pleased with the new finale: "It gave the show a mystique which the other ending did not have, and that made it much more interesting."

The anemone-like aliens designed by Marcel and Victor Delgado.

MOONSTONE

Broadcast 9 March 1964
Written by William Bast. Story material by Joseph Stefano and Lou Morheim.
Directed by Robert Florey
Assistant Director: Robert Justman
Director of Photography: John Nickolaus

CAST: Prof. Diana Brice (Ruth Roman), Gen. Lee Stocker (Alex Nicol), Major Clint Anderson (Tim O'Connor), Dr. Phillip Mendl (Curt Conway), Lt. Ernie Travers (Hari Rhodes), Grippian Voice (Ben Wright), Scanner Unit Voice (Vic Perrin).

> *In Man's conquest of space, his own moon must be the first to surrender. From there he will step his way across the heavens to the edge of Infinity. Each step will be as uncertain as the last, yet each will bring him closer to ultimate truth. Lunar Expedition One: Here a handful of brave scientists and technicians pave the way to the future. Their mission: To collect information that will eventually enable Man to inhabit the Moon;*

to use the Moon as a springboard to the stars. Once during each twenty-four hour period, a force of three commanded by General Lee Stocker and including Lieutenant Travers and Major Clint Anderson makes its slow, uncharted way across the lunar surface, a surface whose depths and desires are, as yet, unprobed . . .

During one of their daily moonwalks, Major Anderson falls into a crater full of quicksandlike moondust and finds a radiant white spheroid buried there. This basketball-sized "moonstone" turns out to be a space vessel containing five fugitives from the planet Grippia—monocular, anemonelike beings who are on the run from the tyrants who have conquered their homeworld and would use their collective genius to create new weapons for the invasion and enslavement of other planets. General Stocker agrees to transmit a signal that will lead a rescue ship to the fugitives, who then begin feeding their vast knowledge into the moonbase's computers. The resident scientists are astounded by the new facts and formulae. But the hoped-for rescue ship has already been wiped out by the tyrants, who follow the signal and arrive in a much larger sphere, demanding the immediate return of the renegade Grippians. Stocker, once faced with a similar no-win situation during the Korean War, refuses, and the tyrants commence obliterating the moonbase. To prevent the devastation, the five Grippians opt to surrender, but before the larger moonstone can absorb them, they blow themselves to cinders. "Well, that's one way to defeat the tyrants," says Anderson. Stocker's fiancée Diana Brice, realizing that Stocker has been haunted by guilt over his identical ineffectiveness in Korea, agrees, "It was the *only* way." The tyrants retreat into space, emptyhanded.

The steps Man takes across the heavens of his universe are as uncertain as those steps he takes across the rooms of his own life. And yet if he walks with an open mind, those steps must lead him eventually to that most perfect of all destinations, truth.

"One time," said Leslie Stevens, "Lin Parsons was walking down a hallway near Joe Stefano's office, carrying a large lightbulb; you know, one of those spherical lampshades. Joe spotted him, pointed at the bulb, and said, 'There's our next show—he's holding a *moonstone!*'"

At first, the seamless Grippian sphere was to have been a large wooden ball, over which optical effects would be superimposed, but Parsons and production manager Leon Chooluck scared up one of the milky, oversized globes they'd seen hanging from the street lamp posts in Beverly Hills. John Nickolaus recalls that choruses of "Bring on the street lamp!" greeted the prop during filming, and that the crew was on guard a tiny bit. They were not exactly sure where the globe had come from, but they had their suspicions.

"My idea was to come up with creatures so small they could fit inside that lamp," said Lou Morheim. The story, unfortunately, is built entirely

The Moonstone, superimposed over a Chesley Bonestell lunar painting titled "The Straight Wall."

around this visual gimmick, and hampered by the same stale "sci-fi" cliches that handicap "Specimen: Unknown." Though the plight of the runaway Grippians seems very momentous, it fails to hang together convincingly. Several times they express a nebulous need for "energy," yet none of the moonbase's forms of power are useful to them even though they somehow intend to energize themselves on Earth. They are too weak to send an SOS to the moonbase, or Grippia, but powerful enough to revive Anderson from an electrical mishap with a brilliant light beam, and blow themselves to smithereens at the finale. They don't seem to realize that the signal beam they aim "in the direction of Grippia" will give away their exact location to any Grippian who cares to tune in. And while they quite loftily advise Stocker that "If you are ever to destroy evil, you must survive to fight it," they have absolutely no qualms about wiping *themselves* out and leaving their human benefactors defenseless and at the mercy of a gang of extremely aggravated Grippian bad guys—who then conveniently turn tail and split without any vengeful aggression, although earlier they stomp the base's scanner unit flat just to exhibit their muscle. Yes, they behave barbarically, but no differently than most bounty hunters might under similar circumstances. In fact, there is no real proof that the Grippians in the little moonstone are benevolent; they could easily be smooth-talking criminals who con the Earth-folk into harboring them from their own police. Stocker never speaks to the supposed tyrants; everything is relayed through those in the runaway moonstone—who don't bother to reveal themselves until long after being brought to the moonbase, and then make a deal with Stocker's people based on a trade of scientific information so far in advance of our own science that it is impossible to verify. Rather than addressing these questions, the script is too busy substituting plot motion for substance by jumping from the tiresome trappings of moonwalking to alien platitudes, from the already-dated Korean War references to lunar soap opera (a love triangle among Diana, Stocker, and Anderson). Even the Control Voice speech is lacking. Beyond telling us what we can already see on screen, there is an oblique riff about questing for truth that relates directly to nothing we see in the episode.

"Anytime we began to get really *science fictiony,* I knew we were in trouble," said Stefano. "'Moonstone' caused a lot of problems, as did any show calling for 'futuristic' qualities. The things we could afford to do were tight, naturalistic dramas and Gothic melodramas." After the strong character motivation seen in "The Sixth Finger" and "The Man Who Was Never Born," "Moonstone" is thin beer indeed, and a big step backward for *The Outer Limits*.

The teleplay was a one-time assignment for writer William Bast, and a one-time job for director Robert Florey, a long-time veteran of the film industry whose work in "Moonstone" is competently done, but flat and uninvolving. John Nickolaus characterized it as "lacking any distinctive style." The cast was headed by another *Outer Limits* Odd Couple. Ruth Roman delivers the only performance with any humanity, and Alex Nicol (who directed the grade Z horror film *The Screaming Skull* in 1958) is stiff and ill-at-ease as Stocker. Tim O'Connor's Anderson maintains a hysterical dislike of Stocker that far outweighs the General's somewhat foggy war crimes. Anderson is repellent and a bit of a stumblebum—it is he who blunders into the pit of "lunar quicksand" and, later, plunges drunkenly into the exposed wiring of a control console. This latter accident, from which the Grippians revive Anderson, is utterly phony-looking. Written in the script as a fall from an overhead catwalk, it was oversimplified, and O'Connor's stunt man appears to purposefully dive right into the machine's guts.

Bast's script contained some spectacular action scenes, most of which were not done for logistical and budgetary reasons. Here is what was to happen when Stocker tries to load the moonstone onto the base's shuttlecraft, to escape:

> (*Within the larger Moonstone*) Hundreds of eyes shine ominously, glowing more and more brightly until their iridescence is nearly hypnotic. Then, suddenly, they attack—hot rays of light zoom downward. One by one, the eyes rotate out of the oval eddy, moving slowly in the direction of the

The eyes of the Grippian tyrants focus on the moonbase dome.

dome. In an endless stream they pour forth. Two spacesuited men have started running now, clumsily, awkwardly trying to win the frustrating battle against near-weightlessness, the lunar dust, and their cumbersome spacesuits. The eyes hover closer and closer. (*One of them steps into a moondust pit and is sucked under. His partner is cornered by the eyes.*) In a pathetic gesture of defiance, he grabs a large rock and throws it with hateful fury at the giant eye. His figure is illuminated by the beam, frozen in negative for an instant—a gallant, defiant statue—then dissolves into nothing.

As originally written, Dr. Mendl dies in a fiery explosion of the base's laboratory dome, but his revised death scene at the hands of the Grippian invaders is still startling. Explosions chase him around the lab, and he bursts through a pair of swinging doors to fall at Stocker's feet. He is momentarily spot-lit by the death-beam, which vaporizes him as Diana screams, then dwindles to a tiny dot of white light on the now-bare floor.

"Moonstone" is partially redeemed by some splendid visuals, including an extravagant "lunar exterior" built by Jack Poplin on KTTV's Stage #2. It is a dark moonscape with jagged mountains and columns of rock, floored in a good five-inch depth of sand. "That 'sand' was a very light material used normally for insulation," said Poplin. "We'd dye whole barrels of it different colors; you'd get differing values on black-and-white film. I designed all the *Outer Limits* sets basically in color; it did something for the actors. I got the moon backdrops from MGM, and we built the rock columns to hide the gaps between them." While technically elementary by today's standards, the life-sized set is a grand achievement considering the small scale of TV, and looks as good as any similar set used in science fiction film up to that time.

Paintings by astronomical artist Chesley Bonestell were used as background plates for the many shots of the two Moonstones cruising against the lunar surface. The Grippians themselves were designed at Project Un-

Clad in environment suits left over from the TV series *Men Into Space*, Alex Nicol (L) and Tim O'Connor examine the benevolent Moonstone on Jack Poplin's lunar set.

limited by the father and son team of Marcel and Victor Delgado. "We worked up a variety of small models with tendrils," said Gene Warren. "The 'eyes' were dressed-up, tissue-papered ping pong balls held on sticks." The Grippian puppets were filmed inside a water tank so that their "hair" would drift about as they swayed and moved.

The mostly ponderous Grippian monologues were dubbed by Ben Wright, and as was customary for *Outer Limits'* more thoughtful aliens, they express several quotable sentiments, such as, "The mind earns by doing; the heart earns by trying." Or: "In the end, it is usually the good minds who enable evil to thrive." But for the most part, the speeches are slow and repetitious. On hearing them again years later, Ben Wright remarked, "What a gabby old poop!"

Stefano suggested Hari Rhodes for the part of Lt. Travers, whereupon one of ABC's brain boys pointed out that Rhodes was black. "Or, at that time, a *Negro actor,*" said Stefano. What ruffled the network was that Rhodes had been proposed for a part "not specifically written for a black actor. So they said, 'Well, write it in the script: *black actor.*'" Stefano scribbled this onto his copy of the teleplay on the spot. Case closed.

It is to be hoped that the lack of a complicated story and the variety of sets and special effects perhaps made this *Outer Limits* episode more accessible to the mass TV audience. But it is no pun to say that, ultimately, "Moonstone" is more a show for the *eyes* than for the brain.

Jeff Corey alongside his sinister alien alter-ego.

O.B.I.T.

Broadcast 4 November 1963
Written by Meyer Dolinsky
Directed by Gerd Oswald

Assistant Director: Lee H. Katzin
Director of Photography: Conrad Hall

CAST: Senator Jeremiah Orville (Peter Breck), Byron Lomax (Jeff Corey), Col. Grover (Alan Baxter), Dr. Clifford Scott (Harry Townes), Barbara Scott (Joanne Gilbert), Clyde Wyatt (Sam Reese), Dr. Phillip Fletcher (Konstantin Shayne), Fred Severn [OBIT Operative] (Jason Wingreen), Capt. James Harrison (Robert Beneveds), Dr. Anderson (Lindsay Workman), Armand Younger (Chuck Hamilton), OBIT Creature (William O. Douglas, Jr.).

> *In this room, twenty-four hours a day, seven days a week, security personnel at the Defense Department's Cypress Hills Research Center keep constant watch on its scientists through OBIT, a mysterious electronic device whose very existence was carefully kept from the public at large. And so it would have remained, but for the facts you are about to witness.*

The Outer Band Individuated Teletracer—OBIT—is a hellishly precise surveillance machine that is thrown into an unwanted spotlight by a murder investigation. While spying on Cypress Hills scientists and dutifully logging their various transgressions, Capt. Harrison spots a "phantom image" on the screen which resolves into a one-eyed albino monster. Its fearsome claws close on air, as if choking a pantomime victim. At that moment, *human* hands slap around Harrison's neck, and he watches the creature on the screen strangle *him*. This killing prompts an investigation into Cypress Hills and OBIT by Senator Orville. The head of the research base, Dr. Clifford Scott, has vanished following a mental collapse, and in his stead is administrator Byron Lomax. The extent and uses of OBIT shock Orville; it has seemingly permeated all levels of society. As the hearings progress, the OBIT creature and other operatives are seen attempting to locate the missing Scott and eliminate all witnesses for the prosecution. One initially hostile witness, Col. Grover, breaks down on the stand in horror at OBIT's true nature and leads Orville to Scott, who is not crazy, but is hiding out at a mental institution because he saw the same monster on the OBIT screen, and discovered it was Lomax himself! The murdered Harrison had been working for Scott, with orders to monitor Lomax. Scott is produced as a surprise witness and uses the machine to expose Lomax to the court, but Lomax holds everyone at bay long enough to deliver a grandiose speech. He gloats that the machines are everywhere, and they will demoralize and divide the population of Earth, making us easy invasion fodder for his race. As he speaks, his gestures are duplicated on the OBIT screen by his alien alter ego. Before sentries can apprehend him, Lomax reverts to his true form and dematerializes.

> *Agents of the Justice Department are rounding up the machines now. But these machines, these inventions of another planet, have been cunningly conceived to play on our most mortal weakness. In the last analysis, dear friends, whether OBIT lives up to its name or not will depend on you.*

"I'm very much in love with freedom," said Meyer Dolinsky. "But I'm also concerned that we do have restraints against extreme totalitarianism. The political focus of 'O.B.I.T.' is all mine; it's a reverse on the H.U.A.C. thing. These people, far from helping a free society, are really its worst enemy, in the sense they breed so much hostility and fear that they curiously accomplish the very thing they are trying to prevent. Witch-hunting is the wrong way to go about it."

The "peeping Tom" nature of the OBIT machine neatly implicates the TV viewer as well, in Dolinsky's slick plot about moral conquest. As the OBIT men spy on their subjects, they are in turn watched by the *Outer Limits* audience, who, by extrapolation, is probably also being monitored. "People with nothing to hide have nothing to fear from OBIT," says Lomax, in an innocuous-sounding policy statement that permits him to psychologically undermine our entire planet. Importantly, "O.B.I.T." demonstrates that the exposure of a sinister plot is not in itself a remedy, and stresses the need for forthright action before it is too late. The decision to act, or to ignore the plot and be destroyed, rests with us.

Stefano had read an obscure book on the invasion of privacy theme, which he passed along to Dolinsky. "Originally, I had the OBIT machine all over the place," said Dolinsky, who submitted a script with a fair amount of globe-trotting action centered around OBIT. "I changed it because they wanted to cut costs; my canvas had been wider. I confined it to the Army base, which helped the dramatics but wasn't as much fun." While working superlatively as both a cautionary fable and a tight courtroom drama, "O.B.I.T." could have worked quite well without its eccentrically designed monster. "*We* didn't need it," Dolinsky stressed. "Our concept was for an X-ray type camera that could see through buildings. It became personified in the monster, and the monster was the sort of thing we had to invent for the network."

"The script had very little action on the page," said Stefano. "But Gerd Oswald transformed it." Oswald had a wealth of experience filming gavel-operas by virtue of his work on *Perry Mason*.* Limited to very basic sets and lengthy inquest sequences, he experimented with chiaroscuro tricks. "Sometimes I'd dare Connie Hall to do something unconventional," he said. "He'd *always* do it. We'd generally opt for the unconventional." One example is how Oswald chose to shoot Jeff Corey, as Lomax: "I kept moving closer to him in stages, until I could focus on one of his eyes through his eyeglasses, and the reflections *in* the glass, to build the menace." This forms one element of a "monster eye" motif that is competently sustained throughout the show. The creature glimpsed through the static on the OBIT screen is appropriately Cyclopean—a thoughtful effect achieved by tilting the actor's head inside the alien mask so that

*Oswald directed many *Perry Mason* segments for Ben Brady, who was later to become the producer of *Outer Limits'* second season.

his real eye peers from dead center. The OBIT's circular screen recalls the earliest round-screened TV sets, and symbolizes the intrusion of this "new" medium by suggesting a more complex technology, such as that of a radar scope. The dull, utilitarian rooms in which the hearings are conducted are broken up by patterns of circular blobs of background lighting. The arrangement of tables and chairs is arenalike, also circular, as are the distortive, bottle-bottom spectacles worn by Lomax. In the show's final shot, Oswald pulls up into a high-angle, omniscient-god point of view, as though everyone is still being quietly watched.

The episode is full of excellent dialogue, powerfully delivered. Here is the jittery Dr. Scott, explaining what he tuned in on the OBIT screen:

> SCOTT: When I told them what I saw, they got very quiet, and looked at me with great, quiet eyes. Quiet can tell you so much. Until they looked at me that way, I was certain that I had seen what I had seen. Dead certain. Of course, I hadn't. It was just that my life had become a nightmare, so naturally I saw the sort of things that inhabit a nightmare world. I saw a monster. When I told them that, they got very *quiet*.

The close-cropped Col. Grover, staunchly militant, approves of the OBIT at first... and then is horrified by it:

> GROVER: It's awful—*awful!* I feel responsible; I should've spoken out.... It's the most hideous creation ever conceived! No one can laugh, or joke. It *watches*, saps the very spirit. And the worst thing of all is *I* watch it. I can't *not* look. It's like a drug—a horrible drug. You can't resist it. It's an addiction.

Thus does Dolinsky smoothly slip his critical scalpel into the old one-eyed monster itself—television—as well. Thanks to the engaging tension between Orville and Lomax, the plot moves briskly, and the gaps left by the lack of TV's usual running around are filled by the well-delivered contributions of the supporting players. As with "Specimen: Unknown," Oswald builds the whole show toward a single climactic moment, but here the payoff is no disappointment, as Lomax holds the court momentarily spellbound.

> LOMAX: The machines are everywhere! Oh, you'll find them all; you're a zealous people. And you'll make a great show out of smashing a few of them, but for every one you destroy, hundreds of others will be built, and they'll demoralize you, break your spirit, create such

> rifts and tensions in your society that no one will be able to repair them! You're a savage, despairing planet. And when we come here to live, you friendless, demoralized flotsam will fall without even a single shot being fired. You're all of the same dark persuasion. You demand, *insist* on knowing every private thought and hunger in everyone—your families, your neighbors, *everyone but yourselves!*

Omitted from the script is one line revealing the origin of the aliens to be a planet called Helos, and the black pun in the Control Voice's tag speech is Dolinsky's.

Years later, the Wah Chang-sculpted OBIT mask turned up on a guest monster in an episode of *The Munsters,* while the OBIT console (*sans* screen) ironically became the center of worldwide communications for Leo G. Carroll on *The Man From U.N.C.L.E.*

"O.B.I.T."'s broadcast caused Daku (the same *Variety* critic who had panned "The Galaxy Being") to opine: "*The Outer Limits* has successfully overcome a mediocre start with a succession of good sci-fi stories that have established this as a unique and interesting series... [this] teleplay has a lot of bite, and the moral is obvious."

Everybody Say Cheese

During "O.B.I.T."'s second day of filming, September 16, 1963, while Gerd Oswald and his crew were working late on KTTV's Stage #4, *The Outer Limits* had its network premiere as TV sets across the country lit

Paul Richards, Eduard Franz and Joseph Cotten try to ignore the Thetan in their midst during this photo session for the 1963 "Fall Preview" issue of *TV Guide.* (Photo by Gene Trindl)

up with "The Galaxy Being." Hyperbolic press releases from ABC claimed: "No, this season on television won't be the same old stuff. There will be television programs of conspicuous excellence. Over one hundred million dollars has been spent in eight months to bring America this completely new kind of television." Other than *The Outer Limits,* only one of the "New ABC"'s vanguard of shows (which included *100 Grand,* the alternating Sid Caesar and Edie Adams variety shows, *The Farmer's Daughter* and a disastrous, two-hour live talk show hosted by Jerry Lewis) remains in syndication today—*The Fugitive,* starring David Janssen.

The Outer Limits was covered in *Look, Time,* and *Newsweek.* Numberless newspaper fillers were written around publicity shots of the monsters. *TV Guide* did several pieces; one, "They Deal in Ideas—and Outer Space" was a career overview of the Stevens/Stefano team intelligently written by Richard Gehman. The Thetan from "Architects of Fear" appeared in the "Fall Preview" issue for 1963, posed incongruously between Paul Richards and Eduard Franz of *Breaking Point,* and Joseph Cotten of *Hollywood and the Stars.* A whole gang of monsters got to mug for a photo feature called "Now, Everyone say CHEESE," published in *TV Guide* the same week as the episode "It Crawled Out of the Woodwork" was broadcast. The series never made the cover of *TV Guide,* except as a blurb above a photo from *The Andy Griffith Show.* Apart from a cartoony rendering of the Galaxy Being used in local TV listings and on promotional billboards around Hollywood, apparently the only piece of publicity art done for *The Outer Limits* was a painting, also based on the pilot, by Charles Schneeman. Considered a "discovery" of *Astounding Stories* (today known as *Analog*), Schneeman was a stalwart of the science fiction pulps whose artwork dated to Hugo Gernsback's *Wonder Stories* in 1934. Today the painting is owned by Stefano's son, Dominic.

ABC tried to evolve a mystique around the *Outer Limits* monsters by never showing them in the earliest commercials for the program. In one spot, the Control Voice spiel plays out against the fluctuating sine-wave pattern used to preface *Please Stand By*; this is followed by the radio tower explosion from "The Galaxy Being" and a slow-motion shot of Nina Foch thrashing around in "The Borderland." In a later, even more confusing ad, the Control Voice tells us, *"Thrill to the awe and mystery of the hidden world."* Then a different voice continues: *"You will journey into strange realms of science fiction. You will journey through uncharted galaxies, from the inner mind of Man to* The Outer Limits... *every week on ABC."* This was backed by a rapidfire succession of clips from eight episodes—none showing a monster (with the exception of the energy cloud wiping out the Finley living room in "The Man with the Power"), making the spot a very odd compendium of characters' reaction shots.

Even stranger was an ABC special touting the new fall lineup. Called

An *Outer Limits* "family portrait" from the early part of the first season. (L–R:) Chill Charlie, from "The Human Factor," *Ichthyosaurus Mercurius* from "Tourist Attraction," Andro from "The Man Who Was Never Born," a Luminoid from "A Feasibility Study," the mangled clay head of William Lyons Selby from "The Hundred Days of the Dragon," The Galaxy Being (note that the suit has been painted silver for publicity photography), and the man with "The Sixth Finger." And no, these are not the original actors. (Photo by Gene Trindl)

What's New, it opened with the *Outer Limits* interference/sine-wave pattern, with a wife-to-husband voice over:

> "Look, Charlie—what's that?"
> "Gee, honey, I don't know *what* it is. . . ."
> "I never saw anything like that before. . . ."
> ANNOUNCER: *Of course not—it's NEW!*

After a tinkly dance-band intro and (no kidding) a song about the new fall shows sung by Edie Adams, the voices of the vapid Charlie and his twilight wife returned.

> "Uh-oh, there it is again, Charlie!"
> "There's nothing to be afraid of, honey; it's only *science fiction.*"

Charlie is cut short by a booming, echo-chambered, haunted house voice that bellows, "OUTERRRR LIMITS!" Leslie Stevens must have been amused and dismayed; here was the awe and mystery of the universe colliding head-on with the audience he had once called "your basic trailer park; the Panorama City Lube Pit." All clips in this preview show were from "The Galaxy Being," most notably the Being's first discourse with Cliff Robertson.

Monster magazines eagerly did their bit. *The Outer Limits* was enthusiastically previewed in *Famous Monsters of Filmland* and even received a few encouraging critical comments (plus good photo coverage) from the inimitable *Castle of Frankenstein*.

A set of fifty *Outer Limits* gum cards was minted by a company called Bubbles, Inc., featuring color-tinted photos from the show backed by the most outrageous captions ever conceived. A shot of the "bear" from "Don't Open Till Doomsday" was titled "The Brainless Glob." The caption stated that the Glob was an alien space pet, left behind on Earth by its owners. The poor thing, though utterly harmless, scares away humans, and pines away from a broken heart.

Though entertaining (in the sense of hilarity), this has nothing to do with the plotline of the episode, needless to say. In 1984, a complete set of the *Outer Limits* cards was listed in a collector's catalogue with a price tag exceeding $1200!

In January, 1964, Dell Publishing commenced a bimonthly series of *Outer Limits* comic books, which ran for sixteen issues worth of original stories done under license from Daystar/Villa di Stefano (the issues from #17 onward were reprints). These stories, with titles like "Battleground of Monsters" and "The Day the Blob Invaded Earth," were presented in a three-chapter format, and were pure pulp nonsense from one cover to the other. Had ABC spotted these plotlines, they might have been ecstatic, but the comics well served the purpose of *Outer Limits* juvenilia. For younger fans of the show, Milton Bradley also produced an *Outer Limits* board game and several jigsaw puzzles. The idea of an official Monster of the Month Club with William O. Douglas, Jr., as the "chief barnstormer," was briefly negotiated with Stefano, but nothing ever came of it.

Around the time of the program's premiere, Stefano did a "guest column" for critic Cecil Smith in the *Los Angeles Times*. Here he laid down his guidelines on "tolerable terror" (derived from the *Canons*) for a readership that would normally not think twice about watching something called *The Outer Limits*. "It was a very prestigious sort of thing to do at that time," Stefano said.

For now, *The Outer Limits* had arrived.

James Shigeta (L) and John Anderson.

NIGHTMARE

Broadcast 2 December 1963
Written by Joseph Stefano
Original title: "Ebon Struck First"
Directed by John Erman
Assistant Director: Robert Justman
Director of Photography: John Nickolaus

CAST: Col. Luke Stone (Ed Nelson), Major Jong (James Shigeta), Ebonite Interrogator (John Anderson), Pvt. Arthur Dix (Martin Sheen), Lt. James P. Willowmore (Bill Gunn), Capt. Terrence Ralph Brookman (David Frankham), Lt. Ersa Krug (Bernard Kates), Gen. Benton (Ben Wright), Commanding General (Whit Bissell), Chief of Staff (Willard Sage), Dix's Mother (Lillian Adams), Krug's Grandfather (Sasha Harden), Krug's Governess (Lisa Mann), Dr. Whorf (Martin Brandt), Ebonite Guard (Paul Stader).

> *A war between worlds had long been dreaded. Throughout recent history, Man, convinced that life on other planets would be as anxious and belligerent as life on his own, has gravely predicted that some dreadful form of combat would inevitably take place between our world and that of someone else. And Man was right. To the eternal credit of the peoples of this planet Earth, history shall be able to proclaim loudly and justly that in this war between Unified Earth and the planet Ebon, Ebon struck first. Ebon: Its form of life unknown; its way of life unpredictable. To the fighting troops of Earth, a black question mark at the end of a dark, foreboding journey.*

A six-man multinational strike force led by Col. Stone is captured and made prisoners of war by the Ebonites, satanic, bat-winged, gargoyle-like aliens who wield control wands that can manipulate the five human senses. The first soldier to be subjected to an "exploratory interview" is the apple-pie neurotic Pvt. Dix, who is rendered mute and led away. He returns with his stolen voice regained after questioning, leaving the group to conjecture as to what he might have talked about. Willowmore, a black officer, is casually blinded by the aliens, and Krug, a German, is softened up with hallucinations of his Jewish grandfather, whom he betrayed to the Nazis while just a child. He never returns, and Willowmore comes back in shock. He had asked for his sight back, and gotten it on the condition that he look at the corpse of Krug, who died during interrogation... and the first thing he saw was the gaping hole left when the Ebonites removed Krug's heart. Stone "sleeps" through his own interview, and Major Jong, a Chinese more emotionally resilient than the others, blacks out after having the bones in his right arm pulverized by an Ebonite wand. After Jong's session the group is allowed basic necessities and "the respect due a conquered enemy." The group's consensus is that Jong has turned traitor, and Stone insists there be no leniency for traitors. Straws are drawn and Brookman is assigned to execute Jong by strangulation. When Brookman cannot bring himself to kill another man in cold blood, Jong illustrates that *all* the men had motives for talking. Dix suffers a mental breakdown, revealing that he confided secrets to a hallucination of his mother. Raving, he cuts and runs from the compound and is scooped up by the Ebonite guards. The Ebonite Interrogator conducts Stone to a cubicle where they encounter an Earth General and his Chief of Staff. The alien explains that Ebon's attack on Earth was accidental, and to make amends, his race agreed to continue with the phony "war" in order to provide the Earth commanders with a test scenario to determine how Earth troops such as Stone's men would "behave or misbehave" in actual conflict. The Ebonite is by now affronted by the immorality of this game, and refuses to sanction it, in an attempt to prevent further harm to Stone's men (Krug died of a coronary and the Ebonites fought to save him, but failed). When the Interrogator returns to the POW compound to expose the charade to the remaining men, he is jumped by Brookman, Willowmore, and Jong. Stone breaks from the cubicle, with the Earth generals in pursuit, and orders his men to release the Ebonite. The Chief of Staff backs up Stone's command with a pistol, but the men no longer believe the evidence of their own eyes. There is a scuffle; Brookman grabs the gun and shoots the Chief of Staff, who dies on the floor. The horrible truth dawns on Brookman, who earlier could not murder a fellow human: "I thought he was..."

"He wasn't," says Stone grimly. "He was *real*."

The exploration of human behavior under simulated conditions of stress is a commonplace component of the machinery called war. So long as Man anticipates and prepares for combat, be it with neighboring nations or with our neighbors in space, these unreal games must be played, and there are only real men to play them. According to established military procedure, the results of the Ebon maneuvers will be recorded in books and fed into computers for the edification and enlight-

enment of all the strategists of the future. Perhaps they will learn something.

Arguably *Outer Limits'* best-written show, "Nightmare" is a *tour de force* of ensemble acting that illustrates just how resourceful the program's cast and crew could be when squeezed by the limitations of time and budget.

Once again, as earlier in "Specimen: Unknown" and "Moonstone" the military was up in space, but Stefano's approach to this topic was different. "I had some very strong problems with the government situation at that time," he said. "Space was not bad; space agencies were not bad. But I had little faith, and virtually no trust, in the people in charge of the Space Age. In World War Two, the military dropped the atom bomb, and everyone thought that was great because it ended the war. If you wanted to give something the stamp of approval, you made it military, and I was attacking part of that faith in the military. I was politically naive in those days, and a lot of what I was writing wasn't based on any great passion or knowledge, but on superstitions, thoughts and feelings about who worried me. 'Nightmare' wasn't written out of cynicism, but out of deep suspicion. If you think of that in terms of 1963 or '64, it's shocking and disturbing. Now, of course, nobody's surprised. It took a few years for the government to prove I was right. The idea of war games was not particularly popular, and there was a lot of stress testing going on just then. I said let's do a *real* game, push these guys to the limit and see how much they can take. A real theatre piece."

The soldiers' ordeal in "Nightmare" is a stage of established scientific method, the experimentation stage that follows simple observation (as seen in "O.B.I.T."). But here the experiment has gone too far; it is beyond corrective measures and can only plummet toward its dark and frightening conclusion. The Unified Earth so hoped for in "Architects of Fear" is here realized in Col. Stone's interracial, multinational crew, but that unity is now subjugated from within. Stefano suggests that for all its deadliness, soldiering is still a childish game. When the Ebonite exposes the generals to Stone, one of them exclaims, "You've spoiled the whole game!" The opening scene of the episode features Stone pep-talking his boys like a football coach: "Whatever the Ebonites are, however they live or die, win or lose..." The pawn-pushing of the officers in charge soon forces Stone's men to resort to games as the only way of asserting their capacity of choice: The selection of Jong's executioner becomes the old straw-pulling game; the men bandy the precise meaning of a code number back and forth, straining for a technicality by which they can justify murdering Jong; Jong calls the planned murder of the Interrogator "the vengeance game." Present in the Ebonite's lines are the games of language soon to become familiar to America with Watergate: Treason is given the euphemistic mantle of "telling *true* things"; ruthless interrogation is "an exploratory interview"; and the worst kind of coercion translates as "Pvt. Dix will be the first to accept my invitation." When the Interrogator calls the disastrous experiment a "charade"—another game—the generals behave like naughty kids caught red-handed, puffing up enough to tell Stone "We're sorry... but we don't apologize." When Dix goes mad, he hums "Twinkle Twinkle, Little Star," which recalls our first glimpse of Ebon, a planet that does not twinkle like the stars in children's songs, but which looks more like an evil black hole punched in the fabric of space. This "game" gives the men no way out, and they succumb to easy bigotry and their animal fear of the unknown.

Stefano deleted a great deal of dialogue from his first draft, and while most of the omissions are not essential material, they broaden the already-deep characters and clarify certain aspects of the complicated plot. Jong, for example, is designated as a "Chinese Independent," which adds a layer to his presumed guilt by associating him with one of America's most recent enemies, the Chinese Communists. He also explains the haiku poetic form to the men, which sets up the scenes we do see—Jong reciting haiku while being tortured, and the Commanding General estimating his potential for treason by saying, "Perhaps. Recites poetry."

After Krug's death, Jong and Brookman have a talk that eerily forecasts what is to come:

> JONG: I feel too sad to mourn anyone.
>
> BROOKMAN: Sad? Or sorry for yourself?
>
> JONG: Myself? No. For you. All of you. I feel ineffably sad for all of you.
>
> BROOKMAN: This sadness, major—does it make you feel like doing something heroic?
>
> JONG: You mean tell all, in the hope of saving all? I thought of doing that. It made me feel like a born and saintly warrior, all warm and noble inside.
>
> BROOKMAN: You wouldn't be the first man who turned traitor over mistaken notions of heroism.
>
> JONG: What would you do to me, then, if I turned traitor?
>
> BROOKMAN: One of us would kill you.
>
> JONG: Which one?
>
> *(suddenly Brookman is paged for his "interview," as if the Ebonite P.A. had just answered Jong's question.)*
>
> JONG: No. Not Captain Brookman. Too civilized. Not a bare-handed assassin at all.

Later, Brookman pulls the short straw, and when asking Stone how he should kill Jong, says, "With my bare hands?"

"If a lot of that stuff had been left in, it would have confused everybody," said Stefano. "It was a joy to write it, knowing that I would be able to cut it out." Only one change from script to film is truly critical, and it involves the unexpected compassion the Ebonite shows Stone's men. He confronts the generals alone (without Stone), realizes he cannot reach them, and so goes to the POW compound to tell the truth to Stone and his remaining men. The seriousness of what occurs then is lampooned by Robert Justman's comedic shooting notes for the scene:

> INT. COMPOUND ZERO–THREE–DAY–1Sc.–1 4/8 Pgs.–(32)
>
> DESCRIPTION: Chief of Staff, him show up & try stoppum fellas who all beat up on Interrogator–Chief, him pull firestick–Brookman, him slip up behind Chief and disarm same—Stone, him pick up firestick and shoot Big Chief in labonza—Chief, him fall down, go to happy hunting grounds–other warriors, they react–Interrogator, him confirm that Chief was real–Commanding General, him show up too late–Chapman Crane, him pull back as Control Voice, him narrate Tagsville–Director, him say "Print"–Assistant Director, him say "Wrap it up"–Everybody, they go home–eat supper–smoke peace pipe with squaw.

The line concerning real men and unreal games originally went to the Ebonite, but Stefano divided it between Stone and the Control Voice. If you watch the final shot of the finished episode closely, though, you'll see the Ebonite speaking as the Control Voice wraps things up.

Stefano's "exteriors" on Ebon, meant to depict only a *milky-white, even sky* and a *flat, vast, empty black surface, slick and glassy-hard as some ebony gem,* were shot on a nearly naked soundstage dressed with a few outcrops of Jack Poplin's plastic, foam, and rubber rocks. Justman hung a lot of black velvet, to transform the set into a featureless kind of limbo area, heightening the impression that the whole show is an experimental stage drama.

Although Byron Haskin was set to direct the episode, the time was right for John Erman, Daystar's casting man, to direct his first *Outer Limits* as part of his agreement with Leslie Stevens. "I inherited John," said Stefano, "but I liked him and wanted him to have one of my scripts, even though he hadn't really directed anything before. That didn't worry me, because *I* had never done anything before, either."

"I had no real technique as a director," said Erman. "And I think one of the deficiencies of that show was that it was done on Connie Hall's off-week. He alternated episodes with John Nickolaus, and while John is a lovely man with whom I've worked a great deal since then, he's very conventional. Unless you pushed him into doing odd or provocative lighting, he wouldn't do it. Whereas Connie would walk onto a set and say, 'Oh God, wouldn't it be interesting if we did *this!*' John *could* do all that—he could do anything, and was very skilled—but the director had to come up with it, and I was not ready to come up with it."

Another problem was the way Erman looked at scripts: "All I saw were the casting problems," he said. "But I knew I would be directing 'Nightmare' by the time I cast it, and I surrounded myself with actors who were my pals, because I was frightened. We did read-throughs of the script at my house one weekend, and the next weekend—in the middle of shooting—at Jimmy Shigeta's house. We'd rehearse, and discuss the characters and their relationships. That was Martin Sheen's first job out here. I'd seen him on live TV, and he came out from New York and rented an apartment here. I'd pick him up each day for work; he used to sit on his stoop at 5:30 in the morning to wait for me."

A former actor himself, Erman was very much an "actor's director," and this partially accounts for the terrific ensemble work on view in "Nightmare."* But while the performances were inspired, the finished film was not what Stefano had envisioned. "It just didn't work," Tom Selden recalls. "It wasn't that Joe was disappointed in the direction; it just didn't *matter*. Sometimes the pace is wrong, the angles are wrong, something is wrong, and a film doesn't jell. So he reworked the show in the editing room, reconstructing it and turning it almost entirely around."

"I was promised a certain number of *Outer Limits* in my deal with Leslie," said Erman. "But after Joe saw 'Nightmare,' he was not happy with my work, and told me he didn't want me to do anymore. In retrospect, I think he was right when he said I dealt wonderfully with the actors, but did not have enough film experience. I asked Al Sargent, who is now a successful writer, what was wrong and he said, 'It looks too much like a play; you approach things from the proscenium arch, and you have to learn the film medium better.' I imagine Joe, in editing, wanted to make it *more* theatrical, and I'd let him down, and he was pulling every trick he could to give it more style than I had. I went to Leslie and said, 'I'm very confused. I really feel I want to be a director, and Joe doesn't want me to direct anymore.' And Leslie said, 'If that's what you *really* want, then you should stop casting. And direct.' Once I made that decision, I wanted to leave Daystar very quickly, before I got truly scared. And I had some very rocky times right after I left. Joe and Leslie and I did not part enemies in any way. It was *go and do what you need to do*. At that time, it was very painful and difficult for me. But if Stefano hadn't done that, I might have potchkied around, just casting, for the next few years because it was so comfortable for me—and I might not have the career I have today. So he did me a huge favor."

Despite its staginess, "Nightmare" is surprisingly intellectual TV drama, and the series' most potent view of phobia and conspiracy. A highpoint of the show's capacity for tension and Stefano's skill as a scenarist is the scene in which Lt. Willowmore has his horrifying breakdown. He is too overwhelmed by the sight of Lt. Krug's heartless corpse to do

*Erman's acting debut was in *The Blackboard Jungle* (1955).

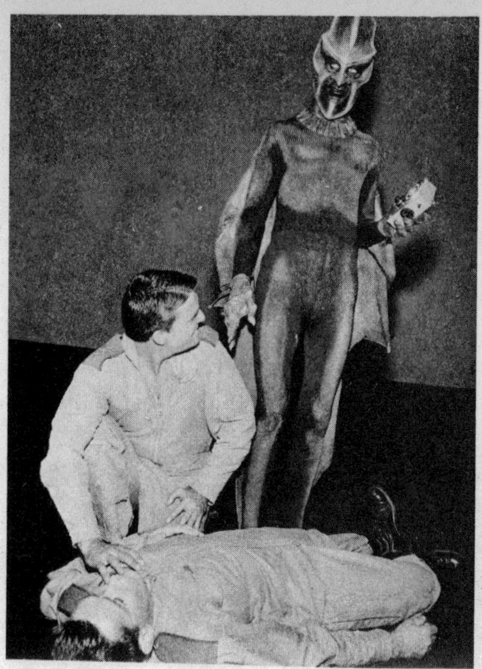

Martin Sheen (prone), Ed Nelson, and John Anderson, who holds an Ebonite translator box. This still is more brightly lit than the episode itself—hence the visibility of the alien's underwear!

anything but grope for words and scream, his nerves flayed raw. Bill Gunn's performance places a cold finger on the soul.

The episode was also a nightmare schedule-wise, according to Wah Chang: "It was a real rush job; we worked into the early morning hours to get the masks done. Paul Pattee worked like a Trojan on the winglike portion of the costume and could *not* get it right. He made duplicates of one wing model rather than trying to do a right and left side, and as it went, we had all right wings and no left ones!" On the second day of shooting, Fred Phillips had a flat tire on the Hollywood Freeway, leaving actor John Anderson to apply his own Ebonite makeup and mask. "He did a fine job," said Phillips.

The "TV cheapness" of the batwinged bodystocking distressed Erman, and was unpopular with the Ebonite actors since "Nightmare" was filmed during one of L.A.'s characteristic September heat waves. The air conditioning on the KTTV stages was negated by the extra lighting required for the totally black sets, and actors began fainting as the temperatures soared. While his fellow Ebonites became sweat-drenched and dizzy, John Anderson took it in stride, smoking cigars and never seeming to need a fresh costume... although later he growled at Erman, "You owe me one because of this!" Anderson also dubbed the Interrogator's bizarre voice, described as "high, reedy, cold, and mechanical" in the script, via the same process used in "The Galaxy Being."

"I took our son, Dominic, to the studio to walk around on the set," remembers Marilyn Stefano. "He was five at the time. When he encountered John Anderson in costume, he cringed and clung to my skirt

... until he looked down and saw that the alien was wearing tennis shoes. That broke the ice!"

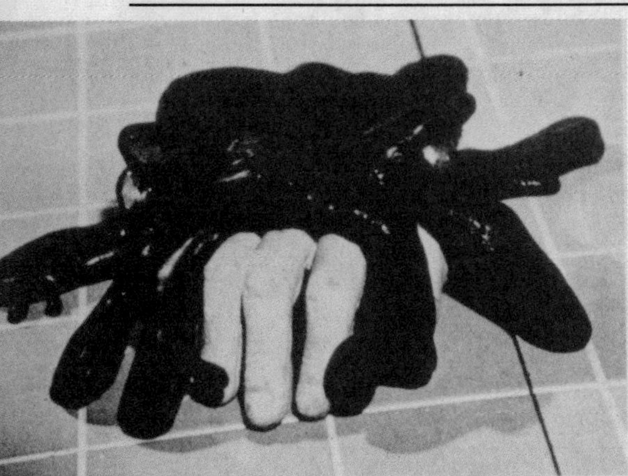

The fleshtone glove with attached parasite, by Project Unlimited.

CORPUS EARTHLING

Broadcast 18 November 1963
Written by Orin Borsten. Some material by Lou Morheim and Joseph Stefano.
Loosely based on the novel *Corpus Earthling,* by Louis Charbonneau.
Directed by Gerd Oswald
Assistant Director: Claude Binyon, Jr.
Director of Photography: Conrad Hall

CAST: Dr. Paul Cameron (Robert Culp), Laurie Hendricks-Cameron (Salome Jens), Dr. Jonas Temple (Barry Atwater), Ralph [physician] (David Garner), Caretaker (Ken Renard), Voice of the Rocks (Robert Johnson).

Rocks: silent, inanimate objects torn from the Earth's ancient crust, yielding up to Man over the long centuries all that is known of the planet on which we live; withholding from Man forever their veiled secrets of the nature of matter and cosmic catastrophe, the secrets of other worlds in the vastness of the universe ... of other forms of life ... of strange organisms beyond the imagination of Man ...

Two unidentifiable rock samples in Dr. Temple's geology lab are actually protoplasmic alien invaders capable of entering and controlling a human "corpus." Thanks to a metal plate in his skull that makes him "defective" and useless to the aliens, Paul Cameron can hear them communicating telepathically. They mesmerize him and gently suggest that this "listener" kill himself. Paul is prevented from jumping out a window by his wife, Laurie, and Temple, but fears for his sanity since no one else can hear the voices inside his head. He and Laurie decide to head for Mexico, for a few days' rest and a second honeymoon in a secluded cabin hideaway. One of the rocks metamorphoses into a spider-like parasite and possesses Temple, sending him robotically in pursuit. He catches Laurie alone and forces the second parasite on her. When Paul returns and crawls into bed with his wife, he finds a gaunt, demonic thing, pasty-white and hollow-eyed, beckoning the "listener" to come closer. Utterly bug-eyed with panic, he flees, holing up in a Tijuana hotel until the cabin's Caretaker summons him back. The alien presence has made Laurie deathly ill. Temple ambushes Paul at the cabin, shooting him in the shoulder; Paul manages to stab Temple to death with a scalpel, and his corpse evacuates the parasite. Then Laurie tries to kill him, and he is forced to shoot her. The two aliens then hypnotize Paul into dropping his gun, but his hand brushes a hot stove, which shocks him back to cognizance. He overturns the stove onto the aliens, setting the cabin ablaze.

Barry Atwater doesn't notice the alien glob about to pounce on his hand...

...and is possessed.

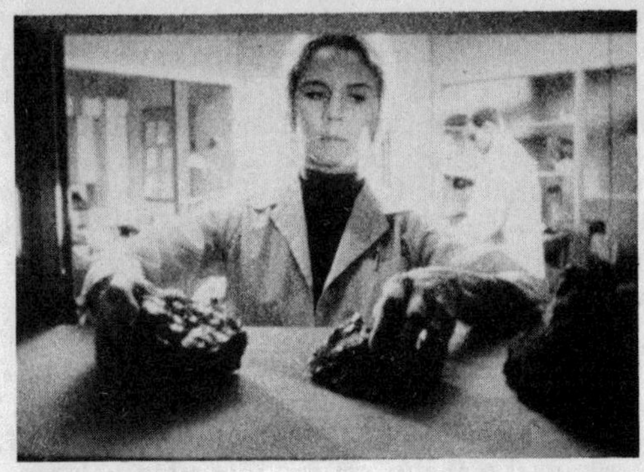

The same fate befalls Salome Jens after she files "two black, crystalline rocks."

The creatures melt to gelatinous goo as Paul carries Laurie's corpse outside, where the Caretaker continues to tend his ring of ceremonial fires.

> *Two black crystalline rocks. Unclassifiable. Objects on the border between the living and the nonliving. A reminder of the thin line that separates the animate from the inanimate. Something to ponder on—something to stay the hand when it reaches out innocently for the whitened pebble, the veined stone, the dead, unmoving rocks of our planet.*

"When 'Corpus Earthling' was finished and the music added, I sat there wishing I could say *don't air this*," said Joseph Stefano. "I had never thought it could be that scary, and I was horrified. It hit me in a disturbing way I never wanted our shows to hit people; it was *frightening* as opposed to *scary*."

"Do you know anything about paranoia?" Paul Cameron asks his wife. "I have several classic symptoms, in case they might have escaped your notice." He says this *before* his friend Temple tries to kill him, before he finds a monster awaiting him in bed, before his world becomes one of absolute paranoia realized. Here Robert Culp plays the flip side of his "Architects of Fear" character, Allen Leighton, who gives up his humanity to save the world. Allen loses his loved ones, and dies. Paul Cameron must sacrifice his loved ones to keep from *becoming* the invader; he fights to retain his humanity and loses everything, but survives... and the world is spared another alien invasion.

"Corpus Earthling"'s fade-out is also an example of how Stefano used the Control Voice to "put the world back in order again by the end of the program," as he says. "I didn't want kids going to bed thinking anything was still hanging around." In a 1963 interview he explained: "I've made it a strict rule for myself never to put children in a frightening viewing situation. I see to it that my own child watches the program, and I'm happy that he hasn't been frightened by a single one of them." The show represents one of the cleanest combinations of adult and juvenile horror ever achieved by *The Outer Limits*. The lurking alabaster zombies that Laurie and Temple become place "Corpus Earthling" firmly in horror film territory. Paul's palpable fear of insanity, the loss of identity implicit in the alien takeover (a la *Invasion of the Body Snatchers*), and his victimization by the people closest to him all squeeze the most common and vulnerable human psychological pressure points. On top of that, there are these squirming, hissing, glob monsters that stick to your face and zombify you.

"During my story conference with Stefano, I gave him an idea for a teleplay," said Orin Borsten. "He passed on my idea, but gave me the paperback novel *Corpus Earthling* (Zenith Books, 1960), to which the series had rights. Would I come back with my own ideas for translating it to television?"

In the novel, author Louis Charbonneau presents Paul as a university instructor with a heavy letch for Laurie, one of his students. He is a latent telepath, and on at least three occasions has been compelled toward suicide by an alien force that calls him "the listener." These invaders were inadvertently brought to Earth along with the first geological samples from Mars (the time is post-1990), and are eager to adapt themselves to the human hosts they find here. Dr. Temple, who at first diagnoses Paul as schizophrenic after hearing about the "voices" in his head, becomes the first person possessed. "With a shudder I thought of the scientist's habit of touching a strange crystal with the tongue," thinks Paul. Eventually he kills the alien advance guard (the first one he burns up when it escapes from its dead human host and into the body of a sand crab), and discovers a telepathic girlfriend living in the trailer next to his. "I found the book uninteresting dramatically," said Borsten. "But the central concept of rocks turning into beings, I decided, could be the basis for an interesting segment."

Strangely, Gerd Oswald claims, "There was no real attempt to accentuate the nightmarish feeling in this particular episode. It was completely subjective. All the characters were isolated, set off, and I kept things very claustrophobic. It was a distorted vision." Conrad Hall concurs: "We may have deviated from Stefano's original intention on that one. The material evoked an ugly and disturbing mood." The result is tense, and plucks at the nerves with Oswald's accustomed "crescendo" effect. "I'll stick with my rocks," Temple says, comparing them to Paul's human patients. "They don't get sick, and they never phone me in the middle of the night." Later, when Paul is afraid to answer his phone for fear of hearing the alien voices, it really *is* a call from the rocks, who have taken over Temple's body. "I liked the rocks," said Oswald, "because it kind of 'juggled' the idea of a weekly monster."

This was Borsten's only *Outer Limits* script. "I visited the set one day," he said, "mostly to talk to Salome Jens, who had been brilliant in a feature film of mine, *Angel Baby.* One thing sticks in my mind: The complaint of the special effects department that there was never enough time to create believable outer space creatures. Everything was thrown together in a wild rush and it was a wonder that it all worked." The parasites themselves were blobs of rubber, fitted with blinking lightbulb eyes and toy armatures that made them writhe as they were pulled across the stage floor on strings. Byron Haskin devised the effect of the rocks "expanding" into parasite form, and sinking into human flesh.

Robert Culp boosts his paranoia quotient.

The *dramatis personae* of "Corpus Earthling" are outstanding, although the statuesque Salome Jens certainly does not look the part of "a very *plain,* unbrilliant lab assistant," as her own dialogue describes Laurie. Robert Culp recalled the scene in which he was required to carry her from the burning cabin: "You try it sometime. She's a beautifully-built, very Scandinavian girl, and she ran a good 160 pounds. After carrying her a hundred feet, I thought I was going to drop her!" Jens later starred in the memorably paranoid John Frankenheimer film *Seconds* (1966), and Barry Atwater (Temple) played TV's most unforgettable vampire, Janos Skorzeny, in *The Night Stalker* in 1974.

"Corpus Earthling" also marked the debut of two important *Outer Limits* crewmen. It was the first of two episodes done as "fill-ins" by Claude Binyon, Jr., prior to becoming a permanent 1st AD on the program. It was also the first episode for which Daystar accountant Robert Johnson dubbed the voices of the aliens (though he was heard previously, as a human, in "Specimen: Unknown" and "The Man Who Was Never Born"). His mellifluous, resonant voice would soon become quite familiar to the *Outer Limits* audience, and would later attain immortality as the tape recorder voice heard in every episode of *Mission: Impossible*.

Oswald and his crew also devised a sly in-joke to give Conrad Hall's dauntless cameraman, William Fraker, a bit of recognition, since he never received screen credit for his *Outer Limits* work. During the scene where Paul refuses to answer his phone, he also warns Laurie not to open their apartment door when a strange thumping is heard outside. Determined to prove his fear is all in his mind, she peeks out and sighs, "It's Billy Fraker—he's been drinking again."

Voices From the Outer Limits

"The only thing an awful lot of young people can identify me with is *The Outer Limits*," said Vic Perrin, who did the famous Control Voice speeches for each episode of the series. "I'll go in for an interview, and people not of my generation will say, 'Tell me about yourself.' These fresh-out-of-UCLA casting directors know *The Outer Limits*, because it's something they grew up with. It always puts me a few notches up in their esteem."

Victor Perrin came out of the heyday of radio drama, and before he crossed paths with *The Outer Limits* he had been doing character voices for twenty years, and TV roles for half that time. His first announcing job was for a Madison, Wisconsin radio station for a tidy $40 per week. Shortly after coming to California he became a junior announcer for NBC. "I did coast-to-coast remotes from the Wilshire Bowl, from the Florentine Gardens, and dance remotes from the Biltmore Bowl," he said.

Vic Perrin, the Control Voice.
(Courtesy Vic Perrin)

"When the government insisted that NBC divest itself of one of its networks, the Blue or the Red, I went with the Blue, which made me a senior announcer." His career ballooned, and by the end of World War Two Perrin was pulling down $400 a week. "That was a *fortune* at that time... and announcing wasn't what I wanted to do! I just walked out on it, sat under a tree, and decided I wanted to be an actor."

He joined Charles Laughton's speech workshop along with such fellow students as Shelley Winters and Jane Wyatt. "Laughton was a great master; he got our minds and bodies involved in the words we were saying. You have to submit to being beaten to a pulp; your ego suffers so, and your ego is what you rely upon when you're performing. To have it ripped to shreds leaves you open to new ways of doing things." He moved into regular parts on the radio dramas *Escape, Columbia Workshop, Romance, Dr. Christian, Masquerade, Mayor of the Town* (with Lionel Barrymore), *The Story of Polly Stone*, and many others. "I was on *One Man's Family* for seven years, playing Ross Farnsworth, a mother-dominated schoolteacher who was very cruel to his wife, Joan. I used to get *nasty* letters! I established my connection with Jack Webb on the radio *Dragnet*, and Norman McDonnell on the radio *Gunsmoke*." Perrin soon branched into television, playing everything from DA's to doctors, from murderers to gamblers. "I did very well as an actor," he said. "I loved doing the sleazy little characters."

During Perrin's audition for *Please Stand By*, his wife was seated in the recording booth next to Leslie Stevens. As Perrin recited, Stevens slapped his hand to his head and exclaimed, "Oh my God!" Mrs. Perrin was aghast. "She told me afterwards that she was sure Stevens had *hated* me," Perrin recalled. But Stevens explained: "It's like me to be going *oh*

Jesus, oh God on the spot, because I remember having good feelings about him the *moment* he spoke."

The Control Voice was born.

"Vic was extraordinary," said John Elizalde, who recorded the Control Voice readings at Daystar. "He'd come in at 11:30 at night, or 1:00 in the morning, because his schedule was so full. It didn't matter. We were there all the time, and were always ready for him. It was remarkable; sometimes he'd pick up the paper and do the speech cold. His comprehension of the printed word was astounding to me. He'd usually do a narration full of twists and turns all in one take." Perrin also contributed voice-over dialogue in postproduction whenever it was needed. "We did the speeches for four or five shows in about two hours," he said. "We'd do them in gangs, and that was it. I have a little trouble, today, recapturing the rather ominous tone I used when I read those. But the interesting thing about florid writing is that if you do it *flat*, without trying to be Shakespearian, you can get away with it. I thought it should be direct, not commanding, but authoritative." He had no input on content—that was Stefano's domain—and often did not know the plots of the individual shows. "There were times when John Elizalde would explain, from the booth, that a speech led *into* a certain scene."

Perrin "conducts" his recitations with a batonlike motion of his right hand, holding the first two fingers pressed against his thumb. Years of this practice have left a dent in his middle finger. "It's like diagramming a sentence, like accent marks, or physical punctuation," he said. "One thing I learned from Laughton was to have an 'instant playback' upstairs, as though there's a little guy sitting on my shoulder, listening. When I get the inflection correct, the little guy says, 'Okay, you can go on now.' So I correct myself before the director has a chance to."

He secures work to this day on the strength of his *Outer Limits* credential. "If God gave me a talent," he says, "it's the ability to sound more intelligent than I am on things that I know absolutely nothing about!"

British-born Ben Huntington Wright emigrated to America in the aftermath of World War Two. "A dull production, World War Two," jokes Wright, who rose to the rank of captain in the British Army. "The costumes were awful; the sound effects terribly loud. A long contract, to be sure, but for terrible money!" To this country he brought his experience as a veteran of the Royal Academy of Dramatic Art, as well as being a seasoned radio actor. His work in the U.S. included a year as Sherlock Holmes for the ABC network (his Watson was Eric Snowden), and a stint on *One Man's Family*, where Vic Perrin was a regular.

Wright's skill with foreign accents led him to many on-camera roles in films and TV, primarily as military officers. His stocky build, ramrod

Ben Wright in human form.
(Courtesy Ben Wright)

posture, piercing gaze, and pencil moustache became his trademarks. "They picked me principally because of my radio background," he said. "Word gets around as to who can do voice-overs, and who knows the dialects." Before turning to *The Outer Limits,* he did a breadth of work ranging from the voice of the young composer in Walt Disney's *101 Dalmatians* to the narration for *Cleopatra* (1963).

Wright lent the overbearing Luminoid Authority a voice in "A Feasibility Study," as well as doing the pacifistic, quietly noble Grippians for "Moonstone." He appeared as an Earth general in "Nightmare," and as a millionaire industrialist a season later, in "Wolf 359."

"Benjy used to work the *Gunsmoke* radio show a lot," said Vic Perrin. "We used to kid him about being a pompous Britisher because he worked the *New York Times* crossword puzzle with a *pen*. You can't get more elegant than that."

"One of the reasons I like voice work is that I love the English language," said Robert Cleveland Johnson. "I love the *sound* of it, and what you can do with the written word."

The man who did the Daystar payroll by day and most of *The Outer Limits'* best-known "monster voices" by night began his career by falling in with a little theatre group called Blue Room Productions, at age sixteen. The company included several attorneys who encouraged the young Johnson to develop his voice. "This was in the days prior to PA systems," said Johnson. "Since there was nothing to give you a boost, you had to have a big, booming voice in court. I admired their vocal ability, and used it as a model." Another of Johnson's models was the famous '30s sportscaster, Ted Husing.

By the end of World War Two, Johnson had worked as a singer, actor,

Robert Johnson: the often-heard, never-seen man of a thousand monster voices.
(Photo: Reed Saron; courtesy Robert Johnson)

a vocal performer with professionals from major symphony orchestras, Broadway, and Hollywood. To support his family he completed a degree in accounting (his father's field), and two days after moving to Hollywood from Portland, Oregon, he was hired by Walter Lantz, of *Woody Woodpecker* fame, thanks to Dallas McKennon, an old friend who did cartoon voices for Lantz. Johnson also sang with the Hollywood Bowl Opera Company, the Guild Opera, and the Los Angeles Opera during this time.

It was while working at Security Pictures, then based at Kling Studios, that he met Elaine Michea, who later hired him for his accounting skills during the formation of Daystar Productions.* His Screen Actors Guild card won him a bit part in *Hero's Island,* when Leslie Stevens needed a fill-in to play the part of a colonial overseer. Michea ultimately pitched Johnson to Stevens as a voice man.

"I *vied* with Vic Perrin to do the Control Voice," said Johnson. "Although I'm sure he never knew it. I'd heard him for years on the radio. But I was still in my 'formative' stage and he was an established voice-over man, so he got it." Since Johnson worked in the Daystar building, he was instantly available whenever dubbing work was needed up on the fourth floor. "When they were ready to have talking rocks, or whatever," said Michea, "Bob would run upstairs, do his thing, then come back down to his desk." Sometimes it was just a line or two, a telephone or intercom voice; other times it was a fullblown alien speech, a major vocal role with many lines. "It was fun," said Johnson, "and I thought I was lucky to get such work. My god, to me it was like play for pay! Often, I would not have seen the script prior to the actual recording session, and Joe Stefano would 'brief' a

*Kling Studios was housed on the old Charlie Chaplin stage in midtown Hollywood. This building today houses A & M Records, and was also an *Outer Limits* shooting stage briefly during the show's second season.

character for me. In a very short time, without filling my head up with ideas and procedure, we'd arrive at a formula for doing the character. Most of my performances are pretty spontaneous because there was no lead time; the most would be a phone call a day beforehand. Stefano was pretty descriptive, explicit and explanatory." Despite his standing in SAG, Johnson never appeared physically in any *Outer Limits* episode.

"Bob was thrilled to death with doing those monster speeches," notes Robert Justman, who later recommended Johnson to *Mission: Impossible* creator Bruce Geller. What began as a onetime reading for the pilot grew into 175 separate assignments on behalf of the Impossible Missions Force. While Johnson retired from accounting in 1975, he remains interested in unlocking the potentials of voice, and in 1983 he released his unique voice-coaching course via mail order.*

"The Outer Limits was a very imaginative show," he said. "You could let your mind roam beyond the script. I'm a fairly smart writer; I know the rules of grammar and I like phrasing and delivering lines, investing them with something more than they had in the beginning. I loved this show because it let your head go where *it* wanted to go. I'm sure that nearly everybody 'added' to those scripts, while they were watching and listening."

The next *Outer Limits* assignment for both Johnson and Vic Perrin would be a suitable challenge, in that it required them to invest some dramatic punch into such dialogue as, *"Ple ben zo a lanz tri ob trinsini!"*

*Send a letter-sized SASE to The Voice Pro Shop, Box 65, Kaunakakai, HI 96748.

The Zanti Regent bugs Bruce Dern outside the penal ship at the Vasquez Rocks location.

THE ZANTI MISFITS

Broadcast 30 December 1963
Written by Joseph Stefano
Directed by Leonard Horn
Assistant Director: Robert Justman
Director of Photography: John Nickolaus

CAST: Prof. Stephen Grave (Michael Tolan), Gen. Maximilian R. Hart (Robert F. Simon), Major Roger Hill (Claude Woolman), Ben Garth (Bruce Dern), Lisa Lawrence (Olive Deering), Communications Operator (Lex Johnson), Radar Operator (Joey Tata), Computer Technician (George Sims), Air Police Sergeant (Mike Mikler), Corporal Delano (Bill Hart), Voices of Radio Newscaster, Zanti Regent, and Zanti Commander (Robert Johnson), Voice of Zanti Prisoner (Vic Perrin).

Throughout history, compassionate minds have pondered this dark and disturbing question: What is society to do with those members who are a threat to society, those malcontents and misfits whose behavior undermines and destroys the foundations of civilization? Different ages have found different answers. Misfits have been burned, branded, and banished. Today, on this planet Earth, the criminal is incarcerated in humane institutions, or he is executed. Other planets use other methods. This is the story of how the perfectionist rulers of the planet Zanti attempted to solve the problem of the Zanti misfits.

Grave, a historian, arrives at the California ghost town of Morgue to document the arrival of a penal ship from the planet Zanti, whose rulers, incapable of executing their own species, have coerced Earth officials into allowing them to exile their criminals to our world. The Zanti government has threatened "total annihilation" to anyone disturbing their cordoned-off tract of desert, but have not anticipated the intrusion of rich, neurotic Lisa Lawrence and her psychopathic paramour, Ben Garth, who run down a checkpoint sentry and trespass into the restricted area. Garth happens upon the Zanti ship, a bullet-shaped affair no bigger than a washing machine. A hatch springs open and he is attacked by the Regent of Prisoners—a large, antlike insect about a foot long, with a humanoid face, round-pupilled eyes, and tiny, mean teeth. Back at the military command post in Morgue, Grave, Gen. Hart, and his men listen in horror as the Zanti radio link transmits Garth's death-screams. While Grave volunteers to enter the Zanti landing area as an emissary, Lisa finds Garth's corpse wedged into the cliffside and is chased back to her car by the Regent. Grave arrives in time to smash the Regent with a boulder, but the Zanti prisoners commandeer the ship and attack the command post, which is set up in an abandoned hotel. A fierce firefight with rifles and grenades ensues, from which Hart's men emerge victorious. When Hart grimly wonders how the Zantis will retaliate, a new transmission comes in from the planet's Commander: "We will not retaliate. We never intended to. We knew that you could not live with such aliens in your midst. It was always our intention that you destroy them and their guards, who were of the same spoiled persuasion. We chose your planet for that purpose. We are incapable of executing our own species, but you are not. You are practiced executioners. We thank you."

> *Throughout history, various societies have tried various methods of exterminating those members who have proven their inability or unwillingness to live sanely among their fellow men. The Zantis merely tried one more method, neither better nor worse than all the others. Neither more human nor less human than all the others. Perhaps, merely... nonhuman.*

An enduring *Outer Limits* favorite more because of its unique alien menace than its underdeveloped themes (the politics of aggression, the capacity of any species for self-destruction), "The Zanti Misfits," according to Stefano, was written "to give some thought to the way we've been killing each other, legally and illegally, throughout all of history."

It was the first of a group of scripts done by Stefano while his *Outer Limits* output was at its most furious pace, from October through the end of 1963. In addition to his *pro forma* touch-ups and revisions on every *Outer Limits* teleplay, he turned out five more original scripts during this period. "I didn't have the time to do treatments or outlines," he said. "I just made them up as I went along, according to a vision in my head—not a step-by-step formula, but more like a dream. This made my analysis more difficult. I'd no longer free-associate, but I'd correct and edit what I'd dreamt the previous night, and spin it into a tale! But this was great for my writing, though, and this was a very lush period for me."

Stefano's claim that he would lock himself into his office in order to complete a script over a weekend is no exaggeration, and the first two scripts thus produced, "The Zanti Misfits" and "It Crawled Out of the Woodwork," introduce cryptic characters who seem to have deep philosophical problems, but little time to address them, or even explain for the audience what they are. Stefano assigns each character a clear value within the aggression theme: Grave is the academic turned killer in spite of his high-sounding morals; Major Hill is the dog of war whose only comprehension of superiority lies in the comparative size of the enemy's stick; the aptly-named Gen. Hart is an old-school soldier (in effect an experienced, wiser version of Hill) who is frustrated by his own idealism and the impenetrability of protocol; Ben Garth represents the human instinct to kill turned rebelliously outward upon the entire world, while his around-the-bend lover Lisa Lawrence is that same instinct, focused suicidally inward. Once established, these symbolic character types do not develop; they remain ciphers, caught up in the whirlwind of events culminating in a conventional action capper, the Zanti attack. This climax is exciting and satisfying, but the business leading up to it is meandering and muddy. The chase between the Zanti Regent and Lisa is hard to swallow (crawling bug overtakes running human). Grave, who comes to preserve peace, kills the Regent as though there is no option—like running away and outdistancing it. Then Lisa dissolves into an incoherent monologue about her own self-destruction that stops the show dead.

Part of the problem was in the script revisions. Hart, for the most part, seems to be merely a harried military peacekeeper. He complains, "If [the Zantis] retaliate, it means death and suffering, broken bodies, and broken hearts. I can't let everybody break." This isn't very meaningful, because it is the tail end of a longer speech cut by Stefano from the original draft:

> HART: I hate war, Steve! I hate the people who cause it and I hate them with every atom of my being! So I pretend to respect the enemy, even like him. I try to minimize him with love! I hate the Zantis. I hate our compromising ourselves. Yet I recommended it. *I* did! Because almost anything is better than a war! Right now, I would like to go in there, pick up that detestable 'Red Special' phone and advise the Chief to destruct! Wipe them off the face of our Earth. Clean the face of our Earth of every hostile, aggressive, coercing being or nonbeing on it! I would like to do that . . . but I can't. Because I'm afraid. And I'm old. And I'm sick of all this!

We are told Grave's father was a war correspondent, that Grave is a "sentimentalist" (he uses his dad's old typewriter), and that he would have liked to have reported live from Hiroshima if he could have *helped*. Presumably he follows in his father's footsteps by turning the Zanti landing into a war in his own mind, then doing everything possible to make this view self-fulfilling. His very first act—flicking an Earth ant from a post, in deadly presagement of what is to come—is hostile. He eagerly volunteers as an emissary of peace, and sure enough, he's the first Earthling to kill a Zanti.

Lisa is the biggest question mark of all. Nothing really justifies her strung-out behavior, but she does momentarily permit the episode to weirdly resemble a Big Bug movie of the 1950s—Hero with Thick Glasses Saves Girl in Familiar Desert Milieu—with the characteristic gigantism of the insect antagonists left out.

And those insect antagonists are what boost this show into the front rank of unforgettable *Outer Limits* episodes. Stefano blithely exploits the human fear of crawling, bristling bugs, and it matters little that we

A gang of Zanti misfits contemplates some interplanetary criminal activity.

Earthlings are much bigger than the Zantis—we, like Lisa, would probably run like hell if confronted by one. While the use of stop-motion animation to motivate the tiny critters endears the show to special effects fans, Leonard Horn's well-planned direction packs the episode with striking visual images—the uneasy expressions traded by the command post soldiers as they listen to the bizarre Zanti voice emitting from a translating computer, for example. Or Ben Garth's face looming hugely in the Zanti ship's porthole as a segmented leg (the first we see of the aliens) squeaks across the glass from the inside.

The loud and chaotic—if terribly one-sided—battle that exterminates the Zantis is doubly interesting due to the fact that it was *not* included in Stefano's first script. Originally, the revelatory Zanti transmission was to precede the slaughter, with the show fading out as the first shot is fired. The inclusion of the battle was a winning gamble, and Horn manages to show a few convincing human casualties amid the somewhat extreme shots of Zantis getting blown to bits by explosions and point-blank gunfire. One shot showing a screaming, Zanti-covered soldier falling down the hotel steps and flailing around packs a wallop even today, and the battle sequence illustrates one way Stefano could present a mass murder on network TV with no interference from the censors—so long as *aliens* were the ones getting massacred.

Luckily, the time Horn lavished on his camera set-ups shows on-screen. "Lenny Horn would *still* be shooting 'The Zanti Misfits' today if I hadn't pulled the plug on him," said 1st AD Robert Justman. "After I knew he had enough coverage it was a matter of saying, 'This is *it;* we can't afford to *stay* any longer!'" Ghost Town Street, a stock Western set on the MGM lot, was used as Morgue, California, and the exteriors of the Zanti landing zone were filmed at the famous Vasquez Rocks formations just outside of Los Angeles (a location almost as prevalent in science fiction films as Bronson Caverns). It was here that Bruce Dern, as Ben Garth (a part originally offered to Burt Reynolds), did his own stunt fall down the rock incline. "Bruce and I were good friends," noted Justman. "Even then, he was training to be an Olympic runner, and he'd use the time between set-ups to run. I'd tell him, 'You've got to be back in half an hour,' and in exactly half an hour he'd be back so I could tell him, 'Another fifteen minutes!'" Dern is the show's most interesting piece of casting (he had been a semiregular on *Stoney Burke*), and Garth, the story's most uncluttered character. As street-lethal as this hood is, he is nonetheless spellbound as he squints toward the Zanti ship and asks the time-honored science fiction question, "What do you suppose that is . . . ?"

Wah Chang sculpted the show's true stars, and after Stefano told the Project Unlimited crew that the aliens were "not *pretty* enough," Chang softened their physiognomies and turned them over to Paul LeBaron for mass production. "We built the main ones around wire armatures because of budget and time restrictions," Chang said. "This made the animation less flexible than we wanted." Stop-motion, a process in which the position of a stationary model or object is manipulated every few frames of film in order to confer the illusion of independent movement when the completed film is projected, usually utilizes complex, jointed armatures that are costly and time-consuming to machine. The stop-motion animation of the four Zantis seen in close-up (Chang gave them differing expressions and hair distribution) was executed by Al Hamm, who had done the Monkey Money sequence for *Mighty Joe Young* (1949). Operating the camera for this time-gobbling process was Ralph Rodine, with whom Hamm had done the animated Speedy Alka-Seltzer commercials a few years earlier in his career. The Zanti voices were the result of John Elizalde working his usual audio magic, speeding up and distorting the voices of Robert Johnson and Vic Perrin reading lines in the Zanti language invented by Stefano: *"Lanz trinsini lobo zan a mang lis lanz ob."* This is the only time in the entire series an alien is heard speaking anything but English.

To Stefano's credit, the show's single most haunting scene depicts the Earth personnel listening to this weird alien tongue and wondering just what the hell they've gotten into. It is a direct contrast to the pyrotechnic action that makes the show hurtle along, and demonstrates that it is very often the *little* things that are the most unnerving.

Monsters, Incorporated

> A little thing that creeps across a desk can cost two thousand dollars to make. Of course, in quantity they become cheaper. A monster outfit—the kind you dress a man up in—can run as high as seven or eight thousand dollars. That's more than you're allowed in most shows for your entire cast!
>
> —Joseph Stefano

Byron Haskin cheerfully characterized Project Unlimited as "a rubber and glue factory that stunk up the neighborhood." The first true "special effects company," Project Unlimited, Inc. designed and developed *The Outer Limits'* visually unique aliens, executed model animation and optical trickery, and served as a catch-all special effects pool that participated in each of the series' forty-nine episodes.

Assembled in the late 1950s (and referred to as "Projects" by most

Another *Outer Limits* family portrait (L-R:) Andro, from "The Man Who Was Never Born," the Box Demon from "Don't Open Till Doomsday," the Empyrian from "Second Chance," Allyson Ames (Leslie Stevens' third wife) of "The Galaxy Being" and "The Production and Decay of Strange Particles," an Ebonite from "Nightmare," and the Bifrost alien from "The Bellero Shield."

of its alumni), the organization's first work was on the George Pal feature *Tom Thumb* (1958). Subsequent assignments for Pal included *Atlantis—The Lost Continent, The Time Machine,* and *The Wonderful World of the Brothers Grimm.* Other fantasy films of the early 1960s heavily influenced by Projects were *Dinosaurus!* (1960), *Master of the World* (1961), and *Jack the Giant Killer* and *Journey to the 7th Planet* (1962). *The Outer Limits* was the company's first TV work, and it was brought into the Daystar fold by Leon Chooluck and Byron Haskin.

The company heads were Wah Ming Chang and Gene Warren, along with Tim Baar, the "gang boss" who assembled the group in 1958. *Outer Limits*' effects coordinator, M. B. Paul, was the liaison between Villa di Stefano and Projects, assigning work to the group at an average ceiling of $10,000 per episode. *The Outer Limits* provided continuous, bread-and-butter money for Projects at a time when feature film work was sporadic, but the series' demands were frequently high-pressure ones. Chang and Warren sat in on the Daystar script meetings, making suggestions and sketching monsters while episodes took shape at the conference table. "I did all the contracting and preplanning," said Warren. "The only way a show like *The Outer Limits* could be feasibly done was if we were in on each show from the beginning. If something looked impossible to do under the circumstances, we advised Daystar and tried to help with rewriting. They appreciated this since we were all under the same pressure. Once they had a start date for shooting, the devices, costumes and so on had to be ready by that date—so Projects had to start working on effects two weeks *before* the scripts were approved by the network, in some cases. Our budgets were adequate; we didn't really make that much money. Unlike *Star Trek,* where 80 percent of the effects shots were stock shots, and reusable, *The Outer Limits* was worse than usual because you needed new creations every week. Sometimes we'd refurbish an old monster suit, just to ease the pressure. I wonder now how we ever did it!"

After the meetings, Chang says, "We would go back (to Projects) and try to figure out how this thing could actually be done." A talented sculptor and designer, Chang was often behind the camera himself, filming effects, when he wasn't roughing out the look of next week's "bear" in wood or clay. Warren used detailed cue sheets to "direct," from his desk, most of Projects' optical effects—warps, shimmers, spaceships, rays, disintegrations, and the like. Once recorded on film, these effects were shipped to either the Ray Mercer or Butler-Glouner companies, for composition with the live-action footage. Very often, the man shuttling the film cans all over Hollywood was Byron Haskin. "I was at Projects a lot," he said. "I remember taking Janos Prohaska over there to see if he could fit into the Thetan costume and be able to work it."

Of the monsters, Warren noted, "We did not always agree with Stefano, but his was a very strong personality, and he made that show hang

From "The Man Who Was Never Born," a Projects optical of the spaceship in Earth orbit.

together. Joe was very definite on what he wanted, but he was always behind. He'd miss early meetings because he was busy finishing another episode, and by the time he *did* show up we were already building something." This accounts for the extremely vague and very adaptable descriptions of various creatures found in many *Outer Limits* scripts. "We had to educate Projects in such things," said Stefano aide Tom Selden. "If a script said that a creature had to push buttons or run a computer, they immediately started designing things with fingers and hands to do all that, and we said, 'No, no, that's not the way to go at all!'" Eventually Projects broke free of this restriction, producing such wild concoctions as the Chromoite ("The Mice"), the phallic being in "Don't Open Till Doomsday," and the amorphous nasties seen in "Corpus Earthling" and "The Invisibles."

Trying to pinpoint exactly who did what at Projects is not only difficult, but ultimately pointless. It was a "grey union shop" where duties were performed by whomever was available; everybody helped everybody else, crisscrossing credits. Ralph Rodine, for example, was both a cameraman and an accomplished animator. "I had a Local 44 card as a propmaker, but not as a cameraman," he said. "Sometimes an outside supervisor would raise a stink, coming down and complaining that I was operating a camera... at which point Wah would step in and say, '*I'm* running this camera, not Ralph, and who are *you* to be telling me how to run my company, anyway?'" Project's sheer diversity lent it an atmosphere that was anything but unionized, and Chang and Warren worked hard to get their people into other facets of the industry. "Jim Danforth tried to get into Albert Whitlock's group, and the matte painters' union," said Rodine. "But even with Projects pushing for him, he couldn't, because the structure at Projects was not in keeping with the established system of ladder-climbing. As far as the unions were concerned, we were

Some Projects folks on the set of *Jack the Giant Killer* in 1961. First row, kneeling: Dave Morick and Don Sahlin. Second row, sitting: Marion the secretary, Marcel Delgado, Bill Brace. Back row: Gene Warren (far left), Tim Baar, Phil Kellison, Victor Delgado, Wah Ming Chang (making "devil horns" over Brace's head), Paul LeBaron (in cap), and Blanding Sloan.
(Courtesy Jim Danforth)

legal, but not entirely on the up-and-up. We kind of scooted along that way."

Another Projects stalwart was Paul LeBaron, a master prop and model-maker who was often called upon to finish up head sculpts done by Chang. "I made molds and cast masks," he said. "I was more mechanical, and as a rule I wouldn't sculpt because I wasn't any good at it. I'd make the armatures and the frames that held things together." LeBaron constructed the fabulous flying machine seen in *Master of the World,* and at Projects built everything from monsters to flying saucers.

Rodine, LeBaron, and Jim Danforth (then only twenty-three years old) were accorded individual credits beneath the Projects mantle in the end titles for *The Outer Limits*. "Tim Baar fixed that up," said LeBaron. "He was a pretty good lobbyist." Rodine elaborated: "Before *The Outer Limits,* the credit would have read, 'Projects, Unlimited: Gene Warren, Wah Chang, Tim Baar.' When both *The Outer Limits* and feature work became steady, Paul, Jim, and I petitioned Gene Warren for a raise. Warren suggested we take screen credit instead. I voted for the money; Danforth and LeBaron for the credit. So our names appeared rather arbitrarily—you'd see them on some show we didn't work on, then you'd see Ray Mercer's name on a show we *did* do."

Apart from Chang, Warren, Baar, Rodine, LeBaron, and Danforth, Project Unlimited included Al Hamm (model animation), Bill Brace (matte paintings), and Paul Pattee, a modelmaker, sculptor and all-purpose assistant who did weird things like submerge himself in six feet of water and breathe through a hunk of hose in order to operate a hand-puppet monster for an episode titled "The Invisible Enemy." The Projects prop shop was run by Marcel Delgado (who worked with Willis O'Brien on *King Kong* in 1933) and his son, Victor. "He was a great all-round effects man," said Warren. "He did molds and sculpts, and he and Victor built most of the actual creature costumes." Jim Danforth pointed out that "Bill Brace was actually the art director of Projects; he did designs, and painted masks and mattes. He did the library shot in 'The Man Who Was Never Born,' and Rodine photographed it." Also with Projects at this time, but not involved in *Outer Limits* work, were David Pal, Tom Holland, Don Sahlin (an animator and artist who went on to work with Muppet-master Jim Henson), Phil Kellison, Blanding Sloan, and Dave Morick. "Sloan was a friend of Wah's who didn't do too much work," said LeBaron. "Dave was an actor who played a lot of Germans on *Hogan's Heroes;* he was more or less a cleanup guy, and a good helper." Working in an advisory capacity was a Disney technician named Bob Mattey, who in 1975 was called out of retirement to devise "Bruce," the mechanical killer shark seen in *Jaws*.

Besides Byron Haskin, Projects also worked in conjunction with Janos Prohaska and *Outer Limits* makeup artist Fred Phillips. "In some cases, Phillips did monsters by himself," said Chang. "I do recall going over designs and making appliances of actors with Phillips." According to Warren, M. B. Paul "was primarily involved with optical effects, while we handled physical effects. He wasn't really an in-between man, because if Jack Poplin, say, wanted to know something, he'd come directly to us rather than Paul."

"Projects, Unlimited was at 5555 Sunset Boulevard," notes LeBaron. "Right down the street from KTTV." Warren recalled, "We had a two thousand five hundred square foot shop, art and conference rooms, and two long soundstages. We had Mitchell and Bell & Howell cameras; we rented anything for bigger setups." Ralph Rodine would often light and shoot effects setups in the parking lot outside the studio. "We were always trying new ways of 'vanishing' people and things on *Outer Limits,*" he said. "We had an Acme Optical Printer left over from the Pal films, and used that to create all kinds of beams and rays."

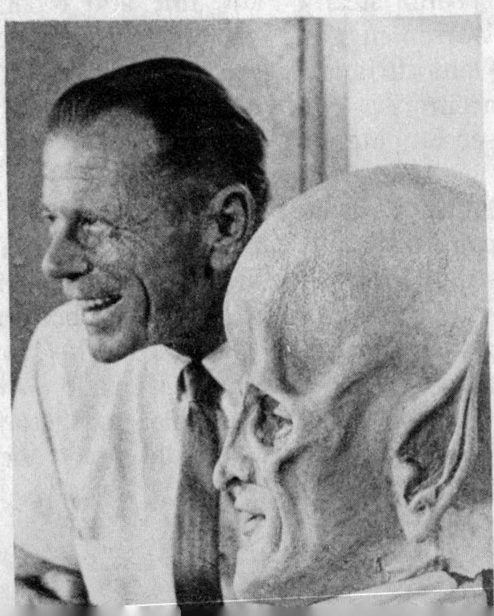

Makeup artist Fred Phillips on the set of "The Sixth Finger," with David McCallum.
(Courtesy Fred Phillips)

As much as Stefano's scripts, Gerd Oswald's direction or Conrad Hall's cinematography, Chang's eccentric monster designs are another of *The Outer Limits'* signatures. As he says, "You try to create the best thing you can within the time and budget." Today, Chang does fine-art sculptures and castings, many of which are sold through a gallery in Mexico run by his old partner, Gene Warren.

"Did Gene ever tell you how we'd negotiate?" said Claude Binyon, Jr., who became responsible for contracting work from Projects during the series' second season. "We'd sit in my office and drink scotch, and I'd gradually work him down to a lower price than it should have been. It was always in fun. And he'd sit there and say, 'My God, I gave the show away *again!*'" Binyon also worked out details on some optical effects with Frank Van Der Veer, founder of the now famous Van Der Veer Photo Effects house.

"Every once in a while, something would go wrong with one of our effects," remembered Paul LeBaron. "And I'd have to go down to KTTV or Paramount and straighten it out. It was a bore; I nearly lost my mind on that deal. I'm tellin' you, we were working on a *shoestring* down there!"

The *Outer Limits* crew prior to a take on the set of "It Crawled Out of the Woodwork." From left, past the balding grip: Stand-in Allan "Whitey" Christie, Gerd Oswald, Gene Darfler, Lee Katzin (with hat).

IT CRAWLED OUT OF THE WOODWORK

Broadcast 9 December 1963
Written by Joseph Stefano
Directed by Gerd Oswald
Assistant Director: Lee H. Katzin

Director of Photography: Conrad Hall

CAST: Jory Peters (Scott Marlowe), Prof. Stuart Peters (Michael Forest), Dr. Block (Kent Smith), Gaby Christian (Barbara Luna), Detective Sergeant Thomas Siroleo (Ed Asner), Prof. Stephanie Linden (Joan Lamden), Warren Edgar Morley (Gene Darfler), New Sentry (Ted DeCorsia), Coroner (Tom Palmer), Cleaning Lady (Lea Marmer), NORCO Intercom Voice (Robert Johnson).

His name is Warren Edgar Morley. For the past six months, he has guarded this gate from eight in the morning until six at night, at which time he is replaced by another just like himself. These are the last few moments of his life.

At NORCO, a top-security energy research facility tucked away in the San Fernando Valley, a cleaning woman working the midnight shift finds a mysterious black dustball stuck against a baseboard, and when she sucks it into her vacuum cleaner, it amplifies into a strobing, chaotic cloud of lethal energy that instantly consumes her. Later, physicist Stuart Peters arrives to accept a position at NORCO, with his younger brother Jory in tow. Morley, the gate guard, tries to warn them away with a message scribbled inside a matchbook, and is destroyed for this attempt by the energy cloud, which shorts out a pacemaker-like box strapped to Morley's chest. Stuart shows the matchbook to NORCO head Dr. Block, who has managed to pen up the energy-sucking cloud in a chamber called the Pit. He has used the cloud to terrify the NORCO staff to death with heart attacks, then reanimates them using the pacemaker boxes to continue research into new ways to feed the ever-hungry cloud. The next time Jory sees Stuart, Stuart is wearing one of the boxes, which shorts out and kills him when he accidentally plunges into a bathtub full of water. With the help of Prof. Linden (another unwilling NORCO zombie), the detective investigating Stuart's death uncovers NORCO's secret. Linden shoots Block, but before Block dies he unleashes the energy cloud from the Pit. It goes amok, killing all the NORCO personnel by leaching the power from their pacemakers. Before Linden expires she tells the detective, Siroleo, that a local blackout will force the thing back into the Pit, which has self-contained power generators. The plan works, with Jory showing up just as all the ruckus dies down. "It's under control," advises Siroleo. "For the moment..."

The Conservation of Energy Law—a principle which states that energy can be changed in form but that it cannot be either created or destroyed. And this is true of all energy—the energy of genius, of madness, of the heart, of the atom. And so it must be lived with. It must be controlled, channeled for good, held isolated from evil... and somehow lived with, peaceably.

Unconventionally structured and staffed with abstruse characters, "It Crawled Out of the Woodwork" nearly demands to be interpreted as allegory, since as a linear dramatic narrative it *does* very little. It does present two typical Stefano touches: A bastille of scientific research presented in Old Dark House terms, and characters that illuminate their oddball backgrounds largely in terms of talkative asides not directly connected to the plot. The show can easily be read for the obvious parable, a caution against the destructive potential of nuclear power, that annihilatory boogeyman of post–World War Two thinking, and the need for the technicians who toy with it to be governed by a human conscience. But paradoxically, the show's basis, and perhaps its message, is the thing least accessible to the viewer, since it has to do with a theory Stefano holds about writing.

"We write, or make films, as a kind of exorcism," he says. "And what keeps us writing is the fact these things never really do get exorcised no matter how many films or scripts we do." Under pressure to deliver complete scripts in whirlwind weekends of typing, Stefano conceived a monster that consumes all forms of energy. The idea came to him from thin air, or, it might be said, right out of the woodwork.

The idea of the energy cloud, first explored in "The Man With the Power," is reprised here as a voracious monster of Lovecraftian proportions, and contrasts Stefano's approach to that of Leslie Stevens. In "Power," the cloud is ominous and lethal, but stately, like a methodical lightning storm. Stefano's literal Thing in the Pit gobbles up everything in its path in an eyeblink of time. "The trick of the show is to put the unreal in the midst of the real," said Stefano. "I try to invent convincing people and put them into real houses, to build reality into other areas of the show so the audience can sit back and be scared in comfort. The terror must always be unreal." The isolated NORCO plant, dark and apparently disused, "was just a restructuring of the old haunted house motif."

"Woodwork"'s problematic characters are complex enough to seem real, but are trapped in a dramatic chaos only slightly less controlled than the madly strobing energy cloud that dispatches many of them by the final curtain. "Jory is the perennial younger brother who doesn't bother to develop because his older brother, Stu, has 'become' that mature personality," said Stefano. "You can get crushed by older brothers." At one point, Stuart suggests to Dr. Block that it might be good for Jory to be independent, on his own, noting that Jory is technically his ward. Stefano cut the following lines from his script:

BLOCK: Is he financially dependent on you?
STUART: No. He came into his trust at eighteen.
BLOCK: He sounds weak. (pause) I didn't mean that unkindly.
STUART: I know. And he is... in the way a wounded deer is weak.

Most of the story's irrelevancies are heaped into Jory's mouth. One of the few meaningful speeches he delivers is a recounting of his parents' death in a boating accident—which connects directly to Stu's death-by-water, in the hotel bathtub.

Death and talk of death abounds in "Woodwork." Several characters—notably Stu—die more than once. "You must get over this repugnance for death," the sinister Block purrs (in a thick Kissinger accent) at Prof. Linden, one of the NORCO scientists he has resurrected. "For you to hate death is as foolish as for a live person to hate life." True enough, but dying is nevertheless shown to be a hideous and agonizing experience—we see the NORCO zombies grimacing and screaming as their pacemaker boxes are shorted out or drained; Stu's death in the Pit, and later, by electrocution in the tub, is protracted and painful. Stefano's macabre black humor tints the scene in which Jory tells Stu he wouldn't be "caught dead working at a place like NORCO"—where, of course, all the workers except Block are *already* dead.

Since the indecisive Jory is too weak to carry the plot past the point of Stu's bathtub death, Stefano brings on Ed Asner as the tough, teddy-bearish Siroleo to deliver some of the best lines in the show. "Stuart Peters had scar tissue as fresh as tomorrow morning's milk," he says. "If he'd been in any better health, they would have given him a morning show on television." When the energy cloud is freed from the Pit to run amok, it is Siroleo who says, "As long as we're in the dark, we're as safe as we can be"—a nice turnabout on the dark fears Stefano wielded so well in other shows.

"We have to find a way to break, or change, the Conservation of Energy Law," Linden tells Stu. It is Block, of course, who needs to create new energy to feed the hungry force in the Pit, so he may investigate it. "Every man wants to solve one mystery before he dies," he says after Linden shoots him. Despite the name-dropping of the Conservation of Energy Law, it is clear within moments that "Woodwork" has no truck with real science. Stefano was more interested in painting a nightmarish picture of what goes on inside top secret, government-funded labs—the type that would never let ordinary citizens past their iron gates. It seems that Block's obsessive plan to study the energy cloud backfires because once he kills his dissident researchers, then reanimates them to serve his needs, they lack the sort of burning scientific curiosity Stu evinces when he first walks into the lab. He is alive, his soul is his own, and he is the new blood Block needs. Linden, on the other hand, is never seen *doing* anything except drifting around the obviously disused and unmaintained lab. If Block really wanted to make a name for himself, he should have marketed those miraculous "pacemaker" boxes with which he revivifies the dead.

The soulless nature of Block's NORCO drones is an aspect of the show's indictment of atomic energy. The only use to which Block is able to put the energy cloud is murder. Like real-life nuclear researchers, he is a slave to the power he is presumably investigating, and no matter what the rationalization for puttering with such power might be, the bottom line is always the struggle to keep it penned up and under control. But Stefano takes great care, in the closing Control Voice speech, to mention such things as genius, madness, and the human heart before getting around to atoms, hinting at the personal demons this script might have helped him to corral and control.

The Energy Creature itself is ingeniously conceived. Smoke effects were used as the basis for matte cutouts which were edited quickly together, providing a kind of zero-to-ninety effect for the cloud's progress. Director Gerd Oswald gave the weak story a heavy coat of gloss by keeping the NORCO interiors morgue-like, and resorting to extreme, bizarre camera angles, particularly whenever Block is seen discoursing on death. "I liked that one," said Oswald. "There was a kind of claustrophobia, a feeling of menace and mystery created by the lady doctor with the pacemaker." Hard and shocking images—the terrified struggles of Stu, and later Siroleo, as they scream for help behind the soundproof glass port in the Pit corridor, or the startling smash cut from Jory's calm discussion of Stu's "nice smile" to a close-up of Stu's death rictus as his corpse lies on a slab at NORCO—help the show seem more portentious and threatening than it really is. Bright, sparking carbon-arc lights called "lightning scissors," along with six-foot-tall, propellorlike wind machines helped create the effect on the monster's passage on the set. First AD Lee Katzin's shooting notes refer to it as *Daystar's answer to the White Tornado,* and *THE (gasp) ENERGY (choke) BEING (shudder).*

For Stefano, this unstable, insatiable, all-consuming vortex was *The Outer Limits*. "It Crawled Out of the Woodwork" chronicles—or cannibalizes—the massive drain on his personal energies and the furious pace that caused some of his midseason scripts to seem foggy, rushed, or imprecise in comparison with his earlier shows. At times, it must have seemed all too easy to become a NORCO-like slave to the demands of producing the series. *The Outer Limits,* one might say, occasionally went beyond control. But as Siroleo demonstrates, this monster might be subdued by a simple phone call and brought under control... for the moment. "I was not unaware of that, and it's true of producing for television," said Stefano. "Am I in control of the show... or does it control *me?*"

Diana Sands in the clutches of the Chromoite (Hugh Langtry) on the MGM backlot.

THE MICE

Broadcast 6 January 1964
Written by Joseph Stefano, based on the script "Exchange Student," by Bill S. Ballinger. Story idea by Lou Morheim. Teleplay credited to Ballinger and Stefano.
Directed by Alan Crosland, Jr.
Assistant Director: Robert Justman
Director of Photography: Conrad Hall

CAST: Chino Rivera (Henry Silva), Dr. Julia Harrison (Diana Sands), Dr. Thomas Kellander (Michael Higgins), Dr. Robert Richardson (Ronald Foster), Haddon (Don Ross), Goldsmith (Gene Tyburn), Chromoite (Hugh Langtry), Prison Warden (Frances DeSales), Dr. Williams (Dabney Coleman), Chromo Transmission Voice (Robert Johnson).

In dreams, some of us walk the stars. In dreams, some of us ride the whelming brine of space, where every port is a shining one, and none are beyond our reach. Some of us, in dreams, cannot reach beyond the walls of our own little sleep.

Faced with life imprisonment for murder, convict Chino Rivera volunteers as a human guinea pig for an "inhabitant exchange" between Earth and the planet Chromo. "It's worked with mice," the supervising scientist, Dr. Kellander, says of the "teleportation agency" built from Chromoite instructions, which beams a native of that world to our planet. A gelatinous, crab-clawed biped, the Chromoite is allowed to roam the lab compound freely while Kellander's group waits for the ideal time to beam Rivera to Chromo. Rivera spends *his* free time trying to escape, and when Dr. Richardson is discovered strangled at a nearby lake, the natural suspect is Rivera (who was missing from his room at the time) and not the alien, which Rivera calls a "garbage eater" even though Chromoites are supposed to live by photosynthesis. Dr. Julia Harrison observes the alien eating a doughy scum that has spawned in the lake shortly following its arrival. The Chromoite chases her back to the lab building, just as the attempt to transmit Rivera fails and all contact with Chromo is lost. The Chromoite murders a guard and tries to commandeer the transporter. Rivera shoots it with the dead guard's pistol, aborting the escape attempt. Then the aliens on Chromo recontact Kellander, admitting that "Chromo's soil no longer yields," and that they have been seeking a new planet on which they may grow vast quantities of their staff of life—the lake scum. The Chromoite is no expendable guinea pig, but the planet's most eminent scientist, and having failed in their deception, the homeworld requests his return. Kellander sees Rivera in a new and honorable light, and tells him that the parole board will take his selfless actions into consideration. As for the thwarted invaders, he tells them, sadly and accusingly, "You should have asked."

> *Hunger frightens and hurts, and it has many faces, and every man must sometimes face the terror of one of them. Wouldn't it seem that a misery known and understood by all men would lead Man not to deception and murder, but to faith, and hope, and love?*

"It was a problem when I'd get a script from a writer, and make my suggestions for changes, and then get back a second draft that was still not good," said Stefano. "At that point, you have a choice. Either you give the writer another shot, or you take it home with you. Which most producers do, because you know it's going to be faster to do it yourself when you need it for next week. You don't *have* to offer the writer a third rewrite, so I didn't ask for one. I just did it the way I wanted it."

In broad outline, both "The Mice" and its genesis script, Bill Ballinger's "Exchange Student," are similar. The original teleplay gives us a vaguely Hispanic convict named Cully, who for the most part acts as a foil for a rain of pseudoscientific gobbledygook endlessly dispensed by Marius Kellander, one of a trio of scientists who have discovered a planet called Soter "in the constellation of Dorado." A Soterian visitor is in residence at the lab, obligingly constructing a duplicate of the teleportation device that "flashed" it to Earth, and simultaneously carrying out its fifth-columnist food-nurturing mission. Cully, the test guinea-pig for the machine, is set up as the fall guy by the alien before it murders a scientist who tampers with the scum food. Kellander's group gets wise to the approaching Soterian invasion fleet, and spends the entire fourth act chasing the renegade alien around before Cully turns hero and subdues it. The Soterian lacks the grandeur of the speech-making aliens native to *The Outer Limits*, and its most interesting lines occur as it sets up Cully:

> SOTERIAN: You have bread. We have this—our "staff of life." Soter is very different. In many ways. Some very horrible. Do not go.

CULLY (calculatingly): What chance have I got? Back to prison. Unless I could... "move around," like you...
SOTERIAN: You would escape? If I helped you?
CULLY: I would escape. But why should you help?
SOTERIAN: Pity. I have already helped you... I have disconnected the power rays (indicates window) in there.
CULLY (as he starts for the door): Just pity?
SOTERIAN: Isn't pity enough?

Technical explanations hang all over the story like Spanish moss, and for the most part, Cully is a one-dimensional thud who supplies the ear into which Kellander pours his windy discourse. Here's a sample:

KELLANDER: The Hecron Institute of Neo-Kinematics (is) sometimes referred to by the newspapers as the T.H.I.N.K. CENTER... At the Center, we work in all scientific fields directly or indirectly related to the theory of motion. That's what part of our name means—Kinematics—motion in the abstract. *Neo* means new, advanced theories of motion. For our purpose, now, we can simply call it space travel.

Stefano jettisoned most of Kellander's leaden verbiage and, in "The Mice," gives us Chino Rivera, obviously named after his good friend and Beverly Hills neighbor, dancer Chita Rivera, whom he was soon to cast in *The Outer Limits*. Chino is a full-blooded, extroverted creation that gives the story a much-needed human focus, and Henry Silva jumps into the role with both feet and quite rightly walks away with the whole show. Bright-eyed, street smart, quick and intense, Chino plays off the straight-arrow Kellander, constantly kidding and dancing around him in ways the poor doctor is just too dedicated to comprehend. When he first sees the teleportation device, he exclaims, "That's my getaway car!" Stamped by society as a misfit, Chino is considered less than human by Kellander, who is harshly determined to ignore any evidence to the contrary. A running commentary on hunger, worked in by Stefano, makes Chino seem more alive than the scientists around him because of that ache in his gut—once a physical hunger, now an ideological one. The scientists are complacent, mentally flattened, and bored. They seek to validate themselves by probing other worlds, and lack the drive to discover the Earthbound lust Chino has for life. His lively, reckless attitude never fails to irritate and perplex Kellander:

KELLANDER: I didn't think you'd try to escape.
CHINO: Neither did I.

KELLANDER: No? I think you had it in mind the minute you walked out of the warden's office. That's probably the only reason you volunteered.

CHINO: Come to think of it... you're right!

KELLANDER (angered): What's the matter with you, Chino? Are you a psychopathic liar? Do you know when you lie and when you're telling the truth?

CHINO: What's the difference if I know? What's important is if *you* know!

Kellander's intellectual blinders disallow even the simple connection of the lake scum with the Chromoite's activities, in the same way they make him automatically peg Chino as Richardson's murderer. In the end, with those blinders slapped away, his rage is as genuine and human as Chino: "You have deceived us!" he shouts toward Chromo.

At cross purposes to such rich and promising character detail in "The Mice" are story cheats held over from the Ballinger script, the overuse of redundant and even repeated footage to pad out the running time, and the physical form of the alien itself. The Chromoite (changed from "Soterian" because it probably sounded less mushy as an alien name) is never described in either script as anything but "humanoid" and "repulsive." Gene Warren of Project Unlimited took those two words to the outer limit by designing one of the series' most outrageous and improbable beings—an alien that looks like a silver Portuguese man-of-war on legs, with dangling, mucoid pseudopodia, weedlike appurtenances poking out of its jellied mass, clutching crab claws, and a slavering mouth hole that snaps wetly open to ingest the thick, alabaster goop growing on the lake. It certainly is a jarring sight when first seen—worrying its claws around in a handwringing gesture and making a liquid gargling noise—but we see far too much of it. Nonfriendly aliens were kept in the shadows in most *Outer Limits* shows, but one thing the viewer gets in "The Mice" is *lots* of the Chromoite. The globular headpiece of the costume was poured slip rubber and solidified glue weighing nearly 150 pounds. It had to be lowered onto stuntman Hugh Langtry using a block and tackle attached to a tree in MGM's Tarzan Forest, where the exteriors were shot.

The Chromoite's whole scheme seems fuzzy and needlessly complicated. The scum food grows so quickly and easily that the whole alien ruse to test it on Earth seems unnecessary and risky. Only the tunnel vision of the scientists allows the plot to get as far as it does, and does the Chromoite honestly expect to escape, once exposed? Not helping matters are the frequent tracking shots of the creature stomping through the forest, used as transitional footage and obviously printed up and stuck in during editing for want of anything better. More time is eaten up by a repeated sequence in which security guards cruise the woods and climb in and out of their car. The same shot of a dead (or unconscious) guard

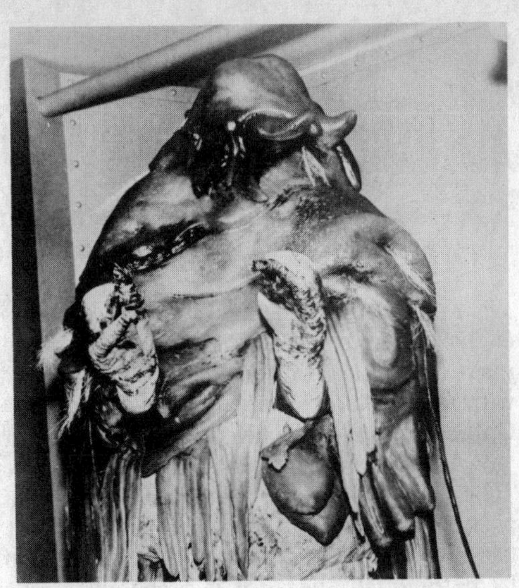

The Chromoite inside the "T.A."—
Teleportation Agency.

shows up, confusingly, in two places in the episode. Another sentry is vaporized during Chino's battle with the Chromoite, but nobody seems to care about him, or even notice he's gone.

Whether or not Alan Crosland, Jr.'s direction is any good is tough to assess—both of his *Outer Limits* shows, "The Mice" and "The Mutant," were heavily compromised on the script level at a time when Stefano's main objective was to streamline production. Crosland did bring off the shoot quickly and efficiently, filming all the woodland and lake scenes, amazingly, in one day. Cinematographer John Nickolaus had just left *The Outer Limits* to work on *The Travels of Jaimie McPheeters* series; with "The Mice," Conrad Hall settled in for a long haul of six episodes in a row, without relief, culminating in a fourteen-day shoot on Stefano's elaborate pilot, *The Unknown*. The opening scenes of "The Mice," set in the waterfront prison milieu, are dark and somber, and ultimately frustrating when nothing follows to match them atmospherically. The degeneration of the story is best summed up by a comparison of Stefano's opening and closing Control Voice speeches—the first is positively lyrical, the second just belabors the obvious.

Cast as Julia Harrison was Diana Sands, a talented yet underrated stage actress who did little TV work. Perhaps this was another case of Stefano writing—or *not* writing—"black actress" into his script. Unfortunately, next to nothing is made of her attraction to Chino, and her role does not grow much beyond the imperiled heroine phase. Sands died tragically in 1972 following the release of one of her infrequent features, *Georgia Georgia*.

"The Mice" finds the *Outer Limits* crew doing their best to make mediocre material work in a hurry, and provides a diverting, if disappointing, hour of television. But Stefano, once having gotten the hang of writing at top speed, now made sure that his next new scripts would be episodes not to be forgotten. And even the Chromoite—or rather, his overblown costume—got a chance to come back and try again.

A wounded Don Gordon attempts to outdistance a hungry Invisible.

THE INVISIBLES

Broadcast 3 February 1964
Written by Joseph Stefano
Directed by Gerd Oswald
Assistant Directors: Lee H. Katzin (preparation)
Claude Binyon, Jr. (production)
Director of Photography: Conrad Hall

CAST: GIA Agent Luis D. Spain (Don Gordon), Genero Planetta (Tony Mordente), Gov. Lawrence K. Hillmond (George MacReady), Gen. Hillary J. Clarke (Neil Hamilton), Oliver Fair (Richard Dawson), Mrs. Clarke (Dee Hartford), Invisibles Recruiter (Walter Burke), Henry Castle (Chris Warfield), Attachment Supervisor ["the Doctor"] (John Graham), GIA Agent Johnny (William O. Douglas, Jr), Sforza Water & Power GIA Agent [Old Man] (Len Lesser), Voice of GIA Chief (Vic Perrin), Invisibles Radio Voice (Robert Johnson).

You do not know these men. You may have looked at them, but you did not see them. They are newspapers blowing down a gutter on a windy night. For reasons both sociological and psychological these three have never joined or been invited to join society. They have never experienced love or friendship or formed any lasting or constructive relationship. But today, at last, they will become a part of something. They will belong. They will come a little bit closer to their unrealistic dreams of power and glory. Today, finally, they will join the hu— I almost said the human *race. And that would have been a half-truth. For the race they are joining today is only half-human . . .*

Three misfits—the stony Luis Spain, the twitchy and neurotic Genero Planetta, and an overeager joiner-type named Castle—are delivered to an abandoned Army base as new recruits to the ranks of the Invisibles, a "subversive and illegal" underground composed of high-ranking men in government and industry who are possessed by alien parasites. Spain is actually an agent of the Government Intelligence Agency sent to infiltrate the Invisibles, who plan to infect other key power brokers with the scuttling, voracious, trilobitelike aliens. The corrupt low lifes who carry out these "attachments" are inoculated against "accidental infection" by the indiscriminate parasites. Once inoculated, Spain is assigned to Washington, DC, to infect an army general named Hillary J. Clarke. As cover, Spain becomes Clarke's new chauffeur, with the endorsement of Clarke's effete aide, Oliver Fair, another Invisible who serves as Spain's chaperone for the mission. But Clarke is *already* an Invisible, and the mission is a setup intended to expose Spain as a double agent. The Invisibles would very much like to have an operative inside the GIA, and Clarke and Fair plan to use the parasite supplied to Spain on Spain himself as soon as his inoculation runs out. Spain escapes from Clarke's mansion but is accidentally run down by a car driven by Clarke's wife; his ankle is smashed in the wheel-well. Crippled and in terrible pain, he later manages to steal the car and drives to a power plant to seek out Planetta, whom he cultivated as an ally back at the indoctrination camp, and whose help he now needs to get back to GIA headquarters. Planetta's "primal target" as a new Invisible, however, turns out to be Spain himself, and having no stomach for the attachment procedure, Planetta unleashes a parasite and abandons Spain. Screaming for help, Spain tries vainly to crawl away as the creature gains on him. Planetta has a last-minute change of heart and returns to pry the thing off Spain's back just as it begins to attach itself. A rescue party of police and GIA men arrives, and Planetta and the parasite perish in a hail of bullets. Spain is escorted to safety, and one GIA man notes that they've apprehended Oliver Fair, who is "cooperating."

You do not know these men. You may have looked at them, but you did not see them. They are the wind that blows newspapers down a gutter on a windy night . . . and sweeps the gutter clean.

A hard-hitting tale of America's power structure in the throes of corruption, "The Invisibles" focuses on subjugation via both deception and force, pain thresholds, and the ugly ends to which human beings

"We've *lost* Mr. Castle." Walter Burke lays down the law of the Invisibles for Don Gordon (center) and Tony Mordente.

can be maneuvered. It renders the military-industrial complex as literally diseased, infected by a cancer-cell-like extraterrestrial, but presses home the point that such a plague would not thrive without the vanity and greed of "men in places so high, no one knows how high they are," as Gen. Clarke says in the episode. While the mistrust of top-dog politicians (unfashionable while the U.S. was in the grip of John Kennedy's charisma) may be taken for routine cynicism today, it was a dramatic forethought by Joseph Stefano, who rates this *Outer Limits* as one of his favorites. "Everyone is so *good* in it," he said. "The way Gerd shot it was disturbing; it's a tight, tense show, and even today, watching a scene by itself makes me uncomfortable. The effect is one of overall, pervading evil."

Stefano's original teleplay was passed without a hitch by ABC Standards and Practices. The finished film, however, brought an immediate phone call from network censor Dorothy Brown. "I really felt compassion for her with that show," said Stefano. "It unnerved and unsettled her. When she saw the rough cut, she said, 'I don't know what to do about this; this film *bothers* me and I can't tell you why, or what to cut.' At that point, I knew I had her—its *body* was frightening to her. And I agreed—but I didn't think it was as disturbing as 'Corpus Earthling,' for which she asked me to make maybe six little cuts."

Gerd Oswald calls Brown "the *real* monster on *Outer Limits!* Some of the notes she wrote Joe were so ridiculous you just wouldn't believe it; objections to anything that might be too gory or spooky. Her superior at ABC was a guy named Adrian Samish, who was a total terror. Stefano threw him out of his office, once." Samish later became president of ABC in the mid-1960s.

"We fought continually with the censors," said Stefano. "I used to put things into scripts *knowing* they'd be taken out, just to save other things from cutting. Normally, we'd get three- and four-page lists of things that 'had to go.' The signals were all crossed. I'd get a call from the network heads, saying, 'Let's have more monsters; we love *this*, do more of *that*.' Generally, it would be the very thing Dorothy Brown hadn't wanted me to do. And every time you get a letter from Continuity, it still doesn't mean they'll okay the show even if you make the changes. It's all 'subject to final viewing.' My ace in the hole was to refuse to air the show. My objective became not to get caught and crushed between the censors and the network heads. So, I'd argue with Dorothy up to a certain point and then say, 'Well, then, let's just pull the show.' Then all the phones would start ringing. As soon as everybody heard that, they'd get time-conscious, and eventually the show would come back okay. They're weird people."

Leslie Stevens maintains that ABC's misunderstanding of *The Outer Limits* was a backhanded asset: "We had a certain leeway because they never quite knew what the show *was*. Were they surer, we'd've had less room to get imaginative material in." Thus, ABC's complaints about "The Invisibles" never really fructified, and we are left to enjoy Don Gordon's superb portrayal of Luis Spain, secret agent.

"Heroes die alone" is the credo by which Spain operates, and he is a loner, isolated in enemy territory, communicating impersonally, by tape recorder and telephone. The GIA insulates itself from infiltration by the Invisibles through the "Spain-is-a-leper-routine," and Stefano describes Spain in the script as a "social disaffiliate." He is confounded by basically decent people—Planetta, Mrs. Clarke—who are too terrified of disrupting their status quo to help him when he needs assistance. When Planetta finally relents, he dies instantly, just after the only constructive friendship Spain has established turns against him. "I *liked* you!" Planetta yells in betrayal, as he tosses a parasite at Spain... the hero who *would* have died alone, had Planetta not come back to save him.

"The Invisibles" treats us to some harrowing images of men pushed to the razor's edge of endurance. We see Hillmond and Clarke writhing and grimacing as their Invisibles wrest control from within. The "attachment procedure" is gruesome but not grisly, and Planetta and Castle scream in fear as the wriggling symbiote is offered their naked backs. Castle becomes the victim of attachment (his inoculation fails), and we soon see the debilitating effects of becoming a host on his face. Spain undergoes the test application of a parasite to *his* back in sweaty, teeth-clenching, barely controlled silence. Planetta is chopped apart by gunfire, for all his good intentions, and Spain's GIA buddy, Johnny, is beaten to death by a rifle butt in the hands of an Invisibles sentry, in a scene that ended up on the cutting room floor. And then there is Spain's smashed ankle—Don Gordon is painfully convincing to watch as he force-fits his shoe onto his foot as it swells, the agony ultimately causing him to pass out. In one shot dropped by Stefano from the script, Spain escapes by jumping from the second floor of the Clarke mansion and hobbling to the limousine on his injured foot.

In November of 1963, the trappings of the secret agent genre were still new, and the only non-British spy show on TV was a trifle called *Espionage*. James Bond was just penetrating the mass consciousness—the current Ian Fleming novel was *On Her Majesty's Secret Service,* the latest film, *From Russia, With Love* (the novel had been a highly-publicized favorite of President Kennedy's)—but secret agents did not come into their own until the advent of *The Man From U.N.C.L.E.* in 1964. Nineteen sixty five would be the boom year, when more spy shows would be on the air than any year since. In "The Invisibles" we get tantalizing glimpses of procedures that would later become familiar, even trite, as conventions of the spy genre: Spain's code number, 0021 (which happens to be three times 007); the rigid method followed by Spain and Johnny for making reports on tape; the jargon used for various gambits like the "kid brother ploy," by which Spain tricks Planetta into revealing his location to the GIA. Referred to as the CIA throughout Stefano's script, the name of the reputation-conscious agency could only be invoked by permission, and thus the "GIA" was born.

The story somewhat resembles Robert Heinlein's 1952 science fiction novel *The Puppet Masters,* in which the United States is invaded by large grey space slugs that attach to the human back, between the shoulder blades, making the victim into a hunchbacked zombie (like the Recruiter and Castle). The protagonist is an investigator for a secret Federal agency. It is possible that someone saw the novel, which has remained in print ever since its serialization in *Galaxy* magazine in 1951, during the early sift-throughs of published science fiction at Villa di Stefano. It is rumored that Heinlein disassociated himself from all films based on his books following a plagiarism suit involving a feature film script written around *The Puppet Masters,* long before *The Outer Limits* ever came along. At any rate, the idea of parasitical aliens invading human bodies, as in "Corpus Earthling," was nothing new.

"The Invisibles" benefits greatly from the veteran actors who play the villainous roles. "George MacReady was my man," said Gerd Oswald. "He was in my first feature, *A Kiss Before Dying,* and was part of the 'Oswald Stock Company,' as were Walter Burke and John Hoyt." Tony

It's all happening so *fast...*" Neil Hamilton gets the drop on Agent Spain.

Mordente, late of *West Side Story* and then married to Chita Rivera, was cast by Stefano. Another Stefano favorite was Neil Hamilton, a leading man of silent films soon to become famous in 1965 as Commissioner Gordon on the *Batman* series. A pre–*Hogan's Heroes* Richard Dawson is featured as the unctuous Oliver Fair, and a brief glimpse of the face that had been behind the Galaxy Being mask is provided by William O. Douglas, Jr.'s walk-on as "Johnny."

Stefano was uncharacteristically specific, in his script, about what an Invisible parasite looked like:

> It is a dark, throbbing creature, about the size of a grown man's back, probably ten inches thick. It is a patchwork of thorns and bristles. Small, nervous paws protrude from its entire circumference. The paws are tipped by a single saw-edged claw, and are spaced about four inches apart. At regular intervals, a large, glowing eye pops up out of the middle of the body, glares, and quickly withdraws out of sight.

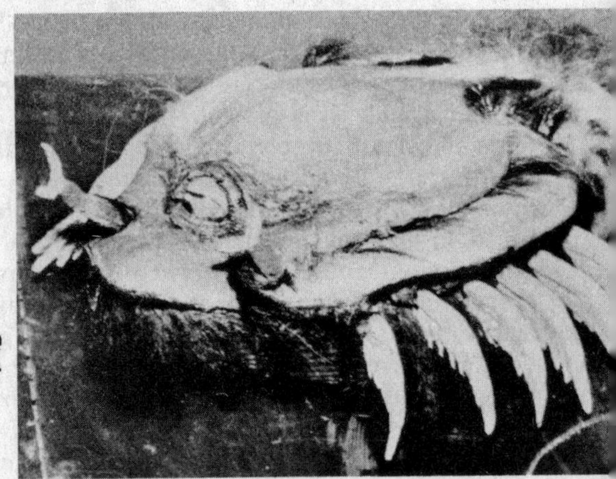

Another pretty disgusting alien parasite by Project Unlimited.

The mechanical monster cooked up by Project Unlimited is adequate, resembling an ambulatory meatball sandwich (indeed, the beasts are seen to be stored in what looks like a large food automat) or a football-sized crab louse. The hungry roar it emits was the Tyrannosaurus Rex sound effect Projects did for *Dinosaurus!* in 1960.

"'The Invisibles' was very effective, I thought," said Oswald. "Stefano remarked during the dailies that the scene with the handball thrown against the wall became unbearably suspenseful for him. That was the mood I strove for—it's nervous and tense as opposed to 'O.B.I.T.,' which was low-key."

The scene to which Oswald refers takes place "under" the prologue, with an Invisibles sentry bouncing a ball against the outside wall of the barracks as the new recruits arrive. The background is barren and grey in the wet aftermath of recent rain. As Hillmond speaks inside, the ball continues *thonking* against the outside wall, timed like the drops in a Chinese water torture.

Unlike the nefarious subterfuge seen in "O.B.I.T.," "Nightmare," or "It Crawled Out of the Woodwork," the "Invisibles" plot is not safely fenced up within the confines of the military, or top-secret research labs. It has sifted down to the common people, using the dregs of humanity as well as its leaders to achieve the final takeover. While the tenor of the times allowed Spain to be a clearcut good guy merely by being a GIA agent, the show itself imparted a note of discomfiture to the TV viewer who, in 1963, was blissfully ignorant of governmental lying, coverups, and rampant domestic espionage, or of the true price paid when souls are traded for power.

Daystar's Revolving Door

"The Invisibles" was produced during a transitional period for the personnel working on *The Outer Limits*. In November, 1963, five key production positions changed hands. The per-show budget was slimmed to $120,000, and soon the shooting schedules would be shortened by an entire day per episode. Some crewmembers moved on to new projects. Others were dismissed.

"I was fired by Joe Stefano after we'd done eight shows," said 1st AD Lee Katzin. "We'd had an argument. I was the victim of industrial sabotage, in a way, but it was personal and had nothing to do with business. Joe was a very dour, taciturn, talented man, and I was not the only one at Daystar who did not take to him. Maybe I was just more vocal than the others." Katzin had prepared "The Invisibles," and parted company with *The Outer Limits* two days before filming started. Claude Binyon, Jr., stepped in as 1st AD on that episode.

"I'll tell you something about that Leslie Stevens was very helpful on," said Stefano. "I fired Lee, and that was it as far as I was concerned. But Leslie said, 'You have to give this man a chance to appeal.' I felt, why? He doesn't deny what he's being fired about. Leslie said, 'Because it upsets the rest of the company. You are the man with the power. If you don't, in your position, give him a chance to appeal, then the crew won't care whether he's right or wrong. It means that if they make a mistake, they won't get a chance to appeal, either—and suddenly, they're dealing with a tyrant, who frightens them.' And I felt Leslie was absolutely right. So I had Lee come in, and I said to him pretty much what I said to my son at times: 'You don't realize that you have the power to hurt somebody bigger than you. You think because I'm the producer, you can say anything you want and it's not going to hurt me.' He was terribly chastened; I mean, I'm sure he thinks I'm his mortal enemy, but the only impression that I wanted to leave Lee with was that he was capable of hurting me, and he'd done it, badly." Five days later, Stevens rehired Katzin as 1st AD for a new Daystar pilot film titled *Stryker*.

Within a week of Katzin's departure, Casting Director John Erman left *The Outer Limits* to pursue his career as a director. "Fortunately," said Erman, "Leslie was willing to let my assistant, Meryl Abeles, take over, and that was the beginning of a career in casting for her."

Shortly after completing "The Zanti Misfits," John Nickolaus left to assume the director of photography position full-time on *The Travels of Jaimie McPheeters*. For the next three months, Conrad Hall would shoot all the work *The Outer Limits* had to offer, and when he left the show to work on feature films in early 1964, Stevens brought in Kenneth Peach to replace him.

Meanwhile, Lindsley Parsons, Jr., had replaced Leon Chooluck as titular production manager. "Leon clashed with Dominic Frontiere and didn't last," said Stevens. "Theirs was a problem of authority, and who made the right decisions. Dom outranked Leon, and won out." Lee Katzin noted, "There was a little bit of folderol going on there, and Leon was sort of 'let go.'" Chooluck went to work for producer Samuel Bronson in Madrid, on the film *The Fall of the Roman Empire*, after appealing his case to Stevens, with whom he had worked since *Private Property*. "In the course of our routine, day-to-day crises, there has to come a flare-up point," said Stevens. "And in this case I simply had to back Dominic."

Come January of 1964, Parsons was also to leave. The cut-rate deal he had engineered in order for *The Outer Limits* to shoot on the MGM backlots came to the attention of MGM general manager Ray Clune. "He came back from a vacation and wanted to know who in hell made this deal," said Parsons. "He figured I was too dangerous to leave on the 'outside,' so he made me an offer I couldn't refuse, and hired me." Taking Parsons's position was 1st AD Robert Justman, who remained in this capacity until the close of the first season. Among Daystar's new 1st ADs was a young man named Phil Rawlins, an ex-rodeo rider who'd gotten his start the previous year, on *Stoney Burke*.

Joanna Frank, *The Outer Limits'* one-and-only Bee Girl. (Courtesy Joanna Frank)

ZZZZZ

Broadcast 27 January 1964
Written by Meyer Dolinsky. Additional material by Joseph Stefano.
Directed by John Brahm
Assistant Director: Robert Justman
Director of Photography: Conrad Hall

CAST: Prof. Benedict O. Fields (Phillip Abbott), Francesca Fields (Marsha Hunt), Regina/Queen Bee (Joanna Frank), Dr. Howard Warren (Booth Coleman), Voice of Mr. Lund/Bee Voices (Robert Johnson).

> *Human life strives ceaselessly to perfect itself, to gain ascendancy. But what of the lower forms of life? Is it not possible that they, too, are conducting experiments, and are at this moment on the threshold of deadly success?*

In the garden of entomologist Ben Fields, a coruscating mass of sparkling lights resolves into the unconscious form of an exotic, raven-haired young woman. No sooner does Ben send his wife Francesca into town to place a newspaper ad for a lab assistant than he discovers the ravishing girl, who, once revived, asks for the job. Her name is Regina, and unknown to Fields, she is actually the queen of a superintelligent hive that has effected her transformation so that she might mate with Fields and produce hybrid offspring. Neither Ben nor Francesca suspect anything, rationalizing that Regina's strange behavior stems from foreign origin—until Francesca spots Regina in the garden at night, drawing pollen from the flowers and metamorphosing into a human-sized bee! After a meal the next day, Regina passes out from horrible internal pain after using a computer translator of Ben's to communicate with the hive. Her cramps turn out to be food poisoning, but the attending physician confides to Ben that "she's the closest thing to a complete mutant I've ever seen," in terms of her body and blood composition. When Francesca later catches Regina at the translator addressing her buzzing subjects, Regina unleashes the hive to sting her to death. Ben discovers tapes of Regina's communications with the hive, and when Regina makes sexual overtures to Ben while wearing Francesca's old wedding veil, he delivers an impassioned speech on the sanctity of matrimony while backing her off the second floor balcony. Regina falls over the rail with a scream, reverts to bee form, and flies away forever.

> *When the yearning to gain ascendancy takes the form of a soulless, loveless struggle, the contest must end in unlovely defeat. For without love, drones can never be men, and men can only be drones.*

"I commissioned 'ZZZZZ' because of Joanna Frank," said Joseph Stefano.* "There was something about her face I thought would photograph beautifully, and so I had Meyer Dolinsky do the script. That business at the end with the wedding veil was mine; it worked even though there was nothing terribly original about the story."

Well-versed in the needs of *The Outer Limits*, Dolinsky quickly executed a script to accommodate the demands of scheduling. Strictly speaking, revisions were not necessary, but the teleplay did not match up with Stefano's sensibilities, and Dolinsky admitted that it was his least favorite episode.

"I wrote it from Francesca's point of view," Dolinsky said. "The beekeeper falls in love with Regina and rejects his own wife, before finding out at the last minute that the girl is a bee." Ben then kills Regina (originally named Doris) with a pistol. "I had a high degree of temptation going, with Ben having the hots for this young chick. Stefano reversed all that. My own thinking was it was because *he* was married, and I wasn't. I did not agree with his ending; in fact, I tried to get him to cut it. It went on interminably, this long, moral speech which I felt was unnecessary. I said, 'Hey, this slows it down, and I don't believe it!'"

Dolinsky's script dealt in matriarchal power, Stefano's, in simple fidelity. The former is definitely the more daring scenario. Consider these lines, excised from the Fields' dinner table conversation:

> FRANCESCA: You mustn't enjoy being dominated by women, darling. Their motives aren't always good for you.
>
> BEN: That's a risk a man has to take in a matriarchal society.... You know it's only after I've checked her

*"ZZZZZ" is the one *Outer Limits* title that the people interviewed for this book absolutely refused to pronounce for reasons of conversational sanity, preferring instead to call it "The Bees." Therefore, all quotations referring to the title have been accordingly modified.

experience, and she's proved her merit, that I let a woman dominate me.

Later, Ben says of Regina's cleanup job in the lab, "You're obviously a very good housekeeper," adding, with a trace of regret, "You'll no doubt make some fellow a meek and obedient wife." When Regina suggestively broaches the beauty of the mating ritual in bee society, Ben responds with:

BEN: My feelings are no doubt colored by the fact that I'm a man, and would *ipso facto* be a drone in a Bee Society, but I feel they stunt their own social development by adhering to such intractable customs and philosophies. Amongst humans, an unwillingness to grow and change has caused some races to become extinct.

Such a sentiment was clearly at odds with Stefano's more customary view of marriage as sacrosanct. Another theme that crops up in his revision is the idea that Regina is just too wrong, too different both biologically and ideologically, for the super-bees' plan of world conquest to succeed. He also pushed Ben and Francesca closer to his own age at the time (forty-one), and one scene remains in the broadcast version wherein the clearly fortyish Phillip Abbott talks about having children "before I'm twenty-five." Making Ben and Francesca older does permit for a brief comparison of Regina to their stillborn daughter, but this reduces Ben's potential attraction to the bee-girl even more, and he never seems to be in any real danger of being seduced. In the end, Regina buzzes away, presumably to pick another entomologist not so emphatically Catholic. At the end of both Dolinsky's script and the Stefano redraft, she goes off the balcony frantically flapping her arms and is crushed to death when she hits the ground.

The bees themselves also had more to do in the first script. "They were commenting on our culture," said Dolinsky, who got the idea for the insect language analyzer from an article in *Time* magazine. "I thought of Ben and the bees discussing their plans intentionally, but that was all cut out, and Stefano went for this very wrong message at the end."

The watered down version does have its moments, though, such as when Francesca describes why people fear insects:

FRANCESCA: We talk more about our fears of the larger forms of animals; we don't think it so cowardly to admit fear of crazed panthers and giant vultures. But I think all of us are uneasy about those tiny things that crawl and fly. You can't see what they're thinking. You can't look into their eyes...

She's watching Regina as she says this, of course, and the mutant counters that while Francesca can be inoculated against bee stings, she cannot be immunized from their *thoughts*.

Neither Regina nor the super-hive seem much of a menace. The food-poisoning incident makes her appear too fragile for the plan of biological conquest, and the revelation that the bee stings were not what killed Francesca kills the threat of the hive instead—the script's intimation that the bees *thought* her to death is not enough. In place of the sinister business of Ben's seduction, and his death (which would come as a result of Regina's use of him as a drone), we have Ben's ponderous declamation, which has the rabid overtones of a religious tract: "Ours is such a beautiful ritual, Regina," he growls in grief. "It happens only *once* in a person's life. It should, anyway... and no one, *nothing* can uproot that memory. No sudden, senseless tragedy, no willful murderer can rip it out and *desecrate* it!"

The contrast between Francesca's barrenness and Regina's thick sensuality remains, and Stefano cast Joanna Frank after seeing Elia Kazan's *America America*. "She had gotten literally cut out of it," he said. "She had maybe three scenes left. I had read her for 'The Man Who Was Never Born,' and didn't really like her for that." As he had with Sally Kellerman, Stefano saw possibilities in Frank's face, "... with those strange, big-almond kind of eyes." Frank met Stefano at the home of Tony Mordente and Chita Rivera. "We were out by the pool," she said, "and Joe Stefano came over the fence—literally!—to introduce himself, and everybody present wound up with parts in *The Outer Limits*."

John Brahm directed "ZZZZZ" while in his seventies. "Like Robert Florey and Laslo Benedek, he was in his twilight years," said Jack Poplin. A German emigré, Brahm is perhaps best remembered for his gaslight thrillers *The Lodger* and *Hangover Square*. His films in the horror field included *The Undying Monster* (1942) and *The Mad Magician* (1954) with Vincent Price. His prodigious work in TV included *Alfred Hitchcock Presents*, twelve segments of *Thriller*, and more episodes of *Twilight Zone* than any other director to work on that series. "When I went into television, it was for the money," said Brahm. "Including *The Outer Limits*, although it was something fresh, creative, and unusual."

"ZZZZZ" is a fragile narrative largely crushed under Brahm's leaden hand. Joanna Frank felt particularly abandoned and alienated on the set. "I didn't get much direction," she said, "except for once—the scene where I embrace the tree." This is the "pollination" scene featuring Regina in the garden. "[Brahm] just said, 'Go with your feelings,' and I went crazy overplaying it."

To Brahm, "ZZZZZ" was memorable for one reason only: "During filming, President Kennedy was assassinated." This news came to the cast and crew on the next-to-last day of shooting. "By the time I got to the studio, it looked like nobody was going to be able to finish the day," said Stefano. "Once they announced Kennedy was dead, I think it was about 11:30, I found that I really had to be the one to say we had to go on shooting and just not think about it. It would have been terribly demoralizing to just let everyone go home; you never would have been able to pick up again the next day." Joanna Frank recalled, "For some strange reason, all I could think of was that the country was going to collapse and all the banks would fail. So when we broke for lunch, I rushed down to my bank, thinking everyone would be reacting the same way, and wound up in line behind Sally Kellerman!"

In contrast, "ZZZZZ" inspired some of the wildest shooting notes ever typed by Robert Justman:

> Regina swings with her leitmotif: 'You Can't Beelieve that You're in Love with Me' –then she does the hucklebuck out the gate, leaving Ben onstage to do a single –beeing fresh out of material, he effoes into the house –Regina reappears and takes cover beehind a beegonia bush –but beefore we beegin Act IV, a few short words from our sponsors, the makers of Beeman's Gum and Beechnut Beebee Foods.*

Regina's attack on Francesca is "Beeological warfare," and Ben's discussion with Dr. Warren is done as a musical duet.

"ZZZZZ" was shot entirely on a massive interior set, including the two-story mockup of Ben's house and the full garden, all built by Jack Poplin on KTTV's Stage #4. Conrad Hall used a "sparkle-plenty" filter to lend Joanna Frank an otherworldly appearance, and devised the white spoke pattern seen in the iris of her eye. "Since her *look* was her performance," he said, "her lack of acting ability was well-concealed." But Regina's voluptuousness was not entirely the product of soft focus lenses. "I've always been rather, how you say, well-endowed," said Frank. "But for some reason I can't remember, I stuffed my bra full of nylon stockings for that show. There was a scene where I was lying on a table, and [Hall] complained that he couldn't see my face! He said, 'Can you do something about your, uh, tits?' And I started pulling out stockings and going, 'How's this?' And then I'd pull two more out."

"I thought the bee woman was extraordinary," said Meyer Dolinsky. "I met Joanna Frank outside the Writer's Guild Theatre, and that look she had, I think she came by naturally. Whether she was talented or not was very hard to tell. So much of talent is fortuitous, the parts you get, or how a director handles them."

"Every time 'ZZZZZ' is shown on TV, I get at least four phone calls from friends," laughs Frank. "And it's been what—twenty-one years, now? In the supermarket, people look at me funny, then they come up and say, 'Aren't you the bee girl?'"

*When a character exits in a Justman breakdown, they "effoe." In a Katzin one, they "f.o." Says Justman: "The object was to be as dirty as possible *without* being dirty, you know."

John Hoyt and Melinda Plowman find out what's in the box.

DON'T OPEN TILL DOOMSDAY

Broadcast 20 January 1964
Written by Joseph Stefano
Directed by Gerd Oswald
Assistant Director: Claude Binyon, Jr.
Director of Photography: Conrad Hall

CAST: Mrs. Mary Kry (Miriam Hopkins), Gard Hayden (Buck Taylor), Vivia Hayden/Balfour (Melinda Plowman), Emmett Balfour (John Hoyt), Justice of the Peace (Russell Collins), Justice's Wife (Nellie Burt), Harvey Kry (David Frankham), Dr. Mordecai Spazman (Anthony Joachim), Box Creature (Frank Delfino), Voice of Box Creature (Robert Johnson).

The greatness of evil lies in its awful accuracy. Without that deadly talent for being in the right place at the right time, evil must suffer defeat. For unlike its opposite, good, evil is allowed no human failings, no miscalculations. Evil must be perfect . . . or depend upon the imperfections of others.

The year is 1929, and somewhere on the outskirts of a town called Winterfield a wedding reception is going full tilt at the just-constructed mansion of young bridegroom Harvey Kry. A gift is delivered to the front door, and after confiding in his butler that he and the new Mrs. Kry are planning to sneak away, Harvey examines the gift, which bears a card inscribed DON'T OPEN TILL DOOMSDAY. Lying on a loveseat in the bridal suite where Harvey unwraps the box is a newspaper bearing the headline, NOTED SCIENTIST DECLARES COUNTRY INVADED FROM OUTER SPACE, with a picture of the man who delivered the gift—Dr. Mordecai Spazman, an ex-associate of Harvey's father, "Daddy" Kry. The gift itself is a box with a lenslike eye hole, into which Harvey peers and sees an amorphous, monocular monster, an alien who transports Harvey into the box and offers him freedom only if he will help it to reunite with others of its kind so they may "blend frequencies," forming a symphony of destruction whose purpose is to annihilate the universe. Harvey steadfastly refuses, and Mrs. Kry spends the next thirty-five years awaiting the return of her groom. To get him back, she needs someone else to replace him in the box. Enter two underage newlyweds, Gard and Vivia, who are directed to Mrs. Kry's house by the scheming wife of the local Justice of the Peace. Mrs. Kry, now slightly demented and still wearing her flapper gear, rents the pair her "unused" bridal suite, dustily preserved exactly as it was in 1929, including the "Doomsday" box still sitting on a table-load of unopened wedding gifts. When Gard steps out to park his car, Vivia peeks into the box and is absorbed. Her father, ex-DA Emmett Balfour, shows up in Winterfield, and using bribery and "big lawyer talk," learns the location of his errant daughter. When Vivia refuses to help the alien, Mrs. Kry tricks Balfour into the box, where Harvey (unaged in the box's timeless void) explains his predicament, and how he prevented Mrs. Kry from helping the alien by threatening to stop loving her. Balfour lies to the alien to free himself and Vivia. Gard gets Vivia clear of the house while the alien, realizing the deception, reabsorbs Balfour. While Gard and Vivia watch, the alien "uncreates" itself, the house, and everyone inside. The gift card reading DON'T OPEN TILL DOOMSDAY stands untouched in the ashes.

> *Without that deadly talent for being in the right place at the right time, evil must suffer defeat. And with each defeat, Doomsday is postponed... for at least one more day.*

"There's a part of me that likes to scare people," says Joseph Stefano. "It's like tickling somebody, the imp of the perverse. You get very evil; you can't stop. And if you really let yourself go, there's a tremendous deviltry in it. A lot of *The Outer Limits* was done to scare, to tickle, to upset people."

This handily sums up "Doomsday," in which the man who wrote love songs earlier in his career turned his eye to the psychology of sex and ritual and composed a symphony of bizarre, disturbing images rooted in Freudian symbology. Janglingly discordant, almost nonsensical as a linear story, it is a tapestry of metaphor representing Stefano at his most eccentric and daringly experimental, as he translates the loss of virginity into a horror story. Rife with free-associations on marital fidelity, nuptial customs, and sexual dementia, "Doomsday" is almost the flip side of the repressed attitude that governed "ZZZZZ."

"I was never really surprised by what I could pull out of myself," said Stefano. "I know myself well enough to have long since dealt with all my personal demons. I no longer hide from them. I think I tended to use, as a writer, things that came out of my sessions of analysis; things I wasn't terribly conscious of. Somebody on the series pointed out to me that all of my scripts have staircases in them—even to this day, to the script I'm working on right now."

The staircase in Mrs. Kry's house winds straight up to a purgatorial limbo of frozen time, where escape for Gard and Vivia (from Vivia's overpossessive father) could mean cosmic oblivion. The forbidding Kry mansion is both an externalization of her madness, like the House of Usher, and a boxes-within-boxes puzzle. The young lovers are drawn first into the Kry house, then the smaller box of the bridal suite, and finally the smallest box of all, where they find a squat monster who wants to wipe out the whole universe—a crystalization of the generalized "evil" mentioned in the Control Voice speeches, as well as a figurative devil inhabiting Mrs. Kry's figurative Hell. The alien is a mad amalgam of phallic/vaginal symbology, the physical nexus for the sexual fears that pervade the scenario. The script also employs darkly purposeful plot twists that lead to narrative dead ends... almost as though Stefano tossed in a few obscure or personal demons that remain inscrutable to the viewer. Small wonder, then, that TV viewers probably shared the confusion expressed by *TV Guide* critic Cleveland Amory:

> The way we understood it (and mind you, a child was helping us all the way), back sometime in the 1920s a young couple is given a wedding present in a box marked DON'T OPEN TILL DOOMSDAY. The bridegroom picks up the box and, looking through a hole in the side, sees a lizard. The next thing you know he is imprisoned inside the box, with the lizard. This greatly annoys the bride (Miriam Hopkins), and she turns into a recluse. She keeps the box in the house, however, for forty years, with her husband inside still in his wedding suit but growing older. Then appears on the scene a young married couple who want to rent a room. Miss Hopkins gives them the room with The Box, and the girl disappears inside. Next her father arrives, and *he* disappears inside. It is now becoming very lonely for those left outside, so the lizard projects some of his boarders back outside, where the young bridegroom and the father have a horrible row. The lizard grabs back the father, and the young honeymooners escape. Meanwhile, Miss Hopkins shows up all decked out in her wedding gown, ready to join her husband, who is still inside with the lizard. She begins to pound on the box violently and, as the boy carries the girl away in his arms to safety, the whole house blows up.
>
> One child we know told us the whole thing was symbolic. We asked him what of. "Why," he said, "it's the story of Lizard Taylor." Anyway, his guess is as good as ours.

Interpreted as a sexual nightmare, the episode becomes a different animal altogether. "It's one of the most overtly sexual shows of them all," said Stefano. "Most of it is conscious and deliberate, but there certainly are a lot of undercurrents in my writing that I don't become aware of until *after* the fact."

For one thing, the action is precipitated by not one, but *three* monsters, one for each "box" in the puzzle. The first is the unseen Daddy Kry, a beastly man opposed to Harvey's marriage, as Balfour is opposed to Vivia's. His box is the mansion, which he built for Harvey, Jr., as Mrs. Kry tells Vivia, because "He wanted us under *his* roof, where he could keep his cold, scientific eye on us." The newspaper in the bridal suite includes a subheadline that is barely readable: DR. MORDECAI SPAZMAN BRANDED 'COMIC STRIP FANATIC' BY ACADEMY PRESIDENT HARVEY KRY, SR.,—RESIGNATION DEMANDED. Spazman delivers living proof of the alien invasion for which Kry denounces him, trapped within a box that is the same kind of prison Kry intends the mansion to be for Harvey, Jr. We are told that the loss of his son broke Daddy Kry's heart, and so Spazman (pronounce it with a long *a* to get the pun) is avenged.

The second monster is Mrs. Kry herself, who is holed up in a house haunted by the past, the ghost of her own bridal suite. Like the house, her 1929 facade has been ill-maintained, and she is a gross caricature of her former self, just as Miriam Hopkins, the beautiful ingenue of Rouben Mamoulian's 1932 *Dr. Jekyll and Mr. Hyde* (itself a study of sexual stress), had put her glory days behind her by 1963. Gard remarks that Mrs. Kry's embalmed bridal suite "looks like a movie theatre somebody forgot to tear down." Mrs. Kry is quite insane as a result of putting her loss of virginity on hold for thirty-five years, and is by now determined to do anything necessary to complete her wedding night scenario, right down to pulling her decaying bridal gown out of mothballs for the climax.

This introduces the concepts of closing, or repeating cycles, and to this end Stefano imposes a consistent duality on his characters. There are two sets of young newlyweds, and the extreme youth of both brides is noted. Both fight to come to terms with their imminent wedding night duties, and both are harassed by overbearing father figures. Emmett Balfour serves as a reincarnation of the hated Daddy Kry, and the measures Gard and Vivia take to elude him call to mind Harvey's plan to escape with his "flaming youth bride." During Harvey's gambit to procure his car, he is sucked into the box, and during Gard's effort to park *his* car so it is hidden from view, Vivia is likewise absorbed. The Justice of the Peace and his hamster-faced wife represent what Harvey and Mrs. Kry might have aged into had their marriage proceeded along the usual mundane path. The Justice is thoroughly dominated by an old biddy who can't even stand up, the physical twin to Mrs. Kry's crippled emotional state (Stefano suggests, in his script, that Mrs. Justice's infirmity is "not apparent; probably nonexistent"). She and Mrs. Kry function in tandem to trap the scared-as-bunnies newlyweds, and both women even use the same phrases—"Let me steal a tiny minute," for example.* Both are

*Stefano also uses Mrs. Justice to harken back to *Psycho,* as she aims the newlyweds toward Mrs. Kry's while clucking her tongue about "those *disreputable* motels on the highway!"

sexless, antifeminine, contrasting Vivia's fresh-faced innocence. They are used up and dissipated while Vivia is positively embryonic, or, as Mrs. Kry would say, "inviolate." Vivia's name, the feminine configuration of the Latin *vivus* ("alive") puts her at the opposite pole from the obvious connotations of Mrs. Kry's name.

Pleasingly, all the male characters muster backbone by the final act. Harvey, Jr. remains altruistic and willful throughout, and it seems that the other men ultimately draw strength from his resolve. He has seen his bride become corrupted and strident over the years, a broken woman by virtue of her unbroken maidenhead. Since the alien has cheated Harvey of his wedding night, Harvey in turn denies it its own kind of consummation. The Justice finally stands up to his wife, and advises Gard to do the same to Balfour. When he does, Balfour has a change of heart and sacrifices himself to save Vivia. These denials of evil build quickly toward a literal climax—the big bang in which Harvey, the alien, and Mrs. Kry at last achieve some kind of release.

"The whole show, to me, was about frustration, about the failure to consummate *whatever,*" said Stefano. "Nobody is quite where they ought to be, or the *way* they ought to be, like the newlyweds who'd not done what they should have."

Seen in this light, the blatancy of the Thing in the Box becomes the hub on which another aspect of the story turns. Harvey quite pointedly falls into the wrong box on his wedding night, after letting his curiosity get the best of him and seeing a nightmarish distortion of the sex act awaiting him, he screams in terror. Gard—or "guard," from his footballing past—is the embodiment of letter-sweatered post–high school virility, and he has a long speech on this topic. It seems he has done battle for the right to deflower Vivia and won—his nose was broken recently by a sexual rival for Vivia's attentions. He proves himself an eligible substitute for Harvey as he breaks the bridal suite's carefully preserved hymen by forcing open its stuck door with his "strong, groomy shoulders." Mrs. Kry intends him to complete this symbolic penetration by trading places with Harvey inside the Doomsday box. But Vivia accidentally becomes a virgin sacrifice, of sorts, to it, and when she, like Harvey, Jr., chooses good over evil, the alien within decides enough is enough. Since it cannot "join" with others of its kind either, it wipes everything out in an onanistic cosmic orgasm that consumes Mrs. Kry not in an act of procreation but of "uncreation."

The episode's third monster is the alien, a feculent blob composed of grotesquely mixed male and female components. In its physical manifestation, the show's sexual double entendre reaches almost comical heights. Here for real is a one-eyed monster, with a stunted, penile "head" interrupted by a wide vaginal mouth. Near its base are a pair of slashlike openings that resemble an organic version of a female electrical outlet. Two pendant, breast-like protuberances hang near the thing's right "arm-

The Box Creature in all his/her/its phallic glory.

pit." The stumpy, waving arms feature three sausage-thick fingers each—pitchforks, perhaps, for this devil that waits inside Mrs. Kry's bridal suite box.

One consistency in the show is that nearly every line of dialogue carries a sexual alternate meaning (especially overt during the discussion of Gard's broken nose, and his command to Vivia to kiss it). Elsewhere, "Doomsday" is often like a cryptogram without a key. Stefano left open wide vistas of interpretation, making the show itself truly free-associative. Though its tone is reminiscent of "It Crawled Out of the Woodwork," it fits no formula seen in previous episodes. One similarity comes when the alien butts in with an explanatory speech, late in the fourth act:

> CREATURE: We came into your universe, each of us in his own ship, each ship containing the nonelements of the void from which we came. Our first target was this planet Earth. We were to rejoin here to blend our frequencies, but I had no experience with time and space; I lost my way. I became separated from the others. You must take me to them. That is what you must do. They are useless without me. I am the fundamental component. Mine is the lowest frequency in the complex vibration...
>
> HARVEY, JR.: The *annihilating* vibration.
>
> CREATURE: He wouldn't do it, but you will... won't you?

This speech is the point at which Leslie Stevens' hard science becomes Stefano's *weird* science. "Their plan was to first blow up the Earth, and then the entire universe," Harvey Kry, Jr. says with an absolutely straight face. Although Stefano deleted a line giving the motive for this alien plot ("Your universe intrudes on our void. We saw the need to uncreate it."), what the creatures gain by blowing up the universe, or why they must come first to Earth to do it, is unclear. How Dr. Spazman managed to capture and contain such a creature is also a mystery. If he imprisoned it inside the box, how did he handle it, and why wasn't *he* beamed inside? If the box is the alien's craft, what restricts it from flying away under its own power? Spazman and his own motivations are so vague that they are themselves almost wholly on the level of inference. More of Harvey's omitted lines help a little: "The man who found [the alien] tried to warn us. And my father branded him a madman. If spitefulness is madness, then he *was* mad. He brought this... this horror here... as a wedding gift." But the "science" in "Doomsday" might just as well be witchcraft, and when read at face value, the entire invasion scenario is laughably dumb and entirely unexplained. Stefano's interest was in a representation of absolute evil—thus, a being who wants to destroy *everything*—and the moral price exacted for defying it . . . or wanting to help it.

"Connie Hall and I gave the film a soft look around the edges which gave it an aged, antique feeling," said Gerd Oswald. "Composition and atmosphere are necessary in this kind of show. The setting was good and the macabre incidents were great, although the costume was a little ridiculous."

"That was the big glob with the eye, right?" chuckled Claude Binyon, Jr. "That was Frankie Delfino, one of the 'taller' little people, inside that suit." Binyon had worked his way up from the *Broken Arrow* TV series to feature work at Fox, and was brought onto *The Outer Limits* as 1st AD by Lindsley Parsons, Jr., his old military school buddy. For Binyon, "Doomsday" was ". . . wild. You know Joe Stefano saw all that stuff. He would never have any problem directing something he'd written, because he'd already 'filmed' the entire show on paper. That must be terrible, to edit your dreams and tighten them up. *The Outer Limits* must have been marvelous therapy for him."

Miriam Hopkins was one of Stefano's heroines from the films of the 1930s, big features like Lubitsch's *Trouble in Paradise* (1932) and *Becky Sharp* (1935). Parsons recalled, "She came in because the material was interesting to her, and she was an old pro who had been given the opportunity to play something other than run-of-the-mill cops 'n' robbers stuff. She never wanted her key light to drop too low; she'd keep telling Conrad Hall to 'Get *that* one up; get *that* one up!'" She also got to croon the only song lyrics Stefano would ever pen for *The Outer Limits: "Don't let your baby wait no more/Doomsday is knockin' at my door!"* This theme, another motif titled "Lonesome Time," and the Kry reception jazz (called "The Daystar Rag" by Roger Farris) were composed by Robert Van Eps.

One rumor that found its way around the set was that the sixty-one-year-old Hopkins "became" the mad Mrs. Kry while preparing for her role. "I got a call that Miriam didn't want to come down to the set," said Binyon. "I had to go up to her apartment and convince her to come. She didn't feel like working that day. And there she was, with cold cream on her face, and it was one of those weird moments, like a bad dream, trying to convince this star who was fading in and out of the real world that it was very necessary for her to come to the set, because there were a lot of people depending on her. She was unhappy with her life, and I was afraid she might decide to end it all any moment. I really didn't know. But she was a lovely person, never *angry* at any point. She had those problems, and depressions, partly because she was once quite beautiful, and it was hard for her to deal with the fact that those days were over for her."

Of casting Hopkins, Stefano said, "I usually had three names, and

I'd go after the top name first." In case Hopkins turned him down, the next name on the Mrs. Kry list was Jayne Meadows. "But I wanted Miriam first on that one. There were a lot of very good actors like her who weren't working, and I could never understand why. *The Outer Limits* was five or six days' work, and there was usually no reason for them *not* to do it. And we were able to get Miriam."

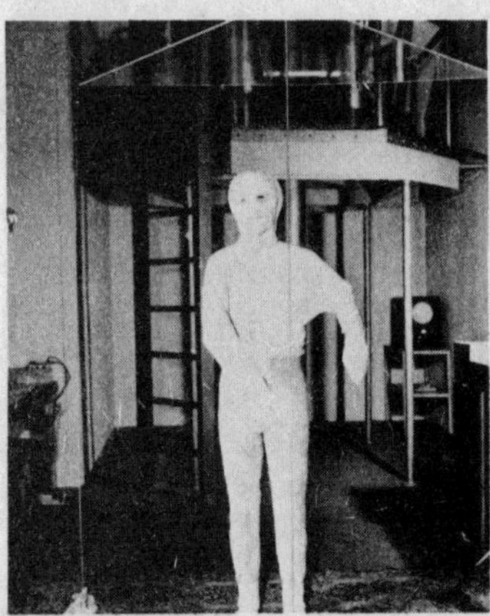

John Hoyt as the alien behind "The Bellero Shield." Note the sandbag stabilizing the Plexiglas screen, lower left.

THE BELLERO SHIELD

Broadcast 10 February 1964

Written by Joseph Stefano. Story by Stefano and Lou Morheim, loosely based on the Arthur Leo Zagat short story, "The Lanson Screen." Developmental writing by Perry Barry and Mort Lewis.

Directed by John Brahm

Assistant Director: Robert Justman

Director of Photography: Conrad Hall

CAST: Richard Bellero, Jr. (Martin Landau), Judith Bellero (Sally Kellerman), Richard Bellero, Sr. (Neil Hamilton), Mrs. Dame (Chita Rivera), "Bifrost" Alien (John Hoyt).

> *There is a passion in the human heart that is called aspiration. It flares with a noble flame, and by its light Man has traveled from the caves of darkness to the darkness of outer space. But when this passion becomes lust, when its flame is fanned by greed and private hunger, then aspiration becomes ambition—by which sin the angels fell.*

Inventor Richard Bellero's newest laser device does nothing to impress his militant-pacifist father, who intends to pass him over for the chairmanship of the Bellero Corporation. But the device *does* accidentally intercept a being from a world that "hovers just above the ceiling of your universe," a radiant creature possessed of keen perceptions and gentle mannerisms. For Richard it demonstrates the impenetrable shielding device that enables it to travel between worlds; clearly, the device could become the ultimate defensive weapon. Richard's greedy wife Judith sees the shield as the means by which to win her husband the chairmanship from Bellero, Sr., with whom she has been feuding hatefully for years. She shoots the alien, steals the device (a palm-button connected to a vein in the alien's wrist), and ditches the corpse in the wine cellar with the help of her sinister lady-in-waiting, Mrs. Dame. Then she demonstrates, to an astonished Senior, his son's "Bellero Shield." Once surrounded by it, Judith proves impervious to bullets and Richard's laser pistol, but her triumph curdles when she discovers she can't *remove* the shield, and her oxygen is going fast. The truth is exposed and Senior goes to the basement to view the alien. Enraged by his vituperative remarks about Judith, Mrs. Dame clouts him, and he tumbles down the stairs to sprawl atop the "dead" alien, whose eyes suddenly snap open! The mortally weakened being staggers back to the lab, still trusting, still innocent of how it has been used: "When she borrowed the thing, she accidentally broke the vein. My fluid is like your blood—the prime ingredient." So saying, it uses some of its milky blood to free Judith, then dies, vanishing in a dazzling burst of white light. A penitent Judith goes to her husband, but stops stock-still two feet short of him and begins rubbing her hands across a barrier that is no longer there while murmuring, "Nothing will ever remove it." Her experience has left her broken and insane, not unlike Lady Macbeth, and a very pointed close-up reveals a glowing smear of alien blood on the palm of her hand.

> *When this passion called aspiration becomes lust, then aspiration degenerates, becomes vulgar ambition, by which sin the angels fell.*

More a *classical* show than a classic one, "The Bellero Shield" is a stylistic vertex for *The Outer Limits*. It combines Shakespeare with ancient mythology, pulp science fiction, quasireligious overtones, and legitimate theatre via its "perfect number" cast of five and the stagey, embroidered quality of their performances. At times the dialogue seems hammy and intemperate, but since good theatre is not a reflection of the world, but a mirror distortion of it exaggerated for point-making purposes, the bigger-than-life nature of the players is fitting.

The episode is a thematic bookend to "The Galaxy Being," or perhaps the Stefano side of that Stevens coin: A starstruck scientist probes the heavens and accidentally intercepts a radiant, innocent, inquisitive alien. Both men have self-centered wives who crave power (Carol Maxwell wants to control the output power of her husband's radio station; Judith wants the power of patrician over prole). In Stevens's story, the Galaxy Being asks what an hour is and gets a dry, scientific calculation based on Earth's orbit time; when "Bellero"'s visitor asks Judith what a minute is, her reply is in poetic terms: "It passes unnoticed when you're content. For the needy it can be a string of endless lifetimes."

And like Stevens's misunderstood Galaxy Being, the alien "monster" here is far less monstrous than the human beings surrounding him. He is sympathetic, blind to the emotional maneuvering that eventually destroys him, and with his ability to sense human feelings and decode language through eye contact, he is *The Outer Limits'* most elegant visitor. While he is not supposed to be here, he nonetheless approaches the human strangers with a courtesy that, sadly, is never reciprocated. While not an obnoxious extraterrestrial invader, he is still doomed to pay heavily for his interaction with human beings.

While examining published science fiction on behalf of *The Outer Limits*, Lou Morheim found a novelette by Arthur Leo Zagat entitled "The Lanson Screen" (first published in the December, 1936 *Thrilling Wonder Stories)*. In the story, one Professor Henry Lanson invents "a dimensionless shell through which energy cannot penetrate." A military liaison named Thompson sets up a demonstration in which Lanson will throw his spherical screen around Manhattan in return for one million dollars. "If knowledge of this were universal," Thompson muses, "there could be no more war." But during activation of his device, the obese Lanson falls from a platform and crushes his skull. Manhattan is cut off from the rest of the world until the shield is finally dissolved in 1997. It is discovered that the imprisoned city suffered a catastrophic fire that burned up all the oxygen within the domed shield.

Morheim and Stefano brainstormed a storyline together, retaining the ideas of the shield itself, and air running out inside of it (while trapped, Judith says, "Movements and words accomplish nothing, and only deplete the oxygen and the soul."). Thompson's pacifistic bent was carried over to the Bellero, Sr. character. The story was given to writer Perry Barry, whose first draft proved unsatisfactory. The script and story were passed on to a second writer, Mort Lewis. "Lewis's draft never materialized into an acceptable script for the show, either," said Morheim.

"When Lou came back with the second writer," said Stefano, "I remember saying, 'What I really want to do here is a 'haircut' of *Macbeth,* and *I'll* do it.' I saw it as a vehicle for Sally Kellerman, as Lady Macbeth." He completed his teleplay four days after "ZZZZZ" began filming.

Apart from rendering the Bard into *Outer Limits* terms, Stefano injected significant jolts of Norse, Greek, and Biblical mythologies into the story, starting with Judith's evocation of the Bifrost, the "Trembling Way" that is a rainbow bridge that leads from Asgard, abode of the Norse gods, to Midgard, the world of mortals. Judith calls the shield "*our* Bifrost ... to what for me would be heaven—power, far-flung holdings, undiminishable authority." The Bifrost is guarded by Heimdall, who, like the alien, is painfully perceptive (Heimdall can hear the sound of grass growing, and see the wool curling out from the flesh of sheep).

The Bellero name seems derived from the Greek story of Bellerophon, son of Poseidon, great grandson of Atlas. His greatest wish was to ride Pegasus, the winged horse, and with a golden bridle given to him by the gods, he tames the creature and embarks on many adventures (he is the man who slays the Chimera). One day he decides that there is only one height left to conquer, and tries to fly over Mount Olympus. Zeus is stunned by Bellerophon's arrogance and literally knocks him off his high horse. Like Richard, Bellerophon "roams the globe in sadness for the rest of his days."*

The straightforward Biblical allusions are framed by the Control Voice speech on sinning angels. The alien is himself an angelic being who falls to Earth from a place of light. He is murdered, entombed and resurrected, to give of his blood in a sacrament-like act that frees Judith. Before seeing the visitor as a "monster," Mrs. Dame calls it a ghost, fearing that it is proof of life after death, and thus, her imminent damnation for previously murdering her "human monster" of a husband. She asks if the alien is "... something dead? That won't die?" Judith replies, "No, it isn't a specter, Mrs. Dame. It's real. And it's alive. And it's *ours*."

The top-notch cast were all veterans of previous *Outer Limits* episodes, save one. "I put the Chita Rivera character in," said Stefano. "Without shoes. No one would've written that part but me." Originally, Rivera asked for the part of Judith, and not her barefoot confidant. We are introduced to the gypsylike Mrs. Dame feet-first, as the camera follows her feline paces at floor level. She always seems to be lurking in the shadows, like a black-clad animus for the white-clad Judith, waiting to dispense advice on homicide and packing a snub-nosed revolver in her garter. Stefano's inspiration for these "white" and "black" murderesses in cahoots (along with the business of disposing of pesky corpses) was drawn from the Henri-Georges Clouzot thriller *Les Diaboliques* (1955), which would soon be addressed on a greater scale in Stefano's script for his supernatural series pilot, *The Unknown*.

Sally Kellerman runs the full distance with the plum part of Judith Bellero. Ambitious and manipulative, Judith infuses Richard with false emotional strength while twisting the psychological thumbscrews that keep her in control. There is a faint whiff of a lesbian relationship with Mrs. Dame that perhaps allows Judith to maintain a normal (i.e., mundane) wife-husband role with Richard. She is a fighter, and down into her world slides a serene alien whose nonviolent honesty undoes her. Here is a being she cannot control, or, seemingly, kill, since she shoots it with both the laser and the revolver and it keeps coming back. We find Judith's worry about the madness that will eventually claim her presaged in two bits of dialogue cut from the script. "Mrs. Dame tells me I see

*Bellerophon is coincidentally the name used for the colony ship in the film *Forbidden Planet*, which is itself a "haircut" of Shakespeare's *The Tempest*.

potentials that don't exist," she says. "Perhaps I'm beginning to see other things that don't exist." And later, as she implores Richard to call Senior as a reliable witness to the alien's passage: "Who'll believe we aren't three benighted idiots, three hallucinators?"

The lustiest, most arch-Shakespearian line of the whole show goes to Neil Hamilton, in his dour portrayal of Senior. "Great men are *forgiven* their murderous wives!" he says proudly, after Mrs. Dame tells him about the dead alien. This is his last line before his own death.

Though Richard and the alien appear victimized by the squabbling, ambitious personalities surrounding them, they are in fact driven by a selfishness of their own—the eager scientific curiosity that blinds them to more immediate hazards. Their intentions are benevolent, though, with the alien's seraphic nature denoted by its gentle speech and radiant presence, which brings a spiritual "light" to the gloomy Bellero manse. "That was one of my favorite aliens," said Stefano. "John Hoyt did a beautiful job of that."

Director John Brahm and Stefano wanted the creature to glow as if illuminated by an inner light. "We did a lot of experimentation on that," said Gene Warren. "We tried Scotchlite, a beaded front-projection material invented at 3M. It reflects light, but the problem was that it has only a one-degree angle of reflection, so if [the camera] didn't hit it at that exact angle, the shimmer effect was lost." Since both the alien and the camera had to move around a lot, Scotchlite was abandoned.* As an alternative, Conrad Hall used a blob of vaseline on a pane of glass, held in front of the camera and kept in line with Hoyt's movements. "The light reflected through the vaseline and spread out in emanating rays," said Hall. "I was careful not to use too much vaseline, so you don't realize that the creature alone is out of focus." Hall called the task of aligning the glass with Hoyt's carefully programmed movements "some of the most incredible technical problems I've ever dealt with." The shield itself was a V-shaped pane of plexiglas upon which the handprints of the actors can frequently be seen, and which wobbles visibly if someone moves past it too fast.

Working with stronger material here than in "ZZZZZ," Brahm's direction is more impressive. "Through my background in the theatre," he said, "I found the humanist approach was more important than the special effects of that show. I enjoyed dealing with human expressions, human emotions." While a broad success in dramaturgical terms, "The Bellero Shield" shunts aside the science aspect as never before—whenever a character is about to illuminate something technical, another character intrudes to shove the explanation into irrelevancy. When Richard offers the alien a quickie rundown on lasers, we cut to Judith and

*This expensive technique was exhumed for filming the glowing costumes worn by the denizens of Krypton in the film *Superman* (1978).

Mrs. Dame before he can say anything meaningful. Similarly, the alien's departure deadline has something to do with the parallax between Earth and somewhere else, but this revelation is overridden by Judith, who interposes to tell Richard he is a fool. More than staying clear of scientific explanations, Stefano was now playfully batting them away. In "The Bellero Shield," the play is definitely the thing.

Getting into the Unknown

The completion of "The Bellero Shield" in mid-December, 1963, was followed by a short Christmas break in production, during which Stefano applied his energies to his last original script for the series, "The Forms of Things Unknown," titled again after Shakespeare. ABC President Tom Moore asked him to convert it into a pilot for a supernaturally-oriented suspense series, and by New Year's Day Stefano had completed two versions—a science fiction one, intended as an *Outer Limits* episode, and *The Unknown*, the sort of densely-packed Gothic fever dream he felt he could really go all-out with.

By early 1964, Moore was very interested in acquiring some of the audience *Twilight Zone* was pulling in for CBS, and later offered to buy that series when it was cancelled at the rival network. *The Unknown*, as it turned out, was not what he was looking for.

But *The Unknown*—both versions—gobbled up most of January, 1964, and Stefano found his hands quite full. Normal *Outer Limits* segments were in production simultaneously, shows that he could spend little time supervising, or editing, due to the attention demanded by his *magnum opus*. The two episodes that filmed in the midst of *The Unknown*—"The Children of Spider County" and "The Mutant"—suffered from this piggy-back approach, and were additionally handicapped by being done by "leftover" elements of the Daystar crew not working on Stefano's two-way episode/pilot.

Stefano's notorious twenty-hour workdays could be stretched no further. "Ideally, if I ever do another series, I would not like to do a pilot at the same time," he said. "Because things *do* get away."

William O. Douglas as Aabel.

THE CHILDREN OF SPIDER COUNTY

Broadcast 17 February 1964
Written by Anthony Lawrence
Directed by Leonard Horn
Assistant Director: Wilson Shyer
Director of Photography: Kenneth Peach

CAST: Ethan Wechsler (Lee Kinsolving), Aabel (Kent Smith), John Bartlett (John Milford), Sheriff Simon Stakefield (Crahan Denton), Mr. Bishop (Dabbs Greer), Anna Bishop (Bennye Gatteys), General (Robert Osterloh), Mr. Greenbane (Joe Perry), Military Intelligence Officer (Roy Engel), Aabel as Eros Creature (William O. Douglas, Jr.).

In light of today's growing anxieties, it has become more absolute that the wealth of a nation consists in the number of superior men that it harbors. It is therefore a matter of deep concern, and deeper consequence, when four of the most magnificent and promising young minds in the country suddenly disappear off the face of the Earth...

Ethan Wechsler, whose unusual mental abilities have earned him the label "witch-boy" among the local hambones in rural Spider County, is being detained on a trumped-up murder charge until a weird, insectile alien shows up to rescue him from his police escort. Assuming the form of a cultured, white-haired gentleman, the alien hastens Ethan away to sanctuary. Meanwhile, the US Space Agency has noticed a peculiar pattern of disappearances among four of the nation's top scientists: All were born prematurely, within the same month, and in Spider County. Ethan is the fifth member of this group, having never left his birthplace. The alien, Aabel, explains that he is Ethan's missing father; that he and others came from a planet called Eros to interbreed with humans to produce male children, something no longer possible on that planet. He has come to take Ethan home, but Ethan resists the idea, having roots and a girlfriend in Spider County. Aabel, who would rather destroy Ethan than abandon him to the "dogs and desperation" on Earth, tries vainly to convince him to make the trip voluntarily. When Ethan chooses to face the "neat and legal" justice of Earthmen, Aabel cannot bring himself to kill his son, who is the better half of himself, the "dream part." Ethan is gifted with the ability to dream—the loss of which, Aabel claims, is responsible for the barrenness on Eros. Aabel leaves emptyhanded (the other four fatherless geniuses also stay behind), and it is clear that the Space Agency plans to intercede on Ethan's behalf in the murder charge.

> *The wealth of a nation, of a world, consists in the number of superior men that it harbors, and often it seems that these men are too different, too dreaming. And often, because they are driven by powers and dreams strange to us, they are driven away by us. But are they really so different? Are they not, after all, held by the same things that hold us—by strong love, and soft hands?*

Unlike the smooth transition from script to film undergone by his previous *Outer Limits* tale, "The Man Who Was Never Born," Anthony Lawrence found his intended followup, "The Children of Spider County," a story about the ostracization of the gifted, to be an experience fraught with problems.

"'The Man Who Was Never Born' was from *me,*" Lawrence said, "whereas 'Children' was blocked out in a sitting with Joe Stefano and Lou Morheim. We had difficulty pinning it down. It was a difficult story, and I had trouble with it."

Having been involved with George Pal's proposed film of Olaf Stapledon's pioneering 1936 novel, *Odd John,* Lawrence began with themes from the book.* "It's one of my favorite stories," he said, "and I've always been intrigued by the 'superman' theory." Stapledon's superman is an intellectually superior being seeking a state of enlightenment and truth called "the way of the spirit." For the inhabitants of Eros in "Children," this became a drive to recapture the lost "dream part" of their makeup, and was summed up in another splendid *Outer Limits* alien speech delivered by Aabel, just prior to his obliteration of Anna's father, Mr. Bishop:

> AABEL: You called my special and gifted son a 'no-good dreamer.' In our world, on the planet Eros, it was the absence and abhorrence of dreaming that made men no good. They worked like insect slaves. They fought

*After seeing David McCallum's performance in "The Sixth Finger," Pal cast him as the lead in the *Odd John* project... which, sadly, was never produced.

> evil wars. They gathered lush riches and splendid pains, but they took no time out for dreaming, and dreaming became a lost art. And, as always happens, they began to die off. For all their riches, they began to die. No male child had been born in many years. The seed that spawns the male had retreated in sorrow, faded out of this dreamless race. The wise ones thought it was the climate, so they sent five of us here to prove that in a more favorable climate, the males of Eros could again produce males. Perhaps they were right. Perhaps it was the climate that enabled us to produce sons... but I do not think so. I think it was because, while here, we once again caught the fashion of dreaming. [Ethan] and the others will start a new race for Eros, a race of men who cannot help but dream, who have the dream machine in their human half, and call it 'soul.'

A series of multiple revisions pared away both good and bad aspects of the story. The first draft, for example, is much more violent. Ethan is being detained for the murder of one Jonathan Stimpson, whose jaw he is said to have broken in three places before setting him afire. This established a recurring fire motif Lawrence intended as a keynote for each appearance Aabel makes in alien form. Ethan and the other Eros-spawned boys are supposed to have burned down the local schoolhouse at age eight, and Aabel is seen "bursting into flame" before running the sheriff's car off the road. All that is left of the sheriffs are outlines of char on the upholstery. Mr. Bishop's original death scene was equally gruesome:

> Aabel raises his arms, begins to glow like a lit coal. Bishop freezes, hand outstretched; he staggers back, shocked. Suddenly, out of the coal-like glow, the monster form of Aabel appears... approaches Bishop, touches him. And Bishop bursts into flames, and is incinerated. Only a charred outline remains on the foyer floor.

Also deleted was an entirely gratuitous attack by Aabel on a Forest Service watchman, who gets fried just for being in Aabel's way. The revised Aabel is determined, authoritative, yet more humane, and even slightly misguided. Kent Smith's sharp Aryan countenance and deep, full-bodied voice lend his portrayal of Aabel a nobility that is darkened by a tinge of dead earnestness.

The original script concludes with Aabel simply wandering off into the woods, with detectives chasing after him. The Stefano-inspired rewrite resolves the Aabel/Ethan relationship by permitting Aabel to admit defeat and go home.

There remains a flabbiness to the story, however. No sense of geography is imparted to Ethan's flight from the lawmen; the viewer quickly gets the impression that Ethan, Aabel and Anna are going around in circles since they never seem to get too far from town. Mr. Bishop never has any trouble finding the fugitives, though—he pops in, gets hypnotized by Aabel, pops out, then pops back in long enough to get killed. Bishop himself is irritatingly inconsistent. Ethan relates how the Bishop family never feared him, and took him on as a farm hand when everyone else in Spider County was superstitiously afraid. Surely Bishop knows of Ethan's romantic involvement with Anna. Yet he goes gunning for Ethan repeatedly, mindlessly, without ever once asking this young man, whom he probably knows better than most people in town, whether he's innocent, or what his story might be.

Aabel ducks in and out of Ethan's flight path without a clue to his location, either, and while there is an attempt to inform this father-son relationship with a sense of Ethan's dawning awareness of his own unique nature, the interminable cut-aways to the alien Aabel stomping through Tarzan Forest at MGM give the impression that the filmmakers just wanted to get on with the monster movie.

Fred Phillips "suits up" Douglas on the "Spider County" set.

"That monster was merely gratuitous," said Lawrence, not surprisingly. "It was added to please the network." The head, hands, and feet of the Eros Creature were another sculpting job by Wah Chang, who took his inspiration from the "insect slaves" line and made Aabel's face an exoskeletal, bug-eyed thing with mandibles. The first time we see this creature incongruously clad in a suit and tie, it *is* a startling sight; thereafter, the immobile mask is intrusive and phony-looking. The angular, armored face creates another plot-hole, to wit: If Aabel is Ethan's dad, why can't Ethan transform into a mantis-faced alien? In "The Man Who Was Never Born," Andro used hypnotic suggestion to appear human; it is never clear whether Aabel does this too, or actually changes his physical make-up. Andro suggested clothing along with his human guise; Aabel apparently brought his coat and tie with him from Eros.

The much-revised teleplay proved too much to handle for one-time *Outer Limits* assistant director Wilson Shyer, and some action described in newer drafts never found its way into the shooting breakdown sheets, meaning that the production crew wasted time setting up scenes that were no longer part of the script. "Wilson Shyer... did not work out," sighed veteran 1st AD Robert Justman. Much of the show looks cheap or hurried, shot on-the-run with no leeway for the artful concealment of mistakes (like the large and obvious shadow of the camera truck speeding alongside Sheriff Stakefield's car). Since *The Unknown* was using up the KTTV soundstages, studio time for "Children" had to be booked elsewhere, and to reduce costs it was decided that all the show's interiors had to be filmed in a single day at Samuel Goldwyn Studios. There was just too much to shoot, so director Leonard Horn restructured some scenes to be done outdoors... and that got him in trouble with Joe Stefano.

"Leonard played what I thought was a very important scene between the father and son with them coming out of a barn, going in and out of doors, and climbing a ladder. When I saw the dailies I was hysterical; I thought, *how* are we going to hear the dialogue when we're watching people running? It was all important stuff, and it was too late to go back and shoot it again, so I was very disturbed. In the script it was a straight scene of two people in a room; Leonard moved them out of that room. Now, I think there are times when you've got to see a close-up of a person saying something so it'll register, just to indicate its importance. Instead, you get the line while a car is running by. I see this today: A director will get bored, or scared he can't maintain interest in a scene where there is nothing to do except sit and watch actors act. So he makes the viewer into two people—one watching and one listening. And that's a conceit I detest. I think Leonard was afraid to play a scene between two people that ran for more than two pages, and that changed the show unproductively."

Allan Balter, who was at this time rewriting the next show on the production roster, "The Mutant," offered an alternate perspective on Horn's dilemma: "Joe was overcome by the authority of being in the captain's chair, and laid down difficult rules, such as *no script changes on the set without his approval*—then he wasn't available when you wanted to follow his rules by clearing it with him. Lenny Horn in particular ran afoul of this." Horn's changes were not wrong, but they were not what

Stefano had envisioned. "I felt secure going in with Leonard," Stefano said, "so I could pay more attention to *The Unknown.* On 'Spider County' I did miss the kinds of conferences I usually had."

As of "Children," the look of *The Outer Limits* also changed permanently as cinematographer Kenneth Peach signed on. Peach had been shooting *The Long Hot Summer* series at Fox when it was cancelled, and Stevens hired him to fill in when Conrad Hall began working on *The Unknown.* Like Byron Haskin, Peach had developed process photography techniques in the 1930s, and brought to *The Outer Limits* his expertise with in-camera optical tricks. With Peach, the visual identity of the show became more standardized and workmanlike, almost monochromatic. When supervised by a director like Gerd Oswald, Peach's work could appear "arty" enough; otherwise he did not attempt to emulate what Hall and Nickolaus had done before him. He had no time to be fancy—he was to shoot all the remaining first season episodes, and all the second season shows yet to come. His son, Kenneth, Jr., became an assistant cameraman on *The Outer Limits* as well.

"In a two-shot, I preferred to face the actor against the key light," said Peach. "In standard lighting, all cameramen use that, with variations. I've always found TV difficult unless I used a reference light to throw off greys; I concentrate toward basic blacks and whites. I did strive to get whatever light effects or mood called for by the script. I listened to suggestions, and my suggestions were always listened to. I did my job and that was that."

Described by Lawrence as "Lincolnesque and loose-jointed," Ethan was played by Lee Kinsolving, known at the time for his portrayals of alienated, rebellious teens in such films as *The Dark at the Top of the Stairs* (1960) and *The Explosive Generation* (1962). Two weeks after "Children" finished shooting, *Twilight Zone* featured him as one of a trio of alien bikers in an episode called "Black Leather Jackets." Lawrence notes that "I named the character after my son, Ethan, who was then just-born. My wife and I are writing together now and we've just named another character Ethan; I must've used that name a dozen times through the years."

Despite the four-script deal Stefano had made with Lawrence after "The Man Who Was Never Born," this would be the writer's only other *Outer Limits* show. Lou Morheim asserts that "We were very impressed with Tony," but Stefano adds: "The problem was that Tony was busy fulfilling four-script deals on other shows, like *Ben Casey,* so he never brought anything else in to us." At this time, Lawrence was also working on the script for the Elvis Presley film, *Roustabout.*

What did Lawrence think of his parting shot on *The Outer Limits*? "It was interesting," he said, "but I wasn't terribly excited by it."

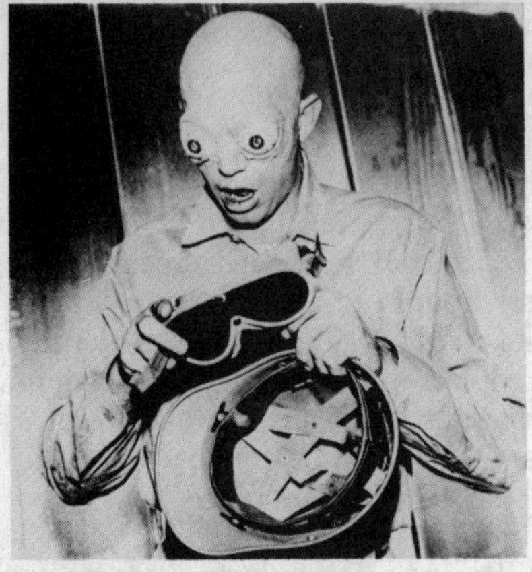

Warren Oates unveils himself.

THE MUTANT

Broadcast 16 March 1964

Written by Allan Balter and Robert Mintz. Story by Joseph Stefano and Jerome Thomas, based on a treatment by Ellis St. Joseph. Developmental writing by St. Joseph, Victor Stoloff, and Betty Ulius.

Directed by Alan Crosland, Jr.

Assistant Director: Phil Rawlins

Director of Photography: Kenneth Peach

CAST: Dr. Evan Marshall (Larry Pennell), Reese Fowler [Botanist] (Warren Oates), Julie Griffith [Biochemist] (Betsy Jones-Moreland), Dr. Frederick Riner, MD (Walter Burke), Prof. Henry LaCosta [Meteorologist] (Herman Rudin), Lt. Peter Chandler [Biologist] (Robert Sampson), Philip "Griff" Griffith [Biochemist] (Richard Derr).

At this very moment, our horizon is menaced by two explosive forces, both man-made. One is a deadly wonder; the other, wonderously alive. Both forces have compelled Man to reach out for worlds beyond his own, new worlds where he may find peace, and room to grow. This is the first of those new worlds. The United Nations of Earth have claimed it, and called it Annex One. It is almost identical to Earth, except that there is no night—sunlight is constant. Early reports from the small expeditionary team stationed on Annex One indicated that the ancient planet appeared suitable for colonization by Earth's overflowing population. But the most recent reports have contained unspoken, oddly disturbing undercurrents, and the United Space Agency has decided to investigate. The man chosen: Dr. Evan Marshall, psychiatrist…

When Dr. Marshall's shuttle lands on Annex One, he is greeted by the outpost team, who all wear densely-tinted goggles to protect their eyes from the planet's fierce sunlight. Philip Griffith, leader of the team, has recently died and there remains no trace of his corpse. During introductions, botanist Reese Fowler refuses to shake Marshall's hand, and with good reason: The radio-isotope "rainstorms" on Annex One have caused Reese to mutate into a bug-eyed, bald semihuman who can exist without sleep, read minds, and kill by touch. When Griffith proposed to abandon Annex One as uninhabitable, it meant leaving Reese behind, and Reese touched him, causing "the atoms of his being to explode." Reese has terrorized the colony into staying mum and remaining on Annex One to keep him company. When he reads the mind of biologist Chandler and finds an intention to slip Marshall a note revealing the truth, he kills Chandler. While attempting to treat Reese's condition, Dr. Riner finds that darkness causes Reese intense pain. Since there is no night, a hidden cave provides the colonists' only refuge from Reese, and when Prof. LaCosta is killed there by a mutant insect, Julie Griffith's screams bring Marshall running to the secret place. There, Riner tries to secrete the facts on Annex One and Reese into Marshall's mind via a posthypnotic suggestion, so that Reese, thinking Marshall knows nothing, will allow him to return to Earth. But the ruse fails; Riner is injured during one of Reese's treatments, and spills the plan before dying. Reese locks Marshall and Julie out of the hut prior to an isotope rainstorm, then chases them to the cave. He attempts to follow them inside, fixating on the single candle flame that is the only light source there. He accidentally snuffs out the candle, and howls with pain as the darkness snuffs *him* out.

> *The forces of violence and the forces of nature compel Man to reach out toward new horizons, where peace and sanity may flourish, where there is room to grow. But before we run, should we not first make certain that we have done all that can be done here to end madness, quiet the disturbers of peace, and make room for those who need so little to grow in?*

To explode the cliche about success, "The Mutant" had many fathers and was *not* one.

"There was a time I called the Hot Period," said Stefano. "It was when I was crazy about a story and felt the writer could deliver a script which we could put into production two weeks later. Now, suppose the first draft comes in and needs work. It's still hot. If the second draft still needed changes, it wasn't hot anymore. I would tell Lou Morheim, 'I have cancelled this script in my mind... but see if you can *ever* get it to work.'"

After completing "The Sixth Finger," writer Ellis St. Joseph pitched two more ideas to Stefano. One was a fragment concerning a civilization held under martial law by a computer. The other was a thirty-five-page treatment set aboard a gigantic satellite in deep space. "It housed terrestrial life and contained an artificial sun," said St. Joseph. A scientist at the outpost has a freak encounter with an alien phenomenon that touches off his psychological disintegration. He does not change physically. "At the end of my story," St. Joseph said, "the Earthlings and satellite are completely destroyed." Though the scenario was too expensive for even a generous *Outer Limits* budget, Lou Morheim bought it and assigned it to Jerome Thomas, who reworked the story with Stefano's input. By the time it sifted down through the typewriters of Victor Stoloff and Betty Ulius (one complete draft each), the Hot Period was over as far as Stefano was concerned.

The interior panoramas of the satellite were rendered down to a more simply-filmed forest world, the hundreds of colonists were reduced to seven, and Reese Fowler's mental breakdown was changed to give *The Outer Limits* the monster that was expected of it. "If you have a good script," said Stefano, "You can take away anything you want and it still works. This was not a good script."

The shuffled pack of ideas was then handed to Allan Balter and Robert Mintz, cowriters of "The Hundred Days of the Dragon." "The Mutant" had been assigned a Daystar production number in June, 1963 (while Leslie Stevens was finishing "Controlled Experiment"), and a finished script was not filmed until March, 1964.

Beyond the mechanical, ten-little-Indians plot, there is a half-hearted attempt at a subtext involving the human need for night, sleep, and dreams, all of which have been denied Reese, with the result that his "dreams" become the thoughts of his fellow colonists, who all want to kill him. Marshall's hypnotic experience is a kind of "sleep" Reese cannot penetrate, and when Julie awakens him from his trance she says, "Maybe you were dreaming when I stumbled upon you in the forest." When Riner dies, his last words are, "Sleep... sleep," as he repeats the hypnotic patter he used on Marshall. When Chandler dies, Reese reads his thought that *"It's only going to be like night... a long night, to dream in."* This is the conclusion of the episode's best scene, a weirdly sadistic number in which Reese unveils his deformity for the first time, then forces Chandler to eat the desperate note intended for Marshall.

Originally, Prof. LaCosta dies from exposure to the isotope-rain in a fallen-to-ruin temple built by Annex One's earlier inhabitants. This was changed to the cavern-sanctuary, where he is killed by the bite of an ant brought unknowingly along on the Earth ship (there is no native animal life on Annex One)—an ant that, like Reese, has mutated. Rather than tripping over LaCosta's corpse, Julie finds him menaced by a recycled Zanti Misfit, which permitted a more frantic Act Two break. The cave itself was the famous Bronson Caverns location in Griffith Park, seen in virtually every science fiction film and TV show ever produced.*

*To cite two examples from hundreds, it is the cave in which the Venusian teepee monster hides in Roger Corman's *It Conquered the World,* and the "mine shaft" in which Miles and Becky hide from the Pod People in *Invasion of the Body Snatchers.* If the science fiction genre is ever to have a shrine, it should be Bronson Caverns. Visit it for free the next time you're in Los Angeles.

Cut from the script was a poignant and frightening speech that expands Reese's human dimension:

> REESE: I didn't want to come up here. In the deepest, truest part of my mind, I didn't want to come. But Griff was my friend, and Julie was my friend... they wanted me to come with them, the way friends always want friends when they go somewhere new, and exciting, and just a little intimidating. And so I let them persuade me. And I was glad I did. I made more friends. I've always liked having lots of friends. I would have died for you—gladly, for any one of you. But when you die for someone, it ought to be fast, sudden. It shouldn't be a lingering death. It shouldn't be lonely, should it? Maybe, before it comes—*if* it comes—one of my friends will find a way to prevent it. One of you might. If you try; if you're *here* to try. That's why you ought to be here, to try to prevent my death. Or, at least, to bury me... if you can't.

Ultimately, the new, improved Reese is too powerful a monster for any gambit by the colonists to succeed, making the business of the cave hideout incredibly contrived, and Reese's death in the darkness, while an evocative image, an unsatisfying conclusion to the story. If any of the colonists had thought to lock Reese in a dark room, or bring along a pistol to Annex One, the whole mess would have been resolved in seconds.

Marshall's shuttlecraft is the spaceship mockup from "The Man Who Was Never Born" with a new paint job, and Project Unlimited did the "isotope rain" effect by sifting metallic dust through a high-intensity light—a technique later picked up for use as the "transporter" effect in *Star Trek*. A more interesting visual tidbit is the presence of a crate clearly labeled "Daystar" seen in several shots beneath the cot of space colonist Robert Sampson.

During this cutback period on *Outer Limits,* Stefano's team handled some procedural problems in the most direct way imaginable. "For instance," said Tom Selden, "we were sending to the network scripts on which Joe had already done two levels of rewrite, and all the pages they saw were white pages. They didn't understand why they weren't getting blue pages, or pink pages.* What we were doing, of course, was saving time and money on mimeographing. Joe sent ABC the drafts he wanted to go with, and they couldn't handle that, and felt that in order to earn their pay they had to pick at *something.* (To ABC, the all-white scripts showed no evidence of having been revised at all.) I don't recall who

*Each generation of script revisions is done on a new color of paper to differentiate it from the like-numbered pages in the previous draft.

came up with the idea, but eventually we'd just divide the script up and mimeo some pages on white, some on pink, and some on blue, and send it in *that* way. Then ABC was happy; then they left us alone."

"'The Mutant' was probably the worst show we did," said Stefano. "Just terrible. I didn't care for the cast on it, either." To be sure, Betsy Jones-Moreland and Larry Pennell are another *Outer Limits* Odd Couple that makes the show look like a dated 1950s science fiction film romance, but Walter Burke's performance as the bearded Dr. Riner is respectable, and that of Warren Oates (another *Stoney Burke* veteran and Daystar regular) is impressive despite the pitfalls of being a literal BEM, or Bug-Eyed Monster. The extreme makeup restricts him to using only his mouth expressions and voice to convincingly portray a man driven crazy by his nearly limitless power over his companions.

The mutant eyeballs described in the script *("huge, oversized orbs criss-crossed with a network of ugly red veins")* were vacu-formed at Projects and delivered to Fred Phillips, who recalled, "I'd first seen the fake eyes the night before shooting and thought, what the hell are we going to do with *these*?" He used mortician's Dumo Wax to arch Oates's brows into the contours of his face, but the heat out in Bronson Canyon caused the wax to "sweat." Melted droplets of it can frequently be seen on Oates's face. Phillips noted that "I had to use a strong sealer to keep the eyes from popping off in the middle of a take." Which they did, many times, to the weary hilarity of cast and crew.

"I or one of the crew would always come up with these pet names for the 'bears,'" said Stefano. "And the right one always stuck. Because of those eyes, Warren was forever known as the Fried Egg Monster."

Janet DeGore and Don Gordon puzzle out their new and improved Space Ride.

SECOND CHANCE

Broadcast 2 March 1964
Based on "Joy Ride," a script by Sonya Roberts, revised by Lou Morheim. Teleplay credited to Lin Dane (Roberts) and Lou Morheim, from a story by Lin Dane.
Directed by Paul Stanley
Assistant Director: Claude Binyon, Jr.
Director of Photography: Kenneth Peach

CAST: Dr./Capt. Dave Crowell (Don Gordon), Mara Matthews (Janet DeGore), Empyrian (Simon Oakland), Arjay Beasley (John McLiam), Sueann Beasley (Angela Clark), Buddy Lyman (Yale Summers), Donise Ward (Mimsy Farmer), Tommy/"Nebs" Shadbury (Arnold Merritt).

When fear is too terrible, when reality is too agonizing, we seek escape in manufactured danger, in the thrills and pleasures of pretending—in the amusement parks of our unamusing world. Here, in frantic pretending, Man finds escape and temporary peace, and goes home tired enough to sleep a short, deep sleep. But what happens here when night comes? When pretending ends, and reality begins?

Amusement park patrons given free passes to Joyland's spaceship ride unexpectedly find themselves aboard a *real* flying saucer, bound for a planet called Empyria and piloted by a pedantic alien prone to lofty speech-making. He has abducted this "psycho-organized" group of people "with the least to lose" to colonize an Earth-type asteroid called Tythra, which is destined to collide with Empyria eighty-two years hence, and set in motion a billiard ball chain of events that will result in Empyria colliding with Earth. Together, the alien reasons, his race and Earthlings suited to Tythra's environment—the abductees—can work to prevent the catastrophe. But most of the passengers aren't too thrilled by the prospect of abandoning their lives on Earth ... with one exception. Dave Crowell, an unemployed astrophysicist who moonlights as the space ride's captain, is intrigued by the proposition, which causes the others to see him as their enemy. When they try to kill him, the Empyrian intercedes. Crowell points out that most people don't *want* a new life, no matter how petty or empty their old life was, or a second chance to redress the failings of those old lives. If the Empyrian was to state his problem openly, Crowell says, he'd reap a whole shipload of willing volunteers, not the "discontented dreamers" currently aborad. The Empyrian agrees, and reverses course to return the abductees to Earth.

*Doctor Crowell was right—they came. Not people in need of a second chance, but those who would give that chance to Earth, and to their children's children.**

"I asked Simon Oakland if he would do an *Outer Limits,*" said Joseph

*When broadcast, "Second Chance" featured no closing Control Voice speech. The lines quoted here are from Sonya Roberts's original script.

Stefano, "and he said, 'Only if I can play the monster.'" Stefano had suggested Oakland to Alfred Hitchcock for the part of the psychiatrist who appears in the final moments of *Psycho,* and though totally unrecognizable except for his distinctive voice beneath his Empyrian makeup, Oakland delivers a sincere and moving performance. The vehicle for this performance, though, was shaky and superficial.

"ABC was looking for some kind of hype that would elevate our ratings," said Lou Morheim. "They felt the way to do it was with monsters and simplistic stories. Some of our shows were extraordinary in concept; the level of imagination was very high—and ABC was afraid of them." "Second Chance" was, therefore, heavily geared toward what Morheim called "the large, young, broad-based audience that would buy more simplistic material."

The original script was Sonya Roberts's "Joy Ride," and its basic plot is identical to that of the ironically-titled rewrite done by Morheim. The difference was that Roberts provided pages of character development, sharply individualizing the abductees; while it approaches the silly plot in a manner intelligent enough to put off anyone seeking a mere hour's worth of monster shenanigans, it is written perceptively enough to be clever rather than offensively smart. In "Second Chance," for example, the Empyrian forces Arjay Beasley to buckle his safety belt by hypnotizing him with his all-purpose alien medallion. Here is how he does it in "Joy Ride":

EMPYRIAN: Would you be good enough to fasten your seat belt?

BEASLEY: Now, ain't no use carryin' things *that* far!

EMPYRIAN: How can you enjoy a space ride if you won't pretend it's real?

BEASLEY: I didn't say that! I'll pretend it's for real. All of it . . . except the belt. Why, heck, I'll even pretend *you're* for real!

EMPYRIAN: That's exactly what I was going to suggest. And if I'm a real space being, then I have to be armed with a real space weapon.

BEASLEY: One of them death rays!

EMPYRIAN: Splendid! Now, let's say this space being—me—points his death ray at you (as he draws a slim weapon from his belt and aims), and says, "I give you three seconds to fasten that belt . . ."

BEASLEY (enjoying this hugely): Or if I don't?

EMPYRIAN (theatrically): Then I'll burn you to a cinder!

BEASLEY: A cinder! (slaps his knee, laughing) I just *knew* you'd say that! (he begins to buckle up, still laughing) I *knew!*

EMPYRIAN: Thank you for allowing me to spare your life!
BEASLEY (gasping with laughter): Don't mention it!
MARA (shaking her head): Talk about a method actor...

"Second Chance" divides into equal parts bathetic soap opera and the galvanic stimuli of TV violence, with its science fiction needs served by the hoariest cliches in the field—such as the obligatory meteor shower crisis, which pitches everyone around and changes nothing, or the man-sucked-out-the-airlock routine, which provides a juicy death to hold the audience through the Act Two commercial break. While Roberts parodies such dramatic standbys, Morheim frequently falls back on them and uses them straight. In "Second Chance," as the Empyrian walks around Joyland handing out free space ride tickets, he scares the wits out of whoever he encounters by appearing suddenly. When Crowell and Mara first spot him in "Joy Ride," their reaction is not knee-jerk terror but growing awe as he saunters up wearing a sandwich board that reads GREETINGS EARTHMEN, I AM FROM THE PLANET EMPYRIA IN OUTER SPACE. "Second Chance," on the other hand, is overloaded with feminine screaming—the kind intended to tell viewers that what they are seeing is a horror movie, instead of showing them. Morheim does acknowledge the thematic richness of Roberts's draft, but conventionalizes the characters and shakes out most of the emotional depth. One place where this worked to advantage was a long speech by Crowell about his disinclination to work as an astrophysicist for the government. Morheim condensed this down into a single pithy and amusing line: "I wanted to go off somewhere alone, where I could unravel the mysteries *I* preferred—the ones that mystify the heart, not the Defense Department!"

"Joy Ride"'s abductees are all young, vigorous, idiomatic American types: Buddy, Donise, and Tommy are the Football Hero, Prom Queen, and Number One Gofer; the Beasleys are illiterate hillbilly newlyweds; Mara Matthews, the "space stewardess," is living the cliche of the actress-between-jobs. Morheim changed the Beasleys to urban burnouts in their late forties, with Arjay becoming a Willy Loman caricature. Mara becomes an artist who cannot sell her paintings—curiously retaining the artistic aspect of the character while removing all her pretentiousness. In "Joy Ride," Tommy is indicted by the Empyrian along with the rest: "Would you ever have learned that a man never stands deeper in shadow than when he attempts to crowd the limelight of heroes?" In "Second Chance," he exists solely for the purpose of getting sucked out the airlock.

The germ of "Second Chance" has nothing to do with kidnapping. It has everything to do with Disneyland. Roberts calls it Jollyland, Morheim calls it Joyland, but the idea for this story could only have come from a person who had visited the Magic Kingdom, strapped themselves obediently in on the Flight to the Moon Ride (since updated to a journey to Mars), and thought, *What if this thing was to take off, I mean,* really *take off*? This was just the sort of "hook" that would appeal to Stefano, and the overlay of the second chance theme sealed the plot, as all the characters work at, or visit, the park to avoid confronting their failures, or the myths they've spun from their lives. Once the "illusion" of the flying saucer becomes real, they attempt to take control of their lives through acts of violence. The abduction theme harks back to "A Feasibility Study," but the show really has more in common with "The Mice," which also featured a lone alien on a mission that is terminated because the aliens do not bother to ask for what they want. Like "The Mice," "Second Chance" also suffers from the "dangling guard" syndrome: The first thing we see the Empyrians (in Roberts's script there are two) doing is vaporizing a night watchman, about whom no further mention is made. The guard is only included in the story as the butt of some monster business, allowing the "bear" to come onstage and do something monstrous right at the beginning of the show, even though this action completely contradicts the Empyrian's basically benevolent character. If nothing else, "Second Chance" is structured to be extremely commercial TV entertainment.

The business of assembling the abductees into the saucer absorbs an entire half-hour, and then Act Three crams so much action into fifteen minutes that the viewer will presumably be too overwhelmed to ask questions... such as how the plywood-and-plastic Joyland flying saucer could ever be made spaceworthy, not in a matter of hours, but years. And surely Empyrian technology could find an easier way to divert Tythra from its collision course than by coming all the way to Earth to seed the asteroid with human beings. It is better to savor Simon Oakland's performance as the Mr. Spock-like alien than to question the hazy and illogical motives for his mission, which are laid down in a typically grandiloquent *Outer Limits* soliloquy.

EMPYRIAN: To me... to every member of my race, the dark airiness of the universe was once an endless, laneless thoroughfare, unrestricted and harmless. In some fanciful flight of evolution, we Empyrians, like the birds of your own world, were given the freedom to soar above our destinies. And, like the men of your world, we chose to discard the greater part of that freedom to confine ourselves to a single star—a planet we call Empyria. In some of us, the soaring freedom still lives, and must be employed to distract disaster from the rest of us... I have been here a long time. I've studied the human specimen. So many long to soar. Great expenditures are directed toward the leaving of Earth. And yet, in all the minds I probed, I found not one genuine desire for total freedom. None

Simon Oakland in 1963.

Wah Chang's sketch of the Empyrian.
(Courtesy Wah Chang)

Simon Oakland in costume.

What the costume looked like with the beak.

of you, it seems, truly wants to leave this troubled star.
And so, regretfully, abduction became necessary.

Apparently, most Empyrians are constitutionally incapable of migrating from their homeworld, thus their need for Earth people to handle Tythra. Morheim dropped Roberts's idea that our atmosphere, and Tythra's, are poisonous to the Empyrians, who have sent one of the few with the "soaring freedom" on a suicide mission, with only six months to live, and, it is hoped, save all of Empyria. This omission confuses the plot and makes the Empyrians seem less noble. Roberts retaliated to the massive changes worked on her script by substituting her pseudonym, Lin Dane (subtract the capital letters) for the onscreen credit line.

Paul Stanley, an ex–*Stoney Burke* director, made "Second Chance" his *Outer Limits* debut via Leslie Stevens. Here his work is competent but flat; he would soon do more visually interesting material in "The Guests." Don Gordon takes his limited role as far as he can, and Simon Oakland has a grand time with the monster role he asked for and got. "The *logic* of human thought evades me," says the Empyrian, shaking his head. "How could I be so wrong about people?" A veteran of *Twilight Zone* and one of TV's most familiar character faces (including a role as the ultimate monster skeptic, Tony Vincenzo, the long-suffering editor of newshound Carl Kolchak on *The Night Stalker*), Oakland here hides his face and credibly portrays a troubled and desperate alien.

Unfortunately, Project Unlimited took a literal cue from the "soaring freedom" speech, and the mask produced from a sketch by Wah Chang was an outrageous feathered contraption that was originally to have sported a beak! The script was no help, describing the aliens only as *slant-featured, stylized, not so much ugly as totally unearthly.* Ugly was the right word for the mask. "I had to rearrange the feathers and add a nose just so you could tell it was a face," said Fred Phillips. Oakland's performance is slightly sabotaged by this mask, and an ill-fitting costume that makes his burly form look spindly-legged and top-heavy, like a pouter pigeon. "That mask got joked about a lot," remembered Gene Warren. "We called it Chicken Little." It was reused in a second season show, "The Duplicate Man," in which a foot-long beak was added—showing how silly the idea looked in the first place. Projects also provided the flying saucer shots, which look majestic as the ship soars away from Earth, and ridiculously cartoony a few moments later, when it ping-pongs around in the grip of the meteor storm.

At worst, "Second Chance" is an unusual script made routine, a procedure that would be reversed with the following episode, "Fun and Games." While "Second Chance" fails to convincingly answer the question of why aliens possessing a superior technology and a sensitive intellect would ever need human beings, "Fun and Games" provides the only answer that makes any sense: They need us for kicks.

Bill Hart brandishes his pre-*Road Warrior* boomerang.

FUN AND GAMES

Broadcast 30 March 1964
Written by Joseph Stefano, from a Robert Specht script titled "Natural Selection." Story credited to Robert Specht; teleplay to Robert Specht and Joseph Stefano.
Directed by Gerd Oswald
Assistant Director: Phil Rawlins
Director of Photography: Kenneth Peach

CAST: Mike Benson (Nick Adams), Laura Hanley (Nancy Malone), Voice of Anderan "Senator" (Robert Johnson), Male Calco Galaxy Primitive (Bill Hart), Female Primitive (Charles MacQuarry), Detective (Ray Kellogg), Poker Dealer (Read Morgan), Sharpie [the assassin] (Harvey Gardner), Sharpie's Voice (Vic Perrin), Poker Players (Theodore Marcuse, Charles Horvath, Jack Perkins, Buzz Henry).

> *There was a moment in time when those who were brilliant and powerful also were playful, and when they took recess from their exhausting and magnificent strides toward glory, they replenished their darker passions with fun and games. On the planet Earth, such games have been civilized, and drained of all but their last few drops of blood...*

The Senator, a sporting alien representing the citizenry of a planet called Andera, abducts Mike Benson, an ex-boxer and small-time hood, and divorcée Laura Hanley, "electroporting" them to an arena planet where they are to be pitted in battle against two hissing, ornithic primitives from the Calco Galaxy. The goal of this contest is survival; the stakes are the home planet of each team, with the world of the losers to be obliterated in a display lasting five years, for the further enjoyment of the Anderans. The male Calco creature takes an early lead by murdering its own partner to double its food supply. Mike and Laura learn some brutal truths about themselves in the thick of combat, and learn to function together instead of quarreling. When the opponent corners Mike on a footbridge spanning a bubbling river of lava, Laura retrieves its weapon, a sawtooth-bladed boomerang, and kills the creature. Mike slips and plummets into the lava after it, but as the Senator points out, "Survivors need survive only a split moment to be considered survivors—rule of the game." He returns Mike and Laura to Earth, intact and wiser, then sets about devising new diversions for his audience of Anderan thrill-seekers.

> *The struggle for survival goes on, on all levels of existence. Surrounded by the vastness of the universe, Man tries to illuminate its pathways and make a place for himself in it. One day he will journey afar into its great darkness. Let us hope he brings with him the human qualities of friendliness, compassion, and love. And let us hope even more that in his future contest for existence, such qualities as these will be of profound and everlasting importance.**

Once *The Unknown* was completed, Joseph Stefano turned his attention to a script purchased in December of 1963. Written by Robert Specht, "Natural Selection" opened with a shot of bacteria greedily devouring each other, and a Control Voice speech on survival of the fittest. Then we are introduced to Mike Adams, a computer expert working for the United Nations, who walks through his office door and into a vortex of blackness where he meets Em, a powerfully-built alien who informs him he is Specimen #172, and is ready for "testing." Mike meets Loris Harper, a medical missionary who has been Em's captive for two days, and together they fight off a flying jellyfish monster as their first test. When Em is satisfied that the pair are hardy survivalists, he tells them that his home world is equidistant between Earth and Andera, one of which will have its population exterminated to make room for the spillover from Em's world. Mike and Loris are to fight two Andrites on an arena planet, armed with pistols that fire explosive charges. The male Andrite murders its partner, and Mike pretends to do likewise to lure it out of hiding. He trips a snare, is gaffed by a homemade spear, loses his pistol, and tumbles over the edge of a cliff. As he hangs onto the ledge, bleeding to death, the Andrite emerges to finish him off. Loris grabs the fallen gun and shoots the Andrite in the chest. Later, Mike tells Em that perhaps his kind could colonize Earth peacefully: "You're not that much different." Em says, "Unfortunately, we are," as he reveals his *true* appearance—that of an intelligent ape. "*Could* our people live side-by-side, Mr. Adams? Or would yours consider us a mistake of nature? Spare yourself the embarrassment. We will leave the answer to the future."

*When broadcast, "Fun and Games" featured no closing Control Voice speech. The lines quoted here are from Robert Specht's original script.

Stefano saw the shortcomings in "Natural Selection" right away. *The Outer Limits* had more than its share of Earth takeover plots. There were so many different aliens and visual tricks called for that costs would have been prohibitive, and Em's degeneration into his anthropoid stage was too much like the ending of "The Sixth Finger." Among the dramatic deficiencies were the testing procedures Mike undergoes, which were too complicated, redundant, or riddled with technical gibberish ("I have an almost perfect specimen; variance of minus .003; 3⁄10 of 1 percent.").

Hart poses with *Outer Limits* Script Supervisor Hope McLachlin on MGM Backlot #3. (Courtesy Darren Raley)

Stefano's revised plot imposed a bread-and-circuses aspect on the humans versus monsters contest; certainly the notion of aliens decadent enough to blow up the Earth "like a firecracker in a black summer sky" just for chuckles is more refreshing than aliens who want to make us slaves, eat us, or claim dibs on our real estate. The plot of both scripts also has a lot in common with the famous Fredric Brown story, "Arena," which may have inspired Specht, although Stefano had never read it. "My knowledge of science fiction at that time was *The Martian Chronicles,*" said Stefano, "so, frankly, you could have sneaked it by me. I don't know whether you'd've gotten it past Leslie or Lou."

As protagonists, Stefano substituted Mike Benson, an ex-pug who turns up his nose at a second chance but turns out to be the tarnished hero type, and Laura Hanley, a scared fugitive from a less-than-sterling marriage. The line that points up the polarity of their relationship was altered by one of ABC censor Dorothy Brown's infamous phone calls. Originally, the Senator says that Laura is "relatively unspoiled, and will reap the rewards of innocence. You, Mr. Benson, are the net result of all the *spoiling* things in your world..." As "unspoiled" and "innocence" struck Brown as being too sexual in nature, the words were changed to "trusting" and "faith" (and as Mark Twain wrote: "Faith is believing what you know ain't so").

The character of the Senator is Stefano's trump card. Coolly mocking, with a bemused humor that is alternately cruelly sarcastic, then penetratingly insightful, the alien cackles like a B-movie villain, relishing an unshakable sense of his own superiority. He never rises from behind his control console, a black spider in an electronic web, who with ringmaster flourish directs attention by pointing his slim baton or twisting his control dials with fingers featuring curved mandarin fingernails of ebony (surely a hallmark of a hedonistic culture). He takes great pleasure in manipulating the conflict so it provides the maximum entertainment value for his Anderan audience. When the boomerang-wielding alien is about to kill Laura, the Senator freezes the time sequence in order to interrupt with some delightfully nasty recriminations:

> SENATOR: Oh, I can't let you kill her just yet. She hasn't *begun* to suffer! Mmm-ha-ha-ha! Miss Hanley? Wasn't it our understanding that you and Mr. Benson were a *team*? You've run away *again*, haven't you? Why have you run away from him... so that he can eat all the food, or so that he can do all the fighting? Your heart is a bottomless box of virtuous motives, isn't it? Whatever you do, you do for someone *else's* good, *don't* you? Your husband didn't want you to *mother* him, *Miss* Hanley, he wanted you to help him! Ah-ha-ha-hah! It hurts to admit that you're afraid you can't help someone, *doesn't* it?

Likewise, he shrugs off Mike and Laura's hard-won victory: "Well, what's the difference who saves the human race? The dull fact is, it's been saved."

The "game" that begins the show is a tense hand of seven-card stud that results in Mike being framed for the murder of the Dealer. "I'm very fond of that poker game," said Gerd Oswald. "I felt I shot that very interestingly." To do it, he cut the center out of a large table and dropped in a camera with an eighteen-millimeter wide-angle lens that imparts a fisheye effect to the visage of each player as it pans in a slow, low-angled circle in the dark and smoky room.

MGM's Tarzan Forest became a primordial alien jungle in which Oswald and Kenneth Peach set up shots of Mike and Laura running with the sun behind them, a tree between them and the camera, and smoke pots. The result is a halated silhouette effect that is dreamy and unreal. Oswald's almost total lack of lighting in the Senator's chamber helps conceal the fact that the alien's head is a recycled mask from "Nightmare." The two alien primitives were done by Projects from specifications in the Specht script. One would reappear (without its bulging rubber eyes and with an added mane of hair) two years later in the *Star Trek* pilot, "The Cage."

Stefano stretched Oswald's minimal footage in the editing room, creating his own sort of "bottle show." Thanks to the plot, which keeps jumping back to the time of the Dealer's murder, Mike's panicked search for a hiding place in Laura's apartment building is seen three times, and many of the shots of the action on the arena planet are seen twice. If you look fast enough, you'll notice that when Laura is "electroported" the second time, she's still wearing her dress from the first trip. Even though the repeat shots are numerous and noticeable, the episode gallops right along.

Nick Adams in 1962.

Nick Adams, as Mike, enthusiastically makes like Brando and epitomizes *The Outer Limits'* brief romance with "alienated youth" characters (like Lee Kinsolving in "The Children of Spider County" and Geoffrey Horne in "The Guests"). Adams, late of *The Rebel* series, got the part after it was turned down by Clu Gulager, Rip Torn, and George Segal, and his performance is aggressive and full-bodied.

But the real star of the show is still the Senator, and the reason is Robert Johnson, who was called to postdub *all* the alien's lines when the actor on the set did not perform to Stefano's expectations. It's easy to imagine Johnson leaping from his accountant's desk at Daystar to run upstairs every so often to tape dialogue. "I remember sweating that show out," he said, "because it involved very long speeches, and I was totally surprised when I got it. I hurriedly read through the script the night before I was to do it, and had no idea of how the guy before me had read it. It was about twenty minutes of straight dialogue! And since Joe had not been too happy with the first guy, he sat over my shoulder while I read. I tried to keep myself inside the kind of feeling he wanted, and I've always had a few reservations on whether I 'hit' the script Nick Adams and the others had already done." Johnson's rendering is sonorous and flamboyant, his derisive laughter gutsy and full-blown, and the alien speeches found in "Fun and Games" are possibly the best of the entire series.

Nellie Burt.
(Courtesy Claude Binyon, Jr.)

THE GUESTS

Broadcast 23 March 1964
Written by Donald S. Sanford. Based on a teleplay by Charles Beaumont titled "An Ordinary Town."
Directed by Paul Stanley
Assistant Director: Claude Binyon, Jr.
Director of Photography: Kenneth Peach

CAST: Wade Norton (Geoffrey Horne), Theresa "Tess" Ames (Luana Anders), Florida Patton (Gloria Grahame), Ethel Latimer (Nellie Burt), Randall Latimer (Vaughn Taylor), Dr. C. Ames (Burt Mustin), Voice of Brain Creature (Robert Johnson).

("The Guests" features no Control Voice narration.)

After nearly running his jalopy over an ancient old man on a country backroad, drifter Wade Norton seeks help and comes upon a foreboding mansion occupied by a quartet of eccentrics: shady financier Randall Latimer; his shrewish, nagging wife, Ethel; faded film queen Florida Patton; and Tess Ames, a young woman pictured inside a locket belonging to the old man. Once inside the house, Wade finds that the doors and windows have been replaced by smooth, blank walls—there is no exit. He is drawn upstairs by a pulsating alien brain in the attic, which lays bare his mind to dissect his emotional reactions to his predicament. The brain means to construct an equation using such human emotions as fear, anger, and despair as factors, with the product equalling the ultimate destiny of the human race. While all occupants but Tess seem content to remain prisoners of the brain, Wade discovers that each has a personal exit door. They stay inside the house because they do not age—for all the years the brain has been calculating its seemingly irresolvable equation. Tess falls in love with Wade and struggles to convince him to leave the house before he is trapped there by his own vanity, as the others have been. She reveals that the old man in the road was her 120-year-old father, and when Wade refuses to leave because of his feelings for her ("There's nothing out there for me, either," he says), she uses her own doorway to escape. In seconds she withers (somewhat inexplicably) to dust. Wade remains inside, where the brain informs him that this new, hitherto undetected emotion—the love between Wade and Tess—is the missing capacity that completes the equation and offers hope for humankind's survival. It commands him to leave. As Wade walks out into the sunlight, the brain vaporizes, consuming the house and the selfless, loveless people still within.

It is no accident that the gloomy, baroque quality that pervades "The Guests" is evocative of an episode of *Thriller,* which had been cancelled about a year prior to the broadcast of this episode. The teleplay was by Donald Sanford, who was commissioned by Lou Morheim on the strength of his *Thriller* work, which included such classic episodes as "The Incredible Dr. Markesan" and "The Cheaters."* The genesis of "The Guests" is about as convoluted as a *Thriller*-type mystery, as well.

Stefano had been on the lookout for story material with a heavier-than-usual emphasis on the Gothic, to provide director Curtis Harrington with an *Outer Limits* vehicle (and perhaps in anticipation of doing *The Unknown* as a regular series). He had been quite impressed with a nightmarish piece of low-budget filmmaking done by Harrington in 1961—*Night Tide,* an offbeat interpretation of the Lorelei myth—and invited the director to visit the *Outer Limits* set during the filming of "Don't Open Till Doomsday."

Fantasist Charles Beaumont, who supplied *Twilight Zone* with many of its most memorable teleplays, had pitched and sold to Stefano a script titled "An Ordinary Town"—dated January 3, 1964, at which time the writer was fast in the grip of Alzheimer's Disease (finally diagnosed in May of that year, he was given three years at most to live). It is possible that "An Ordinary Town" was written from a Beaumont outline, or completed by one of his many ghostwriters, which at the time included Richard Matheson (who approached Seeleg Lester, *The Outer Limits'*

*Sanford scripted fifteen episodes of *Thriller,* some of which were directed by Laslo Benedek, John Brahm, and Robert Florey, all of whom participated in *The Outer Limits.*

second season story editor, seeking to write a script on Beaumont's behalf in order to help pay his friend's enormous medical costs), William Nolan, Jerry Sohl, John Tomerlin, Ray Russell, and Ocee Ritch. The storyline hews quite closely to that of an hour-long *Twilight Zone* Beaumont had written a year earlier, "Valley of the Shadow," in which a newspaper reporter becomes trapped in an isolated rural community that keeps the benefits of a miraculous technology (possibly brought by aliens) stringently to itself. "An Ordinary Town" substitutes two protagonists and makes the alien influence a gigantic brain that controls the town. The only thing carried over from Beaumont's script to Sanford's is a shot of the alien brain sitting massively atop a hill where a mansion is supposed to be.*

Except for this image, "The Guests" is entirely Sanford's story (he asserts that when he sought a second season *Outer Limits* assignment, the Beaumont script was again offered to him for revision by Seeleg Lester). His final draft needed so little revision that Stefano neglected to tack on the customary Control Voice speeches. Like many *Outer Limits* shows, "The Guests" adds a monster element to a story that does not really require it; unlike them, the gargoyle in residence at the mansion forms a subplot almost totally apart from the main story, a meditation on dreams and self-deception in a house where time stands still. The brain creature's quest for emotion-factors is motivated by scientific curiosity, making the alien the seeker for a change, although an aggressive, obnoxious one, and making the house a sort of petri dish into which it has unfortunately collected the wrong ingredients. Occasionally, the episode has difficulty balancing the two extremes—the musty, drawing room drama versus the quivering, gelatinous brain that chuckles like an Inquisitional torturer and belts out lines like, "Let me *dissect* it! Let me *absorb* it! *Bring your brain here!*" But the swing between what goes on in the attic and in the parlor is rhythmic, pendulant, itself dreamlike.

Dreams and illusions are the story's main concern. Latimer preserves the illusion of his innocence on fraud charges by remaining in the house and not completing a 1928 business trip that surely would have resulted in a guilty verdict. Ethel stays with him because, as she says, "A wife's duty is to share her husband's life sentence." She really stays to needle the others with their pretensions. Florida Patton stays to preserve, or rather, embalm her lost stardom, and freeze in place the beauty that had begun to deteriorate in 1935. As for Tess, she explains, "My father was a resigner. He saw this as a way of resigning from the human race. He asked me to stay, and I stayed because he needed me to."

One of the first things Wade says after entering this house is, "I feel

*It gets even more curious. Frank Belknap Long, a poet, horror writer and confidant of H. P. Lovecraft, claims (in an interview published in the January, 1982, issue of *Twilight Zone* magazine) the episode is based on his short story, "Guest in the House," although there is no similarity between it and "The Guests."

as if I'm having a bad dream," and this becomes the story's *ostinato*. When the brain creature "anesthetizes" Wade's fear, he enters a state of dreamlike passivity, and the alien's pat explanation of its purpose sounds as insane as the tacit lunacy of nightmares. After his first brain-picking session, Wade asks, "Have I lost my mind?" The others agree enthusiastically, just as they did when he asked if he was having a bad dream—since to them, it's all the same thing. "My husband thinks you and I and this fine actress are figments of his imagination," chirps Ethel. "He expects to wake up one day and be right back where we were when this grisly dream started. We've been in this house since 1928—*no* dream could last that long." When Wade takes her to task, she hits him with a hard dose of reality as well:

> ETHEL: Are we deliberately remaining here, complaining, fighting, and clawing at each other's souls? Why should *you* care? You're not one of us; you're *above* us! You're a special and gifted dreamer chasing a rainbow no one else believes in, much less sees. The reason you drift is there's nothing heavy in your noble heart to anchor it in reality. But you're *scared*, young man. You begin to suspect *you*, don't you? You're not so sure you won't just plunk yourself right down here and dream a life. And live a dream..."

Geoffrey Lewis and Gloria Grahame.

Wade's "dream" is Tess: "I looked at your picture in the watch case," he says, "and I heard a pain in my heart that was the sweetest hurt in all the world. Is that when the dream began? This *is* a dream—isn't it?" Tess urges Wade not to live this dream, saying, "Go now, while your life can still be lived, while you're *real*... I'm an illusion. They're so easy to lose." Then she proves it by crumbling away to dust. It seems unlikely that she would disintegrate if her father was only 120 years old, unless she really is a figment of Wade's imagination, his literal dream girl. Then the brain sends him away, saying, "Go out of this dream, Mr. Norton," before "undreaming" the mansion, just as it undreamed the doors through which Wade enters.

Apart from Robert Johnson's lusty vocal performance for the brain creature, the best of "The Guests"' fine performances is that of Nellie Burt, a stage actress of long standing Stefano had also cast as Mrs. Justice in "Don't Open Till Doomsday." She is perfect as the punishing Ethel, and sometimes, perfectly beastly. "Shut up, Randall," she warns her husband, "Or I'll be *nice* to you." Gloria Grahame is an eerily appropriate choice for Florida. An ingenue of the 1940s, she won a Supporting Actress Oscar in 1952 for her role in *The Bad and the Beautiful.* Geoffrey Horne is adequate as another of *The Outer Limits'* Angry Young Men, and Luana Anders was cast through Curtis Harrington, who'd used her in *Night Tide*. She'd also appeared in Roger Corman's *The Pit and the Pendulum* (1961) and an early Francis Ford Coppola film, *Dementia 13* (1963).

But Harrington was not to direct the episode. "Curtis would have been fantastic," said Stefano. "But Leslie still had a lot of directing commitments to people from *Stoney Burke;* he owed Paul Stanley shows. He kept telling us we didn't have room; could we wait until next season? Paul Henreid was going to do a show for us; that fell apart, too." Another *Outer Limits* directing hopeful at this time was Stefano's assistant, Tom Selden.

Paul Stanley availed himself of some unusual techniques, proving he was no slouch with Gothic trappings, either. The "corridor of lights" in which Wade gets hopelessly lost was a small glass painting. "We literally 'built' that set with lights," said Claude Binyon. "We used a piece of glass about ten inches by six, representing a set that would have been about eighty by twenty *feet.* The corridors were painted on the glass. We had to film very carefully, because any camera motion would have caused our 'set' to shake all over! Kenny Peach came up with the idea." Another cost-cutting measure was the reuse of the top portion of the costume from "The Mice," oiled down and given the benefit of low-angled horror movie lighting for its new role as the pulsating brain creature. For the shot of the house dissolving, a Project Unlimited painting of an actual, hemispherical brain was superimposed over the mansion on the hill.

Sanford secured a two-story deal with Daystar, but his second *Outer Limits* treatment never appeared. Years later, while both Stefano and Harrington were connected with Universal Studios, Stefano would do some developmental writing on a film project for the director. "It was the story of a man who invites a group of people to a weekend house party and blackmails them all," said Harrington. "But all the things he blackmails them for, nobody cares about today because there is so much more freedom now. The times made the story completely invalid."

The title of the film? "The Guests."

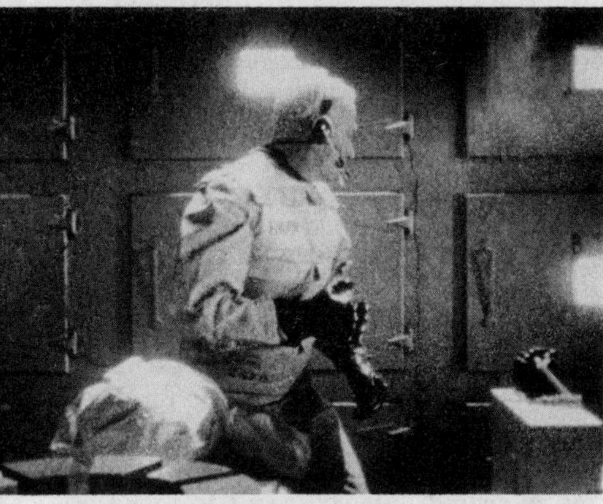

George MacReady suits up in the "hot room."

THE PRODUCTION AND DECAY OF STRANGE PARTICLES

Broadcast 20 April 1964
Written and directed by Leslie Stevens
Assistant Director: Phil Rawlins
Director of Photography: Kenneth Peach

CAST: Dr. Marshall (George MacReady), Laurel Marshall (Signe Hasso), Dr. Paul Pollard (Robert Fortier), Dr. Terrel (John Duke), Griffin (Rudy Solari), Collins (Joseph Ruskin), Coulter (Willard Sage), Arndis Pollard (Allyson Ames), Official (Paul Lukather), Konig (Leonard Nimoy).

> *In recent years, nuclear physicists have discovered a strange world of subatomic particles, fragments of atoms smaller than the imagination can picture, fragments of materials which do not obey the laws of gravity. Antimatter composed of inside-out material; shadow-matter that can penetrate ten miles of lead shielding. Hidden deep in the heart of strange new elements are secrets beyond human understanding—new powers, new dimensions, worlds within worlds, unknown...*

A cluster of intensely radioactive subatomic particles pulled fresh from the cyclotron by Dr. Marshall accidentally comes into contact with an isotope of Nobelium-238, resulting in an emergency in the Broadridge nuclear plant's furnace reactor. The result is a seething, crackling magnesium glare that fills up the radiation suits of the furnace personnel, obliterating them. Marshall concludes that a dimensional hole has been torn open within the reactor, and the force-creatures that are seeping through and "inflating" the suits of the dead workers plan to cause a chain reaction that will blow the doorway to their dimension wide open with an atomic explosion. As the creatures implement their plan, Marshall overcomes his characteristic cowardice and reverses polarity in the reactor core, resulting in an implosion that causes "time-reversal effects" that put everything neatly back into order.

> *As Man explores the secrets of the universe, strange and inscrutable powers await him. And whether these powers are to become forces of destruction or forces of construction will ultimately depend upon simple but profound human qualities: Inspiration. Integrity. Courage.*

"At the beginning of a series, you try to do your absolute best as a dramatist," said Leslie Stevens. "But gradually, you become the fire department; you wind up writing bottle shows to bail the series out of trouble, because the trouble gets horrendous. You get so far into deficit that the front office kills you. You're scared, but you *want* to make a show happen, so you use every bit of your skill to do one that will be enormously inexpensive and still be as effective as you can possibly make it. And I hate working under that kind of pressure. That's happened to me on every series I've ever worked on, and that's really why I'm not doing series television anymore."

As long-winded and technically opaque as its title, "The Production and Decay of Strange Particles" presents another of Stevens's lone scientists (since all of his helpers are neutralized) battling impossible odds and his own fear of inadequacy to pull a scientific hat-trick that saves the world. The scared and frustrated Marshall could easily be seen as Stevens, fighting to whip out a low-budget show while the clock ticks relentlessly away, and ultimately succeeding, though at the expense of story values. Marshall's sole character trait is cowardice, which he overcomes, to his credit. His fellow workers are all straw technicians who march dutifully into the firing line and get their suits filled up with crackling blue lightning. Laurel functions as Marshall's cheerleader, and Arndis (Stevens's then-wife, Allyson Ames) plays a stock-issue screaming female. "That script was a desperation measure," said Stevens. "It started out okay, but didn't go anywhere because I couldn't get a decent monster."

What Stevens fell back upon was an attempt to dazzle his audience with a hive-mind of energy, a "monster" produced by a vagary of science . . . but this is defeated by the yards of Space-Age-ese needed to explain it, dialogue that sounds like a Giant Golden Book on quantum physics run totally berserk. The viewer is drowned without a struggle from the moment that Griffin shouts, "[The atomic weight is] somewhere over

256! Marshall says some cosmic particles penetrated the shield—the gold foil disappeared and a lambda process set in!" Here is Marshall, explaining the danger to his own wife:

> MARSHALL: I know what's in there—something from another dimension, invading our space-time continuum. Laurel, I did it! I placed the heavy elements in the cyclotron; particles from out there, from quasistellar radio sources... bombarded it, split a crack in time and space. It'll widen and tear. Gravity will collapse. Radiation. Contagion. It'll burn us—*burn us!*

This confusing exposition opens the door for some scattergun theorizing about time-reversal, and extra-dimensional intelligence. Such extra notions accumulate until the story its pushed to its own sort of critical mass. Perhaps the Control Voice is correct when it proposes the whole thing is beyond human understanding, and surely the viewer's sympathies are with Marshall when he buries his head in his hands, crying, "It's no use!"

Stevens's final verdict? "I did the best I could on the thing, but I don't think it was worth a damn." Like Marshall's equation, "Production/Decay" just would not solve.

"That was not an episode I would've bought if anyone but Leslie had come in with it," said Joseph Stefano. "I don't think even Lou would have shown it to me, because it just wasn't where we were. It was Leslie's show." The lumbering, Frankensteinian nature of the force beings, and the dark, ominous interiors of the Broadridge plant seem to be Stevens's homages to where Stefano was "at"—namely, the Old Dark House approach. The struggle to tame the growing nuclear menace (plus the allegorical implications of controlling *The Outer Limits* itself) make the episode a close parallel to Stefano's own "It Crawled Out of the Woodwork."

The show was successfully on-time and under budget. "The only optical effect in the whole show was laying in some lightning, the same sort of little thing done in 'The Man With the Power,'" said Stevens. "The radiation lights floating around on the set were just reflected from a dance hall mirror ball, you know, a disco globe." Gene Warren of Project Unlimited filmed the electric chaos that was overlaid onto the faceplates of each of the suits occupied by force creatures. Production Manager Robert Justman called this show "difficult, because we had no idea what the postproduction effect was going to look like."

"The only thing that makes that show interesting," said Stevens, "is that it's the first and last time, that I know of, where footage of an atomic bomb explosion has been run forward *and* backwards."

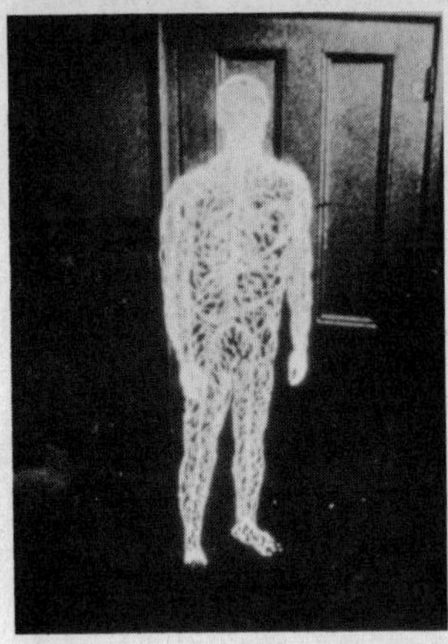

Mr. Zeno—an optical effect shortly to become Richard Ney—materializes from the lymph glands out, courtesy of Project Unlimited.

THE SPECIAL ONE

Broadcast 6 April 1964
Written by Oliver Crawford. Some material by Joseph Stefano.
Directed by Gerd Oswald
Assistant Director: Claude Binyon, Jr.
Director of Photography: Kenneth Peach

CAST: Mr. Zeno (Richard Ney), Kenny Benjamin (Flip Mark), Roy Benjamin (Macdonald Carey), Agnes "Aggie" Benjamin (Marion Ross), Mr. Terrence (Edward C. Platt), Bill Turner (Jason Wingreen), Joe Hayden (Burt Freed).

> *There is a belief that Man's fullest potentials were sealed into him at the dawn of all life, and unfold themselves according to a carefully prepared timetable, to keep him in harmony with his surroundings. This can mean that we are all carrying, within us, now, the seed of not only the man of tomorrow, but the man beyond him. The nucleus of the atom, which has been dormant for millions of years, has been exploded, to explode the future man—the superior man—from within our germ cells, so as to bypass the intervening generations. An explosion requires a catalyst. And such a catalyst can come from strange places, with dark and evil purpose . . .**

Since young Kenny Benjamin is already enrolled in a government-sponsored program to develop gifted children, it's a pleasant surprise to his parents when a private tutor named Mr. Zeno shows up to provide at-home

*When broadcast, "The Special One" featured no opening Control Voice speech. The lines quoted here are from Crawford's original script.

instruction. But when Zeno clocks in after dark to school Kenny in such skills as controlling the climate, walking through solid walls, and cataloging elements that have yet to be discovered, Roy Benjamin gets suspicious. When he sees Zeno dematerialize in the corridor outside their apartment, he becomes fairly sure that the rude, patrician tutor has nothing to do with the educational enrichment program. Zeno's mission on Earth is to indoctrinate intellectually precocious children in the logistics of conquest, as a prologue to invasion by his homeworld, Xenon, gifted children supposedly being more mentally malleable than adults. When Roy's interference causes Zeno to hypnotize him into a suicide attempt, Kenny rigs the alien's climate-control machine to bleed xenon gas out of the local atmosphere, nearly suffocating Zeno, who withdraws in defeat. Kenny reveals he had been leading Zeno on by cooperating with the invasion effort, in order to learn how to use the machine to repel the Xenons. He plans to turn the machine over to the government, suggesting that they "expand the principle so that it can repel a whole army at a time."

> *The mold of a man stems from the mind of a child. Educators and emperers have known this from time immemorial. So have tyrants.*

The not-so-subtle Earth takeover plot spearheaded in "The Special One" by Mr. Zeno (whose austere, Bond Street manner suggests a Klaatu gone bad) is chancey and overcomplicated. He admits to Kenny that Xenons can only survive for 120 days in Earth's atmosphere, and the idea of governing Earth long-distance using a handful of grownup *kommandants* leading an army of child prodigies seems suicidally bad planning. Why doesn't Zeno hypnotize Kenny's parents to sleep to avoid detection during his midnight visits? Why doesn't Roy Benjamin press Kenny for details instead of allowing himself to be repeatedly shrugged off by his own fourteen-year-old son? Why would the Xenons be stupid enough to put a machine that can cause their downfall right into the hands of the enemy?

Rather, the episode is an interesting one because it plants *The Outer Limits* right into the home of the typical 1960s family, and the young *Outer Limits* viewer of whom Stefano so often spoke became Kenny Benjamin—no longer reacting to the aliens he sees on TV, but interacting with them in person. One reason the alien invasion plot is so nonsensically cut and dried is that Mr. Zeno is intended to represent a *threat*—and the threat is really television itself. Being a guy from outer space localizes that threat to *The Outer Limits,* which was being transmitted into the average American home in a fashion very similar to Zeno's method of materialization from electrically-charged thin air.* At a time when pop analysts were bombarding parents with the question of whether

*It is probably overzealous to mention at this point that xenon gas is an essential element to the function of a cathode ray tube—that is, the picture tube of a TV set.

TV was good for their children, "The Special One" asks that question of *The Outer Limits*, and gets a negative reply: Mr. Zeno invades the Benjamin household and does his best to corrupt Kenny, but the boy's absorption of Zeno's lessons allows him to intelligently neutralize the threat that Zeno represents. In the end, the "message" of "The Special One" is that watching *The Outer Limits* might actually do your kid some good . . . which was what Stefano had been saying all along.

The Benjamins are a determinedly normal, damned-near ideal post–World War Two family: Aggie is a shining model of prefeminist housewifery; Kenny's sole concerns are school and (what else?) Little League —which seems to be the only interest his father shares or can comprehend, since Kenny's homework is all Greek to Dad. Roy is a comfortably drab man, a breadwinner of the pipe-and-slippers school, whose concerns are limited to the evening newspaper and his own receding hairline. When the pointedly Aryan presence of Zeno (who looks like an SS *oberleutnant* in an Ivy League suit) causes Kenny to forsake baseball, the "All-American sport," Roy's ire is roused. The idea of Nazis from space is gently introduced through Zeno's program of world domination and youth indoctrination, and his speeches concerning Kenny's "ultimate destiny." At the point Kenny begins talking the same way to Roy, scriptwriter Oliver Crawford tips his hand by adding the descriptive line, "One almost expects to have him finish with a '*Heil, Hitler*'!"

Crawford's inspiration for "The Special One" was personal. "In the early 1960s, my son was placed in a high-aptitude 'cluster group' sponsored by NASA," he said. "He was chosen from his peers as a child of high intelligence, and NASA worked him into a program of advanced learning." Lou Morheim thought the idea of aliens recruiting children as the future leaders of the planet was a natural for *The Outer Limits*, and Stefano wrote the prologue, in which we see Zeno kill the father of another child prodigy. "Stefano and Morheim changed my suburban location to an urban one," said Crawford, "and the house to an apartment." Perhaps Stefano did this to accommodate Zeno's penchant for making uppity fathers jump out high-rise windows, since in Crawford's script, Zeno declares he will burn Roy to death with a shower of sparks that emit from his own skin: "In thirty seconds, you will be little more than an *ash*," the tutor snarls. Zeno's defeat was originally more showy, as well—Kenny uses the climate control machine to chase him around the apartment with a heat beam, then freeze him, then imprison him in a cocoon of vapor from which he withdraws the xenon. In the episode, a superimposition of swirling feathers somewhat ridiculously depicts air without xenon gas. On the other hand, the Project Unlimited effect of Zeno's materialization, in a snap-flash of lightning that "builds" his human form from the skeleton and organs outward, is marvelous.

"I wasn't too involved in that show," said Stefano. "I liked the story originally, but it did not come off the way I thought it would." It also ran short, so he added the prologue, and retarded Zeno's demise down to Sam Peckinpah-style slow motion. This padding only handicaps the show's already laborious pace. "It really didn't *belong* in *The Outer Limits,"* said Gerd Oswald. "It was too pedestrian; not one of my favorites. I've only seen it once, and the most interesting thing in it is Richard Ney."

"Richard Ney was a broker who was very big in the stock exchange," said Claude Binyon. "He was always giving stock quotes to everyone on the set." As Mr. Zeno, he is imposing and quietly sinister. Ney currently hosts a daily stock spotlight, *The Ney Report*, on the Cable News Network. Marion Ross's performance holds a peculiar resonance, since she would later become famous for playing essentially the same role on TV's unending *Happy Days* series. Flip Mark is droning and dull as Kenny, although, curiously, he had recently had a similar role, helping Ray Walston construct a cyclotron in an episode of *My Favorite Martian*.

One amusing touch, also TV-related, occurs when Zeno is welcomed into the apartment for the first time by Roy. The TV is on, and the Benjamins are watching a Leslie Stevens pilot called *Mr. Kingston*.

"The Special One" was the last show on which Stefano, Oswald, and Binyon were to work together after doing *The Unknown*. Said Binyon: "We used to have these seances at Joe's house—me and my wife, and Gerd with whoever his wife was at the time, and Joe and Marilyn. We 'made contact' during the seances. I don't know who was spoofing who, but Joe really loved playing with people. For him, the whole world was therapy."

William O'Connell on the saucer dome.

THE CHAMELEON

Broadcast 27 April 1964
Written by Robert Towne. Story by Towne, Lou Morheim, and Joseph Stefano.
Original title: "The Seamaness Drug," also "The Drug."
Directed by Gerd Oswald
Assistant Director: Phil Rawlins
Director of Photography: Kenneth Peach

CAST: Louis Mace (Robert Duvall), Leon Chambers (Howard Caine), Gen. Crawford (Henry Brandon), Dr. Tillyard (Douglas Henderson), First Alien (William O'Connell), Second Alien/Stunts (Dean Smith), Agent with Pistol (Roy Jensen), Mexican Guitarist (Roy Olvera), Loudspeaker Voice/Voice of Chopper Pilot (Robert Johnson).

The race of Man is known for its mutability. We can change our moods, our faces, our lives to suit whatever situation confronts us. Adapt and survive. Even among the most changeable of living things, Man is quicksilver—more chameleonlike than the chameleon, determined to survive, no matter what the cost to others . . . or to himself.

A flying saucer of unknown origin has crash-landed in a California canyon, and a patrol of soldiers sent to investigate it has been massacred. Assassin Louis Mace emerges from deep cover to accept the mission of infiltrating the spacecraft—a mission requiring his literal "alienization" at the hands of Dr. Tillyard, who uses scrapings taken from beneath one of the dead soldiers' fingernails as a genetic template for altering Mace "via supersonic sound." Once transformed, Mace enters the saucer, equipped with an audiovisual transceiver and a flimsy cover story that doesn't fool the real aliens for a second. They are decidedly nonhostile, however; they killed the soldiers because "they tried to kill *us*," and are hurrying to repair their malfunctioning ship and get away before the "destructive society" of Earth forces them to do more harm . . . or before the authorities realize that the ship does not contain nuclear material, and decides to shell it with artillery. Mace agrees to return with the aliens to their home planet, and is released from their forcefield. He immediately grabs a weapon, kills one of the beings, and chases the other out into the forest before he realizes *he* is a perfect example of Earth's "destructive society," and relents. Instead of returning to his killer's existence on Earth, Mace chooses to help repair the ship and venture to the "warm, yellow planet" from which the real aliens, a nonviolent race, hail. The surviving alien is surprised, but happy for the companionship, and the government men willingly allow Mace to leave and embrace a new life.

A man's survival can take many shapes, and the shape in which a man finds his humanity is not always a human one.

Killing is Louis Mace's personal art form, and we are fittingly introduced to this extraordinary man in the midst of an act of murder, as he distractedly smashes a fly with a swatter he will use a moment later to strangle an enemy agent. His detachment is the same in both cases; like his medieval namesake, Mace is a weapon waiting to be used, and his case is stated simply and eloquently: When CIA man Chambers, after

O'Connell lunches between takes with the Daystar crew.

witnessing the death of the enemy agent, offers Mace his unusual new assignment, Mace says nothing and holds up his empty killer's hands, palms up, as if to indicate "this is all," and at the same time offer the service of those hands to Chambers. It never occurs to him to turn down the job, and while waiting on Dr. Tillyard's operating table for an injection, he clarifies his position to General Crawford:

> MACE: I don't think you understand me, General. I'm not interested in becoming a hero. Nor do I have an overdeveloped sense of duty. I'm doing this because I'm nothing more than an instrument for action. Mr. Chambers knows that, also. Between missions, I cease to exist. I am what I've done, and that's not always very pretty. But being ugly is better than being nothing. I have no one, I care for no one, and I'm cared for by no one. So all I have is what I can do.

The deception-of-appearance theme in "The Chameleon" is not limited to Mace's bizarre charade, for once under sedation he reveals a submerged aspect of his *true* personality—one that wishes he could do "*one* constructive thing... build something for a change." His altered perspective on humankind is not filled with vengefulness for the small prejudices of Earth; rather, his interaction with the real aliens invests in him a sympathy unknown to his killing-machine persona, even though his assassin's reflexes overcome the pull of his new genes long enough for him to make the aliens pay for their accidental contact with us—as did the Galaxy Being, and the Bifrost alien of "The Bellero Shield."

"That story shattered the provincialism of the audience," said Lou Morheim. "And it's even more topical today—what happens to a 'compromised' CIA agent with a mercenary attitude. What most appealed to me was that he chooses to leave with the creatures, to go and live with them on another planet. All science fiction that I can recall always did the reverse: Either the aliens go home, or we kill them off because they're malevolent. Our position was always that *our* planet is the best place to live, even if others may be more intelligent or super-advanced. I decided to stand that thinking on its head."

Scriptwriter Robert Towne had begun his career working for Roger Corman with *The Last Woman on Earth* (1960), in which Towne also played the second lead as "Edward Wain," a stage name he had also used while acting in *Creature from the Haunted Sea*. He would later write the last of Corman's *nuevo*-Poe films, *Tomb of Ligeia* (1964), a draft of *Captain Nemo and the Underwater City,* and *Villa Rides* (1967), before moving uphill to the successes of *Chinatown* (1974), *Shampoo* (1975), and his own *Personal Best* (1982). "The Chameleon," perhaps unfortunately, is Towne's only *Outer Limits* script. It is virtually ideal for the series, written cost-consciously for a small cast, featuring the requisite monsters, but in Stefano's "sympathetic and sophisticated" mold; it offers an action-oriented plot buffered with subtexts examining the loss of identity and deception of appearance themes. According to Morheim, "The reason that Towne did not do other episodes was because he was involved in so many other projects, many of a more personal nature. It took a *long* time to get that one script from him."

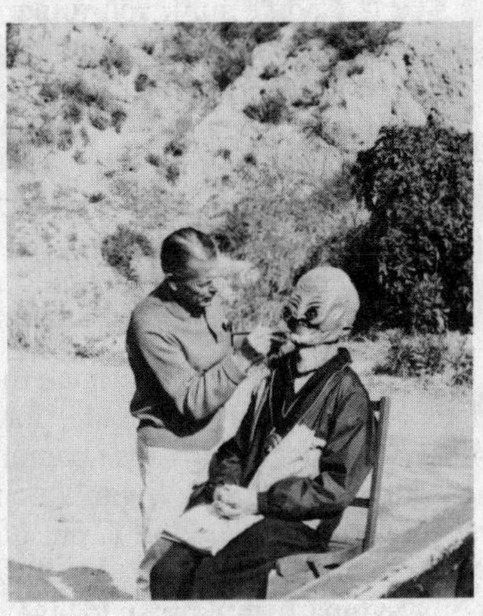

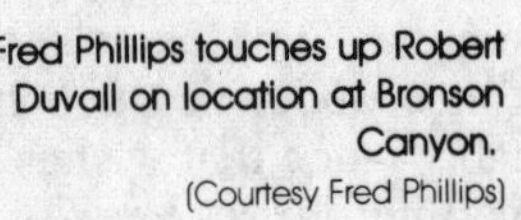

Fred Phillips touches up Robert Duvall on location at Bronson Canyon.
(Courtesy Fred Phillips)

In "The Chameleon," humans are once again the aggressors, but they redeem themselves by being honorable and decisive—as opposed, for example, to the venal and grasping specimens we see in "The Bellero Shield," who destroy themselves with their aggressions. Dr. Tillyard gives Mace every chance to refuse the inhuman proposition of the transformation. Chambers, the squirrely government man, concedes happiness for Mace's new future even though he's losing a crack agent, because he knows how bleak Mace's former existence was. And General Crawford calls off his military dogs against what must have been inviolable orders, and cannot bring himself to blitz the alien ship as it lifts off with Mace, because he senses that Chambers is right about Mace.

Like "The Bellero Shield," this story presents optimistic "monsters" whose personalities transcend the man-in-the-mask illusion. They *smile*, and evince a visceral trust in Mace. "We want you to *want* to share our lives," says one, with perfect candor. Towne's initial description of these creatures is colorful and specific:

> They are bulky, squat, with small unblinking eyes. The face is a fixed grin—smooth, cartilaginous, with a mindless malice suggested by that fixed slash of a grin. Their bodies seem covered with something very like hair, but it's more bristle than mammalian hair. The most humanoid feature about them is a wide belt they wear with some kind of large cluster where the buckle would be... we see... the expressionless eyes, the smooth but hideously tessellated skin of the face...

The Wah Chang designs omitted the hair, but incorporated widely-spaced, catlike eyes that lend a guarded benevolence to the aliens' expressions. Stuntman Dean Smith, with only the slitted "forehead lines" of the mask to see through, does some incredibly energetic running through the underbrush of the Bronson Canyon locations—another touch that helps erase the impression of a man in a monster suit, since such costumes generally hamper the vision and restrict movements to more cautious choreography. As played by Smith, William O'Connell, and leading man Robert Duvall, these aliens really grow on the viewer, and are a total success.

One amusing idiosyncracy of the script is that whenever Chambers or Crawford refer to the alien ship, they shy from calling it a flying saucer, tempering this term every time they use it by adding, "... or *whatever* it is," almost as if they won't admit it's real, or are self-conscious of the public craze for *discos volantes* in the early 1960s.

"The Chameleon" was the final *Outer Limits* episode on the production roster, and filmed in early March, 1964, while some trade papers were prematurely announcing the cancellation of the series. Others stood by its renewal. In *Look* magazine, the following September, Leslie Stevens promised that the new season would be "wilder, woolier and more chilling." In a bit of in-joke dialogue in "The Chameleon," the producer is referenced as the trigger-happy "Colonel Stevens," the man General Crawford keeps ringing up on the hot line... and putting on hold.

Aired next-to-last in the first season lineup, "The Chameleon" was a safe distance from its conceptual antecedents, "The Architects of Fear" and "The Sixth Finger." Here, the "alienization" process of the first is accomplished using the "sonic chamber" of the second. Another curious echo from "Architects" is the use of actor Douglas Henderson as a doctor in both shows; here it looks as though he's quit United Labs to go into private practice turning men into aliens! In earlier drafts of the script, Dr. Tillyard alters Mace with an injection, as in "The Hundred Days of the Dragon."

"It was a compassionate story, very moving," said Stefano. "The Chameleon" might also be considered the calm before the extremely stormy show that was to close out the first season.

PART THREE
Fear of the Unknown

Fear of the Unknown

The dancer figurine seen in Colas' mansion. The base of this silver curio is formed by two Brazilian coins.
(Photo by Marilyn Stefano)

THE FORMS OF THINGS UNKNOWN

Broadcast 4 May 1964
Written by Joseph Stefano
Pilot version title: "The Unknown." Working title: "Lovers and Madmen."
Directed by Gerd Oswald
Assistant Director: Claude Binyon, Jr.
Director of Photography: Conrad Hall

CAST: Kassia Paine (Vera Miles), Colas (Sir Cedric Hardwicke), Andre Pavan (Scott Marlowe), Tone Hobart (David McCallum), Leonora Edmond (Barbara Rush), Old Frenchman (Wolff Barzelle), Old Frenchwoman (Madeline Holmes), Young Frenchwoman (Gabrielle Rossillon); AND: Clive Halliday as Timothy R. Edmond [in deleted sequence].

"The Forms of Things Unknown" features no Control Voice narration.

To free themselves from the domination of playboy blackmailer Andre Pavan, his two mistresses—the scheming Kassia and the meek Leonora—poison him with "a leaf from the Thanatos tree" and stash the corpse in the boot of Andre's Rolls-Royce. Amid a sudden, pounding rainstorm on the road to Aux-les-Bains, the trunk lid pops open and Leonora, panicked into thinking Andre is still alive, flees into the woods. Kassia pursues her, and they chance upon the warm sanctuary of a mansion presided over by Colas, a blind old man dressed in a houseboy's jacket. His guest at the house is the childlike madman Tone Hobart, who "tinkers with time" using a roomful of clocks, all connected to a central control shaft by a webwork of silver wires. It is with this device he claims to have resurrected Andre from the dead, and when Kassia sneaks out to the car to bury him, she finds the trunk empty. Soon enough, Andre appears in the foyer, grinning evilly and requesting a refill of the poison cocktail that did him in. "It was wrong to bring *you* back," Tone says of Andre, but Andre is not about to oblige his desire to return him to death. Finding little to amuse him in the mansion, Andre proceeds with his original plan to pay an extortion call on Leonora's wealthy father, taking Kassia and the car and leaving Leonora behind. Kassia has second thoughts (she can't bear to abandon Leonora), and jumps from the car; when Andre tries to run her down, the Rolls catapults over a verge and he is killed against the wheel. Inside the house, Tone tries to explain his time-tilter to an increasingly hysterical Leonora. He wants her to destroy it after he has used it to return to the "safe, dead quiet of the past" from which he also came. Kassia arrives back at the mansion and gets upstairs just in time to see Tone embrace the time-tilter's control shaft and vanish, proving that the device was *real,* and not the concoction of a lunatic's dreamy imagination.

"And then we came to clocks, and running around in lakes, and lots of tyings of bits of wire," David McCallum muses in his best Tone Hobart tone. "That script seemed very Shakespearian; I didn't know there were two versions of the film, and I didn't see it at all for many years."

"That show was one of Joe's bad dreams," said 1st AD Claude Binyon. "I don't know whether audiences can appreciate it as much as the people who made it; unless you understand Joe Stefano, it may not make any sense to you. It's a world unto him, wholly, and he tries to translate it into lay terms so the rest of us can understand it."

"The Forms of Things Unknown" is definitely a disorienting experience on first viewing; it doesn't run against the grain of normal TV fare so much as attack it outright. It is *The Outer Limits'* most dreamlike show—wispy and unclear, but crammed with arty compositions and startling images. Its stylistic inspirations run from *Hamlet* and *A Midsummer Night's Dream* to Val Lewton, *Les Diaboliques* (again, as in "The Bellero Shield"), and Stefano's own screenplay for *Psycho.*

After reading the script, ABC rejected "Forms" cold; it was just too different, too strange. Then network executive Edgar Scherick gave Stefano a surprise phone call. "Out of the blue," said Stefano, "they suddenly felt that they would like to try an *un*science fiction series, kind of scary, spooky, and mysterious. They asked me to take the script and do it for *The Outer Limits,* but to also do another version with no science fiction element, to give them an idea of what a series called *The Unknown* would look like. It really wasn't possible to shoot 'Forms' and just edit out the science fiction parts, so key scenes were written two ways to accommodate the changes. I wrote them as facing pages in the shooting script." The pilot teleplay for *The Unknown* was completed on New Year's Eve, 1963, eleven days after the script for 'Forms' was submitted. "Adapting the second version was easy," said Stefano, "because the science fiction really didn't belong there in the first place."

Stefano was enthused at the prospect of using the *Outer Limits* crew to produce a show that focused on Gothic horror and suspense, and intended *The Unknown* to be his debut as a director. ABC balked at the idea of Stefano becoming a "triple hyphenate" like Leslie Stevens (writer-director-producer), who had suggested the idea to Stefano after reading the "Forms" script. "It was Joe's turn," said Stevens. "I thought he was ready for it, and I fought for him."

"When a successful producer says, 'Now I'm going to direct,' the top-level executive reaction is *always* 'Watch out—he's trying to do too much!'" said Stefano. "It's automatic. The report I got from the network was that a producer should not stop producing for six days just to direct a script. And I thought, bullshit, Leslie directed a *lot* of *Stoney Burke*s while he was producing it."

But ABC was growing more interested in disciplining Stevens and

Vera Miles, Barbara Rush and Sir Cedric Hardwicke. Note the actors' marks, in chalk on the floor.

Stefano than in indulging their individualistic tastes, and had begun to make noises about shifting *Outer Limits* from its Monday evening slot at 7:30 P.M. PST (where it was opposite the *NBC Monday Night Movie* and CBS's *To Tell the Truth* and *I've Got a Secret*)—first to Wednesdays, against *The Beverly Hillbillies,* then to a kiss-of-death berth on Saturday nights, against the popular *Jackie Gleason Show.* The idea of Stefano becoming a director met with a firm negative response that only fanned Stevens's fire. "We thought, how dare they not let Joe direct," said Stevens, who, with Dominic Frontiere, fired off a telegram of protest to ABC. "We told them that Stefano had goddamn well *better* direct, or else we wouldn't deliver the next six *Outer Limits* episodes. I almost ruined myself forever with the network by doing that. Incredible earthquakes went all over the place; the William Morris reps were coming in with ashen faces, saying, 'You just don't *do* stuff like that!' It meant lawsuits, and millions of dollars in production money at stake. To close down a show because a friend isn't allowed to direct—they'll burn you with blowtorches if you try that too much. That's why networks don't like artists in control. A business manager never would have dreamed of opposing the establishment that way. At the time, we saw that they intended to tear the whole house apart if we weren't careful, so we backed down."

"If Leslie had told me he was threatening to close up shop, I would've thought he was kidding," said Stefano. "I would've laughed. He can be very frightening if you don't know and understand him, and it's very much like him that he'd go out on such a limb, just to insure I'd get my shot at directing. ABC was very threatened by what is, basically, his viable enthusiasm." Stefano bowed out of the conflict to avoid trouble, and Gerd Oswald was appointed to direct the show. "I was not *afraid* to direct," said Stefano. "But I was much more concerned with the overall *Outer Limits* series than I was with directing a single show."

Daystar's first project for 1964 was the ten-day shoot for both the "Forms" and *The Unknown* versions, which commenced January 2nd, four days before "The Children of Spider County" began filming.

> *There is a fear that is unlike all other fears. It has a special, clammy chill, a deadly gift for inspiring deeper, darker dread. It is the fear of unentered rooms, of bends in lonely roads. It is the fear of the phone call in the middle of the night, of the stranger you recognize, perhaps from a nightmare. It is the fear of the unexpected, the unfamiliar. It is the fear of...* The Unknown.

This is the opening to *The Unknown*, rendered in appropriately sepulchral tones by the Unknown Voice, over a succession of bleak images described in Stefano's script as "*slow, oily dissolves of scenes of lonely streets, deserted houses, dark and empty rooms, long twisting corridors,*

Wayne Fitzgerald's "rip-through" title.
(Courtesy Gerd Oswald)

Gerd Oswald's directorial credit "rips through" to the opening shot of the pilot verison.
(Courtesy Gerd Oswald)

long staircases leading up to dark-black landings, desolate backroad motels, quiet and malevolent-still lakes, etc."

"I had to read the script seven times and have the cast over to my house so I could explain it to each one of them," said Gerd Oswald. "Joe and I had many 'shrink sessions,' so I could find out what was *really* on his mind when he wrote it."

Stefano harkens back to *Psycho* territory with his "back-road motel" reference, and by focusing on two women in flight. Like the ill-fated Marion Crane, they have committed an illegal act and chance upon a bizarre, remote refuge. Vera Miles, from *Psycho,* was cast as Kassia Paine by Stefano.

In *Les Diaboliques,* the sadistic headmaster of a French boys' school is murdered by his meek, cowed wife, Christina, and his strong, forceful mistress, Nicole, who trick him into drinking drugged whiskey, then drown him in a bathtub. His corpse is hidden in a disused swimming pool, and later, when the murky water in the pool is drained, the corpse has vanished. In "Forms," we have another pair of desperate murderesses, who spike the martini of their tormentor/lover and cause his watery death in a lake. Leonora, like Christina, is dark-haired and wears dark clothing; she is weak-willed, skittish, and thoroughly subjugated by Andre. Kassia is willful, decisive, resentful of Andre's domination (but clearly a match for him) though attracted to his animal power and lack of scruples; she is blond, like Nicole, and wears a tight white sheath dress matching Leonora's—a "light" to her "dark." The central question of *Les Diaboliques*— is the victim really dead, or alive and seeking revenge?—is the hub on which the plot of "Forms" turns, with the water/death symbology of the Clouzot film heavily emphasized in the eventful first half.

"Such tricks hath strong imagination," says Tone to the women, reciting Shakespeare. The lines he quotes are from a longish speech by Theseus in *A Midsummer Night's Dream,* from which Stefano drew all three of his script titles, as well as some major thematic sentiments. In keeping with Theseus' observations, the characters in "Forms" are all lovers, poets, or madmen in multiform combinations. Colas, for example, appears to be a servant when he is in fact master of the house, and Tone's caretaker. He is blind, and thus given to perceptive asides that seem beyond the grasp of the sighted characters. By choosing to look like a houseboy, he assigns himself a minor role in this drama, because all the *major* players are engulfed by madness, and he knows it. He is the rock around which all the turbulent happenstances and people swirl.

Then there is the matter of the twirling silver figurine in Colas's parlor. Tone and Leonora are both drawn to it, and mesmerized by the tiny dancer's perfect balance and endless pirouettes. While staring at it, their eyes become wide and unblinking; Leonora reveals the details of Andre's murder, and Tone becomes trancelike, which allows Andre to relieve him of a pistol with ease. The figurine was a curio bought in Rio de Janeiro by Stefano; its base is formed by two silver coins, and it sits in his office to this day.

Two more curious puzzle pieces are the French peasant funeral witnessed by Kassia and Leonora, and the clown-faced clock that sits on the parlor mantle—the only clock in Colas's house that *doesn't* work. "Why do you keep a useless clock?" Leonora asks Tone, after comparing Andre's death-smile to that of a "crushed clown"—a great, alliterative image, one thereafter perpetuated by repeat reference to Andre as a clown, but one that has no context since Stefano removed it from the already-dense story. In the original script, Tone's response to Leonora's question is, "Why do you keep useless memories?" Leonora tells him:

> LEONORA: My mother had taken my sister and I to Brighton for the day, and she met a man on the boardwalk. He wanted her little girls to like him, so he threw some balls and won a clown for us. Like any prize won on the boardwalk, it was cheap and very tawdry. My mother ran off, soon afterwards, and my father could never bear to look at that clown.

The clown becomes Andre, the spoiler, when she recounts his murder. The visual image we see is of a young girl's legs, clad in ankle socks and Mary Jane shoes, pushing the pedals of a bicycle that crushes the clown doll's face. (In both versions of the film, we see a simple replay of Andre's death at the lake.)

The peasant funeral is encountered while the women are on the road. Having just caused a death herself, Kassia stops the Rolls so that a young French widow and her parents may push her dead husband's casket past. The old Frenchman holds a baby. When Leonora relates Andre's murder to Tone, she experiences a nightmarish flashback to the funeral procession—only now Kassia wears the cerements of the old woman, Leonora herself is the widow, and her father, Timothy R. Edmond, carries the clown doll instead of a child. "Leonora," he says, "If you didn't really kill him, the scandal will finish off my heart." This scene was actually filmed by Oswald, but dropped by Stefano during editing.

In "Forms," Tone's time-tilter actually does resurrect Andre; in *The Unknown,* Andre's death is a sham, and Tone's device only works in his mind. The notable differences between the two filmed versions do not occur until the last two acts, and most are simple adjustments of dialogue accounting for Tone's insanity... or lack of same. Here is how Colas relates his discovery of Tone to the women, in "Forms":

> COLAS: His lifeless form had been hanging there nearly a week. He had died for want of more than bodily

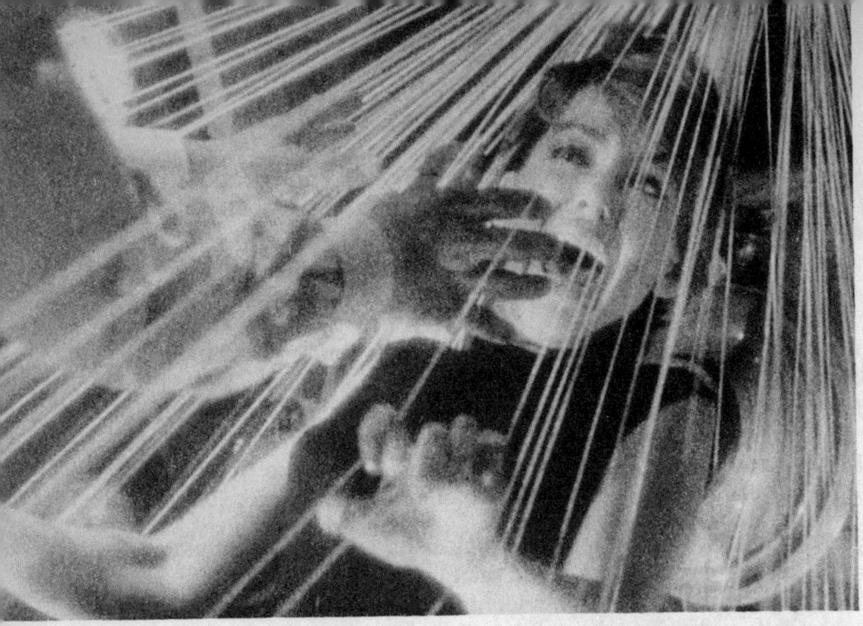

The never-broadcast climax of *The Unknown.* Barbara Rush backs into the wires of the time-tilter, recoiling from David McCallum, who is shot in the back by Vera Miles.

Following an extreme close-up of the pistol discharging, McCallum grabs the central pole for support and slumps to the floor, dead.

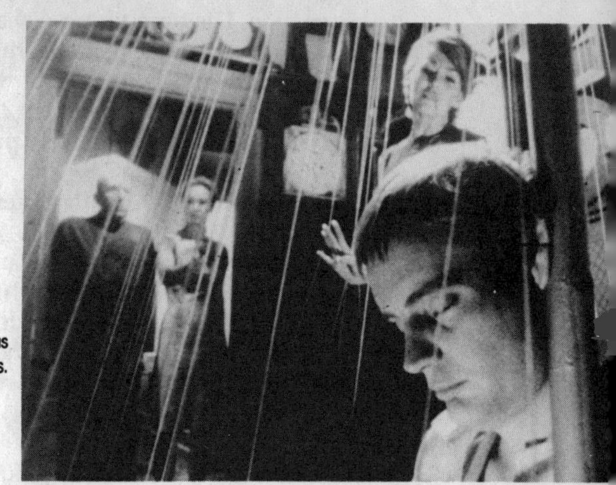

Sir Cedric Hardwicke enters as McCallum expires.

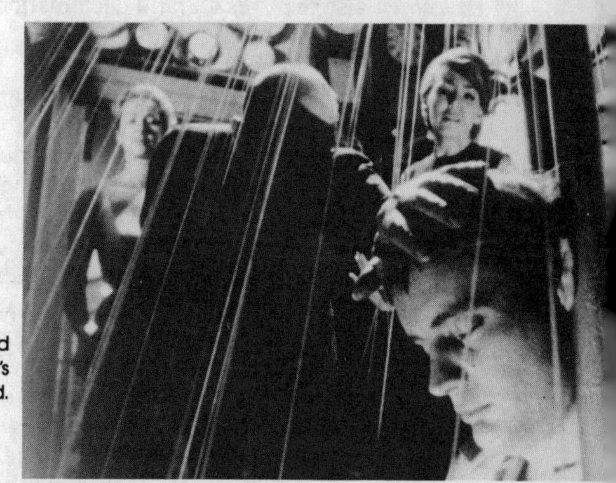

He crosses the chamber and places his hand on McCallum's head.

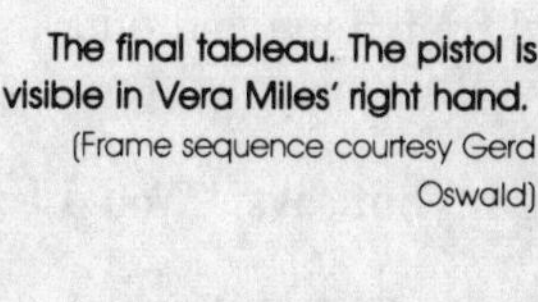

The final tableau. The pistol is visible in Vera Miles' right hand.

(Frame sequence courtesy Gerd Oswald)

> sustenance. His time-tilting device had done it. Somehow, almost accidentally, his genius had broken the fixed laws of the science of time. His device caused the cycles of time to tilt... and he slid out of the dead past, and into a lively present.

In *The Unknown,* the story is slightly different:

> COLAS: He'd been hanging there nearly a week. He believed his time-tilting device had done it. He still believes that. He is convinced that he was dead during (his) comatose days, and that the cycles of time tilted, and slid him out of the dead past and into a lively present.

In "Forms," as Leonora leaves, she thanks Colas for his hospitality; in *The Unknown,* fittingly, she says, "Thank you for your rationality." *The Unknown* also features a grand declamation of Tone by Andre, following his "resurrection":

> ANDRE: Do you know what a madman you are? I detest the blitheness of madmen! Why are they so fortunate? Why don't they hurt the way the incurably sane hurt? Why doesn't reality twist *their* vitals? Who are you, madman, that everyone should humor you so? You're not a curly-headed child; your delusions are not games! Your 'workshop' is not a nursery; it is a fool's cluttered madhouse, a trash-heap of clocks, a cobweb of common household wire! You stole me out of the warm little trunk of my car, and you propped me against a cold, useless pole, and you actually believe such solemn silliness has brought me back from the dead? Well, I was not dead! There *is* no Thanatos tree! I spun them a tale of it—and they believed it! Do you believe that I would allow myself to die at the hands of such inept, fancy murderers? But oh, the fun of pretending! It tickled me to the pit of my soul to peep through my lashes, and watch them shiver with guilt, just as it tickles me now to break your hold on unreality! (He snatches the pistol from Tone and puts it to Tone's temple) Shall I do you this one small favor?

In "Forms," Andre does likewise with the gun, but says, "Would *you* be willing to go back?"

The gun makes an encore appearance in *The Unknown,* mainly

because Tone cannot vanish into a time-tilter that only works in his imagination. He forces the door on the clock room and advances on Leonora as if to choke her; he really only intends to keep her from harming the device. She recoils into the wire-work in terror as Kassia appears in the hallway behind them, with the gun she has removed from Andre's body in the wrecked Rolls. She shoots Tone in the back. He slumps forward, grabbing the pole of the time-tilter and sliding to the floor, dead. "I thought he was trying to kill her," Kassia says ineffectually to Colas. The irony is now that Andre is truly dead *without* the help of the women, they have just precipitated a genuine murder nonetheless.

"We played it very *Hamlet*-like, with me wearing the black pants and white shirt," said David McCallum. The stark chiaroscuro in *The Unknown* is a superb example of the use of a film frame as a compositional canvas. Many shots are divided fifty-fifty between black-and-white values, as in one shot of Tone speaking to Kassia—his face is in shadow, hers, in light; she is front-lit, he is back-lit, and behind them is a white wall divided diagonally by a slash of darkness. Often the effect is so subtle as to be subliminal; other times, the artiness is more obvious. Conrad Hall put in twenty-four hours at a stretch, as the episode neared completion, to make it what he called "a catalogue of Gothic effects. It was very hard, tiring work under adverse conditions." Much of this was accomplished in the dead of night and the cold of January, in a freezing barrage of artificial wind and rain on the MGM backlot. Clad only in their tight, light-weight dresses, Vera Miles and Barbara Rush were drenched to the core for the woodlands scenes; you can see the chilly steam of condensation rising off them in almost every shot. "Those girls were real troupers," said Claude Binyon. "I remember them sitting in the rain, eating ice-cream sundaes brought by Barbara's husband."

Stefano had been anxious to use McCallum again ever since "The Sixth Finger." "David can read any line," he said. "You take one look at his face, and hear his voice, and you *know* you're going to get away with murder!" The star casting coup, though, was Sir Cedric Hardwicke, originally Stefano's third choice for the Colas role after Peter Lorre and Joseph Schildkraut—both of whom died before any contract could be signed. 1964 was also to be the final year of Hardwicke's life. "He used his inhaler on the set constantly," recalled Binyon. "It never seemed to do any good. I was afraid he might die on us at any minute."

"In the beginning of that show, you see what must be the fastest zoom ever attempted," said Gerd Oswald of the shot where Leonora sees the trunk lid of the Rolls pop up in the rearview mirror. "It skipped maybe sixty frames. For the shot where Barbara runs into the clock room at the end, we pulled Billy Fraker along on a furniture pad." Binyon recalls helping drag cameraman Fraker down the length of the hallway. "He was doing a hand-held Arriflex shot that looked like it was on a gear-head," he said. "As we opened the door, he rolled over and did an upside-down point-of-view shot of the time-tilter room—really torturous."

This upstairs "Caligari Hallway" was a forced-perspective construction of Jack Poplin's, with inward-slanting walls, a very high ceiling, and naked lightbulbs strung at head-level at three-foot intervals. This terminates in a tiny room with a tiny skylight, containing, as described by Stefano, an iron pole, a web of "rare magnetic wire," and *"clocks, clocks of every size and variety, so many that we cannot see the ceiling or any part of the walls."* "That was Chet Bayhi's baby," said Poplin. "He spent *hours* on that set, tying each individual wire, which was just sash cord."

"That whole Val Lewton school of filmmaking—the shadows on the wall, the sounds—is absolutely fantastic," said Stefano. "And I knew what *I* was going for. To see this man, Andre, in a bathing suit, ordering these two women to serve him his drink with their clothes on, and to see those two beautiful women wade into that dark water in their 'fine stiletto heels'... that's right out of the most sadistic side of me you're ever going to hear from!"

"It was an extraordinary and peculiar piece," said Leslie Stevens. "But not a coherent thing for an ordinary audience to grab. It was perceived as being far too 'arty.'"

ABC's rendezvous with *The Unknown* was a fizzle, and, in the matter of Stefano-as-director, Stevens's retreat under fire had not placated them. "We had to be disciplined, cut down, and pushed back into our place," noted Stevens. Whether or not *The Outer Limits* was pulling its weight in the ratings race suddenly became a hot topic, as did the proposed time slot change.

"When a series is a runaway hit, the network only sees the numbers and could care less about what happens *on* the show," said Richard Dorso, Stevens' United Artists liaison. "When a series flops, the obvious occurs. But when a series is in-between, the network will take a long look at it to see what can be done to push those numbers up into a real success. *The Outer Limits* had close to a thirty share in those days. Although *any* show could stay on today with that percentage, things were different in 1963."

Meanwhile, Stefano steadfastly refused to continue as producer on the series if it was moved. "I just didn't fancy putting in eighteen-hour days on a series that was doomed," he said. "I mean, I love challenge and competition, and I also know where a wall is, and I'm not going to bang my head against it. Seven-thirty on Monday nights was ideal—the weekend was over, and the kids and everybody else could dig in and watch the show. I certainly would have considered doing it on Wednesdays, but I was furious when they wanted to use it as ammunition against Jackie Gleason. I had really worked my ass off, and I knew that Jackie Gleason was *not* going to be brought down by *The Outer Limits.*"

Gerd Oswald noted that after ABC turned down *The Unknown* as a series, "I suggested an eighty-minute cut, to be shown theatrically in

David McCallum as Tone, with his "clocks... and lots of tyings of bits of string...."

Europe, but ABC wouldn't let Stefano do that." Oswald achieved Tone's disappearance into the time-stream for the "fallback" version, "Forms," by adding a strategic dissolve just after Tone grabs the pole of the time-tilter. "Forms" aired as the final episode of *The Outer Limits'* first season, but the Unknown Voice would never be heard in prime time. Dominic Frontiere's lavish original score and Wayne Fitzgerald's unique title design (in which the credits succeed each other through "rips" in the TV screen) would be reprised in 1967 as the opening for another ABC science fiction series, Quinn Martin's *The Invaders*.

"ABC said, 'Come to New York; we'll talk about it,'" remembers Stefano. There was no room for haggling with the network at a time when he was double-teaming *The Unknown*/"Forms" with his usual overload of production duties on regular *Outer Limits* episodes. ABC's idea of "meeting him halfway" was to ask, "'Well, will you meet us in *Chicago*, then?' And that struck me as so funny, because I was not against going to their offices; I just could not take time out to go to New York for meetings that were simply never going to amount to anything, because they'd *made* their decision already. They seemed to think there was some sort of power-play going on. I would have stayed with the show another year, at least, but I didn't want to put in more twenty-hour days on a show that was stuck in the wrong time slot. I stuck to my guns. ABC stuck to theirs—so I walked away."

Stevens, meanwhile, had begun to view the entire *Outer Limits* production machine as an airplane on which he was no longer the copilot, merely a passenger. "And when that plane touched down in Chicago, I got off," he said. "ABC figured the show wasn't going to get the numbers they wanted, and were willing to let it die. I think they *wanted* to throw it away." On top of this, his salvo of assorted new TV pilots had all been shot down, preventing him from becoming a "mini-mogul" like Quinn Martin, and jeopardizing Daystar's reentry into the movie business. "There were some pretty deadly piranhas at ABC," said Jack Poplin. "Personally, I always thought that Leslie had gotten a little too arrogant for them, and the network brass decided they were going to squash him." Stefano added that, "There were people who wanted to get *The Outer Limits* totally away from Leslie, and once it was clear that I wasn't going to stay, a lot of stuff went down. It was like the show went up for grabs, and a lot of jockeying was done."

"The artist sometimes puts art above anything," said Stevens. "And when he does that, he's not in the industry anymore."

"We were all really burned out by the end of the first season," notes Stefano assistant Tom Selden. "I'm rather glad Joe *didn't* go back for another year, because I don't think he could have. He put so much into the show that he got very ill, just from exhaustion. And when it came time for the second season to start, we were all already busy doing other things, new projects."

One man who continued on to the new season was director Byron Haskin. "*The Outer Limits* could have been one of the biggest hits on TV, if only it had had a little *impetus,*" he said. "But I don't hold much credence for any network attitude, though. If you want the truth, they're all fucking idiots. Really! How they can stay out of the way of bicycles, I have no idea."

Murder, madness, and other lurking horrors are the raw certainties that await you in the depths of the Unknown. And no switch of time, no twist of plan can cancel your meeting with it. For some night, in some blind panic, you will venture into the world of dark reality. And on that night, you will keep your meeting with... The Unknown.

PART FOUR
The Devil's Puppeteer

Man looks up at the stars, and dreams his futile dreams. Child of the universe, his toys are ignorance, his games, fantasy. Not even master of his own fate, it is the Devil's Puppeteer who stretches his fingers to answer the question... What will happen next?

—Control Voice epilogue from "The Inheritors," by Seeleg Lester, Sam Neuman, and Ed Adamson

If you want to pinpoint the bridge between what has transpired on television from the Golden Age to today, *The Outer Limits* is a good transition. It illustrated the problems of trying to do a creative show, while fitting creative things into some kind of budget.

—Seeleg Lester

It has been suggested that Ben Brady and *The Outer Limits* did not work their way toward each other so much as collide. Some say that Brady's appointment as the new producer of *The Outer Limits* was a matter of calculated timing, or convenience. Still others suggest that it was part of a premeditated plot to show the door to the Stevens/Stefano regime before commencing the 1964–65 season.

An independent TV producer prior to becoming a programming vice-president for ABC, Brady had been one of the executives who had given the green light to *Please Stand By* in 1962. When *The Outer Limits* became a series, Brady dealt with it as an advisor: "I sat in creative control for ABC, and read and annotated every script," he said, "as I did on other shows. It was strictly a supervisory position." He advised Villa di Stefano on possible problems before the scripts went to the censors, and was of more or less equal status with Dorothy Brown's superior, Adrian Samish, with whom he worked under ABC's president of West Coast programming, Elton Rule. Brady did not have the power to override Continuity's objections regarding scripts. "I was unable to function creatively," he said. "And I was frustrated over creative aspects of shows I could not alter. Being unable to be a part of it wore me down. My desire was to actually *work* on the shows; to implement changes." He had previously done this for four years straight, while producing *Perry Mason* at CBS.

Like the Erle Stanley Gardner character who almost never lost a court case, Brady began as a lawyer. His parents put him through law school in the 1940s, and after about a year in professional practice he decided to try writing for radio, building a name for himself by scripting such shows as *Mr. Keene, Tracer of Lost Persons*. In the mid-1950s he entered the fledgling industry of television. One early show he initiated in 1951 was a quarter-hour musical variety series for NBC (it preceded the network newscast) called *Those Two,* hosted by Pinky Lee and featuring orchestra music by Harry Lubin, whom Brady would bring into *The Outer Limits* to replace Dominic Frontiere. Red Skelton's first TV series was under Brady's guidance, as were early episodes of the Richard Boone western, *Have Gun Will Travel.* In 1957 came the indefatigable *Perry Mason,* and CBS Executive Producer Gail Patrick Johnson hired Brady to do the show based on his familiarity with the legal field. The series was a prestigious success for Brady, and represents his best work in the medium. While on hiatus in 1960, he attempted a situation comedy called *Oh, Those Bells,* starring a German comedy team, the Wiere Brothers, with former Three Stooges collaborator Jules White as executive producer. Thirteen episodes were filmed, and shelved until 1962, when the show was critically annihilated as a failed attempt to resurrect vaudeville on television.

It was as an ABC executive that Brady first encountered Leslie Stevens, during the preparation of *Stoney Burke,* and his first impression was that Daystar's head man was "a real charmer." But the two would soon be at odds. During *The Outer Limits,* Stevens would frequently try to circumvent Brady's dictates by appealing directly to higher-ups in New York. "You may have been able to gather some of his imperious overtones," said Brady. "He had the impression that what he was doing was of enormous importance to ABC. He was terribly aggressive, and we just did not get along. It was only a matter of time before he was on his way out."

Stevens, in turn, saw Brady's appointment to *The Outer Limits* as a case of the gargoyles taking over the cathedral: "It was ABC, saying, 'If we can get one of our guys down in there, put some sensible people in control who can get this show *done,* then everything'll be all right." The program's ratings were not spectacular enough to justify ABC putting up with the Stevens regime at a time when they wanted to cut back the per-show budget even further, and were inclined to cancel the series outright. "But it was *so* popular," said Brady, "especially with kids and college audiences, and United Artists indicated they would like to continue it." At the same time, ABC still owed Brady the remainder of his contract as vice-president, which Brady was willing to give up in order to get back into active producing. When Stefano vacated his position due to the timeslot dispute with ABC, Richard Dorso recommended Brady as a replacement. UATV knew that Brady, a former executive, would be budget-conscious, and agreed to renew their *Outer Limits* contracts if Brady was made the new producer. This decision allowed ABC to usefully discharge their contract with Brady, and permitted Brady to get out from behind his desk job. It was very convenient timing for everyone involved . . . except Stevens and Stefano.

"When Brady took over," said Stevens, "I was both relieved and offended. It was a relief to finally wash my hands of the show, and to do that is being a very bad boy—the network expects you to stay and work with the new group. But I just didn't have the heart to. In the first place, I couldn't talk to Brady. He didn't know the first thing about science fiction, and it seemed, to me, to be terrible miscasting to put him anywhere *near The Outer Limits*."

Brady was also party to the decision to change the show's timeslot. "A good deal of the first year was a banner year in terms of art and product," he said. "Stefano was a great writer. But there was a violent schism between what he wanted and what ABC wanted. The network won't let go of a man they are happy with, so if they truncated their relationship with Stefano, they must have been unhappy." It is clear that Brady knew little of the circumstances surrounding Stefano's leave taking; his quarrel was with Stevens: "I just didn't want him around."

Stevens and Stefano moved on, retaining their ownership points in the series and leaving behind no prepared material for a new season. Stefano began work on *The Haunted,* a supernatural series pilot for CBS, and Stevens busied himself with what was to be Daystar's final feature film, *Incubus*. Daystar's accounting department remained involved in budgeting the new season, and the craft union people signed to Daystar (the costumers, construction crew, editors, etc.) stayed on, as did Fred Phillips, Project Unlimited, and most of the other below-the-line personnel. "I didn't resent the new people," said Phillips. "But I had in the first season people a sense of trust. Not so, in the second season. When I'd ask them for something, they'd frown on it even though I needed it, as though I was going to pocket their money or something." On the other hand, Vic Perrin, the Control Voice, noticed no difference between the old guard and the new: "Ben Brady told me, 'Just keep on doing what you've been doing.'"

Stevens received a copy of every script, memo, and censorship notice, and several Daystar people tried to talk him into staying. "I felt unwelcome," he said. "And I could only mess things up worse by getting involved, and asserting authority, so I disengaged myself. The network put a stranger in our midst, in a position of authority, and that's enough to kill you as far as the creative group is concerned."

Far from being an errand boy for ABC's creative mandates, Brady soon found himself beleagured by the same frustrations that had hampered his predecessors. The budgets were cut down to about $100,000 per episode. Gerd Oswald, a personal friend of Brady's from their work together on *Perry Mason,* noted, "Whereas Stefano would say of an idea, 'Great, let's do it and I'll fight the network later,' Brady would say, 'I'd like to—but I can't.' After Stefano was eased out by the network, scripts were not improved upon, as they had been during his regime. Scripts during the first season were far superior to those of the second."

Having seen the series progress from *Please Stand By* to *The Unknown*, from Stevens's stainless steel technological showcase to Stefano's murky Gothic fever dreams, Brady's initial intent was to pull in the mass audience by seeking out, as teleplay fodder, "published works by established science fiction writers," he said. "We looked for a marriage between intelligent science fiction and good, sound showmanship." This marriage turned out to be a rocky one, since the cutbacks in budgets required the chosen stories to command fairly low royalties. Sometimes the scripts from these stories required multiple rewrites to shoehorn them into an acceptable episode budget... but the revision process often ran the show over budget anyway. "We were torn between the desire to find stories we could adapt," said Brady, "and the insertion of quickly written originals that would enable us to survive until we found the next good published story." His hand was also forced by a telegram from ABC President Tom Moore's assistant, Alfred R. Scheider, which read in part, "We want to see a monster early and often [in the show]." According to Brady, "During the first year, audience appeal shot right up when a monster was used. ABC showed us graphs and charts indicating that the highest point of interest in *any* science fiction play occurred when a monster appeared, or a 'monstrous' situation of some kind. They made an issue of it, to the point where we could not proceed without considering a monster. The episodes with monsters struck some note of excitement in the audience, yes, but they were artificially construed to carry that appeal. They were of lesser value."

At the beginning of his tenure, Brady contracted several shows that had no obvious "bear" at all, while others had them specifically to placate ABC. Still others had monsters thrust upon them. Brady's unfamiliarity with the show's milieu led him to interpret many of the new shows into a *Perry Mason*–like whodunit format, or superimpose a murder mystery framework in which the plot is advanced via the question-and-answer method of a police procedural, with the characters receiving the explanations serving the function of filling the viewer in on the plot. "Behold, Eck!," "Expanding Human," and "Counterweight" are prime examples of this style, and "I, Robot" would take *The Outer Limits* right into the dock. Brady's administrative expertise made his function more that of a line producer. He was rarely seen on the sets, and conveyed most of his edicts through subordinates. He did some writing, but deferred most script revisions to his new story department.

Brady *did* go into the second season of *The Outer Limits* with a game plan, but his attitude became polarized with that of ABC from the moment production began, despite the fact that his network liaison was Adrian Samish, who had taken over Brady's slot in Programming once

Brady vacated it. "Adrian and I used to meet at lunch to discuss *The Outer Limits* at great length," Brady said. "We talked each other's language, [and] I went into producing the show with great glee."

The Brady Bunch

"I met Ben in 1957, on *Perry Mason,"* said Seeleg Lester, *The Outer Limits'* new story editor. "I came in as a writer, then became story editor, and when Ben left I became an associate producer. In *Perry Mason*'s fifth season, I became a producer. Five years later, Ben called me from ABC. He was working in administration, but wanted to go back into producing, and there were two shows he could do. One was a mystery show of some kind, the other was *The Outer Limits,* and I told him that was the better of the two. We took it over, and I think we made it intriguing and a little more literate."

A scenarist who had graduated from radio to TV and would soon move on to feature films, Lester recognized the severe restrictions under which he was to operate: "The 'minds' at the networks have to justify their salaries, so they formulate theories about 'what the public wants' and turn them into directives. ABC wanted monsters and they were *always* at our throats about it; it became a continuous battle between us. Samish, the ABC liaison, was an idiot. For the first five weeks, we were allowed our heads to buy stories, and I got in some men with some decent ideas. Along about the sixth week, ABC began insisting on a monster in every show, so I tried to make them as innocuous as possible, as an offshoot of the drama. We wanted to grab ahold of the audience with unusual, imaginative material. The network just wanted to frighten people."

Then came the new, reduced budgets. "Ben and I were always conscious of how little money we had," Lester said, citing, as items that vampirized funds, inflating studio overhead and "administrative supervisory costs"—this nebulosity being the per-show percentage drawn by Daystar/Villa di Stefano, the William Morris Agency's eternal 10 percent cut, and Brady's expense account.* "Stevens and Stefano had a much freer hand," claimed Brady. "If their budgets looked like they were going out of control, ABC was willing to risk it on the chance the show would

*"I used to make out Brady's expense accounts," said Brady aide B. Ritchie Payne. "That was some of the greatest creative writing I've ever done in my life."

be 'big.' In the second year, ABC killed *me* with the budget. It was driving us all crazy."

The cutbacks forced fast shooting, fewer retakes, and less time to cover technical slips. Extravagant casting was avoided. Costly optical effects were limited, for the most part, to the first few shows filmed, with Project Unlimited falling back on a number of hand-puppet-style "bears," and "stock shot" footage from 1950s science fiction films filling several gaps. "The effects of the first season would have been impossible in the second," said Lester. "We had to design scripts for cheapness, and find ways to do it all indoors, or with magic instead of production values."

"The one guy we thought the new group was so lucky to have was Seeleg," said Stevens. "He really cared; he had both the drama and the science concepts." Lester, who was to work with Stevens ten years later on the *Invisible Man* series, noted in turn that "Leslie is a victim of his own good nature. He has vision, ideas, concepts... and somebody always comes along and messes it up for him." Of Brady, Lester said, "He was not an 'absentee producer' on *Outer Limits*. He's a good nuts-and-bolts man, with his fingers on all the physical costs of production. He wasn't active in story content—I think that's why he wanted me."

When Daystar disengaged and the soundstage deal with KTTV ceased to exist, 1st AD Claude Binyon became the show's new production manager after Robert Justman returned to his old AD duties. "I went over to Paramount," said Binyon, "and said to Frank Caffey, the head of production, 'I've got a problem: I need a studio and I have no idea of how to go about getting one!'" Caffey, a long time friend of Binyon's father, had given Claude, Jr., his first job in the industry. "UATV scrutinized the deal we made and said there was no way they could have bettered it." Binyon secured the use of "Paramount Sunset," a bowling alley turned soundstage on Sunset Boulevard, formerly owned by Warner Brothers. "It smelled of years gone by," said Binyon. "We had one office I believe used to be Sam Warner's; it had a little portico that extended beyond the wall and looked right down onto a large shooting stage, like a balcony, so Sam could view the ongoing filming from this 'closet' in his office."

"We were in a funny little corner at one end of that studio," said Brady's assistant, B. Ritchie Payne. "To my knowledge, we were the only show shooting there. It was where we did most of *The Outer Limits* because locations cost so damned much money. It was a working office, not exactly plush. Binyon had the layout on the first floor." This was roughly equivalent to Daystar's ground floor. On the second floor were editing facilities, "a little half-assed screening room," and the offices of Brady, Lester, and associate producer Sam White. "Seeleg was down the hall, in his 'darkroom,'" said Payne. "He had a fascinating work habit. He'd pull every shade in his office, and turn on his desk lamp throughout the day to work. He told me, 'I don't know why, Ritchie, but I just can't work in the daylight!' People used to wonder what the hell was going on down there. He was a learned man; I enjoyed talking to him. The apocryphal story about Ben's office was that it had once belonged to John Barrymore. It had the biggest goddamned bathroom I'd ever seen. I remember saying to Ben, 'Now that I've visited this bathroom, I know why it's carpeted—this is probably where Barrymore made love!'"

"We had a series of offices with interconnecting doors," said Binyon. "We put a dart board at one end and threw darts through the rooms. Bob Justman and I had a kitty; you'd get three darts for a quarter and anybody who hit the bullseye would get the pot. We were *lonely* down there!" Binyon's principal task was deciding how to wisely spend the no-frills budgets. "Claude used to break his butt trying to bring the damned shows in under budget," said Payne. In these matters, Binyon dealt not with Brady, but with Sam White.

"Sam had been an associate producer on *Perry Mason,*" said Lester. "He came in after we'd started on *Outer Limits,* and did what an 'ass-prod' does—odd jobs, whatever Ben laid off on him. He was just an errand boy." Brady recalled White as "a line production type, who knew the workings of cameras and technical stuff, more like a production supervisor." Gerd Oswald shares Lester's unfavorable view: "He seemed to be Brady's best and oldest friend, but he was actually his number one handicap, a sort of hatchet man. His taste was dreadful, and he persuaded Brady to use a bunch of writers that weren't of the caliber Stefano had had." White's brother, Jules, had done dozens of Three Stooges shorts at Columbia, and had brought Brady into *Oh, Those Bells*. "Well," said Binyon, "*The Outer Limits* was *not* the Three Stooges. We wound up with a terrible Us and Them situation between the people left over from the first season and Ben, Sam White, and Seeleg. The year before, you could speak to Leslie and Joe; they were like family. Ben and I never had a whole lot to say to each other."

One factor insulating Brady from his crew was his habit of sending underlings to deliver his edicts. "Ben would often send me on such missions," said Payne. "And I thought, Ben, this is important, why don't *you* go? Later, Sam White told me, 'When you deliver the message, it's softer. When Ben walks onto the set, everybody *stops,* and thinks, what the hell's happening *now?*" Though Brady was not dictatorial, this contributed an atmosphere of tension to the new season.

Another sticky situation was ABC's hostility toward the crewmembers carried over from the first season. Although Brady acknowledged that Dominic Frontiere's theme music was fine, Frontiere was a Daystar executive and confidant of Leslie Stevens . . . and so Harry Lubin, an old coworker of Brady's was summoned to provide new *Outer Limits* music. Casting Director Meryl Abeles was quickly and gracelessly fired, and replaced by Harvey Clermont. Brady ran afoul of this bias when it came to using his old friend, Gerd Oswald. "I had directed some thirty *Perry Masons* for Ben," said Oswald. "When he came onto *The Outer*

Limits, he called me for dinner and said, 'I'm going to have trouble using you for the first few shows,' because Adrian Samish had said to him, 'Oswald? Forget it!'"

"Samish was a fellow who could, quote, *command,*" said Payne. "He was one of those schizophrenic network personalities who could be charming, generous, and wonderful one moment, and the next, sir, be quite willing to conduct a personality castration of you right in front of God and everybody. When he walked into the room, you got the general impression that he was in *charge* of something. When you heard him speak, you got the impression he did not like to be disagreed with. When he was dissatisfied with costs or ratings, and called Ben, the conversation would be less than warm and understanding, and Ben would be in a lousy mood for the next two days. Samish was not a stupid man; he came out of Princeton, if I'm not mistaken. But he had a commercial personality quite different from his regular one. He produced half the shows at ABC but never wrote or directed one damned teleplay."

"Samish was of the opinion that 'Forms of Things Unknown' was a *terrible* show," said Oswald. "Brady was forced to go a more prosaic, down-to-earth route. Haskin and I were both on Samish's shit list, and it took Brady four or five weeks before he could say, 'Well, I want Gerd, period, and I want Bunn Haskin.'"

A more bearable go-between with ABC was the new production coordinator, Calvin Ward. "Cal was my representative," said Brady. "He made sure that ad copy wasn't abused, and inserted commercials into the shows." According to Payne, Ward was "a real gentle-man, a do-what-needed-to-be-done kind of fellow. He was quite good at mediating disputes. If Ben wanted to get a message across to Seeleg, very often Cal would go in, sit down, have a cup of coffee, and say, 'Gee, regarding this scene, I wonder if we couldn't change this.' If a negative was supposed to be in to the lab, Cal would jump in his car and deliver it. He was very capable at story conferences. Sometimes he'd sit in the corner for two or three sessions with nothing to say, then make one suggestion that everybody would buy."

Of the crewmembers who worked both seasons, Jack Poplin noted: "The first season was far more creative and esoteric than the second, which was much more commercial. Ben Brady is a capable man, but an executive, not a creator. He was doing what he was told, and grinding them out. He was out of his depth, with the onus of the heavyweights that had preceded him."

Robert Justman said, "With Leslie and Joe both gone, the series degenerated into Monster of the Week... which is what ABC had wanted all along."

"I had no problems with the new regime," said Elaine Michea, who relocated to Paramount Sunset to budget the new shows. "I was involved with Ben a little more than I had been in the first season, and we got along beautifully."

Byron Haskin's description of the season switch was typically apocalyptic: "I had heard that Ben Brady was a fair-haired boy in the top, heavy circles, the rarified air where the masochists and maiming pimps who operate networks work. He left ABC, and was in limbo when along came this network decision to switch producers, and *boom!* We got the guy, and I didn't know who in hell he was. He didn't impress me as too stupid a guy, and seemed to know a lot of the glib answers most producers seem to have for any questions."

"I must say that Seeleg Lester tried very hard," said Binyon. "But he was no Stefano. Sam White worked hard, but he was from the old, three-reeler Columbia school. They all had their positions in the industry, and performed well. But Ben's concept was to look *first* at the dollar, then at what we were trying to do. I don't think you should hinder a writer that way; I always say go for it and then try to figure out how to fit it into the budget."

"ABC obtruded too much," said Lester. "The money Ben *could* have used for production was curtailed. When they flubbed around with the time slot, the show became an orphan. We could not do the things we wanted to do, and it became very frustrating, especially for a producer who can't even control the stories."

"Brady and the second season were not aimed in any specific direction, because ABC was unclear as to what they wanted," said Gerd Oswald. "They wanted the first season concept... yet they didn't. Although Ben had no real writing background, I recall both of us spending hours going over scripts line by line. He was very active."

"At that time, ABC had already instituted a study group to research the effects of programs on the audience," said Brady. "Their success was carefully gauged after many years of this research; it didn't just start when Fred Silverman climbed aboard. Based on those surveys, I was interested in reaching the largest possible audience with *The Outer Limits*, and I think Seeleg was, too. ABC didn't just come over and say, 'Look—you do this.' They can't talk to people of our stature that way. We don't function as automatons, we function by motivation, because we seek objectives. If you're seeking an objective and the research is there, you pursue it. We did whatever we could to avoid scraping the bottom of the barrel to appeal to the masses, but if it's proven they like something, you give it to them. If they like the Fonz, and you can't stomach the son-of-a-bitch, you still write for the Fonz. And week after week, I saw the audience appeal shoot up when we used monsters, and mind you this was in the *first* season. ABC wanted the monsters. You don't agree with anyone but your employer, and if you didn't support their position, then I guess you could afford to leave."

Production on second season episodes for *The Outer Limits* commenced on June 25, 1964.

PART FIVE

Man's Endless Thirst for Knowledge

> On every series you look at, the production operation knows that out of sixteen episodes, say, four might be good ones. Five, if you're lucky. And most of the rest is run of the mill. We know that a lot of the episodes we did were not what we *would* have done, if we'd had more time. But any producer who's honest will tell you that if he *has* those four good shows that satisfy him... then he's in happy-land.
>
> —Ben Brady

The Outer Limits' new season was more properly a *half*-season of only seventeen episodes. Of these, roughly half were derived from the sort of published science fiction Brady had originally favored as a story source.

As had Stefano, Lester talked with science fiction authors who were not used. "One of my favorites is A. E. Van Vogt," he said. "We had lunch one day, but couldn't come up with a good dramatic story. I'd read some of Theodore Sturgeon's work and found it a little pontifical. I would've loved to have had Richard Matheson. In fact, he called one day on behalf of Charles Beaumont, and said, 'Can you get Beaumont an assignment? *I'll* write it if I have to.' But Beaumont was a horror writer, and what he submitted to us was just not usable."

Along with the diminishing budgets came a reduced sense of the fantastic. It is not that the new members of the team were inadequate craftsmen, but when compared to the baroque opulence of Frontiere's music, or Hall's camerawork, the contributions of Harry Lubin and Kenneth Peach naturally sound and look more spare.

An alternate perspective on the new season came from Harlan Ellison, who had not been hired by Stefano, but who had sold scripts to the Brady regime: "The first season, I thought, was garbage, the usual monster bullshit. They were doing 'the bear on the beach,' in which you open with a bear on a beach, then you ask *how* the bear got on the beach. It was a lot of funny rubber masks, and basically silly ideas. Until Brady came in, there were no science fiction writers working for the show. In the second season, nobody paid any attention to what we were doing; nothing was left for production, so they left us alone to do what we wanted, and we were able to do scripts that were considerably more complex. We were allowed to experiment, because after Daystar and Villa di Stefano and everyone else had taken their cuts, nobody had an eye on us, and the ratings were already so low that no one gave a damn. And that's how the *best* stuff gets on—absolutely by accident. It slips through when no one's looking."

The Control Voice speeches became part of the individual writers' assignments, although many were appended to finished scripts by Seeleg Lester. In place of the first season's sometimes overblown moral messages, the new speeches became maddeningly alike in tone, opting for pseudo-Biblical profundities and the timeworn science-fiction-as-prophecy angle. Difficult to tell apart, they pounded the noble sentiment of Man's Endless Thirst for Knowledge into the ground like a tent peg.

The introductory narration was also given a final pruning. No longer was the viewer required to "*sit quietly and*." The edited speech used for most of the first season is heard in "Soldier," "Cold Hands, Warm Heart," "The Invisible Enemy," and "Behold, Eck!" The rest of the second season shows used the final version, which, like the budgets, had been cut back to the barest minimum.

> *There is nothing wrong with your television set. Do not attempt to adjust the picture. We are controlling transmission. For the next hour, we will control all that you see and hear. You are about to experience the awe and mystery which reaches from the inner mind to* The Outer Limits.

The Venusian—a Project Unlimited puppet filmed underwater so its "hair" would waft aloft.

COLD HANDS, WARM HEART

Broadcast 26 September 1964
Written by Milton Krims
Based on a Dan Ullman script titled "Project Vulcan"
Directed by Charles Haas
Assistant Director: Robert Justman
Director of Photography: Kenneth Peach

CAST: Brig. Gen. Jefferson Barton (William Shatner), Ann Barton (Geraldine Brooks), Gen. Matthew Claiborne (Lloyd Gough), Dr. Mike (Malachai Throne), Botany (James B. Sikking), Medicine (Dean Harens), Construction (Lawrence Montaigne), Electronics (Henry Scott), 1st Reporter (Julien N. Burton), 2nd Reporter (Peter Madsen), Security Chief (Hugh Jensen), Guard (Lou Elias), Steam Bath Attendant no. 1 (Ray Kellogg), no. 2 (Patrick Riley), Chairman (Tim Huntley).

The most brilliant planet in our solar system is Venus, named for the goddess of love. It is closer to Earth than any other planet—twenty-eight million miles away. Until sometime in the last half of the twentieth century it is still a planet shrouded in mystery, enveloped in a heavy blanket of clouds and steam. Because its surface temperature was believed to be several times that of Earth's, it was not thought possible for Man to reach Venus and come back... until one day, somebody did it.

Project Vulcan is a planet-colonization program designed to culminate in a human settlement on Mars, and astronaut Jeff Barton achieves its first victory by successfully landing on Venus. Upon returning home he is unable to recall what transpired during a brief radio blackout, but his body temperature drops to ninety-one degrees and he begins to crave heat. When he passes out in a superheated steam room, he flashes back to the Venus mission and has a nightmarish recollection of a plantlike denizen of that world, an ethereal creature with glowing eyes that peered through the porthole in Jeff's ship. He emerges from the steam room with scaly forearms and webbed fingers, his body now adapting to the Venusian climate, but he is determined to conceal his ongoing mutation until he can ram the remainder of the Project Vulcan package through channels to the green light stage. When he accidentally sets his arms on fire trying to get warm, his friend Dr. Mike alerts NASA specialists, who isolate Jeff in a pressure chamber at two hundred-plus degrees and discover an extraterrestrial hemoglobin changing his metabolism. They crank up the heat and prolonged exposure exorcises the alien influence. Barton presents Project Vulcan to the brass—wearing gloves—and is approved. When he reenters the chamber for another treatment, he sweats—the first sign that his ugly transformation has been reversed.

The eternal, never-ceasing search for knowledge often leads to dark and dangerous places. Sometimes it demands risks not only of those who are searching, but of others who love them. These, in their own special way, know that knowledge is never wasted, nor is love.

Dehumanization is the immediate concern of "Cold Hands, Warm Heart," the first show filmed for the new season. Jeff Barton is so obsessed with Project Vulcan that he sacrifices his own body to it, either ignoring his horrendous biological changes or requesting "a pill" to forestall them. Through at least four redrafts of the teleplay, this intelligent kernel idea was smothered in a mediocre and lazily-developed story that is motionless and uninvolving.

"It was the first script I bought," said Seeleg Lester of Dan Ullman's original teleplay. "The focal point of the astronaut's physiological changes was his need for more heat. Later on, I had to rewrite it; that he became a monster with talons was just ABC, wanting monsters." Ullman's story was similar to early drafts of "The Mutant," and the first and heaviest revisions were done by Milton Krims, another *Perry Mason* alumnus brought in by Brady. Lester describes Krims as, "a rather effete man who shouldn't have been doing science fiction; he was a different *kind* of writer. He did every other *Perry Mason*. But I didn't appreciate his talent." Totally at sea with the oddball subject matter, Krims ultimately did what he knew best by condensing the script to a question-and-answer procedural, a static, talking-heads drama to which the "bear" is awkwardly tacked on. Instead of brilliant courtroom thrusts and parries, the heads

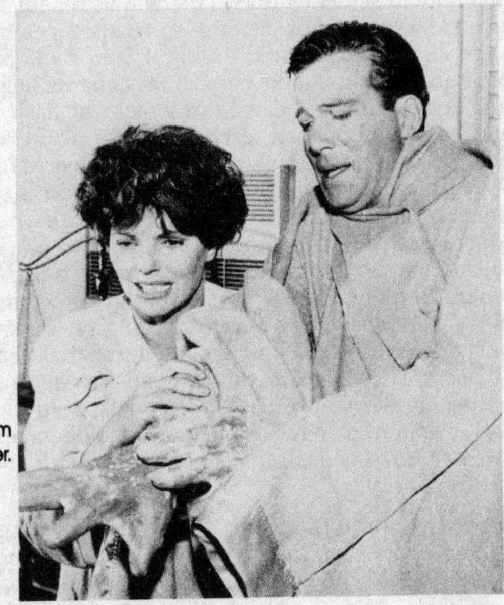

Geraldine Brooks and William Shatner.

were now reciting technological rigamarole, and in "Cold Hands" we first hear Harry Lubin's hysterical musical "sting," which was often tracked in at the end of an act to artificially confer some weight or urgency to the sometimes soporific events onscreen.

Hoping to speed past production setbacks by surrounding himself with old pals, Brady brought in Charles Haas, a former *Perry Mason* director who had done such exploitation quickies as *The Beat Generation* and *Platinum High School* in the 1950s. Unlike Sam White, Haas got along well with the *Outer Limits* crew, although his episodes are among the least successful new ones. Robert Justman, 1st AD for this and two other Haas shows, noted that, "Haas was a nice man, but not a good director."

Lester inserted into the teleplay the aspect of Barton's private investigation into his own worsening condition. He checks the construction of his capsule for conditions that might have led to his "hallucination" on Venus, and (in a deleted bit) checks the composition of his space food to see whether he might have glimpsed something he ate. To his wife, Ann, he delivers a speech that is supposed to encapsulate his character for us:

> BARTON: You married a man, not a headline. A man with certain peculiarities. Even as a boy, he'd spend hours watching the leaves fall from the trees, studying how they fell. His head was always up, looking at the birds. He even made himself a pair of wings and jumped off the barn—darn near broke his neck. That's how much he wanted to be a bird. So he became a bird... started flying higher and higher. August 6th, 1956, remember? Then one day he broke through the troposphere, into the stratosphere, and right then, for the first time, he understood the purpose of his life. It was to lead the way to new worlds, new life, new knowledge. That's the headline, Ann. That's Project Vulcan.

Then, before he can add "to boldly go where no man has gone before," he's off to the steam room. Aggressively American, Barton finds himself subjugated from within by an insidious invader who, if Jeff becomes an alien, will prevent the colonization of Mars by guys with the right stuff. William Shatner's usual obsessive performance is the show's main point of interest, and one of his last TV roles prior to signing on as *Star Trek*'s Captain Kirk.*

*Shatner's first TV space voyage, ironically, is in furtherance of a project called "Vulcan," after the Roman god of the forge. In earlier drafts of "Cold Hands," it is called Project Colossus.

Geraldine Brooks returns to *The Outer Limits* as the wife of yet another man turning into an alien, but this time (unlike "Architects of Fear") she gets her man back. Her characterization is limited to a strident and pathological wifely devotion, culminating in an excruciating speech she makes to the heavens to indicate, "He loves *me* better than you! I'm his *best* world!"

The wispy plant creature done by Project Unlimited was featured in the early commercials for the program's new season along with clips from "Soldier," "Keeper of the Purple Twilight," and "Counterweight." It was a puppet, filmed underwater to impart a dreamy, slow-motion quality to its movements. As a menace, it doesn't stand up to extended scrutiny, and we see far too much of it. The tilting POV shots of outer space seen by Barton as he blacks out were from Leslie Stevens's original end-title footage for *Please Stand By, sans* credits.

"Cold Hands, Warm Heart" was deemed too weak to use as a season opener. Fortunately for Brady, the premiere show of *The Outer Limits'* new look and new season would be "Soldier," an episode that vindicated his theory regarding the use of published science fiction.

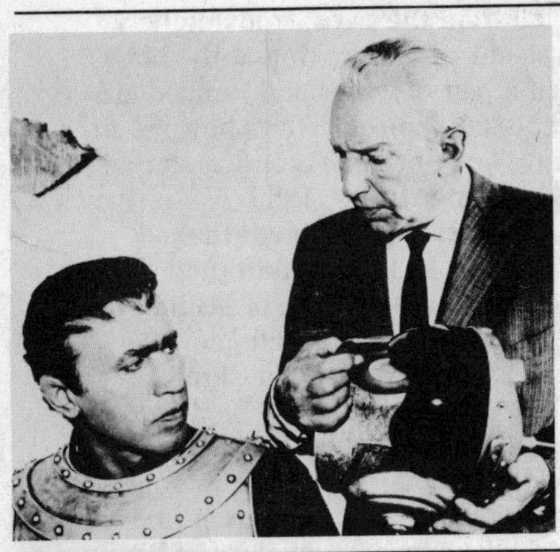

Lloyd Nolan (R) checks out Michael Ansara's helmet. Note ripped padding in cell wall.

SOLDIER

Broadcast 19 September 1964 (season premiere)
Written by Harlan Ellison, adapted from his short story. Some material by Seeleg Lester.
Directed by Gerd Oswald
Assistant Director: William P. Owens
Director of Photography: Kenneth Peach

CAST: Qarlo Clobregnny (Michael Ansara), Tom Kagan (Lloyd Nolan), Paul Tanner (Tim O'Connor), Abby Kagan (Catherine MacLeod), Loren Kagan (Ralph Hart), Toni Kagan (Jill Hill), Doctor (Ted Stanhope), The Enemy (Alan Jaffe), Sgt. Berry (Marlowe Jensen), Old Newsvendor (Jaime Forster), Woman (Mavis Neal), Helmet Voices (Vic Perrin, Tim O'Connor),

Night comes too soon on the battlefield. For some men it comes permanently; their eyes never open to the light of day. But for this man, fighting this war, there is never total darkness. The spidery beams of light in the sky are the descendants of the modern laser beam—heat rays that sear through tungsten steel and flesh as though they were cheesecloth. And this soldier must go against those weapons. His name is Qarlo, and he is a footsoldier, the ultimate infantryman. Trained from birth by the State, he has never known love, or closeness, or warmth. He is geared for only one purpose: to kill the Enemy. And the Enemy waits for him...

On a blasted, radioactive no-man's-land sometime after the year 3000, footsoldier Qarlo Clobregnny meets an enemy infantryman head-on in the middle of a crossfire of death beams. The energy propels both men backward in time to 1964, with the Enemy stuck halfway between the present and the future. Qarlo's materialization causes immediate urban panic and he is apprehended after disintegrating a police car with his energy rifle. Kagan, a philologist, is summoned to decipher Qarlo's gibberish and realizes the soldier is speaking permutated English. He and government liaison Paul Tanner deduce Qarlo is from the future, and while Tanner runs interference against other agencies eager to get their hands on Qarlo, Kagan patiently establishes a rapport with him. Kagan convinces Tanner to allow Qarlo to experience "normal life" by moving in with Kagan's family, but Qarlo, craving his missing weapon, soon breaks into a gun shop and secures a hunting rifle. Kagan talks him out of the shop, without violence, but upon their return home, the Enemy (having successfully squirmed through the time warp) flames away Kagan's living room wall and attacks. Qarlo rushes him, the Enemy's rifle discharges, and both men of the future are vaporized.

From the darkest of all pits, the soul of Man, come the darkest questions: Did the soldier finally come to care for those he protected? Or was it just his instinct to kill? Questions from the dark pit. But no answers. For answers lie in the future. Is it a future in which men are machines, born to kill, or is there time for us? Time. All the time in the world... but is that enough?

When editor Hans Stefan Santesson bought "Soldier" for the October, 1957, issue of *Fantastic Universe Science Fiction,* he paid writer Harlan Ellison $91. Published as "Soldier From Tomorrow," the tale dealt with a footsoldier of approximately eleven hundred years hence who is accidentally time-warped from the thick of a skirmish with his "Ruskie-Chink" enemies to the present. Those who discover him eventually put him behind a podium to outline the horrors of future warfare in gruesome detail, hoping this information might deter humankind from what seems an inevitable path to destruction. For adapting the story for *The Outer Limits,* Ellison was paid $5000. "Soldier" was his first-ever science fiction teleplay. After selling a story to *Route 66* in 1962, he had broken into scriptwriting doing episodes of *Ripcord* and *Burke's Law.*

In Ellison's first draft, Qarlo materializes on a New York subway station platform and is subdued by the pounding noise of an arriving train. He is tossed into a bullpen full of winos and derelicts, at their mercy without his sound-baffled helmet. A goofy cop named Zimmerman inadvertently vaporizes a wall of the precinct house while toying with Qarlo's rifle, and a professor named Charney proposes a method for sending the soldier back to the future, utilizing the "cross-polarization of laser beams." Qarlo also experiences a mild attraction for Kagan's daughter, Toni:

> QARLO (suspiciously): What do you want from me?
> TONI: What do *I* want from *you*? Oh, brother, how it saddens me to know men haven't changed a bit, even eighteen hundred years from now.
> QARLO: You're'a one more danger to me than Kagan. What do you want from me?
> TONI: Don't you trust *any*one? Can't you even see we're trying to help you? Didn't you ever want to get near someone, to talk to someone?
> QARLO: That isn't possible. We can't close to each other; anyone can't. Thinkspeek comes best, not to touch.
> TONI: You don't know what you're missing, friend. And I thought *this* was the worst of all possible worlds, because *nations* can't get together. What a lousy, lonely life you must lead.
> QARLO: That's *my* world. It's fine.

In the treatment, she gives Qarlo his first kiss. The Enemy also has a lot more to do after breaking free of the time-lock. He marauds about the countryside, obliterating a plane in flight and blasting a radio tower to slag (because it interferes with the homing signal on Qarlo), wiping out an old man in the control shack. When he tracks Qarlo to Kagan's home, Qarlo reverts. *"His face becomes something terribly alien,"* the script notes. *"He is the ultimate killer now, as he was when we first saw him. The softness that has been in his face for most of the last scenes is gone. He BELLOWS IN FURY."* He hurls a steaming pot of coffee, which the Enemy picks off while Qarlo runs the length of the dining-room table

Tim O'Connor (L) and Lloyd Nolan scrutinize Qarlo (Michael Ansara) through the padded cell's ceiling grate.

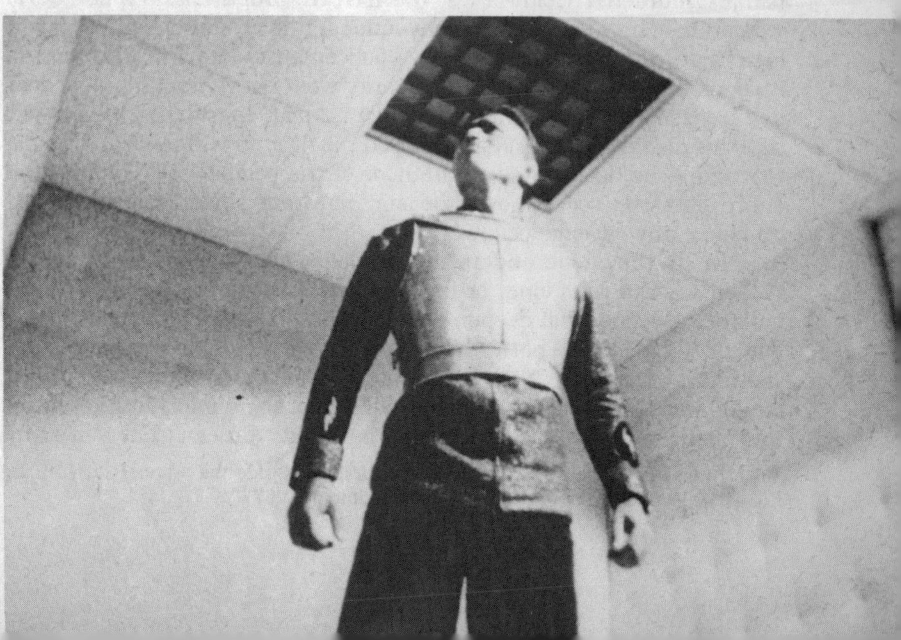

and springs. He strangles the Enemy and a spurt from the energy rifle kills but does not disintegrate him. All is silent, save for the Enemy's helmet on the floor: *"Kill... kill... kill..."*

"Ellison got as close as a TV writer can get to having complete control over his material," said Brady. "He was truculent, and extremely difficult; he *vanished* all the time. It took him weeks and weeks to deliver a script, but once we got it, it would be pretty goddamned exciting. If we wanted to change it, he'd be dying to do it, and what are you going to do with such a talented writer—let someone else screw around with the dialogue?"

The second draft dispenses with most of the one-shot or superfluous characters, and makes the most of a calculatedly small number of special effect shots. The flood of background on Qarlo is condensed, and the Kagan family recedes in importance. At the end of this draft, Qarlo and the Enemy zap out of existence.* Since most of Qarlo's interaction with Kagan's family was removed from Act Four by Seeleg Lester, who substituted the scene where Qarlo robs the gun shop, the "questions from the dark pit" asked by the Control Voice became something of a non sequitur.

"Harlan could pitch the ideas, but he couldn't get the script in on time," said Lester. "He thought the concept of 'Soldier' was novel and earth shattering, and the whole thing was just about this guy who becomes an automaton and follows orders. The production company was entitled to one rewrite. If we wanted any more, we'd have to pay Harlan some more, and when I turned in the second draft, Ben would have shot me if I'd called Harlan back. It *still* needed work!" Lester inserted the gun shop scene to try and impart a sense of action, the lack of which had just murdered "Cold Hands, Warm Heart." But the assumption Qarlo would know how to operate a conventional rifle is a much larger leap of logic than expecting a modern-day policeman to know how to work a flintlock. Further, a cop notes that Qarlo "went right through a steel door like it wasn't there"—a pretty spectacular feat, considering he doesn't have his disintegrator. And if he ripped the door off with his bare hands, why didn't he do likewise to the door of the padded cell? Finally, the entire digressive scene moves the story nowhere, since Qarlo is scooped up before any violence occurs.

"In TV, they don't understand subtleties of character," said Ellison. "When a script runs long, or has production problems, the first things cut are the scenes that deepen characterization. Those changes tore the gut out of that show. That's why, for me, it's a less attractive or interesting show than 'Demon With a Glass Hand.' One of the things that pissed me off was Qarlo's serial number, which for some inexplicable reason was changed to serial *letters,* which is stupid. You can't have an army

*Interested readers may examine this draft alongside the original story in the Ellison collection, *From the Land of Fear* (Belmont, 1967).

HPR 10

SHOOTING SCRIPT REVIEW

American Broadcasting Company

CONTINUITY ACCEPTANCE DEPARTMENT • WESTERN DIVISION • HOLLYWOOD

Dorothy Brown, Director

STUDIO DAYSTAR DATE June 3, 1964

CONTACT Messrs Stevens, Brady, Lester SHOOTING DATE

PROGRAM TITLE OUTER LIMITS EPISODE TITLE "Soldier"

The above indicated shooting script, received this date, has been reviewed by ABC Continuity Acceptance. The following comments are made in conformance with current ABC and NAB program and advertising policies.

Kindly forward such revisions as are necessary and please note that written approval for revised pages will not be forthcoming unless the new pages contain material unacceptable to ABC Continuity Acceptance.

This review is applicable only to the shooting script as submitted. A separate screening report will be issued upon viewing the film. *Kindly advise me at such time as this episode is available for rough cut/ first trial screening.*

COMMENTS (Confidential):

Page 1, sc 1 - here and through-out script the "radiation burns that mar his face" must not be too repulsive.
Page 5, sc 23- As you were advised in the OUTLINE REVIEW - keep the screams to a minimum in d.b. through-out the entire episode.
Page 8, sc 35- Delete the directions referring to "a toilet with no seat".
Page 9, sc 36- DERELICTS - keep smoking to minimum necessary for story purposes. GIRLIE MAGAZINES must be acceptable graphically - with fictitious titles.
sc 43- delete or substitute for "change your underwear".
Page 10,sc 43- Re-write the line "...that beep-beep kind".
Page 11,sc 45- 1st COP's line "...assassinate one of the candidates; we got elections coming soon, y'know" is untimely. Please substitute.
Page 13,sc51 - Usual caution re use of identifiable commercial airlines stock footage.
Page 24, sc 66-PICTURE BOOK - use fictitious title.
Page 25, sc 67-Delete "Damn". and "Dammit". (If dammeeooo, pp 17 sc 57 - is damn you - DELETE
Page 29, sc 73-No commercial brand of gum package.
Page 32, sc 77-Delete "helluva".
Page 41, sc 82-The "camp follower - Joy-girl" is good - but unacceptable.
Page 50, sc91 -Since the death of the OLD MAN is not a story point - let him fall as a result of something hitting him - fainting - fright - etc. His death is not necessary.
Page 55, sc99- Bleeding - deep furrows where claws have ripped at him - please perform this in your usual good taste.
Page 63, sc116-QARLO's death - scream - advise your dubbing editors to keep this down in d.b.

On your use of the FBI - other than the phone call in sc 48, you do not identify anyone as being an FBI agent. Please keep it this way as any further identification would require FBI clearance.

cc: Johnson, Heilweil, Gamson, file

Thomas Kersey
ABC CONTINUITY ACCEPTANCE EDITOR

ABC Television Standards & Practices advisement memo re: "Soldier" from the personal files of the author, Harlan Ellison. Used by arrangement with, and permission of the author and the Kilimanjaro Corporation.

with serial letters because there are fewer combinations, but they did that because they thought they were being very modern, very futuristic. And I had nothing to say about it, because by then I was off writing 'Demon.'"

Michael Ansara's performance as Qarlo is striking. His mien is halting, predatory; he reflects a volatile confusion of fear, curiosity, and barely tethered violence that makes each of Kagan's attempts at communication a scene of touch-and-go tension. "Michael and I go a long way back, to when he was playing Cochise on *Broken Arrow,*" said Claude Binyon. "'Soldier' was a good show. It's the old samurai story, with a time warp." The rest of the cast, unfortunately, is not up to the level of Ansara's singular work. Kagan's family, edited down to a few lines per member, is plain and forgettable. As Tanner, Tim O'Connor has a few sharp, snappy lines, but fails to characterize beyond them.

The casting of Lloyd Nolan was an attempt to emulate the "star casting" seen in the first season, and the $5000 paid to Nolan was more than any other actor received for a single episode, with the exception of Cliff Robertson. As Kagan, Nolan is dunning and monotonous, and shouts most of his lines without inflection because he is working from cue cards. "His lines sound stilted because he's *reading* them," said Ellison. "He was deaf. And no one knew it."

Qarlo and The Enemy are caught in the crossfire of special effects on the "war zone" set at Paramount Sunset.

Gerd Oswald's direction is taut, and the visual gimmicks, as abundant as *The Outer Limits'* new parameters allowed. The scene in which the Enemy burns down Kagan's living room wall from the outside is a real show-stopper. To create Qarlo's "war zone," the Paramount Sunset stage was converted into a fogbound valley of skeletal trees and battle debris. "It was gigantic; the size of three stages put together," said Oswald. "We had a sky cyclorama running all the way around it, and a horizon line of mountains in front of that, in diminished perspective. We filled it up with the fog machine. It was a no-man's-land, very flexible and changing, to contrast with Kagan's family life, which was very stable, as opposed to the uncertainties of the future world. It was open and dark, and I wanted to contrast that with the blinding brightness of Qarlo's closed-in padded cell. We did the hallway shot (as Qarlo leaves with Kagan for home) right there in the studio corridor—you can see Sunset Boulevard through the open door at the end. The gun shop sequence we shot on the actual Paramount lot, on New York Street. 'Soldier' is my favorite second season episode."

It is also the only show besides "Tourist Attraction" to use the Control Voice as a narrative linking device, when the Enemy is trapped halfway through the time vortex:

> *Time is fluid. The waters of forever close—and passage may not be completed. The present and the future are for a moment united. And the Enemy, half-today, half-tomorrow, is locked between...*

Qarlo's peculiar helmet was stashed in the prop closet at Paramount for a decade or so, then resurfaced as Robin Williams's alien headgear on *Mork and Mindy.*

While "Soldier"'s climax is dynamic and effective, the final image of Ellison's earlier draft is quietly unsettling. As the two corpses lie on Kagan's living room floor covered by body tarps, the camera closes in on Qarlo's shrouded form. *CAMERA HAS COME DOWN to an EXTREME CLOSEUP of Qarlo's hand. It is a fist. Even in death, he is ready to fight.*

The hand-puppet "sand shark" in its cork tank at Project Unlimited.

THE INVISIBLE ENEMY

Broadcast 31 October 1964
Written by Jerry Sohl, based on his short story. Some material by Byron Haskin, Seeleg Lester, Ben Brady.
Directed by Byron Haskin
Assistant Director: Robert Justman
Director of Photography: Kenneth Peach

CAST: Major Charles "Lucky" Merritt (Adam West), Capt. Jack Buckley (Rudy Solari), Capt. Paul Lazzari (Peter Marko), Capt. Frank Johnson (Robert DoQui), Gen. Winston (Joe Maross), Capt. Fred Thomas (Mike Mikler), Col. Hal Danvers (Chris Alcaide), Mr. Jerome (Ted Knight), Lt. James Bowman (Anthony Costello), Technician (James Tartan).

In the vast immensities of cosmic space, bold adventurers streak their way to join battle with strange enemies on strange worlds—the alien, the unknown, perhaps even the invisible, armed only with Man's earthbound knowledge...

The four-man M-2 probe lands successfully on Mars with a mission to uncover the fate that befell the two men aboard the M-1, three years earlier. According to monitor tapes, they were gobbled up by an unknown antagonist shortly after venturing out of their spacecraft, and a twilight computer back on Earth suggests, based on the evidence, that a ghost got them. The first M-2 man to investigate the M-1 wreckage is crunched up within minutes of landing; now the computer rather more intelligently opines that the Martian killer is invisible. During a more cautiously mounted sortie, Capt. Buckley discovers diamonds littering the landscape, and his excitement causes him to momentarily lose sight of his spotter, Capt. Johnson, who quickly becomes victim number four. When Buckley later sneaks out to collect more diamonds, he learns that the "invisible" enemy is an enormous dragon that emerges from beneath the Martian surface—"living in the sand like a shark in the ocean!" Mission commander Merritt, the only other M-2 crewman left, doggedly tries to drag Buckley back to the ship, but instead gets marooned on a rock escarpment in the middle of the sand-sea, with the "tide" rising and a hungry monster nearby. Using a blood-soaked garrison belt as a lure, Buckley fakes the creature out, and Merritt runs to safety while he obliterates the dragon with a nuclear-tipped bazooka shell. Six more very miffed creatures poke up their heads, roaring, but Buckley and Merritt make it back to the M-2 intact... and with a substantial haul of gemstones.

> *Battle joined. Casualties? Yes. Resolution: Victory, of a sort. A painful step from the crib of destiny. On another day, a friend, perhaps, instead of a deadly peril—part of the saga of the space pioneers.*

Perhaps the best example of how Brady's story-to-telefilm edict did *not* work, and a sharp contrast to the successful rendering of "Soldier," was "The Invisible Enemy," based on a story by *Twilight Zone* scenarist Jerry Sohl. "There was *nothing* to it," said Byron Haskin, who directed the show as his first assignment of the second season. "They handed me this dog with no cast and no script, just lousy. Of course we *had* to shoot it; they had it on the schedule, and it was coming like a railroad train down the track, and you've gotta get out there, start firing, and do the fucking thing in four days. God!"

"It was *Jaws,* actually, on Mars," said Sohl. "But the way it came off on *Outer Limits* was ludicrous because you saw the monster right off the bat. In the story, you didn't know what was killing those people until the very end."

As published in the September, 1955 issue of *Imaginative Tales,* "The Invisible Enemy" takes place on the fourth planet of a faraway star, where the fifty-man warship *Nesbitt* touches down to investigate a string of vanished vessels. After a ten-man expeditionary force is consumed from *inside* a forcefield, the ship's computer suggests "invisible birds" are responsible. Twenty-nine more men are killed and a lone survivor, Lazzari, is found in the desert. The final transmission from his unit: "No! No! They're coming out of the *ground!*" Lazzari kills himself by bashing his brains out against a bulkhead, and the remaining crewmen gather to give him a military burial. The computer advises against it—Lazzari's corpse is bloody, and blood is what seems to provoke each attack. Allison, a civilian computer expert, protests and is locked into the *Nesbitt* by Warrick, the stiff-starched mission commander. Allison watches helplessly as the entire funeral party is eaten by "large, heavy, porpoiselike creatures... swimming up out of the sand as if it were water."

Seeleg Lester rewrote Sohl's first draft when ABC decided the monsters did not appear soon enough to suit them. "I set up an absolute cover for every action that took place," said Lester. "I had cameras going all the time, and *still* they couldn't figure out what was making the crewmen disappear."

"Lester tried to get me to write a script incorporating the camera in scenes *underneath* the sands of Mars," said Sohl. "We wasted a lot of time over that."

"The script needed a lot of extra pencilwork," said Ben Brady. "Even *I* wrote some of it, which was the last thing I wanted to do." He rewrote the final act into what he termed "a calm fourth quarter," then turned the script over to Byron Haskin. "Haskin saved what could be salvaged."

"If I'd gone ahead and directed it as originally written," said Haskin, "the show would not have been aired. I had to sit up all night and rewrite it. After twenty-eight hours at the typewriter, I tore it apart and brought it up to a fine mediocre. Only a disorganized production team could let something so terrible survive long enough to warrant a full production job."

Just why the sand-sharks cannot pluck Merritt off his tiny spur of rock is never clear, especially when we've already seen the creature's elongated crab claws and the torn-apart shell of the M-1. The monster roars constantly (the same sound effect used in "The Invisibles"), yet is never heard on the radios monitoring the men as they die. The final draft eliminates the Sohl/Lester idea of remote cameras, which would have saved the M-2 crew a lot of grief. In Sohl's script the sand is exactly like the ocean, with an abundance of other life forms and flora; in the film we wonder what the creatures must eat normally, since they are so responsive to human blood.

Since the sand-shark was added in postproduction, Haskin was frustrated not only as a director, but as an effects technician: "I never shot anything that approximated the effect they put in later, beyond my control."

"It was probably the most challenging effect we did for *The Outer Limits*," said Gene Warren. At Project Unlimited, finely-ground cork was spread atop a tankful of water five feet deep, and Wah Chang's hand-puppet sand-shark head was manipulated from beneath the surface by Paul Pattee, who maneuvered according to a code tapped out on the side of the tank by Tim Baar. "You want to know what Paul's 'scuba suit' consisted of?" laughed Paul LeBaron. "We hooked a tube into the air-compressor of a spray gun and fed him oxygen through a paint-gun hose!" Mattes and rear projection imparted enormous size to the monsters when they were "married" to the footage of actors on the full-sized Martian set. "One of the biggest sets we ever had was that sand-ocean," said Warren, speaking of the sixty-five hundred square foot Paramount stage where the Martian backdrop (similar to the set used in "Moonstone") was laid.

To depict the M-2 landing near the M-1 wreck, the opening shot of

Adam West comes face-to-face with the not-so-invisible Enemy.

the 1958 thriller *It! The Terror From Beyond Space* was spliced in. Coincidentally, *It!* also deals with a murderous Martian monster, and was shot by Kenneth Peach. Haskin later used Adam West in one of his last features, *Robinson Crusoe on Mars,* in 1964. "He was an adequate actor capable of small roles," said Haskin. "It was the supporting cast on 'Enemy' that was poorly chosen—that was often the case during the second season shows." West is amusing as a weary space-dog for whom this new frontier is mostly a bore, and Rudy Solari injects some smart-assed verve into his part as Buckley (he is reminiscent of Chino Rivera in "The Mice").

But nothing cripples a show so much as the producer, story editor, director, and writer *all* hating it. "We tried to make that show attractive," said Brady. "But it came out all wrong; we just couldn't lick it." Haskin maintained, "It wouldn't have mattered if you'd've put the goddamned invasion of Normandy in it—it was *still* a dog!"

"The 'invisible enemy' was not so invisible, and so the suspense was shot right off," said Sohl. "On the other hand, people tell me it was a good show, so who can tell? Lester thought the fault was mine, and told me that while he'd buy more stories from me, they did not want me writing the scripts. I have nothing against any of the people on the show—only that they exhibited the syndrome so many TV people do when they discover science fiction: They think it's an invention of their own and don't pay attention to what anyone who has followed it over the years can tell them. If *The Outer Limits* stirs the imagination of youngsters the way *Science and Invention* boggled their minds back in the 1920s, then it is certainly a positive thing, even though we might carp about how it was put together."

The very next show on the production schedule was based on another Sohl story. "What surprised the hell out of me," said Lester, "was that Jerry wrote a book called *The Lemon Eaters* which I read and liked, after we did *The Outer Limits*. It was much, much better written than the teleplay he did for us."

"The plant creature was *not* my design," says Jim Danforth of the monster he animated for "Counterweight."

COUNTERWEIGHT

Broadcast 26 December 1964
Written by Milton Krims, based on the short story by Jerry Sohl.
Directed by Paul Stanley
Assistant Director: William P. Owens
Director of Photography: Kenneth Peach

CAST: Joe Dix (Michael Constantine), Dr. Alicia Hendrix (Jacqueline Scott), Keith Ellis (Larry Ward), Michael Lint (Charles Hradilac), Margaret O'Hara [stewardess] (Shary Marshall), Dr. Matthew James (Crahan Denton), Capt. Harvey Branson (Stephen Joyce), Prof. Henry Craif (Sandy Kenyon), Antheon Voice/Surface Control Voice (Robert Johnson).

> *The great unknown: Limitless heavens crowded with sparking mysteries, challenging Man's curiosity. But the heavens are not oceans. Man cannot push a boat into its currents and set sail for the next horizon. The heavens are a mystery only science can solve, as it penetrates the unknown.*

Weblor One is a 261-day colonization flight to a planet called Antheon, and to prove themselves constitutionally capable of making the trip, six candidates must endure a simulation run, locked up inside a spaceship mockup that travels the length of a desert tunnel, without pressing the "panic button" that ends the test and disqualifies them for the first of the actual interplanetary voyages. Various weird occurrences from meteor storms to physical attacks are presumed staged by the ship's crew; but some of the mishaps are overseen by a stowaway ball of whirling light that works to turn the passengers against one another. Prof. Craif, an ecologist, reveals that he engineered some of the occurrences from a control panel secreted by his bunk, but says some of the other ominous happenings were totally unplanned. Frightened, he goes for the panic button, but is prevented from pushing it by loudmouthed engineer Joe Dix, who stands to make millions off construction contracts on Antheon. The light-ball occupies a plant specimen brought aboard by botanist Michael Lint, turning it into a human-sized monster that warns the self-destructive humans away from Antheon: "You'll destroy us, too, if we let you. We will not allow this." Then it forces Dix himself to press the panic button.

> *Panic button pressed. Passengers returned. One side always in the sunlight, the other always in darkness; the known and the unknown. Frightening to each other only when they are both unknown...and misunderstood.*

"Sure, I'm a Nilly, and I've died seven times..."

First published in the November, 1959 issue of *Worlds of If,* Jerry Sohl's "Counterweight" traces the activities of a "Nilly," or a scapegoat placed intentionally aboard a long-term space colony flight. "It was my job," he says, "to see [the passengers] directed none of their venom against each other or the crew, only toward me." Known to the colonists only as an interloper called Red Mask, he maintains an atmosphere of terrorism that keeps the cooped-up colonists from killing each other. *"We are a theme, with variations, in the endless stretches of deep space, objects of hatred and contempt, professional heels, dying once a trip when the time is ripe, antidote to boredom, and we'll ply our trade, our little tragedies, on a thousand ships bringing humanity to new worlds."*

"I liked the idea of it being a test flight," said Seeleg Lester, "and the viewer not knowing, until afterwards, that they were still on Earth. But I would've held that back, used it as the climax. Instead of exploring that concept, Milton Krims went off into a stupid mystery...."

Like the Empyrian delving into the psyches of his abducted passengers in "Second Chance" (also directed by Paul Stanley), the Antheon being extracts similar skeletons from the mental closets of the Weblor One participants, and late in the last act it cuts loose a speech reminiscent of the aliens seen in the first season. But "Counterweight" is barren, talky, and illogical. The inner fears or doubts of the passengers are terribly obscure, except for Alicia Hendrix's frustrated sexuality, which is too forced and obvious. The script describes her necklace-twirling change of face as being *"like Shirley MacLaine in* Irma La Douce, *but...more like Mae West."* When she spills such glop as, "I must work to forget the children I've never borne," it's a surprise that no one tries to strangle her. The panic button, the psychological fallback of the story, seems none too scientific, since it disqualifies the whole compliment of passengers regardless of who pushes it or why. The closing Control Voice speech makes no sense whatsoever.

With the isolation training/simulation run angle laid bare upfront, and the plot twist of one of the passengers being a "ringer" reduced to a background detail, Krims's "mystery" consists of waiting through three long acts to find out what the alien light-ball is up to. The only performances providing relief from this tedious wait are Michael Constantine's loudmouthed and abrasive Joe Dix (who steals the show from his catatonic fellow guinea pigs), and Larry Ward's predictably cynical reporter, who only deals with the ho-hum facts (and establishes a lesser conflict, with Dix, of intellectual versus blue-collar). Dix fancies himself a pioneer, a survivor. "In this movie, we're the heroes," he says. "We *know* it ain't real—what do we gotta be scared of?" He has a clever speech dealing with belief in such "movies" as unreality:

> DIX: Look, nobody's gonna push that button unless they blow their top, right? This whole deal, for real, is just like a movie, see? Now, you take the hero—everybody's out to kill him—the bad guys, the floods, blizzards. Even in those kooky horror pictures, the most awful monsters. They're all after his blood or something. But is the hero scared? No. Why? 'Cos he *knows* it ain't for real.

Dix's talk of monsters is presumably where the Antheon creature gets the inspiration to turn into something that would appeal to ABC in "bear" terms. Of the fanged, glowing-eyed plant bogey that addresses the passengers in Robert Johnson's voice, Gene Warren said, "We had a full-scale one about six feet tall, motivated by wires, and a small model that Jim Danforth had to animate." The brief shots of the plant uprooting and killing another plant, and crawling out onto the floor of the ship, were *The Outer Limits*' first use of stop-motion animation since "The Zanti Misfits." "The plant creature was *not* my design," asserted Danforth. "And it's quite difficult to animate a puppet you don't find aesthetically pleasing, especially when you must concentrate on it for hours at a time."

Great pains are taken to inject science fiction gimmicks to the prosaic story, but they remain appendages—just like the monster. There's an encore of the go-nowhere meteor shower crisis from "Second Chance." The restriction of storage area compels the group to eat bland paste from tubes, with the proper aroma supplied by a selection of spraycans, yet these Space Age meals are served on a conventional dining room table with a full china service. The book and music libraries are too conventional and cumbersome for a ship that can only afford six passengers a sleeping space the size of a closet.

One curious piece of film is a lengthy boarding sequence, designed to introduce us to each character as they check in for the flight. We see it at the *end* of the episode, under a wailing Harry Lubin motif with no dialogue, and an individual "showcase" credit for each actor. This was done for no other episode. The footage was dropped during editing, then hurriedly reinserted as a credit sequence when the special effects footage came in short. The quick shot of the needle-nosed spaceship hissing through the void was taken from the George Pal film *When Worlds Collide* (1951).

A brief glimmer of first season grandeur comes when the alien upbraids the humans: "You are *children* who still believe in monsters!" But, as Ben Brady said, "'Counterweight' was another victim of budgetary limitations."

"It was a depressing thing," said Jerry Sohl of pitching stories to *The Outer Limits*. "I even offered them the TV rights to my novel *Costigan's Needle,* which, to my relief, they did not take. As a result of 'The Invisible Enemy,' 'Counterweight' was corrupted. I could not stand to watch it when it appeared, and have not, to this date, seen the finished product."

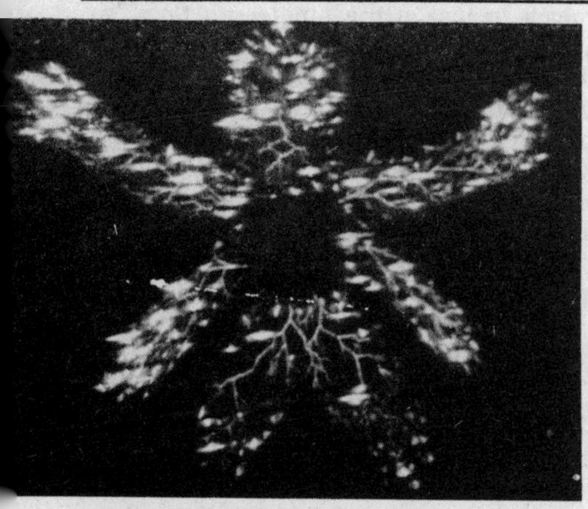

The "electrified" Eck (Lou Elias), beheld.

BEHOLD, ECK!

Broadcast 3 October 1964
Written by John Mantley. Originally titled "The Reluctant Monster." Story by William R. Cox, based on the novel *Flatland* by Edwin Abbott.
Directed by Byron Haskin
Assistant Director: Robert Justman
Director of Photography: Kenneth Peach

CAST: Dr. James Stone (Peter Lind Hayes), Elizabeth Dunn (Joan Freeman), Dr. Bernard Stone (Parley Baer), Det. Lt. Runyon (Douglas Henderson), Sgt. Jackson (Jack Wilson), Miss Willet (Marcel Herbert), George Wilkenson (Sammy Reese), Fire Chief

Rogers (Taggart Casey), Grayson (Paul Sorenson), TV Newscaster (Richard Gittings), Eck (Lou Elias), Eck's Voice/Radio Announcer Voice (Robert Johnson).

Since the first living thing gazed upward through the darkness, Man has seldom been content merely to be born, to endure, and to die. With a curious fervor he has struggled to unlock the mysteries of creation and of the world in which he lives. Sometimes he has won. Sometimes he has lost. And sometimes, in the tumbling torrents of space and time, he has brief glimpses of a world he never even dreams...

"Eck" is a four-eyed, four-armed, cartoonish alien from a two-dimensional world who, after falling to Earth through a dimensional tear, cannot transpose Earth's "alien" perspective into 2-D to find his way back out. Instead, he doggedly vandalizes optometric labs all over New York, and attacks anyone wearing Prescription 109 glasses, which are made from a meteoric quartz that renders him visible. Since Eck can pass through any Earthly solid (as long as he turns sideways first), he also accidentally glides through a thirty-seven-story office building, shearing it in half at the nineteenth floor "so cleanly that it has not yet toppled." Dr. James Stone spots Eck in his lab before he gets the Prescription 109 lenses slapped from *his* face, and after theorizing the existence of a 2-D creature, makes friends with Eck. Eck wants to repair the dimensional tear so none of us plop suddenly into *his* world. Stone's militant brother Bernard leads the police to the lab. Assuming Eck is invisible, they incinerate the lab with flame-throwers in the name of civil good, but Eck survives, revealing himself after the aggressors have left. Stone hastily prepares "glasses" for Eck, and once back at the tear, the creature thanks him and gratefully escapes this inhospitable plane.

Paradoxically, Man's endless search for knowledge has often plundered his courage and warped his vision, so that he has faced the unknown with terror rather than awe, and probed the darkness with a scream rather than a light. Yet there have always been men who have touched the texture of tomorrow with understanding and courage. Through these men, we may yet touch the stars.

"The second season was panics-ville; everybody knew the show was croaking," said director Byron Haskin. Following the aversive experience of "The Invisible Enemy," he decided he wanted out of *The Outer Limits*. "Lou Morheim had moved into a power seat at MGM, and told the executives there that I had the touch to bring some subtlety to programs like *Mr. Novak* and *Dr. Kildare,* which were very mechanical shows with no sentiment. Now, to me, this meant joining the 'inner circle' of directors who did *all* the TV. But Sam White told me I couldn't go because we had a show to do—this silly damned thing called 'Behold, Eck!' I only did it because White and Ben Brady wouldn't let me out of my *Outer Limits* contract. It was an alleged comedy that was just a *bomb*. They laid that script in my hands; I got one sniff of it and damn near fainted. Most of it I either rewrote or made up on the set. Peter Lind Hayes was able to do light comedy, but that script didn't even give him a chance."

According to Seeleg Lester, Haskin's disaffection for the new shows was reflected in his lackadaisical direction: "As soon as Haskin started to direct, it looked bad. When I tried to straighten out something in a script, he'd tell me, 'What the hell: Take your money and run'—that's the kind of director he was."

Lester drew the core idea of "Behold, Eck!" from the Edwin Abbott novel *Flatland*, first published in 1884. "It had no relation to our story other than the idea of a two-dimensional world," he said. "Bill Cox talked it over with me until I sparked to something." Cox wove a lighthearted comedy treatment around the 2-D concept, which was assigned to John Mantley, then a very successful scriptwriter. "John had a portion of some island in the Caribbean," said Lester, "and used this assignment to buy another little piece of it. Before he could retire there, he got caught up in producing *Gunsmoke* and became *too* successful." When a monster had to be added to the stew, Lester created one. "It was a *frightened* monster, doing terrible things just because it was not aware of what it was doing."

Makeup artist Harry Thomas with both Eck costumes—"Before" electrification (on floor) and "After" (on wall).

Much of the intended comedy in the show was to derive from Eck's understated and apologetic nature. "I'm sorry to have caused so much difficulty," he says after Dr. Stone reels off a page of dense gook about optical coefficients and aplanatic surfaces so complicated that even Eck doesn't fathom it. It's meant to be funny, but the show has neither the flair for wit nor the subtlety of delivery that distinguishes light comedy. The direction is weak and the script is padded and boring, and the fact that Eck is a literal "four-eyes" who needs glasses is another joke easily missed. Since Eck is too obviously a superimposed special effect (a la the Galaxy Being), it is impossible for the onscreen principals to play off him in terms of comedic timing—and difficult for the TV viewer to relate to him as a character, since he is so flashy and cartoonlike.

The two Eck suits were full-body affairs in black velvet, filmed against a black background. The first featured the white "lightning bolt" outline of Eck, and the second was decorated with glittering triangles of metal that imparted a sparkling effect to the creature (a consequence of Eck's run-in with a TV set, which "electrifies" him). While unusual and eye-catching, these suits are nothing like the creature described in Mantley's script:

> There are long, overpoweringly muscular hands and arms attached to a short body. The head is huge, with four eyes. The face is rather sad-looking, set on a body with no neck. The legs and thighs are huge and muscular... and reach almost to the chest.

"That was my old buddy Lou Elias playing Eck," said Claude Binyon. "I met him on a picture called *Enemy Mine,* on which I was the Second AD. He played a German sailor. He was an excellent stunt man." Peter Lind Hayes was an acquaintance of Ben Brady's who flew out from New York City to appear in the episode. "After a couple of days' shooting, Peter became very insecure and wanted to see the dailies," said B. Ritchie Payne. "Ben's rule was that no actor could see them, because they'd want to reshoot everything. After they had a heartfelt conversation, Ben said, "All right, Peter, I'll let you see the rushes, but you must understand that I make the decision as to whether we reshoot, and you know that with our damned budget we can't *do* that.'"

"Behold, Eck!" is a dramatic fiasco that had no place on *The Outer Limits,* and it is difficult to imagine it as anything but dreadful tedium for the adult viewer. "It was supposed to be light, with a good-hearted monster," noted Brady. "It was a very cute idea that was hard to control. Haskin did the best he could with it."

"In that particular show, you can see where the production values were not what they should have been," said Lester. "I would've loved to *see* that building actually being sliced in half! We were going to have the creature slice through an aqueduct, pouring water over the whole city. Those would be the things that would have made the show memorable."

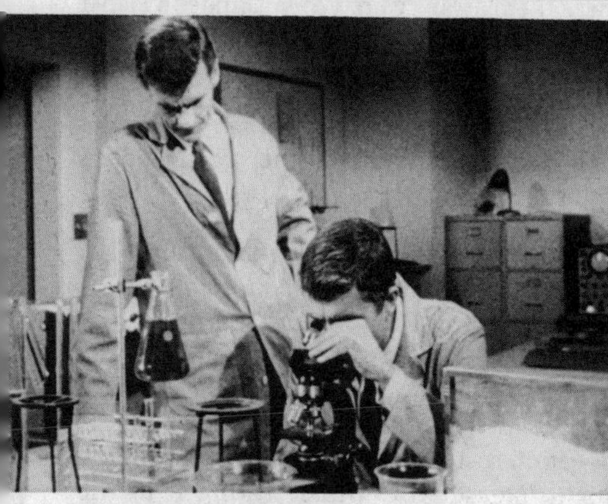

Peter Haskell (L) and Patrick O'Neal at the microscope.

WOLF 359

Broadcast 7 November 1964
Written by Seeleg Lester. Based on "Greenhouse," a story treatment by Richard Landau.
Directed by Laslo Benedek
Assistant Director: William P. Owens
Director of Photography: Kenneth Peach

CAST: Jonathan Meredith (Patrick O'Neal), Ethel Meredith (Sara Shane), Philip Exeter Dundee (Ben Wright), Peter Jellicoe (Peter Haskell), James Custer (Dabney Coleman).

Outward stretches the quest for truth. Stars without end. Timeless infinities. A billion, billion galaxies. Man's imagination reaches out and out, while betimes the farthest reaches of knowledge are found in the smallest places…

Dundee's Planet is an ecologically synthesized sample of a world in the Wolf 359 star system, implanted into an environmentally-regulated "greenhouse" in the desert lab of Prof. Jonathan Meredith. One second equals eleven days in the miniature Dundee world; Meredith introduces human DNA into the ecosystem, and he and assistant Peter Jellicoe settle back to observe the process of evolution with their microscopes and time-delay cameras. Dundee's Planet begins to parallel the most negative aspects of Earth's development at high speed, and also exudes a malignant, wraithlike entity that seems to dominate the goings-on in the capsule world. It is also able to project itself outside the greenhouse to terrorize Meredith, who sends his wife Ethel packing and fires Jellicoe to spare them from the creature's sinister influence. Jellicoe returns (with financial backer Dundee) and unknowingly saves Meredith when the bright headlights of his car banish the attacking creature. Meredith obsessively drives them away again. When Dundee's Planet catches up to Earth's nuclear age and Meredith is about to witness and record what he believes to be the fate awaiting *our* world as well, the entity attacks again. This time he is saved by Ethel, who returns in time to smash the greenhouse glass, killing Dundee's Planet and forcing the creature to withdraw. Meredith's recommendation: Only evil awaits on the *real* Dundee's Planet, and our spacemen should not be sent there.

> *There is a theory that Earth and sun and galaxy and all the known universes are only a dust-mote on some policeman's uniform in some gigantic superworld. Couldn't we be under some supermicroscope, right now?*

Seeleg Lester's first full script for the second season intelligently danced around budgetary and location restrictions instead of succumbing to them. It supplied a monster to please ABC while casting it in the metaphorical role of anti-God, and was informed throughout with an inquiring sense of wonder... even if some of the questions it raised remained unanswered.

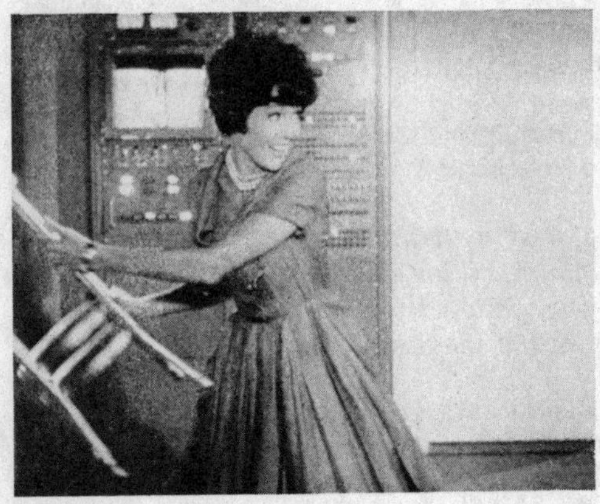

Sara Shane breaks on through.

"Dick Landau came in with a story idea about a far-off planet that had the same evolutionary 'plan' as Earth," said Lester. "I made the other planet without a God, completely evil; then that evil comes out of the greenhouse. I used the monster for the purposes of the story rather than making the story subservient to the monster."

In Landau's draft, the parallel chain of evolution on Dundee's Planet produces a humanlike civilization overlorded, in effect, by the Devil instead of his mythological opposite number. This entity, called a Plag, cheats scientist Jonathan Wragg (later Meredith) out of his bid to become Dundee Planet's resident god. Lester's revision added the aspect of accelerated time (originally the greenhouse was to contain a re-creation of the entire planet Mars, in extreme miniature). The ABC censors returned this draft as "too horrible," and he softened it with another rewrite. One twist he added was the gestalt formed by the Plag among Jonathan, Ethel, and Jellicoe—a group empathy which sends the latter two to rescue Jonathan not by convenient happenstance, but because of the psychic link they share (much like the one Yvette shares with her husband in "Architects of Fear"). "Some of Theodore Sturgeon's work dwelt on that theme," said Lester. "Like 'Baby Makes Three'—a central entity uniting many different types of people." "Wolf 359" is also quite similar to Sturgeon's "Microcosmic God," "Fessenden's World," by Edmund Hamilton, and the novel *Edge of Time* by Donald Wollheim (writing as David Grinnell).

"One thing not exploited in the film was the idea of watching evolution proceed at breakneck speed due to the miniaturization," said Lester. "I wanted to show pictures every so often, depicting the birth of civilization, the time of Moses and the Persians, the Renaissance, the nineteenth century, and thence to the present." The only high speed photo we actually see (as Meredith shows it to Ethel) is a shot of the sand-shark from "The Invisible Enemy," here doing stand-in work as a Dundee Planet dinosaur. "There was never any real intent to try to depict Earth's future," said Lester. "We wanted to keep it a mystery. Besides, what could we show?"

"Wolf 359" places its human drama in microcosm as well by isolating Meredith's ranch house/laboratory in the desert. Jack Poplin and Harry Redmond suggested the tiny planetary sample using little more than a sheet of glass and a cloud of fog, into which Meredith gazes using his various lenses.

Apropos of Brady's and Lester's desire to bring *The Outer Limits* down to Earth, the Merediths are a married couple whose security, stability, and viewer-identification are wrapped up in the accoutrements of middle class life: Steaks on the grill, a spacious and fashionable home, and a martini mentality that considers the best things in life to be "bright lights, champagne, dress shops, diamonds, mink coats, yachts, Monte Carlo," as Jonathan says. Like the determinedly normal marriages depicted in "Cold Hands, Warm Heart" and "Soldier," the romantic relationships supplied as character background throughout the new season are mundane, almost realistic—in the first season, such relationships barely existed unless they served a specific turn of plot, as in "Architects" or "Don't Open Till Doomsday." While it is difficult to imagine Ian and Eva Frazer of "The Borderland" doing something as ordinary as watching TV, it is easy to see the Merediths putting up their feet to catch *The Outer Limits* or *Perry Mason*. While the first season's by-rote love interests resulted in a large number of sore-thumb *Outer Limits* Odd Couples, standardized husband-wife teams like the Merediths fit right into the second. These vital mid-Sixties types, with their cigarettes and five o'clock cocktails, were believably bourgeois.*

The Plag itself is deadly and slow-moving, first manifesting as an amorphous, transparent white mass that "blooms" open like a flower to unveil an evil little mouthless face—sort of a distant cousin to the Galaxy Being by way of "O.B.I.T."'s Helosian. It was a puppet of thin, flexible rubber. "It was a 'hand-mask' for two hands," said Wah Chang, "with a head which was actually where your thumbs stuck through." (Perhaps "Plag" was a condensation of Platex Glove, which is what it looks like.) Skeletal extensions on the fingers give the webbed petals a bat-wing appearance, and the puppet is filmed to good effect against black velvet through a number of diffusion filters that lent it a ghostly aura. We see a bit too much of it, and wonder why Meredith doesn't simply run away (as Jellicoe does, early in the show). The creature remains in the background for the most part until the finale, and the effect was more subtle than anything yet seen in the new season.

"It was so difficult to get something that would be realistic instead of just being another gargoyle," said Lester. "I thought 'Wolf 359,' for all the restrictions of our production, came off very well."

*And director Laslo Benedek found a novel way to circumvent the censor's rule of thumb requiring even married couples to sleep in twin beds on TV at that time. He pushed the beds to within a foot of each other and shot the bedroom very darkly, so the viewer can just barely perceive the gap separating them. It looks like Jonathan and Ethel are sharing a queensize.

Wah Chang's sketch for the "Plag" creature.
(Courtesy Wah Chang)

How the effect looked onscreen next to Patrick O'Neal.

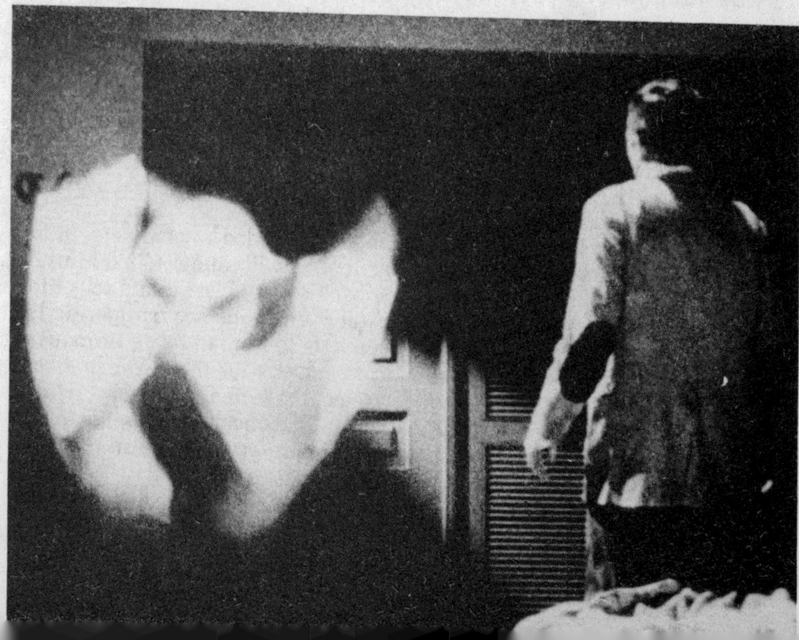

"You gain nothing by suicide." Ikar (Mike Lane) plays backseat psychiatrist to Warren Stevens.

KEEPER OF THE PURPLE TWILIGHT

Broadcast 5 December 1964
Written by Milton Krims, based on a teleplay by Stephen Lord
Directed by Charles Haas
Assistant Director: Robert Justman
Director of Photography: Kenneth Peach

CAST: Prof. Eric Plummer (Warren Stevens), Ikar [human form] (Robert Webber), Janet Lane (Gail Kobe), Franklin Karlin (Curt Conway), David Hunt (Edward C. Platt), Ikar [alien form] (Mike Lane), Alien Soldier #1 (Hugh Langtry), Alien Soldier #2 (Gene Wiley), Alien Soldier #3 (Leroy Ellis), Stunt Ikar [human] (Fred Stromsoe), Stunt Eric (Fred Krone).

> *There is no limit to the extension of the curious mind. It reaches to the end of the imagination, then beyond into the mysteries of dreams, hoping always to convert even the dreams into reality, for the greater well-being of all mankind...*

The nagging lack of two crucial equations needed to complete an antimagnetic disintegrator nearly drives scientist Eric Plummer to kill himself, until a dome-headed alien appears in the back seat of his car and tells him, "You gain nothing by suicide." Eric's unstable emotions are hampering his research, and back at his lab the alien converts to human form, introduces himself as Ikar, and offers a swap: Eric's emotions for the two equations. After the finished disintegrator is demonstrated, Eric's financial backer, Hunt, is overjoyed, but his colleague, Karlin, calls it "diabolical" and swears to axe the project. Ikar shows up with three hulking alien soldiers and "takes"

Karlin's mind, rendering him harmless. But Ikar's newly acquired emotions cause him to reveal to Eric's girlfriend Janet that he is the advance scout of an invasion force that requires a disintegrator so large that "we needed someone to build it for us here on Earth." Ikar's race is rigidly logical; he finds his plan of assuming human emotions in an attempt to comprehend our disorganized and illogical society backfiring, by giving him *feelings* about the invasion plan. The soldiers realize Ikar is getting out of hand and order him back to their home planet. He defies them and escapes to the lab, where he admits that he duped Eric out of his emotions, and gives them back. When the soldiers arrive, Ikar disintegrates two of them before he is killed; Eric uses the model disintegrator to kill the third. Then, his regained compassion causing him to realize Karlin was right, he vaporizes the support machinery and smashes the disintegrator pistol to junk.

> *The curious mind cannot be chained. It is a free mind, endlessly searching for the greater freedom that must eventually make every living being joyfully complete within himself, therefore at peace with himself and his neighbors.*

The monsters were back, full force, in "Keeper of the Purple Twilight," a wild potpourri of science fiction stereotypes including a neurotic mad scientist, extraterrestrial invasion, alien storm troopers, a death ray, and a terminally logical, pointy-eared offworlder falling victim to chaotic Earthling emotions—a gimmick *Star Trek* would make a big deal out of a few years later. The overplotted scenario runs long on momentum and, like the irrational humans in the show, short on logic.

Stephen Lord, the only writer to work both seasons of *The Outer Limits,* did the original draft of "Keeper," as part of a multiple-script contract. "It was so butchered I cannot recall much about it," he said. "It was more of an intellectual melodrama, which was mutilated by a hack and overloaded with monsters. Ben Brady had little feeling for cerebral entertainment."

"The idea was beautiful," said Brady. "To have an alien pick up human emotions. All I can tell you about Stephen Lord is that he wished to Christ he could whip it, but he just couldn't pin it to the mat. Everything he tried was no good." The focus of Lord's script was Ikar's difficulty with the human emotions that turn him against his own invasion plan. There was no dome-headed alter-ego, nor alien troops. "I had nothing to do with 'Keeper,'" said Seeleg Lester, who was busy writing "The Inheritors" at the time. "Ben passed it on to Milton Krims, and I did not intrude on the rewrite." Of the revision, he adds, "Monsters coming to destroy the world is junk. What was there to attract you, to stimulate the imagination? Nothing."

"Krims made it a joke, a worthless Saturday-matinee kind of thing," said Lord, who sent Brady a six-foot funeral wreath when the show aired.

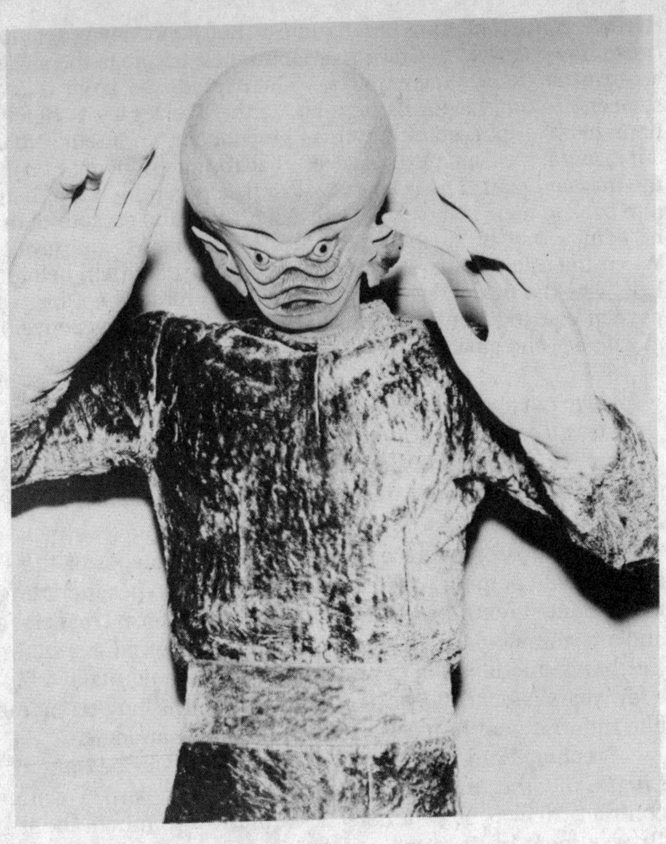

Mike Lane recoils from the publicity photographer.

The card on the floral arrangement read: MAY THE KEEPER OF THE PURPLE TWILIGHT REST IN PIECES.

"I thought it was very funny," said B. Ritchie Payne. "I put the wreath up in the office, then had to take it down because Ben came in and *didn't* think it was funny!"

Nevertheless, there are some striking images in "Keeper." The scene in which Ikar gets his first taste of Earth-style fried chicken by gobbling up a large piece, bones and all, is memorably odd. A scene in which Eric gets a jagged hunk of glass embedded in his forearm is surprisingly explicit (overall, we see much more blood in the second season shows). And the sudden materialization of the alien bully-boys, in broad daylight in an open field, is fantastic in the pulp-thriller sense. In comparison to the spare or barren set decoration in previous Brady regime shows, Eric's workshop and lab are convincingly and interestingly cluttered. The seriocomic interchanges between Ikar and Janet, held over from Lord's script, are still entertaining:

> IKAR: I want only that love which belongs to Eric Plummer.
> JANET (certain she is dealing with a lunatic): Oh... well, I've... uh, given that away. To others.
> IKAR: Why?
> JANET: Because that's what love is for.
> IKAR: Then we must get it back. Now.
> JANET: No. That's impossible. (groping for an answer) The others are asleep. That's true. Now, all good people are asleep and dreaming.
> IKAR (scowling): Then I will come back in the morning.

There is the slimmest hint that Ikar is rekindling Eric's dammed-up love life by proxy, and it scares the hell out of him: "I don't *want* to feel what's happening to me!" he protests. But these attempted subtleties are quickly lost in the circus of illogic and pointless running around that fills up the rest of the episode. Charles Haas's direction is so unimaginative, devoid of soul, and detached from the action that it is almost nihilistic—as though Ikar were behind the camera instead of in front of it, doing his damnedest to make the characters wooden, the dialogue monotonous, and to shoot potentially attractive scenes in an expedient, pedestrian, suspenseless fashion. A catalogue of the episode's plot-holes could easily fill another book.

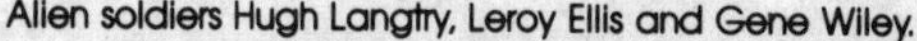
Alien soldiers Hugh Langtry, Leroy Ellis and Gene Wiley.

"We needed tall actors to play the soldiers," said Claude Binyon, "so we recruited Gene Wiley and Leroy Ellis from the LA Lakers." Another was Hugh Langtry, a member of Lowell Thomas' *Outer Limits* construction crew (under Jack Poplin) who had played the Chromoite in "The Mice." The two different mask designs by Wah Chang evoke the best and most outlandish monsters of the previous season. The exertions required of the alien soldiers as they chase Ikar all over Bronson Canyon make the football pads they wore a bit obvious, but they're still a startling sight to behold because there are so many of them–in "Keeper," the TV screen is literally filled with monsters. Ikar was used extensively in promotional 8x10s for the new season.

Warren Stevens (*Forbidden Planet*'s "Doc Ostrow") essays the one-note role of Eric in the manic/hysterical style of William Shatner. He would soon play an Ikar-like role as an emotionless alien in the *Star Trek* episode, "By Any Other Name." Gail Kobe is earnest and energetic in the unfortunate role of Janet, who must faint conveniently whenever Ikar shows up and whose worst crime is the outrageous dress she is compelled to wear during the latter acts. As a couple, Eric and Janet could easily be the happy-hour neighbors of the Merediths, in "Wolf 359." Robert Webber is admirably uncomfortable, stoic, and stuck-up as Ikar. But the struggle of the cast against the material is still clear.

Once "Keeper" was completed, the budget axe fell again, chopping away another $10,000 from each remaining episode. All those monsters had cost money, and "Keeper" would not affect *The Outer Limits'* sagging ratings against Jackie Gleason. When asked about it in retrospect, Ben Brady's first reaction was, "What the hell was 'Keeper of the Purple Twilight?' Did *I* do that?"

Keith Andes (R) reacts to Homeier's altered state.

EXPANDING HUMAN

Broadcast 10 October 1964
Written by Francis Cockrell
Directed by Gerd Oswald
Assistant Director: William P. Owens
Director of Photography: Kenneth Peach

CAST: Dr. Roy Clinton (Skip Homeier), Dr. Peter Wayne (Keith Andes), Lt. Branch (James Doohan), Dean Flint (Vaughn Taylor), Lee Morrow (Peter Duryea), Dr. Henry Akada (Aki Aleong), Mrs. Merrill (Mary Gregory), Susan Wayne (Barbara Wilkin), Coroner Leland (Jason Wingreen), Mark Lake (Robert Doyle), Det. Sgt. Alger (Troy Melton), Receptionist (Shirley O'Hara), Elevator Operator (Bill Cort), Hart Bellaire (Sherwood Keith), Night Watchman (Owen McGivney).

As far back as men have recorded their history, veils have been lowered to disclose a vast new reality—rents in the fabric of Man's awareness. And somewhere, in the endless search of the curious mind, lies the next vision, the next key to his infinite capacity...

Soon after the murder of a night watchman at a university lab devoted to researching "CE substances" (consciousness-expanding drugs), one of the instructors is found clinically dead in his apartment... but he sits up on the slab during his own autopsy, alive and piqued. Mr. Bellaire, a corporate magnate who plans to cut off funding to the CE lab because of the bad publicity of the murder investigation, is himself killed by the same hulking specter that literally crushed the breath from the night watchman's lungs. Dr. Clinton, head of the CE program, reveals to Dr. Wayne that the mystery killer is his own CE-altered ego—a schizoid Mr. Hyde persona with inflated musculature, superhuman strength and learning skills, and a disappointingly predictable fascist craving to rule the world, populating it with similarly "expanded" humans while consigning all contrary parties to death camps. The normal Clinton is unaware of the dictates of his expanded form due to self-imposed hypnotic blocks that permit the Hyde version to function freely and use the Jekyll version as convenient alibi material. Now it's time to recruit Wayne, but Wayne resists the pitch and Clinton must force him to imbibe the CE mixture. When Branch, a thoroughly befuddled investigating cop, stumbles in at the wrong moment, he shoots Clinton, who catches the slugs with a smile and does not bleed. Clinton attempts to escape past a police cordon by holding Wayne by the scruff of the neck and keeping Branch at gunpoint, but his CE dose wears off and his wounds begin to gush blood. When Clinton falls to the ground in death, the vials in his pocket containing the chemical mix are destroyed. Then Wayne tells Branch: "You'd better get me to a hospital—this drug is starting to take effect."

> *Some success, some failure, but either way the gnawing hunger to know is never sated, and the road to the unknown continues to be dark and strange.*

"With Brady, I'd ask for certain scripts, or time off until a script I wanted came along," said Gerd Oswald. "On some shows, like 'Expanding Human,' I got stuck; it was my turn and that was the only script ready. It's a case of saying you'll try to do your best with a story... and then you can't come up with much."

The episode perpetuates the *Dragnet* syndrome seen in most second season shows: Characters stand around interminably, asking questions and droning answers, while a twilight policeman (in this case James Doohan, later *Star Trek*'s "Scotty") vainly struggles to figure out the obvious. Unlike "Keeper of the Purple Twilight," it doesn't even offer the diversion of funky rubber monsters, just a mild rehash of the Jekyll-and-Hyde theme that obscures, for the most part, the more intriguing business of awareness-enhancing chemicals—touchy business indeed, in the early 1960s. "I didn't take that story, either," said Seeleg Lester. "I have a very hazy memory of it; it sounds like a real quickie."

Francis Cockrell had written many cause-and-effect mysteries for *Alfred Hitchcock Presents* (some in collaboration with his wife Eustace), and later conceived a superb *Outer Limits* story, "The Watchbird," which was never filmed due to the show's cancellation. The teleplay for "Expanding Human" reads well, but does not play well. Dr. Clinton is essentially ridiculous, and his foolish explanation of the killings to Lt. Branch (he points out convenient newspaper squibs on weird occurrences that *just might* be CE related) telegraphs the fact he is the culprit very early on. Most of his rhapsodizing on the wonders of his expanded outlook sounds like verbose filler, and his CE pitch inelegant when compared with the explanation of the process by Dr. Akada, who trips out and wakes up in the morgue.

AKADA: Perhaps visions *are* involved. But it becomes a question of whether what we see in everyday life is 'reality'... or whether reality is actually our vastly improved perception, and these so-called "visions." Let's say you see a leaf, falling. In expanded consciousness, I see *all* leaves falling, in time past, in time to come; I see not only their origin, but their... ever-changing, never-ending role in everything.

While Oswald's staging of the laboratory break-in is the closest this episode comes to the dark, atmospheric quality of his first season work, the balance of the show is trapped in Clinton's boring, basic, barren apartment courtyard—the series' furthest remove from normal *Outer Limits* territory. Even with this blander material, Oswald's work is never less than assured, time-conscious and capable; many *Outer Limits* crew-people assessed him as a good technician and journeyman director. In his book *The American Cinema*, Andrew Sarris would later note:

> Gerd Oswald has shown an admirable consistency, both stylistically and thematically, for a director in his obscure position. A fluency of camera movement is controlled by sliding turns and harsh stops befitting a cinema of bitter ambiguity. Oswald's success in imposing a personal style on shooting schedules ranging from five to seven days should serve as an object lesson to young directors who complain that they lack the time to get their films "just right."

"Gerd was a workhorse, always through at six o'clock," said B. Ritchie Payne. "Then he'd come up, and we'd break out the J&B and discuss how the shooting went, and how things were going to go tomorrow. Gerd was always finished—by God—by the last day of the shooting schedule." First AD William Owens recalled Oswald as "the short, redheaded fellow who would tap the camera with his swagger stick."

With "Expanding Human," Oswald had a fight on his hands even though the teleplay was not badly written. "The manner in which we did a great many interiors—Christ!" lamented Ben Brady. "We'd grab whatever we could and throw it in front of the camera as cheaply as we could, and a lot of things looked ridiculous. 'Expanding Human' started out as a good idea, but our budget killed it. Gerd did well with it, but there was just no way to develop it imaginatively."

"Skip Homeier was an excellent actor who wasn't being employed very regularly," remembered Payne. "He was a nice man who had a beautiful voice, and he needed the work." Homeier is another unfortunate victim of a procedural storyline flatter than the EEG of a bean sprout. "Skip was a tragic man," said Claude Binyon. "Forever identified as being a Nazi, since he played the kid who turned in his parents in *Tomorrow the World.*" This 1944 film, done when Homeier was fifteen, cemented a lifetime pattern of typecasting that reached a low ebb with a *Star Trek* episode about Nazis in space called "Patterns of Force."

"Expanding Human" was an equally low ebb for *The Outer Limits,* and is unrelentingly dreary. "It's one of those shows you would not want to spend a lonely evening looking at," said Payne philosophically. "Some shows you would sooner forget, because you knew when you made it it wasn't right, and you just didn't have the time or money to fix it, and so you let it go. Those shows just pass my mind with, *oh, my god!*"

"I was born ten days ago... a full-grown man...." Robert Culp in the prologue to "Demon With a Glass Hand."

DEMON WITH A GLASS HAND

Broadcast 17 October 1964
Written by Harlan Ellison
Directed by Byron Haskin
Assistant Director: Robert Justman
Director of Photography: Kenneth Peach

CAST: Mr. Trent/Voice of the Hand (Robert Culp), Consuelo Biros (Arline Martel), Arch (Abraham Sofaer), Breech (Steve Harris), Battle (Rex Holman), Budge (Robert Fortier), Kyben/Stunt Arch (Wally Rose), Durn/Stunt Budge (Bill Hart), Kyben/Stunt Battle (Fred Krone), Stunt Trent (Dean Smith).

Through all the legends of ancient peoples—Assyrian, Babylonian, Sumerian, Semitic—runs the saga of the Eternal Man, the one who never dies, called by various names in various times, but historically known as Gilgamesh, the one who has never tasted death... the hero who strides through the centuries...

Circa 2964, Earth is conquered in nineteen days by an alien race called the Kyben. The world's entire population vanishes overnight, after loosing retaliation in the form of a radioactive plague that will render the Earth uninhabitable by the invaders. The agent of humankind's salvation is a vigorous, enigmatic, white-clad man named Trent, who escapes into the past—1964—through a Kyben "time mirror." He possesses a prosthetic computer hand that "holds all knowledge," but the Kyben have three lobes—glass fingers—of the device, and they chase Trent into the past because they need the completed hand to tell them where the seventy billion people of Earth have hidden, and how to defeat the plague. Trent, in turn, needs the lobes to enable the glass hand to reveal more of his own identity and purpose, which are blanks to him. Using a "force bubble," the Kyben seal Trent within the confines of a dilapidated office building, where he finds an unwitting ally in Consuelo Biros, a garment worker also trapped inside. Together they commence killing aliens and collecting glass fingers. When the computer coolly advises Trent that his best course of action is to permit the Kyben to shoot him, he complies without hesitation... and Consuelo later obeys the hand's directions for bringing Trent miraculously back to life. He then tracks down the remaining Kyben and destroys the time mirror so that no more aliens will follow. Just when things begin to look romantic, the now-complete hand informs Trent that he is a robot built to look like a man, that the seventy billion refugees are transcribed onto a wire inside of him, and his job is to wait twelve hundred years, then release humankind back into its own era *after* the plague has exterminated the Kyben. A shocked Consuelo quickly makes tracks for home while Trent, totally alone, begins his long wait.

Like the Eternal Man of Babylonian legend, like Gilgamesh, one thousand plus two hundred years stretches before Trent. Without love. Without friendship. Alone; neither man nor machine, waiting. Waiting for the day he will be called to free the humans who gave him mobility. Movement, but not life.

Winner of the Writer's Guild Award for Outstanding Script in the category of Television Anthology for the 1964–65 season, "Demon With a Glass Hand" was a definite high point for the Brady regime. It featured no rubber monsters and is arguably Harlan Ellison's best-realized science fiction teleplay to date. "I think that 'Demon' certainly was the best show of our season," said Brady, "while 'The Inheritors' was the most ambitious." Byron Haskin, who parted company with *The Outer Limits* after directing this episode, agreed: "By far, 'Demon' was the finest show of the second season," he said. "I was amazed that it came through, considering our budget... or *lack* of a budget."

Following "Soldier," Ellison had become enmeshed in no less than seventeen rewrites of "Mealtime," a script for Irwin Allen's *Voyage to the Bottom of the Sea* that aired as "The Price of Doom." Concurrently, he was expanding a novelette begun in 1957, "The Queer File," to novel-length under the new title, "Obituary for an Instant." "I couldn't do both projects at the same time," he said. "My thinking about the latter half of the novel was misty and incomplete, only directional, not specific. So I turned the disadvantage of not being able to work on my book to my advantage by writing a mental memo to myself in the form of the TV script for 'Demon With a Glass Hand,' which outlined the rest of the book for me."

The treatment done by Ellison in June, 1964, opens with Breech, one of the Kyben kamikaze assassins, trussed up amid the gears inside an old clock tower. When midnight strikes, the clockworks will grind him apart unless he answers the questions posed by the Trent character, here named Mr. Fish. The Kyben cat-and-mouse with Fish through the sewers, alleys, and deserted buildings of an unnamed city. In a closed-down penny arcade on an amusement pier, Fish is shot in the heart and his ally Jody Morell is taken hostage. Fish's body is removed to safety by Big Betty Salamagordo, a three hundred-pound fat woman, and her gnomelike lover, Pinook. He wakens from death unharmed, inside a tattoo parlor. Fish's glass hand directs him to raid the Kyben stronghold, an abandoned caboose on a railroad siding outside the city, where he saves Jody and the truth is revealed. When Jody sees the whirring robot machinery in Fish's chest, she flees into the night. The story closes on Fish, as he types one-handed:

> My curse is my humanity. They made me not man, not machine, but something in between, and I am alone, forever alone. To live out all my days, and all the days of unborn generations, walking this planet like a shadow. I walk among you now... and I dare not even ask for your pity. My mission is to remain alive, for 20,000 years. And all I fear is that when my mission is ended, in that future still unborn, they will not bless me with death. After 20,000 years of loneliness, all I can beg of them, those billions I carry in my heart-coils, is that they turn me off... let me sleep... let me sleep...

The chase aspect was enthusiastically sold by the treatment as "a deep, long-winded run a la Hitchcock."

"Originally, I wrote 'Demon' as a cross-country chase, my homage to *North by Northwest*," said Ellison. "The real problem with the plot was physical; it was a chase in a linear fashion. And, like a bolt out of the blue, I thought, 'Why can't it be a chase in a *vertical* fashion?' All I had to do was figure out a way to keep the characters in a contained space. It was a very important lesson to me: You could make the action more intense by *enclosing* it, and providing no escape."

The site chosen for the office complex in which Trent is trapped (called the "Seeleg Building" in an early Ellison draft) was Los Angeles' famous Bradbury Building. Inspired by a work of science fiction and designed with the help of a ghost, its construction was commissioned by mining and real estate tycoon Lewis Bradbury in 1892. After vetoing a disappointing blueprint by architect Sumner Hunt, Bradbury engaged one of Hunt's draftsmen, George H. Wyman, who accepted the job after receiving the message "Take the Bradbury Building. It will make you famous" from his brother Mark—who had been dead for six years! The advice came during one of Wyman's sessions with a planchette board. His design was heavily influenced by the Edward Bellamy book *Looking Backward* (1887) which described a typical commercial building in the Utopian civilization of the year 2000 as "a vast hall full of light."* The landmark building features a wealth of ornamental ironwork, Mexican tile floors, Belgian marble staircases and a glass roof that floods the five-story atrium with daylight. Its two open-caged elevators are smoothly driven by pillars of water. Ellison recalls, "Bobby Justman phoned me and said, 'I think I've found the building!'"

"I drove Harlan down there to see if he could rewrite around the location," said Justman. "Otherwise, the show would have been too expensive to make. I was familiar with the building because I'd worked there in 1950, on Joe Losey's remake of *M*." The baroque edifice is seen in countless TV shows, films and commercials, from 77 *Sunset Strip* to *Banyon* to *Blade Runner*.

"I came to think of that building as a character in the script," said Ellison, "and I very consciously made it a climb-through hell, bottom to top. I walked it from the basement to the water tower. In the film, when Trent enters the building, you have no idea how he got in; all you see is dripping water. But he comes in through the sewer, and winds up going through the window on the very top floor." The first revision also included a rooftop shootout near the water tower, later omitted. "You know the scene where Culp races the elevator? I did that, to see if it could be done." Accordingly, Ellison's script notes the time it took to dash down the stairs from the top floor as seventeen seconds. "I found the only way you could *beat* that damned elevator to the ground floor was to jump from the first floor landing," he said. "I did it—and landed on my left leg so hard I fractured my ankle." Robert Culp's stuntman, Dean Smith (a former Olympic runner with a time of 19.4 in the hundred-yard dash, last seen sprinting his heart out as an alien in "The Chameleon") duplicated this jump for the film... and hurt both *his* ankles upon touchdown.

"Demon"'s revision pages bear dates for nearly every day of August, 1964. Much dialogue and business was stripped away, altered, or con-

*Wyman was also the maternal grandfather of science-fiction super-fan Forrest J. Ackerman.

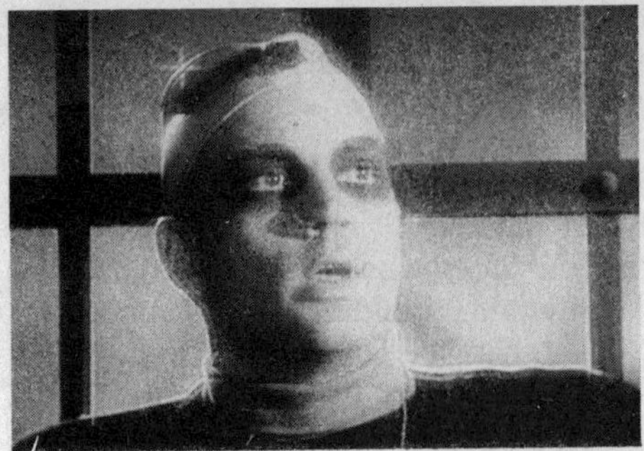

One of the Kyben, Breech (Steve Harris): "terrified, trapped, feral."

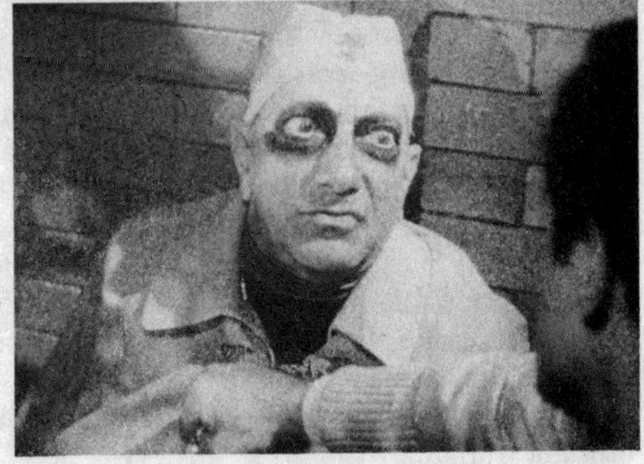

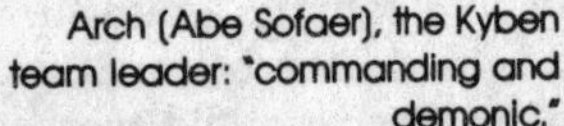

Arch (Abe Sofaer), the Kyben team leader: "commanding and demonic."

densed. But first, Seeleg Lester needed a completed draft. "Ben got after me and told me to goose Harlan or take the script away from him," Lester said. "We're talking six, eight, ten weeks' delay. Ben said, 'Cut him off!' because nobody could reach him. Harlan would call and say, 'I'll bring it in tomorrow'... then there was nothing for another week." Brady noted that, "I had to periodically toss Harlan on his ass because he was so erratic. If he didn't want to work, then I'd be wasting my time that day; if we worked, nobody did it better. How can you live with a genius? All you can do is sit around and wait for him to *gene*."

By far the most significant change was in the character that originated as Jody Morell and became Consuelo Losada, described by Ellison as follows:

> Late thirties, Mexican, lonely. She is not beautiful, but is arresting as a peasant woman in an Orozco painting is arresting, exhibiting those features of nationality and personal strength that tell us this is a woman who had to get dirt under her nails to get along in the world... this is no young girl, but a mature woman who has had to work to stay alive, and then been forced to wonder if it was worth the trouble. But there is an intelligence in her face. She is no peon. She thinks.

"I had written her into the script as a black woman," Ellison said. "The network said she couldn't *be* black. 'Why not?' I said and they answered, 'Because it's *relevant!* We did relevance *last* year and it didn't work!' So I said, 'How about making her a Puerto Rican?' '*NO!*' Finally, she wound up as some sort of nameless Middle European, and they gave her a blonde wig. But Arline Martel played it as a Chicana."

"The Consuelo character was endlessly rewritten," said Robert Culp, "to bow to the pressure to make her less overtly ethnic." Her last name was changed to the racially ambiguous "Biros" by Lester, who said, "Harlan had some kind of *message* he wanted to get out through this Mexican girl, as though his most prosaic thoughts were these illuminations from on high, and he exhibited a lot of grief when this wasn't brought out in flaming colors. It was ridiculous! The script was not about the girl. It was a perfectly beautiful chase. I thought the concept of the show was just stunning."

"We called it '*Demon* With a Glass Hand' to give ABC a monster," said Ellison. "Our monster was in the title, a demon, as in a Fury. I worked closely enough with Ben and Seeleg that they would say, 'Who do you see?' for a part. We'd look through the Player's Directory, and if they agreed, I'd write a part for a specific actor."

"Ellison wrote the Trent part for me," acknowledged Robert Culp, "and wouldn't hear of anyone else playing it." In his final *Outer Limits* role, Culp imbues Trent with a feline grace and a Fury-like ineluctability that deeply etches the mythic stature of this fascinating being into the viewer's mind from the first few frames of film. "I thought Culp was hot," said Ellison. "But I'd never met him. The first night of shooting at the Bradbury, I walked up to the third floor, which was pitch-dark. And there, sitting in a little cul-de-sac, was Culp, reading a book on pre-Colombian art. That knocked me out, since most of the actors I'd met before were dips, purely *non compos mentis*. And Culp and I have been friends ever since. To this day he still wants to make 'Demon' as a feature film, but so much time has passed that he no longer wants to star in it. Now he wants to *direct* it."

Paired again with Culp was Byron Haskin, who had directed him in "Architects of Fear." Whereas his previous work for Brady held no charm for Haskin, "Demon" clearly inspired him. "Byron was one of the exceptional directors of science fiction," said Brady. "He also worked closely with the company I appointed to do the optical effects the second year, Van Der Veer. He was always around to help with ideas and technical things. Once 'Demon' got to the Bradbury Building, Byron was responsible for everything you saw."

"Ellison was nuts!" grinned Haskin. "We met so I could interpret what he had written, because it was pretty wild and didn't look workable to me on paper in terms of finding a continuity from shot to shot. It was 'doubletalk' writing; he and I argued about it, and I got edgy and chased

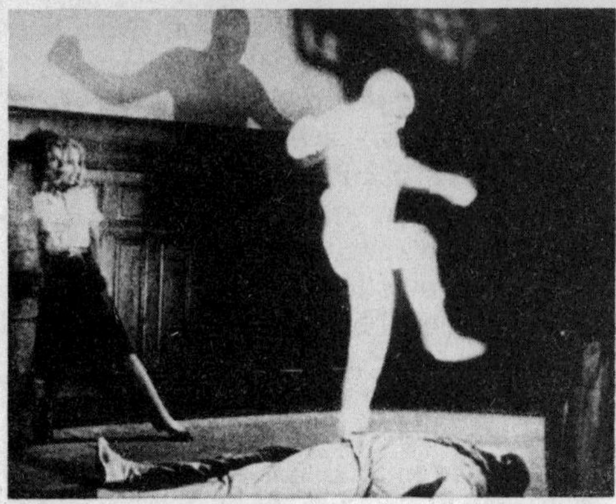

Arline Martel hastens the demise of Dum (Bill Hart) by yanking off the medallion which anchors him in our time, before he can stomp on Robert Culp. The double-exposure on her face is due to the disintegration effect.

him out of my office. But we later became friends. Out at the Bradbury, we had to wait until it was dark and we were sleepy before we could shoot. We had to eat at a nearby beanery, and the gastric problems developed by the whole crew caused quite a stench during the longer setups. One night we surprised a pair of thieves who were burglarizing an office there—I guess they didn't foresee a camera crew showing up."

One of Haskin's ideas was to shoot much of the show using peripheral, rather than direct lighting, and Kenneth Peach was largely responsible for the film's sharp, stark look. Gene Warren recalled, "We built the glass hand at Projects out of plastic, with a tape recorder device in it, and a lot of gadgets to make it look computerized. We shot a closeup of the 'works' and superimposed it over Culp's chest (for the shot revealing Trent as a robot)."

"Once the rough cut returned from the lab, I arranged for Harlan to see it," said B. Ritchie Payne. "This was before the sound effects and so on were inserted. He was very upset, and wanted his name taken off the film. I told Ben, 'Well, boss, you've got another problem today...'"

"I wasn't given a chance to integrate some of the changes so they'd make sense," said Ellison. "There's one shot I've always felt [it] should have. When Trent is told there's a force bubble up, in the film he takes this for granted. In the script, he rushes for the door and tries to get out. And why the black circles around the Kyben's eyes? Some of them look like human beings; some of them look like weirdos with cheesecloth over their faces." A secretary's typo caused the Control Voice to read "Sumerian" as *"Sumerican"* in the prologue. "Oh, it's in the script all right," said Ellison. "But it's not in *my* script."

"Once the editors worked on it and the effects were in, it turned out just fine," said Payne. "Culp gave it some class upfront, and Ellison cannot write a dull story. After we broadcast it, I picked up our office phone and the caller said, 'Hello, my name is Ray Bradbury, and I want to compliment you on "Demon With a Glass Hand," which I saw last night.' I said, 'I can't imagine receiving a compliment from anyone we could appreciate more than you.' Ben thought the call was a phony, at first, then was delighted."

Another person watching was Leslie Stevens. "We'd get literally envious, and say it was an unjust world, when somebody like Brady could pull off a show like that," he said. "All I can say is, when it worked, our reaction [at Daystar] was a combination of gladness, because the show was 'ours' in a way; envy at their bringing it off, and absolute astonishment that they *could* bring it off. In other words, all the bad human response you could ask for in one package, we had."

"If we hadn't gotten 'Demon' early on, I'm sure ABC would have opted not to do it," said Brady. "I would've liked to have opened the second season with that show."

"I would rate 'Demon' pretty high in terms of fidelity to what I wrote," said Ellison. "And it's one of the most remarkable pieces of acting I've ever seen from Culp." Years later, the episode would win an award at the Trieste Film Festival. As for what befalls Trent in the novel version of the "Demon" saga, the author will only say, "When the book comes out, you'll know..."

June Havoc and Eddie Albert ponder the plot twist of sentient tumbleweeds.

CRY OF SILENCE

Broadcast 24 October 1964
Written by Robert C. Dennis, based on story material by Louis Charbonneau.
Original title: "Mind Over Matter"
Directed by Charles Haas
Assistant Director: William P. Owens
Director of Photography: Kenneth Peach

CAST: Andy Thorne (Eddie Albert), Karen Thorne (June Havoc), Lamont (Arthur Hunnicutt), Stunt Karen (Helen Thurston), Stunt Lamont (Richard Farnsworth).

> *In the not-distant future, the sound of Man will invade those unknown depths of space which as yet we cannot even imagine. In his own world there are no places left beyond the reach of his voice. His neighbor is no longer just next door, but anywhere at the end of a wire. And it all began when prehistoric man discovered the art of communication...*

Checking up on some out-of-the-way real estate, Andy Thorne runs his convertible into a boulder blocking a remote country road. His wife Karen gets out of the car and promptly falls ass over teakettle down a hillside, twisting her ankle. They are cut off from their car by a gang of apparently sentient tumbleweeds that locomote sans wind, and explode instead of burning, as Andy learns when he ignites a few. After nightfall, the couple is rescued by a torch-bearing rustic named Lamont, who saw a meteor fall to Earth two weeks previously. After that, the weeds started capturing his livestock. When the three attempt to escape Lamont's farmhouse together, they are cut off by a new threat—a bouncing invasion wedge of sinister bullfrogs. A similar gambit the next morning is foiled by mobile boulders, one of which crushes Lamont. Andy improbably surmises that an alien intelligence is clumsily trying to make contact—*any* contact—long-distance, by animating what it thinks to be representative Earth life-forms. Just then, Lamont's corpse shuffles back to the farmhouse, but like the weeds, the frogs and the rocks, he cannot communicate. Rigor mortis has frozen his larynx, and he scrawls only a few patternless symbols before locking up completely. Eagerly, Andy hypnotizes himself, leaving a list of questions for Karen to ask should the alien force wise up and possess *his* body for awhile... but all it does, through Andy, is lament its own failure: "Consciousness *does* exist on this strange pebble in the drift of space, but its nature remains a mystery." Then it gives up for good and goes away.

> *"And the light shineth in the darkness, and the darkness comprehended it not..." The sound of Man probes the dimensionless range of space, seeking an answer. But if it comes, will he hear? Will he listen? Will he comprehend?*

Usually remembered with derision as *The Outer Limits'* "monster tumbleweed" episode, "Cry of Silence" is actually an intelligently-founded story that marked the debut of scriptwriter Robert Dennis. "That was a good case of our manipulating a meaty story around a scant budget," said Brady. "Bob Dennis brought that one in when I was really stuck for a script. He wrote it in four days!"

Since pulp science fiction writer Louis Charbonneau never authored a story called "Mind Over Matter," we can only assume at this late date that his name was among those handed to scriptwriter Milton Krims by

Brady, via his staff of readers. "Ben started the story with Krims, who couldn't solve it," notes Seeleg Lester. B. Ritchie Payne recalls director Charles Haas's first reading of the Krims teleplay: "After every fifth page Charlie would look up at me and say, 'We're gonna shoot this? And *this?*' I said, 'Stop bitching, Charlie—we've got Eddie Albert, and we've got Gypsy Rose Lee's sister, what more do you need?' And Haas said, 'We need a good story—and this ain't it!'"

"I recall Bob Dennis with great affection," said Lester. "He'd been a very prolific pulp writer, and had begun TV work with a series called *China Smith* in 1952. It was quite well-written, so when I went to work on *Perry Mason,* I called on Bob. He always seemed to do two great acts, then peter out in the third, as though he'd lost his enthusiasm." Payne added that "Dennis was the fastest writer I'd ever seen; to watch him pitch, you'd think he was selling insurance. He was also our 'script doctor.' Cal Ward used to say, 'He ain't great, but goddamn, he's fast.'"

There are no frogs or tumbleweeds in the Krims script, which substitutes an invisible force as the culprit. Lester insisted to Dennis that the story's essence lay in the alien force getting into the first *moving* thing it finds. "I feel it was the best of the four *Outer Limits* scripts I did," said Dennis. "The only real change I made was adding the scenes where the stones attack." This links the plot directly to that of Charbonneau's *Corpus Earthling* (more alien-controlled rocks), and provides the show's one credible threat.

One virtue of "Cry of Silence" is that it keeps its characters in motion, in comparison with the static, petrified quality of shows like "Behold, Eck!" or "Expanding Human." While Andy's off-the-cuff theorizing is a bit wild, even with Lamont's cryptic journal to guide him, the journal itself provides for some nicely eerie recitations:

> ANDY (reading): Seventh day: The Lord rested after Creation, but here there is no rest. Now I am certain that there is a malignant intelligence behind the weeds. No, not behind them. *In* them. Where it comes from or what it wants, I cannot fathom. Perhaps if I could reason clearly... I might understand... but my grip on sanity grows weaker by the day...

As soon as Andy notes, "I don't think it *was* malignant," a huge boulder hurls itself into the farmhouse, shaking the whole building. When Lamont (played by the gangly Arthur Hunnicutt, who made a career out of such hayseed roles) comes stumping back to the farmhouse, not breathing, his eyes glazed over in death, the scene is properly menacing even though Haas did nothing to heighten the sense of impending danger. "That poor man," said June Havoc. "They put *things* in his eyes to make them look milky. He could only keep them on a short time, and was in such pain that tears were running down his face." The stunt man standing in for Hunnicutt when Lamont gets pasted by the avalanche was Richard Farnsworth, the 1984 Academy Award nominee.

The lame direction leaves the actors largely to their own devices. Eddie Albert energetically conveys both wild curiosity about the alien force, and intelligent fury at its fumbled attempts at contact. "Why doesn't it try to communicate instead of playing a lot of stupid tricks?" Andy shouts, shaking his fist at the sky. *"At least act logical!"* While his wife is repulsed by the frogs, Andy is fascinated: "I want to find out what makes it go!"

As written by Dennis, Karen Thorne is nervous and tightly-wired, but June Havoc over-inflates the part to out-and-out bugeyed hysteria, coming unhinged every time a tumbleweed twitches or a frog croaks. We begin to wonder how someone as sharp and methodical as Andy Thorne could have married such a shrieking basket case.

On the day the frog attacks were to be filmed, a Humane Society representative showed up at Paramount's Stage #7 with three large burlap bags of live frogs. "Knowing something *awful* was going to happen, I said, 'What have you got in the bag?'" remembered Havoc. "They said, 'We're going to throw these at you,' and I said, '*Real* frogs?'" She approached the animal supervisor and said, "I don't want to be the heavy in this case, but I can't run through these frogs. I'd squash a couple, and if they throw them, they'll hurt them, and if you're standing by watching, it'll be too late—I'll step on them and they'll be dead." Gene Warren said, "We had to go out to the frog farm to get these gunny sacks full of frogs, and the frogs didn't want to jump around on the set when the hot shooting lights were on." This, presumably, was why they were going to be thrown. But as soon as they got out of the bag, they hopped for cover. "Within two minutes—bingo, not a frog in sight," said Havoc. "So the special effects department came up with fake frogs that were *this* big, and beautiful. There were men on the back of the camera dolly, and lined up down the set, throwing these things at my face. They were wet because they'd just come out of a tub of water, and had to shine. But they were fake frogs... so I made it."

Nina Link (Marianna Hill) consults Adam.

I, ROBOT

Broadcast 14 November 1964
Written by Robert C. Dennis. Based on stories collected in *Adam Link, Robot,* by Otto Binder.
Directed by Leon Benson
Assistant Director: William P. Owens
Director of Photography: Kenneth Peach

CAST: Thurman Cutler (Howard Da Silva), Judson Ellis (Leonard Nimoy), Nina Link (Marianna Hill), Adam Link (Read Morgan), DA Thomas Coyle (Ford Rainey), Fred (Robert Sorrells), Judge (Ken Drake), Prof. Hebbel (John Hoyt), Sheriff Barclay (Hugh Sanders), Prof. Charles "Doc" Link (Peter Brocco), Evie (Christine Matchett), Mrs. MaCrae (Mary Jackson), Truck Driver (John Hudkins), Adam's Voice (John Caper, Jr.).

> *God looked upon his world and called it good, but Man was not content. He looked for ways to make it better and built machines to do the work. But in vain we build the world, unless the builder also grows.*

A crochety, misanthropic defense attorney named Thurman Cutler is coaxed out of retirement to take on a singular case: The defense of a robot, Adam Link, against the charge that it willfully murdered its creator, Dr. Charles Link. Testimony reveals that once Adam was activated, he began a trial-and-error process of learning much like that of a human child, which suggests that some of his later acts, construed as violent, were merely a matter of the mechanical man not understanding his own strength, or misunderstanding sometimes opaque human thoughts and emotions. But the defense is never fully able to recover from the revelation that Adam read the novel *Frankenstein* while absorbing all the books in Doc Link's library, and the innocent robot is ultimately pronounced guilty even though Doc Link's death was accidental. Before Adam can be hauled away to be dismantled as a menace, he breaks his bonds in order to toss a child out of the path of an oncoming truck and gets bashed to scrap metal in the process. Cutler notes sardonically that "that terrible monster won't ever harm anybody again."

> *Out of every disaster, a little progress is made. Man will build more robots, and learn how to make them better. And, given enough time, he may learn how to do the same for himself.*

"I, Robot," the first of the "Adam Link" stories, was published in the January, 1939 issue of *Amazing Stories* under the collaborative byline of "Eando Binder"—*E*-and-*O* standing for brothers Earl and Otto, although Otto Oscar Binder did most of the writing. The stories were of historic note because each was told from the point of view of the main character, a robot named Adam Link—"Adam" because he is the first of his kind, and "Link" after his creator, though he is also a sort of Missing Link between the machine and the human being.

"I remember writing to the Binders to buy the rights," said Seeleg Lester. "They were so pleased that they said, 'We've written a dozen Adam Link stories, and you can take any of the ideas from any of the other stories and incorporate them into your show.' That was very nice

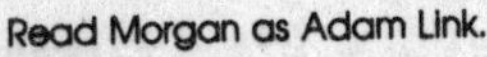

Read Morgan as Adam Link.

of them, and it was one of our better shows because we tried to bring in a serious theme."

It also planted *The Outer Limits* unabashedly into the *Perry Mason* courtroom setting so familiar to Brady and most of his crew. The legal fencing is fun to witness and has the timbre of authenticity, but the promise of the first act—dealing with a robot whose very strangeness scares the hell out of the people trying it for murder—is obscured by the pedestrian business of bringing on witnesses for the prosecution. "It *was* somewhat conventional," said Lester. "But I think we gave it an unusual slant. When I told ABC the story, I'll never forget Adrian Samish saying, 'Who the hell cares about a pile of tin?' And when the thing finally played on TV, I got a lump in my throat watching that pile of tin throw himself in front of a truck to save that little girl."

Robert Dennis delivered his adaptation of "I, Robot" the day after completing revisions on "Cry of Silence," and noted, "I recall reading tear sheets of the story from an old pulp magazine." Dennis created the Thurman Cutler character, greatly expanded a nameless newspaperman mentioned in passing in the Binder story into Judson Ellis, and changed Doc Link's surviving relative to a woman. Cutler's wisecracking banter with the smart-assed cynic, Ellis, and old-warhorse rivalry with DA Coyle are straight out of *Inherit the Wind*, and Howard Da Silva and Leonard Nimoy chomp wholeheartedly into Dennis' engagingly sharp dialogue:

> ELLIS (as Cutler enters City Hall): A Daniel, come to judgement. Yea, a Daniel...
>
> CUTLER: Little Judd Ellis, isn't it? The young man of great promise—and all of it broken.
>
> ELLIS: You're still at it, huh, Cutler? Well, for once we're gonna be on the same team. And, brother, you'll need me!
>
> CUTLER: It seems I didn't retire a minute too soon. With the *Herald* behind me, I'd be ruined!

Cutler's resentment of the town's backwoods hypocrisy, and his need to grandstand the trial, seem to foredoom Adam, until he and Ellis redeem themselves in the last act by evincing a deeper understanding of the true meaning of the trial. Everyone else in the show is defined in terms of rough-hewn cliches. Nina Link is decorative (Ellis's courtship of her was dropped). The denizens of the town are all kissin' cousins to the hicks in "The Children of Spider County." Doc Link, seen in numerous flashbacks, is an eccentric-but-lovable bachelor scientist, a suspected misogynist, quaintly grumpy and absent-minded. Dennis's script and the performances breathe as much life into this scenario as possible, but it is still a bringdown from what "O.B.I.T." had already achieved in a similar setting.

No one at Project Unlimited will take credit for the cumbersome robot suit worn by Read Morgan, although Gene Warren recalls it as "already available," possibly from the prop closet at Paramount. The gaffer's tape holding it together is visible in many shots.

"Leon Benson was another *Perry Mason* director," said Lester. "He did a good job on 'I, Robot,' but really struggled with it because of the budget." This was Benson's only *Outer Limits* assignment.

As of "I, Robot," *The Outer Limits* itself went on trial. On the second day of shooting, September 19, 1964, the new season premiered with "Soldier" in the Saturday evening time slot against Jackie Gleason. *Variety*'s "Daku" wrote: "*Limits* will have to come up with better stuff than it did on its debut to make it any kind of a race. It was, on the whole, unsatisfactory fare."

Gleason's season bow stole away most of the audience for "Cold Hands, Warm Heart" the following week, and at this time ABC's monstermania peaked, as "I, Robot" wrapped and all eyes turned to the next show scheduled for production—a two-parter without a monster in sight.

Robert Duvall and James Frawley: "This is motive power like nothing you've ever seen!"

THE INHERITORS

Part One broadcast 21 November 1964
Part Two broadcast 28 November 1964
Written by Seeleg Lester and Sam Neuman. Story by Lester and Neuman, from an idea by Ed Adamson. Scripted as "The Hui Tan Project" and "The Pied Piper Project."
Directed by James Goldstone

Assistant Director: Robert Justman
Director of Photography: Kenneth Peach

CAST: Adam Ballard (Robert Duvall), Lt. Phillip J. Minns (Steve Inhat), Ray "Art" Harris (Donald Harron), Sgt. James Conover (Ivan Dixon), PFC Francis Hadley (Dee Pollack), Pvt. Robert Renaldo (James Frawley), AIO Capt. Ngo Newa (James Shigeta), Randolph E. Branch [Secretary of Science] (Ted DeCorsia), Prof. Andrew Whitsett (William Wintersole), Surgeon (Robert J. Nelson), Oriental Soldier (Yoneo Iguchi), Steelmaking Shop Super (Leon Askin), Mr. Jessup (Robert Cinder), Nurse (Linda Hutchins), Hospital MP (Sy Prescott), E. F. Larkin (Dabbs Greer), Johnny Subiron (Kim Hector). ADDITIONAL PART TWO CAST: Minerva Gordon (Suzanne Cupito), Agent Grainger (Jon Cedar), Mrs. Subiron (Jan Shutan), Nurse [Children's Hospital] (Paulle Clark), Miss Steen (Joanne Stewart), Daniel Newton Masters (David Brady), Boy with Ball (Charles Herbert). WITH: John Harding, Michael Petit, Earl Brown, H. Faber, M. Finochio, G. Estes.

In the troubled places of the world, the Devil's Hunter finds rare game. For man-made savagery is only the instrument for a secret terror, stirring from its dark place of ambush...

After catching a bullet in the brain in Vietnam, Lt. Minns becomes of special interest to Department of Science investigator Adam Ballard. His EEG now shows a dual brainwave pattern exactly like those of three other similarly wounded soldiers who "should've died and didn't." The alien patterns in all four EEGs match, and Ballard finds that the bullets that wounded the four were smelted from a meteorite whose ore, when magnified, reveals a honeycomb effect reminiscent of the configuration of the human RNA factor. While recuperating, Minns develops a skyrocketing IQ and a new interest in high finance—just as Sgt. Conover, before him, applied his two hundred-plus IQ to metallurgy, PFC Hadley to biochemistry, and Pvt. Renaldo, to physics. Soon enough, Minns hypnotizes his nurses and guards and simply walks out of the hospital... and onto Wall Street, where he generates a fast $400,000 on the stock market and sends funds to each of the other three men. Ballard traces Hadley to Wichita and finds his workshop, where research on inert gases and ducting systems is proceeding. Hadley himself has vanished up the Amazon, looking for rare herbs. Ballard next misses Conover in Stockholm, but discovers his vehicular design, which employs

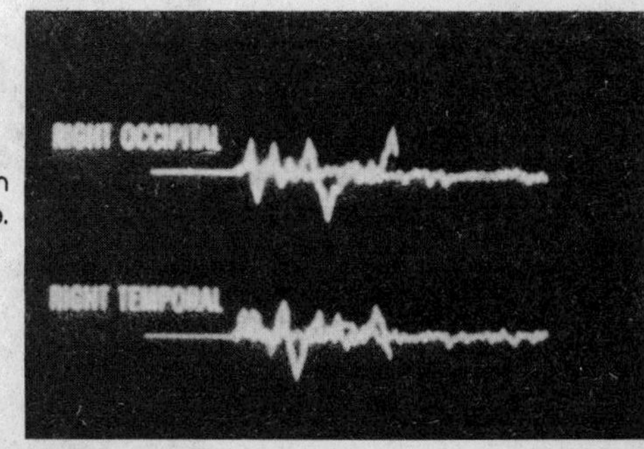

The dual brainwave pattern indicating the alien presence.

an alloy lighter than wood but stronger than steel. In Tokyo, he catches up with Renaldo, who demonstrates his newly-completed antigravity drive. It becomes clear that while the "intruder brain" governs the actions of the quartet, it does not interfere with their attitudes. "If you need to know, suddenly you learn!" an anguished Renaldo tells Ballard. "If you need money, suddenly you get money. Anything to finish the Project. But if you want to get it off your back... you can't do that. You do what's inside your head, no matter how your insides are busting!" And the next thing Ballard knows, it's two weeks later and he is in Minneapolis! Federal agent Harris locates Minns's apartment headquarters and stakes dozens of G-men around it, and while he and Ballard wait to ambush Minns, Minns initiates the next step of the unfathomable plan: He contacts children, promising to take them "far away ... on a starship."

> *Man looks up at the stars, and dreams his futile dreams. Child of the universe, his toys are ignorance, his games, fantasy. Not even master of his own fate, it is the Devil's Puppeteer who stretches his fingers to answer the question... What will happen next?*

PART TWO

> *The Earth: Tumbling grain of sand in the darkness of unending space, plays host to a strange and awful guest, unsought, uninvited, possessor of fearsome power, purveyor of dark deed, a relentless traveler on the road to its mysterious goal...*

Minns evades the trap using "Renaldo's Barrier," an impenetrable force-field developed from the antigravity device. Unable to stop or touch him, Ballard and Harris converge on Wichita, where the other three men are constructing a starship from their combined research. Minns arrives with a station wagon-load of children: The blind Minerva, the deaf-mute Danny Masters, leukemia victim Johnny Subiron, and others crippled or retarded.

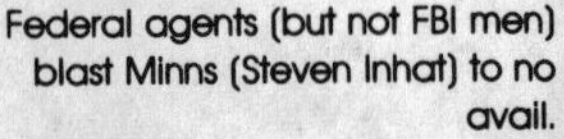

Federal agents (but not FBI men) blast Minns (Steven Inhat) to no avail.

An enraged but helpless Ballard watches Minns guide the trusting kids into the ship; his protests, plus the vocalized self-doubts of the other soldiers, prompt Minns to announce that the four of them will accompany the children into space—of their own free will. Then, with words "that come without my knowledge," Minns relates the story of a benevolent race of humans on a faraway planet—rendered incapable of procreation, they dispatched a galactic SOS long ago, in the form of meteors filled with their RNA factor, in the hope that "a course would follow much like this course has followed with us." Ballard says no one has the right to kidnap helpless children, and Minns surprises him by admitting him and Harris into the spacecraft, where Hadley's "air conditioning," his synthesis of the alien planet's atmosphere, has reversed the children's afflictions. Minns points out that these children are "the hopeless ones, the ones who never had anything on Earth. They will inherit a bright new world of wonder and greatness." Ballard is overwhelmed beyond objection, and the three other soldiers happily agree to go to the stars with the kids.

> *The Inheritors are on their way. In a universe of billions of stars, there are places of love and happiness. On this Earth, in this spot, magic settled for a moment. Wonder touched a few lives, and a few odd pieces fell smoothly into the jigsaw of Creation.*

"I loved 'The Inheritors,'" said director James Goldstone. "It was a marvelous statement on the politics of misunderstanding in the world. Mankind's assumption is that anything not totally understood is, by def-

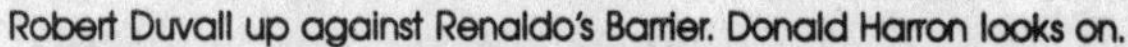
Robert Duvall up against Renaldo's Barrier. Donald Harron looks on.

inition, bad; the suspicion of the Bobby Duvall character is that the Project *has* to be malevolent. It's real drama, and a valuable story to be told. What I liked best about it was that it used science fiction as the jumping-off point: *What if* there was this place that needed people, where the physical constituency was such that blighted children could be healthy, and repopulate the world in a positive way?"

"The Inheritors" absorbed nearly all of Seeleg Lester's work time following the completion of "Wolf 359." It was an all-consuming project, like that undertaken by Lt. Minns. "Sam Neuman came into my office," said Lester, "and said, 'Seeleg, I need some money, and I've got an idea for one of those *Outer Limits* shows. But I've just got the opening; I don't know anything else.' His idea was that a bunch of doctors are watching an encephalograph during an operation, and suddenly two brainwave patterns appear on the screen. One doctor says, 'some entity has entered the brain of that man.' Sam and I entered into *weeks* of discussion on how to use that, and finally came up with a concept."

"Sam was also from *Perry Mason*," Ben Brady noted, "and he was always better at generating ideas than working them out. This was a very appealing idea." The story is still recognizable as a Brady regime plot—a step-by-step accumulation of facts by Ballard, who solves the mystery. But here the gimmick, instead of a conventional monster, was the unconventional ending, a resolution that was sentimental without being cloying. It was titled "The Hui Tan Project," after the Vietnamese province where the alien meteor is found.

"Ed Adamson wanted to sell me a story about a Pied Piper figure who lures away a lot of children," said Lester. "So I incorporated that idea into the story." Accordingly, Part Two was titled "The Pied Piper Project," while in-work. But as Sam Neuman relates, "Seeleg inserted the character of the scientific investigator, to use the script as a possible series pilot, and that took the whole show away from the Pied Piper message."

"Seeleg got bogged down starting with 'The Invisible Enemy,' and never really recovered his pace," said Brady. "He worked on the first draft of 'The Inheritors' for nearly ten weeks, and we just couldn't afford that. These things had to come out faster, and that's why I brought in Milton Krims and Bob Dennis. Seeleg *labored* over every script and got way behind. We had been the best of friends until *The Outer Limits* brought us to some very harsh scenes, and that's a recollection that's rather unhappy."

"We had the goddamndest trouble with ABC because they didn't understand the story," said Lester. "I told Ben we should put it in work as a two-parter, that we could fight for it, and that if ABC wanted monsters we could put them in the *other* shows. Adrian Samish fought me on many, many points in the story, and then, when Ben called me into his office to talk with Samish about the script, Samish said, 'You know, this

"It *is* good... isn't it, God?" Ivan Dixon as Conover.

could make a damned good story—let's not fuck it up!'"

While the Lester/Neuman script concludes Part One by suggesting the mild telepathy by which Minns selects the children (Johnny Subiron runs to greet him as "The Lieutenant" even though Minns is not in uniform), ABC wanted to end with agents raiding Minns's apartment, guns flashing. While Neuman considered the four soldiers to be the leads, Lester gives the story from Ballard's point of view. "The script was better than the finished film," said Neuman, whose narrative opened chronologically in Vietnam and included such scenes as Hadley expressing his extreme alienation to Minns, upon their first meeting in an airport. "There was also a scene where a young girl falls in love with Hadley," said Neuman, "and he realizes he must tell her it cannot be. He doesn't even know why himself. But that was emotional; it got discarded."

Most adjustments were wrought by Lester. In the film, when Ballard is asked if the strange goings-on might have an innocent explanation, his response is a flat *no*. Here is what he says in Lester's earlier draft:

> BALLARD: Innocent? I hope so. But then, why did those three men *disappear*? Do you disappear when you're doing something innocent? How can we know what they may be up to when they've got that "invader brain" in their heads? What if they *aren't* innocent? What if they're enemy-inspired, or a mutant of some kind, or—I hesitate to say it because it sounds so theatrical—but, what if those men are now joined in some dark venture, bent on some evil purpose, controlled by some malevolent extraterrestrial influence? Maybe they *are* innocent, sir, and maybe not... but I think we ought to find out, and fast!

"When you've done a story you think is extraordinarily good, then see the film, I don't think the writer is *ever* satisfied fully," noted Lester. "The sharp limit to the production costs made the spaceship look like some carnival thing. The *menace* didn't come out as much as I would have liked. But I think what did come through was the emotional quality, and the surprise of the ending."

"As the world has seen, there is no limit to how much money you *could* spend on a science fiction show," said James Goldstone, who found in "The Inheritors" the right script to mark his return to *The Outer Limits*. "I certainly recall everyone feeling it was a very special show even though we did it inexpensively. That's why I wanted Bobby Justman with me when I did the second *Star Trek* pilot; he had an understanding of how to get the most onscreen, on schedule. I have a memory of the question of *how* to get that plywood starship to go up into the air at the end of 'The Inheritors.' We couldn't do it optically, and didn't have the time or money to shoot it any other way, so Ken Peach and I just dollied the camera back until we were off the stage, then tilted up to the sky. That was my solution to *that* insoluble problem. There are many TV shows I feel angry about, or apologetic. But you can tell Seeleg for me that I have nothing but good feelings about 'The Inheritors.' I was proud of it, and it stood me in good stead."

Goldstone surely gives a lift to an episode that would have been flattened by a lesser director. The globe-trotting nature of the plot is convincingly conveyed despite the microscopic budget, as the plot takes us, more or less convincingly, from Wall Street to Stockholm to Tokyo. One subtle motif of the narrative is that the closer Ballard drives to his objective, the further he is pushed back. He just misses Hadley, is ducked by Conover, and when he finally corners Renaldo in the flesh, he loses two weeks. Goldstone has a soft spot for society's outcasts—the soldiers and the children—and the gentle way in which they are filmed undercuts

(L-R:) Dee Pollack, Ivan Dixon, James Frawley, Donald Harron, Robert Duvall, and Steve Inhat next to the spaceship ramp.

Steve Inhat leads the children toward the starship.

the sense of menace that is supposed to follow Minns around. Since he never really seems threatening or evil, Ballard looks a bit monomaniacal in his relentless pursuit. He is the hero figure by default, devoted to the erasure of evil, and he turns out to be dead wrong in his assessment of Minns' purpose. When he slams nose-first into Renaldo's Barrier, he shouts, *"I hope you rot, Minns!"* Once he is admitted past the barrier, he is speechless with surprise, and this lends the ending much of its impact.

High marks are due the entire cast, which Goldstone rehearsed for two days before shooting. "Steve Inhat's role is *the* part in that show," he noted. Robert Duvall's performance as Ballard lends the character some compassion. James Frawley (later director of *The Muppet Movie*) is a terrific Renaldo—bearlike, mad as hell at being pushed around by the intruder brain, yet powerful and sympathetic. It is difficult to believe that the mad-dog Fed, Harris, is played by an actor with Shakespearian training. "Donald Harron is enormously talented," said Goldstone. "He had performed at Stratford on Avon; he has his own talk show now, in Canada." Ben Brady's son David appears as young Danny Masters, and Suzanne Cupito, seen previously as an insufferable brat in several *Twilight Zone*s (and today known as Morgan Brittany), has a more touching turn as the blind Minerva, saying, "Look what my hands look like," to a flabbergasted Ballard.

Lester's intention to use "The Inheritors" as a series pilot actually dates back to his tenure on *Perry Mason*. "I developed two series ideas for CBS," he said. "One of them was a mystery series, set in the Caribbean, called *Jamaica Ginger*. The other was *Century 21*, for which I got someone at RandCorp to give me a decade-by-decade prognosis of life in the US, leading up to the year 2000. I wanted to have a 'Secretary of Science' character in the President's Cabinet, and he and his assistant would investigate things of a scientific nature. For example: Someone discovers a drug that will prolong life to 180 years. Who's going to use it? How do you apportion it? It might become the object of theft or murder. That problem would go to the Secretary of Science. I used that character in

'The Inheritors,' and got my ownership of him written into the contract. But CBS wouldn't do the series. They had no imagination. And all the things that RandCorp guy predicted in 1962 have been coming to pass ever since."

The Megasoid costume—looking much better than it did onscreen—backstage at Paramount.
(Courtesy B. Ritchie Payne)

THE DUPLICATE MAN

Broadcast 19 December 1964
Written by Robert C. Dennis, based on the Clifford D. Simak story, "Goodnight, Mr. James."
Directed by Gerd Oswald
Assistant Director: Gregg Peters
Director of Photography: Kenneth Peach

CAST: Henderson James/James II (Ron Randell), Capt. Karl Emmet (Sean McClory), Laura James (Constance Towers), Megasoid (Mike Lane), Zoo Guide (Alan Gifford), Murdock (Konstantin Shayne), Policeman (Jeffrey Stone), Basil Jerichau (Steven Geray), Miss Thorson (Ivy Bethune), Pedestrian (Jonathan Hole), Stunt Emmet (George Robotham), Stunt James (George Paul).

Since the first day that Man stared up at the stars and saw other worlds, there has been no more haunting question than this: What will we find there? Will there be other creatures, and will they be like us? Or when that ancient dream comes true, will it turn into a nightmare? Will we find, on some distant, frozen planet, an alien life of unimaginable horror?

The year is 2025, and renowned academic Henderson James has smuggled to Earth a Megasoid—highly dangerous, illegal to possess, and, in the words of space smuggler Capt. Emmet, "always thinking about killing, unless it's in its reproductive cycle"—which this one is. When it escapes (to hide out amid the stuffed extraterrestrials in a nearby space zoo), James cannot summon the courage to track it down and kill it, and so has a clone of himself illegally made for the purpose. Strict deadlines govern the minting of such "duplicates," which are destroyed before vestigial memory renders them indistinguishable from their originals. James's bootleg duplicate botches his mission at the zoo, and the pregnant Megasoid gets away. A shred of memory leads James II to Emmet's home. When Emmet panics and tries to phone the police, James II bludgeons him and finds his way to "his" home, accumulating more of Henderson James's memories every step of the way. When he confronts James's wife, Laura, she sees in him a younger version of her husband, before he was consumed by ambition and obsessed by his study of the Megasoid. The real James, meanwhile, has gone to bribe Emmet into murdering James II once his task is accomplished. While Emmet waits in ambush at James's home, he is slaughtered by the Megasoid. James meets his duplicate, and the hard truth of seeing a more compassionate version of himself gives him the courage needed to kill the alien, since he realizes Laura would be happier with James II. Both of them hunt the Megasoid, and James shoots the monster as it tears James II apart. Then he discovers that James II was dying all the time... from a timed-release poison in his bloodstream, a precaution provided by Basil Jerichau, the clone bootlegger. A less cynical Henderson James is now reconciled with his wife.

In all the universe, can there be creatures more strange than the species called Man? He creates and destroys; he fumbles and makes mistakes. But the thing which distinguishes him is the ability to learn from his mistakes.

Clifford Simak's "Goodnight, Mr. James," first published in the March, 1951 issue of *Galaxy,* begins and ends with the "duplicate" of Henderson James, who awakes on a street of an unnamed city (much like Trent in "Demon With a Glass Hand") with a mission to kill an alien called a puudly. The alien, using telepathy, fills in some blanks about the clone's origin before he exterminates it. He then decides to try to talk the real Henderson James into letting him live, perhaps after some plastic surgery to differentiate them. Through a fluke of timing, he arrives at James's house after the gardener, whose job is to murder the clone, kills the real James instead. As the duplicate prepares to settle into James's life and routines, he takes a phone call from Allen, the clone bootlegger, who advises him of the poison: "Like a time bomb. No antidote for it even if he found out somehow." The duplicate says, "It was good of you to let me know." Allen responds, "Glad to. Goodnight, Mr. James."

"The Duplicate Man" is both Robert Dennis's most successful story adaptation, and his best *Outer Limits* teleplay. "The Simak story really

Ron Randell.

didn't incorporate the creature in the sense of a subplot," said Dennis, "and I recall altering it to bring the monster back, mostly for the network." Dennis invented the term *Megasoid,* gave James a disenchanted wife, and gave flamboyant names to the background characters (a trademark of his script work). No reason is given as to why the Megasoid, noted as being a creature of extreme intelligence, wants to kill everything that isn't a Megasoid, but as Seeleg Lester put it, "The story really wasn't about this alien on the loose. It had human interest, and logical reasons for the plot turns."

Dennis interprets James, who is never glimpsed in the Simak story, as an acquisitive, self-centered, status-conscious academic. The duplicate yearns to feel and live, while his original has become robotic and unemotional, and the show's best scenes depict the duplicate's accumulation of the real James's memories, and the feelings awakened in the clone by Laura, who laments the fact her husband doesn't love her enough to squire her to social obligations, or drifts around tragically, a second-season drink in her hand. This subtheme (James's responsibilities) extends to the drunken Basil Jerichau and Capt. Emmet (who was mauled smuggling James's Megasoid to Earth), who upbraid James for his cowardice and willingness to let others take risks—the character trait that leads him to have the duplicate created.

Apart from "Soldier"'s war zone scenes, "The Duplicate Man" is a rare attempt to redress 1960s people and places for the future. Here we see primitive videophones that chime instead of ring, automobiles with louvers and turbine engines, a drinking fountain activated by a ray of light, and a world to which the importation of Megasoids has been prohibited "since 1986," as Emmet says. "I dressed everyone a little bit differently from custom," said Gerd Oswald. "No one wore a knot in their tie, the fountain idea was mine, the cars were odd, and the story didn't dwell on the monster." Scouting futuristic-looking locations led Claude

Binyon to an elaborate, toadstool-shaped Hollywood Hills residence known as the Camisphere House, which was used as the home of Capt. Emmet, and was accessed by a mine-car–like lift that ran up the hillside on tracks.*

"The problem with that story was that it was too big for an hour show," said Lester. "A lot of things had to be explained that were essential to the story, but not to the drama of *Which man is the right man*?" One example is the complex set of regulations overlaid on the duplication process, which was moved from the beginning of the show to the middle, probably for the benefit of pacing. As in "Expanding Human," academia is in for another beating here, through the depiction of James as an amoral obsessive, and Jerichau (one of the men who originated the duplication process) as an obsolete alcoholic holding forth from a cobweb-festooned lab.

The Megasoid is the most absurd and ridiculous-looking "bear" ever conceived for *The Outer Limits*. Mike Lane slouches about wearing a floppy velour gorilla suit with a long tail, and the "Second Chance" mask, sloppily modified with a bulging forehead and a foot-long beak. It has claws that are oversized, formless, and silly-looking; when the creature is not speaking in perfect (though phlegmatic) English, it snarls via a dubbed-in dog's growl. Oswald struggles to keep the creature in the shadows to conceal its overwhelming inadequacy (Lane's T-shirt can be seen poking out of the suit), and perhaps too little time was invested in this get-up due to the other aliens Project Unlimited had to whip up for the brief zoo scene—one of which looks like a crawdad four feet long.

Signing on for "The Duplicate Man' was 1st AD Gregg Peters. "He was probably one of the best ADs that ever worked for me," noted Oswald. "A great personality—he knew what he was doing and could adapt himself to whomever he worked with." Some unannounced extra characters appear in one shot of the Camisphere House's ascending tram-car—namely, the whole camera crew, whose shadows are seen jumping around on the hillside in the lower right of frame as the car goes up. This was typical of the technical slips caused in part by the hurried pace of the second season. In "Cry of Silence," avalanche scenes were shot through a pane of protective glass that also betrays the ghostly reflection of a crew hand wearing a cowboy hat, moving along the top of the hill. "Boom shots"—a visible microphone or its shadow intruding on the frame—became prolific, and repeated usage of props, notably the "pressure chamber" from "Cold Hands, Warm Heart," were almost comical. As Jack Poplin said, "If it was big enough to fill a hole, we'd use it again and again."

*Most recently seen in the film *Body Double*, the Camisphere House went up for sale in 1985 for $1,000,050.

Wesley Addy confers with the Paul LeBaron-designed "brain jar."

THE BRAIN OF COLONEL BARHAM

Broadcast 2 January 1965
Written by Robert C. Dennis. Story by Sidney Ellis. Original title: "The Brain of Donald Duncan."
Directed by Charles Haas
Assistant Director: Robert Justman
Director of Photography: Kenneth Peach

CAST: Major Douglas McKinnon (Grant Williams), Col. Alec Barham (Anthony Eisley), Jennifer Barham (Elizabeth Perry), Gen. Daniel Petit (Douglas Kennedy), Dr. Leo Hausner (Martin Kosleck), Dr. Rahm (Wesley Addy), Major Locke (Peter Hansen), Ed Nichols (Paul Lukather), Guard (Robert Chadwick), Stunt Nichols (George Robotham).

> *With the world growing more crowded, the great powers strive to conquer other planets. The race is on. The interplanetary sea has been charted; the first caravelle of space is being constructed. Who will get there first? Who will be the new Columbus?*

Since robot solar system probes cannot deal with unexpected crises in space, Dr. Hausner proposes installing a living human brain as a component that can resourcefully resolve random factors. He finds a perfect volunteer in terminal leukemia victim Alec Barham, an irate and hotheaded astronaut more than willing to abandon his wife Jennifer to the sympathies of project psychiatrist McKinnon. Once Barham's brain is removed and hooked up to computer and life-support equipment, it begins to generate new brain matter and supply its own power. McKinnon quickly diagnoses it as paranoiac. Angry at Jennifer (for not visiting), and McKinnon (for obstructing the project), the brain uses bolts of electricity to zombify technician Nichols into assaulting Jennifer, and Dr. Rahm into emptying a pistol at McKinnon. When the brain traps McKinnon and Jennifer in its room, Gen. Petit ventures to an outside balcony with a sniper's rifle and puts a bullet through the bubbling brain jar. McKinnon's final verdict: "Col. Barham died on the operating table."

> *Progress goes on. One experiment fails, but even out of failure valuable lessons are learned. A way will be found, someday, somehow. It always is.*

After *Frankenstein* and *Dr. Jekyll and Mr. Hyde,* one of the most often-reprised themes in science fiction for film and TV is the one originated by Curt Siodmak in *Donovan's Brain* (1943). If *The Outer Limits* must have a brain-in-a-tank episode, it might as well be "Barham," which at least stands some marginally interesting characters up against the all-too-stock plotline.

"I took my original idea to Ben Brady," said Sidney Ellis. "He requested a full script and I delivered it, and Brady turned around and handed it to Bob Dennis, who changed all the characters' names, and rewrote it to be played mostly in one room. The story remained basically the same, and a friend later pointed out the similarities to *Donovan's Brain* to me."

The intramural conflicts among the large cast of principals is ultimately more engaging than the pound of hamburger the audience expects to see floating in an aquarium by the third act. Dr. Rahm, for example, calls McKinnon a juvenile and a charlatan, for daring to suggest the ground-breaking operation might not be a healthy thing. When McKinnon diagnoses Barham's disembodied brain as having delusions of grandeur, Rahm wryly returns, "Delusions, Major? Col. Barham has *achieved* grandeur." And Barham himself assesses each of his ministrators, in a clever scene with McKinnon:

BARHAM: Major, do you remember the old fable about the blind men trying to describe an elephant by the part they were touching?

MCKINNON: Yes. Does it apply here?

BARHAM: General Petit is a blind man. He thinks I volunteered out of patriotism, dedication to the service.

MCKINNON: That's a soldier's viewpoint.

BARHAM: Then take Dr. Rahm. He sees it as good, common sense. I was going to die anyway; why not gamble?

MCKINNON: Weren't there *three* blind men?

BARHAM: Hausner. To him, it's intellectual curiosity. I think he envies me. (sarcastically) You're not taking *notes,* Major...

MCKINNON: Let me get below the surface...

BARHAM: You see? You're the only one with eyes, and still you can't see the obvious. You keep looking in dusty corners.

Additionally, Petit has the race for space against the Russians on the brain, while Barham's wife Jennifer is oddly moralistic about her emasculated husband, an admitted philanderer who strives to be as emotionally cruel to her as possible. When she expresses her sorrow at his condition, Barham can only think of himself, in rage: "Why *me*? Why do I have to die, with the world full of useless slobs?" Despite McKinnon's repeated and well-grounded warnings that Barham is unfit for this duty, the team persists in ignoring the facts for the good of the project. As Barham says, they really *don't* see the obvious. When Dr. Rahm shuffles off on his Barham-controlled mission of assassination, Jennifer spots him and notes that he looks the same way Nichols did just prior to attacking her. Major Locke shrugs and says, "He's a scientist, Mrs. Barham—they walk around in a daze most of the time."

The fuzzy-headed scientist is not the only bromide Dennis invokes. Like "I, Robot," the show takes the position that amalgams of man and machine are somehow wrong, and the show's editorial position is little better than that time-honored sci-fi party line of the 1950s—There are Things Man Was Not Meant to Know/Do. Dennis's inspiration for changing the title of the show seems truly on the spur of the moment, since Barham Boulevard was a street passed by many a writer on his way to Paramount (use of the name Donald Duncan posed legal problems).

The parts are well-played, considering the limitations and inevitability of the tired story line. Grant Williams, star of the 1957 classic *The Incredible Shrinking Man,* here resurfaces after a four-year stint on *Hawaiian Eye*. Martin Kosleck, a stalwart of many 1940s monster melodramas, plays the monomaniacal and Nazi-like Hausner, a role perhaps epitomized by his similar part in *The Flesh Eaters* (1967).

"Barham" also spotlights a peculiar trend which dogged both seasons of *The Outer Limits*. Here, the scientists are preparing to send a probe to Mars (guided by Barham's brain), prior to sending a manned mission. In "Cold Hands, Warm Heart," we've already gone to Venus and are poised to go to Mars; no probe is needed. In "The Invisible Enemy," we went to Mars three years earlier, and in "Counterweight" and "The Duplicate Man," we are already capable of traveling outside the solar system. These contradictory messages extend even to the Control Voice speeches, which tell us in "Barham" that "*the interplanetary sea has been charted,*" while earlier, in "Counterweight," we are told that "*the heavens are not oceans.*"

Grant Williams.

Paul LeBaron recalled building the brain tank seen in the episode: "I made a dome to go on top of a three-gallon jar and drilled holes to run in all the tubing and wires and stuff. We got a calf's brain from a slaughterhouse and stuck it in there. I still have that jar out in my garage."

Ben Brady tried to toss ABC one of the monsters they were demanding in "Behold, Eck!"—the third show broadcast, while "Barham" was being filmed. "After that third week," said Brady, "I had a clear sense that the ship was sinking. There was no rating. Today, if a show doesn't do well in three weeks, it's off the air in three weeks. Back then, it took as long as a season to get cancelled. ABC gave us all kinds of reasons *not* having to do with ratings as to why they wanted to kill *The Outer Limits*. The bottom line is that there are no abstruse reasons *why*. If there's no rating, the sponsors leave!"

With two shows yet to be filmed to take the series to the halfway point in the season, as Gerd Oswald said, "ABC pulled the plugs."

Dewey Martin in the cockpit of his ship.

THE PREMONITION

Broadcast 9 January 1965
Written by Ib Melchior and Sam Roeca, from a story by Sam Roeca.
Original title: "Gordian Knot"
Directed by Gerd Oswald
Assistant Director: Gregg Peters
Director of Photography: Kenneth Peach

CAST: Jim Darcy (Dewey Martin), Linda Darcy (Mary Murphy), Gen. "Baldy" Baldwin (William Bramley), Matron (Dorothy Green), Janie Darcy (Emma Tyson), Gate Sentry (Coby Denton), Limbo Being (Kay Kuter).

On the fabulous spawning grounds of Man's ever-increasing knowledge of science and technology, ancient, half-forgotten legends seemingly have no place. Except one: The legend of the Gordian Knot, a knot so intricate and convoluted that no man could untie it. For there are problems so perplexing that they are seemingly impossible to solve, when Man ventures to the outer limits of his experience...

Test pilot Darcy is putting an experimental, X-15 type craft through high speed maneuvers when he loses control and abruptly finds himself on the ground, his ship cracked in half in the desert. Nearby, his wife Linda, looking up to see his jet, has rammed her car into a boulder. The couple find that besides the jet, the car and themselves, all objects and creatures seem immovably frozen. They return to the air base on foot and deduce that they've been displaced backward in time a few minutes via their simultaneous accidents, and that the people around them are actually moving, with imperceptible slowness. Time is gradually catching up with them—and the moment of Darcy's malfunction. They discover their daughter Janie will be run over by an improperly parked truck at the same moment, and a shimmering "Limbo Being" wearing a suit and tie conveniently informs them that they must each be in their places (the jet, the car) at the moment time resynchronizes, or they'll be stuck forever... which makes it impossible to save Janie, until Darcy uses a splinter of metal from his jet and all of the seatbelts from Linda's car to rig a contrivance that will yank back the handbrake of the truck as the front wheel turns. They reinstall themselves on schedule, avoiding the Limbo Being by using flares to hold it at bay, and when time catches up all three tragedies are averted.

Man is forever solving the most perplexing problems as he ventures ever further into the unknown. But where are the outer limits of his ingenuity? Will he ever encounter a problem, a Gordian Knot, which he cannot ultimately cut?

Historically, the convoluted knot tied by Gordius, king of Phyrigia, could only be untied by the future ruler of Asia. When Alexander the Great, who considered himself king-to-be, was confounded by the intricacies of the knot, he hacked it apart with his sword. In "The Premonition," Darcy unties his personal Gordian Knot fair and square; he doesn't "cut" it, as the Control Voice suggests.

"The Premonition" is another *Outer Limits* episode frequently confused as a *Twilight Zone*. It expands what might have been a taut half-hour show into an hour that is flabby with redundancies and padding. The problem set up for the Darcys to unravel is interesting, but the Janie

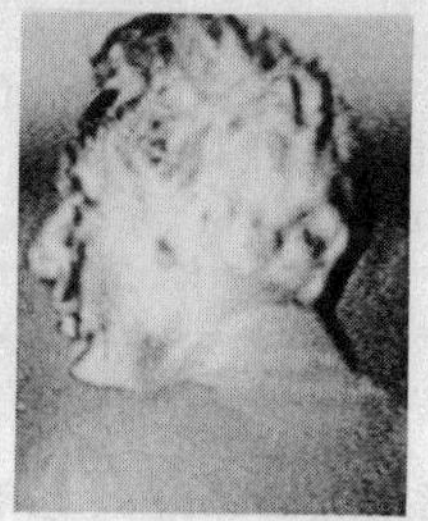

Kay Kuter as the Limbo Being.

subplot (which reinforces the "family" subtext running through the second season) is irritatingly heavy-handed, and the totally extraneous "Limbo Being" waltzes into the story just long enough to tell the Darcys everything they need to know to escape, which runs contrary to the problem-solving theme.

"Ib Melchior brought in the idea for that show," said Seeleg Lester. "His 'timeslip' was a concept left over from *The Time Travelers,* a film he'd done that year. He also showed me his script for *Robinson Crusoe On Mars,* which intrigued me. Sam Roeca did the final script, and that show illustrates how I managed to combine a monster and a dramatic situation. You didn't *need* that creature trapped between two worlds, but I brought it in because ABC needed *something*. I made the 'horror' of it the situation, rather than making the monster itself horrible. You feel kind of sorry for its predicament."

"Ib, as you know, is a science fiction freak," said Ben Brady. "He did the most *science fictiony* stories I'd ever heard of. I liked that episode a lot."

Some viewers fault "The Premonition" in the mistaken belief that Darcy uses the seatbelt from the truck, which is itself frozen in time, to save Janie. Just how immobile everything is was punched home a bit harder in the script, when Darcy tries to shove a field radar man, and impales his hand on the man's frozen-in-time crew cut. Blood seeps from the fifty tiny holes the absolutely rigid hairs make in Darcy's palm. Another excised scene explains that Darcy's mission "has something to do with high-velocity directional changes, like making a ninety-degree turn when you're going several times the speed of sound," as a gate guard explains.

But by the time shooting commenced on "The Premonition," ABC had decided to consign *The Outer Limits* to its own limbo as of mid-January, dead in the middle of the 1964–65 season. "This was the last show I did," said Gerd Oswald. "Don Gordon had originally been cast as the lead, but he got sick the night before the first day of shooting, and we scrambled around trying to find a replacement. At four o'clock in the morning, we found Dewey Martin. Then we found out the show had been cancelled, and the pressure was really on since we'd already lost a day by replacing Gordon. Martin literally learned his lines the moment before we shot them, and getting him through was a struggle. And I'm not a big fan of Ib Melchior in the first place. Don Guest, the overseer from United Artists, told me we had to bring that show in on schedule even if we hadn't shot the ending yet."

The episode's exteriors were shot at Palos Verdes Air Force Base. "We got that X-15 mockup from Palmdale," said B. Ritchie Payne. "The Air Force viewed our use of their mockup as promotion for the armed forces. Most of the time, unless you wanted the entire 7th Fleet, they were very accommodating."

Though poorly developed, the show's time-out-of-kilter theme is engaging, and as in much science fiction, the *idea* overrides any significant characterization. The concept of frozen time as an intermediate dimension also appeals to the imagination (and was clearly one of Melchior's favorite springboards), but the suspension of disbelief is wounded by the severe padding. We see doubles for the Darcys running hand-in-hand, back and forth between the airbase and the crash site, no less than four times. The camera lingers overlong on still photographs, nonmoving tableaus, and Space Age-ese countdowns in both real time and slow motion.

"The Premonition" 's strangest story has to do with the ultimatum delivered to Oswald by Don Guest. "We *had* to shut down on Monday evening," Oswald recalled. "Monday afternoon rolled around and there they were, asking if I'd finish on time. I told them I thought I could. And they told me that if I did, I could have *anything* I wanted and United Artists would pick up the tab. So I said, 'Well, I've never slept with a Japanese broad.' I said that facetiously, of course; I was indulging in a lifelong fantasy. I finished the show on time, and at six o'clock met my wife, and Ben Brady and his wife, for a dinner date. And Guest signalled me wildly—they'd actually gotten me this Japanese girl, and she was waiting in my office!"

"May I tell you the story?" said Claude Binyon, chuckling. "We couldn't *give* that poor girl away! You see, we had this one particular transportation captain, a beautiful man who'd put his life on the line for you. Whenever you had some dirty job that needed to be done, you'd say, 'Uh, I have a problem.' He was the one who went out and came back with this, uh, very attractive Oriental girl. She was driving a green Cadillac. So we were all down on the set, ready to present Gerd with his 'gift' for finishing on time, and in walks Gerd's wife, and Ben, and Ben's wife. And Gerd goes, 'Get rid of her!!' and left for dinner. And no one else on the set would take the girl. It was all heavy, macho-image stuff, I guess; no one wanted her for free. Eventually, the transportation captain paid her; he said he 'collected' later, but I don't know how true that is."

A cheesy photograph of an even cheesier set. L–R: Ron Hays, Mark Richman (note the "Borderland" pylon behind him), Peggy Ann Gardner.

THE PROBE

Broadcast 16 January 1965
Written by Seeleg Lester. Story idea by Sam Neuman.
Directed by Felix Feist
Assistant Director: Rusty Meek
Directors of Photography: Kenneth Peach and Fred Koenekamp

CAST: Jefferson Rome (Mark Richman), Coberly (Ron Hayes), Amanda Frank (Peggy Ann Garner), Dexter (William Stevens), Beeman (William Boyett), Radio Engineer (Richard Tretter), "Mikie" (Janos Prohaska).

The persistence of Man's curiosity led him into new worlds. Without conquering his own, he invaded the sub-world of the microscope, and the outer-world of space. It is said turnabout is fair play . . . but is it?

Enroute to Tokyo, pilot Coberly decides to fly into a squall and winds up ditching his plane in the eye of a hurricane. His passenger, Amanda, and crew awake minus Beeman, the copilot, in their life raft on a fogbound "sea" that turns out to be a floor of solid plastic! Nearby is a large cylinder that first emits a foul mist that dries their clothing, then light-beams that carve off a chunk of their raft and suck it in. Through an overwhelming degree of supposition and on-target blind conjecture, they determine they are trapped inside of a gigantic, completely automated, Voyager-like alien space probe . . . and that the amorphous, sofa-sized silver glob menacing them is a mutated, overgrown stowaway microbe—the "mikie." Poking around, they discover oversized lab facilities, where the piece of raft and the local seawater are being analyzed, and a rudimentary control room featuring alien hieroglyphics. Using the equipment that sends telemetry back to the home planet, Amanda begs for their release as the probe prepares to lift off for the next planet on its itinerary (presumed to be Venus) with them trapped inside. The light-beam protects them from the mikie and herds them out, while summoning a rescue ship. From the ship's deck, the group watches the probe ascend, then explode. It seems the aliens have heeded Amanda's warning about extraterrestrial contamination. "They'll be back," she says hopefully, looking up at the sky. "I'd like to think *we'd* be as smart. Compassionate. Human."

> *A few days, a week, a month... Will the Earth be visited by a stranger from the universe? A warm, compassionate stranger, to tell us of wonders beyond imagination, of life beyond comprehension, of secrets from the treasurehouse of stars?*

"The Probe" is the ultimate *Outer Limits* "bottle show." Almost devoid of production values, it was written at the eleventh hour by Seeleg Lester and is a bit of a minor miracle in terms of his dedication to getting *something* onto the shooting stages and into the can.

"We were tight all the way," said Ben Brady. "We fought ABC all the way. At the end of the season, Seeleg and I did one show designed to cost nothing—it was just people floating around in a vacuum. We did it for something like $70,000 when our average budget was $125,000."

"Once again, Sam Neuman needed money," said Lester. "He brought in the idea; I paid him the story fee and gave him story credit." Neuman recalled, "I had a group of four with one girl, flying over the ocean during the war. During a terrible thunderstorm, lightning hits their plane and they fall into the sea. They wonder why they're not sinking and it turns out they're on a gigantic space probe."

"It wasn't that we couldn't understand the aliens," said Lester. "It was that they *could* understand us—a reverse on the theme of 'Cry of Silence.' Finally, they understand what we're trying to tell them, and they destroy the probe so that no harm will come to Earth. Sam White could never understand what the hell that show was about, but I thought it had moments of good drama."

The show is also a reverse on "Wolf 359"—this time it is Earth, under an alien microscope. This approach was popular with science fiction writers who had been inspired by the early models depicting the structure of the atom, which resembled miniature solar systems. We later learned that atoms don't really look like that, but the concept prompted a great deal of fiction about microscopic worlds-within-worlds; one of the oldest being Ray Cummings' "The Girl in the Golden Atom" (1919).

The main problem with the story's believability is that once the people get inside the probe, they begin making wild and extreme assumptions, all of which are right on target 100 percent of the time. The procedural question-answer approach of the second season is here, but this time the folks giving the answers really have no idea of what they're talking about. Pointing and squinting, Jefferson Rome rattles off the following:

> ROME: That piece of raft back there is being examined; it is, in bits and pieces, being subjected to a variety of tests. And like I said, the information is being sent along to this 'analog room.' Here, it is decoded and classified and sent along to its destination... [the probe] landed here on Earth, just by chance, in the eye of a hurricane, scooping us up and depositing us ... where, did you ask? Under a microscope. Right on the other side of this hollow center shaft. And those light-beams that operate in so many ways, that activate all these tests, are to examine, to scrutinize us, to probe our world. I think... we're inside a gigantic space probe of some alien civilization, and this whole plastic flooring is the base of a microscope inside this hunk of machinery!

The likelihood of all this being true is injured further by the show's obvious cheapness. The sets for "The Probe" are mostly naked soundstages, with movable sections of blue wall impregnated with glitter serving as the probe's interior. The shots of Coberly's toy plane pitching about in the rain are done with a hose and a hand-held model. Janos Prohaska took a final "monster turn" as the "mikie" inside what had to be one of the most uncomfortable costumes ever devised—a bloblike smattering of silver-painted latex (it looks like a giant Luminoid scab) operated from a car mechanic's flat dolly. It is so formless it never seems very threatening.

Janos Prohaska as the microbe monster—the "mikie."

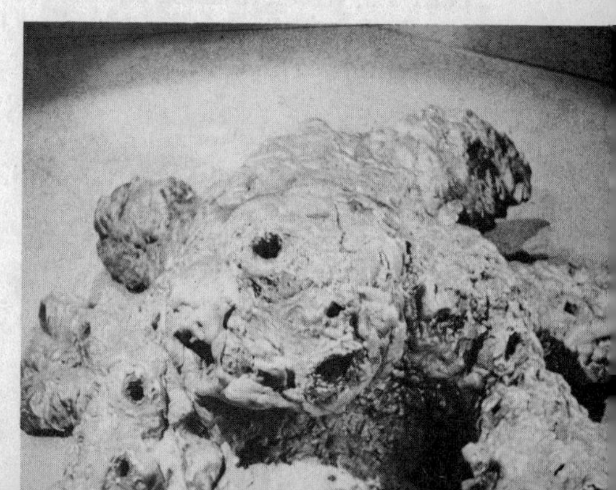

Felix Feist was brought in to complete *The Outer Limits'* final show. "Feist had been suggested to me by an agent who sold me a bill of goods at the time," said Brady, "so I used him." He had directed *The Deluge* for Merian Cooper and Ernest Schoedsack of *King Kong* fame in 1933, and various features through 1955. "He was a marvelous man, and fell in love with 'The Probe'," said Lester. Feist died in 1965, shortly following the only network broadcast of "The Probe." Since Robert Justman walked off *The Outer Limits* following "The Brain of Colonel Barham," a 1st AD also outside the series, Rusty Meek, was brought in to assist Feist.

Mark Richman, who starred in *The Outer Limits'* first regular episode, "The Borderland," fittingly appears in its last, as Jefferson Rome, but he and his companions are at the mercy of a plot too aware of its own need to fill time. "I grew up with Ron Hayes," said Claude Binyon. "He later became a tree surgeon. Peggy Ann Garner came out of oblivion for this show, too. It was all pretty terrible. The people were trying, of course, doing their best, but I don't think anyone was interested anymore. By this point, everyone was leaving."

"Good, bad, or indifferent, it doesn't matter," said Brady. "As a producer, it never bothers me that the network will give you a hundred-and-one reasons why they're dissatisfied with a show. They are only capable of being dissatisfied by one thing, and it's childish to think otherwise. If the show needs a twenty-two share of the ratings and it's only pulling an eighteen, it ain't about to stay on the air. The bottom line I finally got from ABC was, was the show paying for itself? No. Each week we didn't get that rating up was another nail in the coffin, and anything else you might hear is poppycock. Just before we went out of production, I showed ABC a room full of letters from viewers, and I told them, 'You can *still* get on with this show.' No chance."

"The shortsightedness of ABC was extraordinary," said Lester. "We remember lots of people wouldn't go out on dates on Saturday nights because they wanted to see *The Outer Limits*. They were intrigued by the imagination, and by a different story every week."

"The Probe" was broadcast only once. The following week *The Outer Limits* was replaced by *The King Family,* ABC's cheapest show, at $60,000 per hour, which finished out the season.

And, as they say in bad science fiction movies, that was the end... or was it?

PART SIX

Beyond the Outer Limits

> Diverting as all these series may have been, none of them compete with *The Outer Limits,* a programme produced by scriptwriter Joseph Stefano and containing the best science fiction ever to be presented on television. Ill-fated and misunderstood, this series was readily accepted by the visually-oriented teenage audience when it was run in early time slots on American television, but when increasing sophistication forced programming at a later time, adults found its odd plots and unconventional narrative style impossible to comprehend, and it folded abruptly. But in its brief life *The Outer Limits* gave television some of its finest moments.... [It] was not a perfect series, but for consistency of imagination it had few equals.... The result is something of which both science fiction and television should be proud.
>
> —John Baxter, *Science Fiction in the Cinema* (Tantivy Press, London, 1970)

A year or so following the cancellation of *The Outer Limits,* Lou Morheim, working as story editor on *The Big Valley,* found himself in the curious, reversed-role position of handing a script assignment to his old boss, Leslie Stevens. Shortly after *The Outer Limits* closed down, Daystar became inert as a production entity because, according to Stevens, it was "constantly ramming into the wall by losing money on deals. It didn't have any competitive strength at all other than its talent—and that's not much help, if you don't have any dealmakers."

In 1969 Stevens completed his first published book, *EST: The Steersman's Handbook.* Not related to the pop-psych of Werner Erhard, "EST" stands for "Electronic-Social Transformation," or the integration of technology with mystic/spiritual disciplines and philosophies. Its aim was to help evolve the "new age" that Stevens was constantly promoting. The book was published by Noel Young's Capricorn Press under the byline L. Clark Stevens. "That was to establish my credibility," said Stevens. "If the Movement people knew about my background as a successful TV producer, they wouldn't have trusted me. They would have thought I was hyping them." According to Stevens, "steersmen" are those rare individuals gifted with "simulsense"—a broad, comprehensive, forward-thinking outlook that permits them to point the way for the rest of society. One admirer to Stevens' approach was R. Buckminster Fuller. *The Whole Earth Catalog* listed the book as "essential," and Bantam Books published a mass-market edition in 1971, the year that Leslie Stevens Productions, Inc., was christened. Stevens also threw in with some fellow steersmen and purchased a former Titan missile base near Lincoln, California. Renamed "Earthside," the base was intended to be an ecological showplace, to aid in infusing Movement thinking into politics, and try to avert the trends toward rampant pollution and impending ecological catastrophe.

Daystar's final feature project was undeniably its strangest—*Incubus* (1965), an abstract horror film in which all dialogue is spoken in Esperanto. In 1968, Stevens signed up with Universal to develop and line-produce pilots; two of his first were *It Takes a Thief* and *The Name of the Game*. In 1973 he created *Search* (for Warner Bros.), a science fiction-flavored affair involving an elite team of international troubleshooters, spies with sensory implants linking them to a vast computer web overlorded by scientist Burgess Meredith. Back at Universal, Stevens developed the series *Invisible Man* (1975), its spin-off, *Gemini Man* (1976), *Battlestar Galactica* (1978), and *Buck Rogers in the 25th Century* (1979). Feature films were assembled from the latter two projects. Stevens is still vitally involved in playwriting (*Babe Ruth, Partridge in a Pear Tree*) and scriptwriting (some of the projects which he worked on, eschewing credit, included *A Change of Seasons* [1982], *Sahara* [1983], and *Bolero*

Joe Stefano (L) in the director's chair at last, for *The Haunted*. Fred Phillips adjusts Dame Judith Anderson's makeup. (Courtesy Claude Binyon, Jr.)

[1984]). Today he is at the helm of Empress Productions (*E*nterprises in *M*edia *P*roduction, *R*ecordings, and *E*ntertainment for *S*tage and *S*creen), in partnership with Dominic Frontiere, whose wife, Georgia, owns the Los Angeles Rams football team.

In 1965, Ben Brady moved back to CBS to produce the ill-fated *Rawhide* revival. Today he is head of the film and TV curriculum at Cal State Northridge.

Seeleg Lester worked with Stevens on the *Invisible Man* series, and contributed to the series at first called *Ghost Story,* then *Circle of Fear.* In 1969 he did a horror feature, *A Change of Mind,* followed by *The Reincarnate* in 1971, after which he became story editor and scriptwriter for *Hawaii Five-O.* Today he is busy writing novels.

Before retiring from the film industry in 1968, Byron Haskin directed the noteworthy *Robinson Crusoe on Mars* (1964) and one last film for George Pal, *The Power* (1967). Between these he assisted in production and special effects capacities for two pilots for a series with the unlikely working title of *Wagon Train to the Stars*... better known as *Star Trek.* Haskin died in 1984, during production of this book.

Gerd Oswald's numerous subsequent projects included two episodes for *Star Trek,* "The Conscience of the King" and "The Alternative Factor." Oswald reentered anthology territory during the 1985–86 TV season by directing two segments of the revived *Twilight Zone* for CBS—"The Beacon," a supernatural horror tale, and "The Star," based on Arthur C. Clarke's science fiction story.

Many *Outer Limits* alumni moved to permanent positions on *Star Trek,* notably Robert Justman, Claude Binyon, Jr., makeup artist Fred Phillips, and Wah Chang. "*Star Trek*, in fact, was an outgrowth of *The Outer Limits*," said Tom Selden. "Gene Roddenberry watched our dailies all the time, and took a lot of phone calls from our screening room. He was spurring his imagination, and checking on the incredible quality control that we had. I wondered *why* he was there, but he was there more often than not, during the time he was coming up with *Star Trek.*"

Several ex-*Outer Limits* crewmembers regrouped in the mid-1970s to do the *Man From Atlantis* series pilot—Robert Justman produced, Lee Katzin directed, Jack Poplin did the sets, and Gene Warren provided the model effects. Project Unlimited dissolved in the mid-1960s and auctioned off most of their *Outer Limits* inventory.

When Gene Roddenberry walked off *Star Trek* in 1968 due to a contract dispute, he offered the producership of the show's third season to Joseph Stefano, who turned it down after screening a few episodes. By his own count, Stefano turned down producing "at least four other series" in the wake of *The Outer Limits,* including another Roddenberry project, *The Questor Tapes.*

In 1966, Stefano wrote and directed a supernatural series pilot in color for CBS, "The Ghost of Sierra de Cobra," which starred Martin

Joe Stefano holds the completed manuscript of his first novel, *Lycanthrope*, in his office at his home in Beverly Hills.
(Photo by J. S. Frentzen)

Landau as psychic investigator Nelson Orion. Though the series, *The Haunted*, never materialized (due to a changing of the executive guard at CBS), the pilot film is still seen regularly on Canadian TV. In 1968, *Eye of the Cat* was finally produced as a feature film for Universal, based on his never-filmed *Outer Limits* script, "The Cats." He wrote the story on which the pilot for the militantly nonviolent adventure series, *The Magician* (1973) was based, and his TV movies include *Revenge* (1971), with Shelley Winters, *Death of Innocence* (1971), *Home for the Holidays* (1972), *Live Again Die Again* (1974)—using cryogenics as a plot basis—*Aloha Means Goodbye* (1974), and *Snowbeast*, a kind of *Night Stalker* treatment of the Bigfoot legend that was ABC's highest-rated movie of the 1976–77 TV season. Stefano spent several years completing his massive first novel, *Lycanthrope*, and in 1985 and 1986 finished up several screenplays, including a big-budget science fiction project entitled *Escort*.

Both Leslie Stevens and Joseph Stefano have maintained an active interest in an *Outer Limits* revival ever since the original series' cancellation. In the early 1970s, Stevens tried a series concept called *The Other Side*, essentially a carbon copy of *The Outer Limits*, which never blossomed.

In 1983, the MGM/United Artists conglomerate approached Stevens with the question, "If you were to do a feature film for us called *The Outer Limits,* what would it be about?"

"I spun them my 'Earth Tapes' thing," said Stevens. "In a nutshell, Earth is visited by an expedition not from outer space, but *inner* space. Beings come up from the inside of a cyclotron; a particle coming from the interior of reality, so to speak. They just come to find out what Earth *is,* to collect samples of our flora and fauna the same way we collected rock samples on the Moon. In doing so, they progress up the Tree of Life, and discover that humankind represents that tree's top level. But to them, humankind is the *worst* possible development, like a dangerous virus. They declare Earth to be a cull; this particular planet and space is not to be countenanced. And the trick of the movie is that the whole thing is a test. The visitors discover they can't judge our worthiness by testing individual humans; they must test us *en masse*. They decide the only way to make such a test is to observe humankind's reactions to various media. And the movie you're watching is that test. It's a *recursive* movie!"

The atmosphere for the production of the proposed *Outer Limits* film was encouraging. MGM/UA and Stevens each owned a third of the original show. The other third was owned by Stefano, who with Gerd Oswald had also recently pitched an *Outer Limits* movie idea at MGM/UA.

"The basic idea was an enlargement of *The Unknown,*" said Oswald. "About a guy who's 'tinkering with time' in an isolated mansion. Several people are stranded there overnight, and he uses them as guinea pigs, sending them into an alternate dimension, another time zone, in order to retrieve someone he loves who has been lost there. He is evil only in the sense that the people can't come back once he's sent them there. Finally, out of desperate love for the person he's lost, he has to go in himself."

MGM/UA was interested in the idea as a TV movie; Stefano stood by his desire to make it as a feature, and moved it to Paramount, where five years earlier he had worked on a film project involving an experimental, "audience participation" approach. "It was a scary script, about fear," said Stefano. "The idea was that you could feel 'leftover' fear, fear that people had felt watching horror movies, in the theatre you've just walked into. The movie opens in *your* theatre. You see a shot of the auditorium you've just entered—which means special footage would have to have been shot for each theatre in which the movie was to play. We were experimenting with an *occasion* in the theatre. It would still be too hard to do." He applied this concept to his *Outer Limits* pitch at Paramount, running a variation on the Control Voice opening.

Gerd Oswald explained: "We would open by showing a film in black and white, very suspenseful, where someone gets chased and, ultimately, stabbed, a la *Psycho*. On the screen, the blood fades through from black and white to dark red, then, *voom!* The film breaks, runs through the projector, and the screen goes black. In the pitch-dark theatre, you now hear the sounds of chains locking up the theatre doors, and then a voice says, '*Don't be alarmed. You cannot leave the theatre. We have locked the doors and taken over the projection booth. Please remain in your seats.*' Then the *real* story commences, with the time-tinkerer."

Then *Twilight Zone: The Movie* opened on June 24th, and soon afterward the *Outer Limits* feature suffered a death by disinterest. "We *had* gotten tremendous interest," said Oswald, "until *Twilight Zone* didn't make enough money to suit Paramount. Two weeks later, we found out that Stevens had his project over at MGM/UA." With their own ideal *Outer Limits* movie scuttled by circumstances beyond their control, Stefano and Oswald were reluctant to involve themselves in the Stevens venture back at MGM/UA—the studio they had just shown the door. The "Earth Tapes" version was quietly killed by the threat of litigation.

Then, in late 1984, a "back-door pilot" for a proposed revival of the *Alfred Hitchcock Presents* series aired on NBC. It was a two-hour show comprised of remakes of four old Hitchcock episodes, with the original Hitchcock introductions computer-colored. The pilot achieved an admirably high rating, and the series—all remakes—was revived in the half-hour format for the 1985–86 TV season. Suddenly ABC, at the barrel-bottom of the ratings without a show to compete with the anthology shows on the rival networks—*Amazing Stories* and *Hitchcock* at NBC; the *Twilight Zone* revival at CBS—became interested in doing *The Outer Limits* one more time.

Stefano credits the new, young group of executives at MGM—the ones who grew up watching *The Outer Limits*—for "making it happen," since the United Artists contingent did not seem particularly interested. A deal was struck among MGM/UA, Stevens, and Stefano to do *The Outer Limits* as a two-hour back-door pilot in the mode of the *Hitchcock* revival, with Stefano as producer. The executives screened ten *Outer Limits* shows recommended by Stevens and Stefano, picking five of them as potential remake fodder. From these, Stevens chose his own "Controlled Experiment" to rewrite and update, while Stefano picked "Fun and Games." "I wanted to do 'Don't Open Till Doomsday,'" he noted. "But you couldn't keep Mrs. Kry in the 1920s. For the story to take place in the Eighties, you'd have to move her up to the mid-1940s."

The script for the new pilot was completed in the fall of 1985; by which time both *Amazing Stories* and *Twilight Zone* had drawn such mediocre ratings that ABC began to rethink the idea of tossing another anthology show into the TV arena. Meanwhile, Stefano's heavy load of writing commitments prevented him from actively producing the new pilot. The script sat, and it was decided that the remake of "Fun and Games" would be replaced with an original story—the first brand-new *Outer Limits* script in twenty-two years.

* * *

Soon after the "Earth Tapes" proposal was killed, "The Galaxy Being" was broadcast in the wee hours of a Saturday morning in Los Angeles on Channel 11—KTTV, the original home of *Outer Limits* studio production. The series has been a stalwart of KTTV filler programming for the last twenty years; rarely scheduled regularly, always severely edited, it seems to hang on, tenuously, like a fuzzy transmission from a faraway planet, or black-and-white images pulled out of the 1960s by some video time machine.

In 1978, United Artists Television announced its plan to withdraw *The Outer Limits* from syndication by 1983, assuming by that time the series would be too hopelessly antiquated to compete with other programs. Yet today the series is still running in many of the thirty "major markets," the prime syndication cities cited by Stevens. It has become historically respectable enough to rate unedited and uninterrupted broadcast on PBS affiliates. It is a perennially hot item with videotape collectors. As Richard Dorso noted, "*The Outer Limits* will run time and time again. It always will, because there's always a new audience for it."

Ideas for popular science fiction films—*The Terminator* (1984) is a perfect example—derive directly from the plots of "old" *Outer Limits* shows. "O.B.I.T." was recently planned as a stage production at Harvard University. And a reunion of *Outer Limits* principals seems in the cards—if not the back-door pilot, then some new permutation, perhaps next year—for no other reason than those studio executives who grew up with the show keep suggesting the idea.

"That *The Outer Limits* has run for an unbroken length of time in the thirty 'major markets' in the United States is phenomenal," said Stevens. "From the pieces of paper that say where it has been syndicated, it expands rather than contracts. A specialized audience has found it. And it keeps growing, until finally, now, it *does* have something approaching the mass audience."

The consensus of the *Outer Limits* group is still very much the same view expressed by John Baxter in *Science Fiction in the Cinema*, which, like most of the flood of books that appeared during the 1970s to scrutinize science fiction as a genre of film and TV, accords the show a brief but uninformed burst of admiration. "I just loved doing a series with original concepts," said Seeleg Lester. "It was a great opportunity for creative talent. Today, science fiction has become a genre on its own, and *The Outer Limits* helped it to mature."

B. Ritchie Payne, Ben Brady's right-hand man, is still proud of the series even though he does not care all that much for this genre. "Today," he said, "a Spielberg or a Lucas would look at the show and say, 'My god, what an amateur effort.' Well, at the time, we didn't think it was so damned amateurish!" The community feeling surrounding *The Outer Limits* was different from today's hypey and merchandise-oriented ap-

Leslie Stevens today, looking forward into the 1990s.
(Courtesy Leslie Stevens)

proach to TV. "Another one of the problems with TV today," said Vic Perrin, "is the same problem now facing professional sports. The stakes have gotten too damned high. There's too *much* money involved, and you have to protect your own little interest. It's too hyperthyroidally professional. There's no longer any team spirit at all."

"Anthological series are still the best kind," said Ben Brady. "You're not forcing a series of dramatic ideas to fit into a mold; you're building a mold to accommodate the ideas. One form is sloshy; the other, artistic."

"It's a constant source of pleasure to me that the show is still running," said Seeleg Lester. "In today's field, if you have a one-hour show, you've got a couple of executive producers, and four or five intermediate producers, and story editors, and writers on staff, and associate producers. In the days of *The Outer Limits,* we had *one* story editor, and we never threw anything away. We did *everything* ourselves."

Leslie Stevens is not slowing down by any means. "I'd like to do something on the order of *Brave New World,* or a science fiction piece on the order of Robert Heinlein's *Universe,"* he said. "Now *that* I could do, say, as a two-hour TV movie or miniseries, something with a very wide vista. I promise you: I'll get something that has a shot at being extraordinary."

"When I went to New York in 1975," said Joseph Stefano, of attending his first science fiction/fantasy convention, "it blew my mind to meet people in their late teens and early twenties who not only knew *The Outer Limits,* but knew things like the original titles of shows I'd changed! They knew more about the show than I did. I heard of someone paying $65 at an auction for a *Xerox* of an *Outer Limits* script—I was floored! I really can't tell you how rewarding it is to have people interested in the show. I would never in a million years think of doing a show like *The Outer Limits* because people would admire me twenty, thirty years later for it—you know what I mean?"

Appendix I

The Canons of PLEASE STAND BY

by Joseph Stefano

PLEASE STAND BY is a one-hour, dramatic television series whose dramas are woven upon the imaginative and inventive loom of Science Fiction.

As with all creative machines, the end-product, the final filmable fabric that emerges from our Science Fiction loom will depend on the thread fed into it.

Theme is the thread.

If you believe in something, if you are angry or disturbed about something, or exasperated with joy or shaken with worry about something, be it Conformity, or Discrimination, or Politics, or Censorship, be it Patriotism, or Capital Punishment, or Disarmament, or Man's Inaccessability to Man, or Fame, or Famine, or Moral/Physical Slavery, or Addiction, or Mass-culture, or Fanaticism or Isolationism, or Peace—if you believe in your need to state your belief, you have the thread.

All the rest is craft and art and intellect.

A high literary style encompassing the bold use of poetic imagery and stunning language is entirely fitting and not unnatural to the Science Fiction form. The very awesome and wondrous nature of Science, especially when fused with imaginative and inventive Fiction, would seem to beg and perhaps inspire high-level thinking and writing.

THE CANONS

THEME

Out of the issues and the human conditions of this our time, out of the north—and south—seeking poles of human impulses and behaviors, out of the world AS WE KNOW IT, come the themes which are the warp and woof of our dramas.

That these themes must be dramatized within the almost boundless framework of the Science Fiction form is secondary to the basic laws and necessities and purposes of sound dramatic entertainment: a theme worthy of the telling is honey to any tongue, be it the language of Ben Casey, of the Defenders, or of Stoney Burke.

A theme must be born of the conceiver's faith or fury or desperation or groin-pain, not of a particular series' framework.

STORY REQUIREMENTS

A. Bearing out the first Canon, which is Theme, each play must reveal something of the inner life of Man. For all the great complexity of modern scientific apparatus and knowledge, feasible and palatable and identifiable Drama begins and ends in the human heart and soul and mind.

B. Whatever is Fictional, or invented, in a play must have a basis in Scientific knowledge as it is available to us today—no matter how small or theoretical or improbable that basis. All that is required to support a dramatic notion is for a Technical Advisor to say, "If such a thing were to occur, it would seem to us, today, that its genesis would have to form in such-and-such a situation under such-and-such a set of circumstances."

C. There must be terror. The viewer must know the delicious and consciously desired element of terror. Enlightenment, Education, Provocation, and Soul-moving are the end-game of all Drama, but to these must be added, for the purposes of PLEASE STAND BY, the experience of terror. It must, however, be TOLERABLE TERROR. It must remain in the realm of fiction, of unreality. When the play is ended, when the Control Voice has returned to the viewer the use of his television set, the viewer, that willing victim of the terror, must be able to relax and know self-amusement and realize that what he feared during the telling of the story could not materialize and need not be feared should he walk out of his house and stroll a night street.

D. Each play must have a "BEAR." The BEAR is that one splendid, staggering, shuddering effect that induces awe or wonder or tolerable terror or even merely conversation and argument.

E. The mad magic of SOUND must be employed as often and as artfully as is feasible. The ear must never be treated as step-brother to the eye.

F. The viewer will follow and care about and at times even identify with a "monster" or an embodied "element" or a strange and unworldly "creature," but this identification cannot be sustained if the viewer is asked to view monsters and creatures and elements exclusively. Somewhere the viewer must see himself; and while he may see himself or a part of himself in a monster, he will resist and lose interest unless we provide him with a real and human and recognizable hero-figure (or nonhero figure, as the case may be). Therefore, each play must deal with Science Fiction in relation to, or against, or to the improvement or detriment of the race that inhabits our own earth.

G. There must be no apology, no smirk; each drama, no matter how wordless or timeless, must be spoken with all the seriousness and sincerity and suspension-of-disbelief that a caring and intelligent parent employs in the spinning of a magic-wonderful tale to a child at bedtime. Humor and wit are honorable; the tongue in the cheek is most often condescending and gratuitous. When the tongue is in the cheek it is almost impossible to speak in anything but a garbled, foolish fashion.

TABOOS

A. Pure fantasy, that is, dramatizations of incidents which do not or can not have a basis in scientific fact.

B. The Supernatural.

C. Satire (unless it is couched in the most supremely artful dramaturgical terms).

D. Dramas in which no human, as we know humans, appears or is of concern or moment.

E. Dramas which take place in their entirety on another planet and which involve only "creatures" or "beings" of another planet to the total exclusion of earth people.

F. Religious and moral concepts which arbitrarily and arrogantly oppose those concepts held by the peoples of the earth. In this area we are dealing with mystery and fear and puzzlement and faith, and it would be both unwise and distasteful to invent a "someplace" in the Universe where "someone" has all the answers—especially if those "answers" are negative or tend to shatter so precious a thing as human faith.

G. All the ordinary taboos set up in the interest of taste and morality.

SUMMARY

With a theme deeply-felt, a style carefully wrought, characters and basic situations that are hard-real and identifiable—with these, all that can be said can be said with the exciting, imaginative, Universe-wide framework of Science Fiction. No idea, no message or statement or plea is beyond the scope of such a framework. The research required to set a particular story in the setting of Science Fiction is not greater nor harder to attain than that research which is necessary to set the same theme in a hospital or a court of law or the dusty chutes of a rodeo.

All that is required of PLEASE STAND BY is the theme.

And the craft and art and intellect.

Appendix II

The Outer Limits That Never Were

Unfilmed Episodes

LITTLE MOTHER OF ALL THE WORLD

Written by Richard Newman, from a story by Joseph Stefano and Lou Morheim. Revised by Stefano 8/5/63

It is customary in these United States to refer to the house in which a Governor resides as the Governor's Mansion. It need not be a mansion, any more than the current tenant need be fit to govern. In this state, the Governor's Mansion is more commonly referred to as "Mother's House." The press—and others who must, or do, or pretend to respect her—call her Madame Governor. The people, those who know and love her, who run to her with all their needs and hurts and wishes, call her "Mother"...

An emergency call brings DR. EDWARD PERRY running to the aid of Mother, whose right-hand man, TITUS McGEE, ushers him to her office. From behind the closed door, weird, chaotic electronic noises emit. Perry enters and DR. WEAVER asks him anxiously, "Did you bring it?" Perry's response is, "Please. Let's stop now. We were going to *study* the people of this state—not destroy them!" In the inner office, Mother is flinging herself madly about, wrecking the room while in the powerful grip of some berserk fit. The doctors subdue her, then Perry removes Mother's head, popping off the wig portion to reveal a blinking computer brain. He replaces a failed component. Mother is well again.

The social "experiment" Weaver's group is conducting on Mother's constituency has to do with the psychology of tyranny. "Why do people allow dictators to dictate?" says Weaver. "Why do they seem to *want* to be under someone's thumb? Without even knowing it, they'll tell us. They love that woman! She's composed of every vile, tricky, magic, murderous trait ever found festering in a real tyrant. And they love that woman!" Perry protests that they've let Mother get too powerful.

Reporter MURRAY SNIDER is summoned to expose Mother by her current gubernatorial opponent, GILBERT HINDS, who calls her "a boil that needs lancing... a blood clot in this state's heart." But not even Hinds dares to oppose the impregnable, down-home "mother image" that makes the governor so popular with the grassroots voters. When Mother learns Snider is in town, she dispatches McGee and two goons to beat him up. Two policemen stand watching nearby, doing nothing. The beating is also witnessed from a distance by Dr. Perry and his fiancee, SUSAN PALMER. "Beat them up," he nods to himself. "Run them out of town on the night train. That's the procedure at this stage." He is disgusted, yet powerless to stop what is happening.

Mother invites Hinds to tea and tries to break him down psychologically. In the midst of their verbal fencing, Snider bursts in, battered and bleeding, and McGee drags him off (presumably to a hospital) until Hinds leaves. After calling Snider a "hatchet-handed newspaperman," she laughs, "I was right. I *don't* need to be afraid of you. Incidentally, we *do* have a good hospital in this town." Snider finds the door locked. "I hope it has a comfortable morgue," he says. Then Mother unscrews her left hand, revealing a battery of tiny capsule missiles. Snider ducks and dodges these as she fires them, finally diving through the French doors and escaping to Perry's research lab. Susan has helped Perry with his little conscience problem, and Perry agrees to tell Snider the whole story after they've rendezvoused at Hinds' mansion.

Mother gets there ahead of them and begins hunting Hinds. "I'll find you, and I'll punish you," she coos. She corners Hinds in the attic and is about to blast him when Hinds unscrews *his* left wrist and blows Mother into a smoking pile of robotic debris. "Forgive me," Hinds says as Perry, Snider, and Susan burst in. "Destruction is such a poor answer." Then Hinds suffers a seizurelike malfunction, just like Mother did earlier. Perry removes one of Hinds' brain components to subdue him. "They were perfect," the scientist laments. "Into her, we put every evil, even evil charm. In him, the opposite—good, all of it, even the harmful good, the weak good. We wanted to see why evil always triumphs, in the beginning. We wanted to learn why the triumph of good always comes after so much horror has been done."

"When you study the people, you have to study them fairly," Snider says, examining the component. "You have to give them a *person* to react to."

Then again, perhaps they did study them fairly. Perhaps they did give the people a person to react to. A robot, after all, is nothing more—and nothing less—than the person who makes it.

AN ORDINARY TOWN

Written by Charles Beaumont (possibly ghostwritten). Submission draft: 1/3/64. See section on "The Guests."

Space is an ocean, we are told. A new, uncharted sea where Man may venture, an Element to be explored and conquered. Peering out from his tiny island, Man sees the fringes—a mere, few hundred million light-years—and challengingly beyond his reach, the glitter of distant shores. And so he builds small, fragile ships to sail the "coastal waters" of his galaxy, thinking them peaceful, thinking himself alone... forgetting that in every place he has ever looked before, he has found life... not thinking that this sea, too, may teem with forms as yet undreamed. Yet he should remember that for ages past, sailors have whispered of Serpents, Monsters, Demons of the Deep. He should, at least, suspect the possibility of travelers other than himself...

VICTOR HARDIN and ERNIE DRUON, field geologists for Regency Petroleum, wreck their truck in the Nevada desert when they swerve to avoid a deer on an isolated backroad. Ernie suffers a severe concussion that jars his brains and blurs his vision; he swears that an odd cloud formation in the sky looks just like a gigantic brain. Vic seeks help on foot, and road signs lead him to the postcard-perfect town of Sandbar, where DARBY SANDERS, an attractive waitress at the local cafe, helps him find DR. SAM RUDIN. But when Ernie looks at Rudin, he sees a nightmare creature with a skull-like head whose upper half is exposed, pulsating brain matter! Rudin sedates him, explaining that Ernie's concussion is causing hallucinations, and Ernie is taken to convalesce at the home of MR. & MRS. ANDRUS. Sandbar and its people are epitomizations of the backwoods/hometown stereotype: Rudin is grey-haired, ruddy-cheeked, penguin-bodied; Darby is the fresh-faced, sexy country lass; the Andruses are rustic yet kindly, laconic yet sympathetic—as though they'd stepped right out of a Norman Rockwell painting. And Sandbar isn't on any map of the area.

While Vic chats up Darby at the cafe, Ernie wakens and is confronted by three of the brain-creatures, who enter his room by walking through the walls and resolve into the forms of Rudin and the Andruses. Rudin introduces himself as an emissary from the planet Bandarus and explains, "The brain operates on electrical impulses... the blow you received merely shifted your 'wavelength,' so to speak, and made it possible for you to 'tune in' on us." The Bandarusians are shopping for a world to which they can relocate when their sun supernovas. Andrus notes that Earth is "ideal... a true paradise of the spheres, which, we have been shocked to learn, you have made rather poor use of... should we decide to colonize, the present inhabitants could not be allowed to remain." When Ernie asks if they plan to kill everyone,

Rudin says, "You're *already* dead—you died shortly after we brought you here." The enormous brain he thought he saw is real, and Sandbar and all its bucolic inhabitants are the brain's thought projections. Since Ernie is within the brain's sphere of energy, he is still outwardly "alive." The aliens need to "catch and hold" a human being for study, to complete their survey, and since Ernie is dead, they settle for Vic.

Vic naturally assumes Ernie's earnest story of alien invaders is more fallout from his knock on the head. "At least do this," Ernie implores. "When you get out of here, start looking around, closely, at everything. Somewhere, they're bound to have made a mistake." When Vic tries to call the home office in San Francisco he is told that the phone lines were downed by a storm. He sends a telegram, but has no way of knowing the telegraph lines terminate at the edge of town. Darby diverts his attention with a picnic, a phony return telegram from Regency Petroleum, and then sedates him, using a needlelike extrusion from her Bandarusian finger.

When Vic wakes up on the Sanders's sofa, he does not realize the aliens have spent all night examining him, and Ernie tries to get him to take his nonexistent pulse. When Rudin prevents this, Vic insists on transferring Ernie to a hospital outside Sandbar. Surprisingly, Rudin agrees to this and Vic leaves. Ernie guesses that, based on their scrutiny of Vic, the Bandarusians have decided the invasion is on, and very shortly the wrecked truck will be found with *two* corpses inside it. He smashes a water pitcher over Rudin's gelatinous head and steals his car. The further Ernie speeds from Sandbar, the weaker and more zombiatic he becomes, but he manages to reach a small rural airfield and make off with a light plane. Vic and Darby catch up, too late. As Ernie heels the plane over and dives straight toward the brainlike cloud, he says to himself, "You may not know it, Vic, but this doesn't cost me a thing!" As the plane strikes the brain-cloud and explodes, Vic sees Darby dissolve waveringly into her true Bandarusian form, then evaporate entirely, "forgotten," as is everything else, by the alien brain.

> *For ages past, sailors have whispered of Serpents, Monsters, Demons of the Deep. Today there is a new sea to be explored, and Man will need new names for what he finds living in it. For travelers . . . other than himself.*

SMALL WONDER (Parts One and Two)

Written by Joseph Stefano. Part One: 5/31/63. Part Two: 6/18/63.

PART ONE

> *Five years ago they had a revolution down here. It was a moral success. From it came good for all. The new Government is a young one. It is composed of noble and naive men. It*

calls itself "The Comitia," which, in ancient Rome, was an assembly of citizens for electing officials, passing laws, and so forth, and the first thing it did upon ousting the Mondo Pagana regime was to revive such ancient customs as Compassion and Equality and Sensible Joy. But these innovations bespoke an esthetic rather than a realistic approach to the indelicate art of government. Disastrous mistakes were bound to be made. The worst of these was the decision to allow the escape of the dictator, Mondo Pagana, and his wife, Stella. The Paganas have lived these five exile years in a high villa that overlooks the Gulf of Mexico…

The Pagana regime was one of astonishing poverty and deprivation, but Stella Pagana was known as "the Star of Love" and considered a saint. "Once a month," notes elderly revolutionary JUAN PRUDENCIA, "she would drive through in her limousine and smile the hunger pains away." The country's new leader, Juan's nephew RICARDO DEL RIO, took an empty hospital built as a publicity gesture by Stella Pagana and staffed and equipped it. He has given the people homes, jobs, voting privileges… but has found the exiled Stella deified. The people respect the new order. They admire Ricardo and are grateful. "But they do not love us," he says. "They love their Star of Love. They mourn her absence, they say her prayers, they apotheosize her memory." The populace has idolized her to the point where they would welcome her back, and with her, poverty, chaos, and tyranny. Juan calls it a "national death-wish." Exposing Mondo Pagana's corrupt regime was not enough. "He is a mannequin!" Ricardo says. "Nothing! *She* is the devil-thing!" To circumvent the seeming inevitability of the Paganas' return, Ricardo decides Stella must be assassinated. But the Pagana villa is an impregnable fortress. Juan then surprises Ricardo and his associates, MARTINI and ARTURO MOLLO, by showing them a cat no bigger than a square inch, and suggesting that an operative of similarly miniature stature could easily get within range of Stella, "like a devil doll." When they all ask Juan where he got the tiny cat, he smiles, "I have been to America. And I have seen the future."

The four men fly to the US to meet DR. JOHN STRAB, head of the Advanced Concepts Division of the Dearborn Aircraft Corporation. They show him films documenting the cruelty and excesses of the Pagana regime and explain their problem. Strab is sympathetic, but tries to warn them away. For one thing, his miniaturization technique has never been tried on a human subject; for another, the effect is irreversible. He is repulsed by the idea of murder. But after much coercion and moral agony, he concedes and allows Ricardo to enter the chamber called the Magnetic Domain.

Thanks to what Strab calls the "offset"—"the difference between the value or condition you want, and what you actually get"—Ricardo vanishes. Thunderstruck, the others prepare to leave in defeat when Mollo claims he can see Ricardo—but he is much tinier than anticipated; Strab must use a magnifying glass to pick him out, and he nearly drowns in a tear shed by his uncle. "He is the size of a speck of dust," says Strab. "Smaller. A microbe." Strab suddenly sees a solution that does not involve killing: Using a miniaturized PA device (since normal speech would shatter Ricardo's eardrums), he proposes that Ricardo is now small enough to enter Stella's brain via the ear canal and use an electrode to obliterate the center of hostility in her brain. "Through the ear to the brain," muses Strab. "Through the brain to . . . madness."

PART TWO

Five years ago, this villa on Dead Man's Bay, an inlet of the Gulf of Mexico, was leased sight unseen by the former dictator, Mondo Pagana, and his wife Stella. They have lost their own country in a short revolution that was long overdue. Like most exiles, they had no fear of the people in whose country they had taken political asylum. Nor would it have been necessary to fear their own people, for they had been ousted by a group of young men who called themselves the "Comitia," and whose concern was more with the making of bread than with spilling the blood of the past. But when the defeated have dreams of a triumphant return to power, and when these dreams are supported by wealth and influence and other political encouragements, the safety and protection of life and limb become not only a necessity, but a mania . . .

Stella Pagana soaks in a huge Roman tub, surrounded by jewels and opulence. Beyond that, guards, cameras, dogs, guns, the trappings of top security. Stella taunts her barefoot servant, SARAMELA, accusing her of reading the day's mail and of a dalliance with her husband, Mondo. Soon the girl is terrified and in tears, singing a rhyme to her "Star of Love" that was once a kind of national hymn to Stella. "I am only having my pleasure," Stella laughs, with sweet viciousness.

There are many styles and breeds of pleasure. Some of these are silly and sick. Some are solemn, very serious. Some are very dangerous. These are the men who are going to destroy the usefulness, and the sickness, of Stella Pagana. The one with the air of command is Dr. John Strab, a scientist, an inventor, a doer of the impossible. The others are leaders of the Comitia, that noble government which must prevent the Paganas' return to power. The leader of these leaders is Ricardo Del Rio . . .

"He is too small to kill her," Strab says of Ricardo. "But he is just the right size to cure her. I would rather be a conspirator in making an evil woman good, than in making a live woman dead." Using a large, detailed map of the human brain, Strab outlines Ricardo's strategy. He must penetrate the cerebral cortex, find his way to the Amygdaloid Nucleus, an oval area encompassing the range of human emotions, and destroy the portion "between six and nine o'clock" by burning it away with a needle filled with Cobalt Sixty. He will breathe using a microminiaturized Momsen Lung.

The group decides to mail Ricardo to Stella inside an envelope containing "the kind of gift a child would send a saint," a small diamond ring. While tucked away in the envelope, Ricardo is nearly boiled alive by spilled coffee, and almost stamped flat by a postal cancelling machine.

The miniaturized cat gets loose in Strab's lab and steps into a floor-mounted electrical socket, screeching as it is shocked. But then it begins to grow back to its normal size. Mollo is elated—they now know how to return Ricardo to normal once his mission is completed. Strab is horrified: "A mere 220 volts of electricity," he says. "The human brain is alive with it! He'll be hit from all sides. He'll start to grow inside her brain!"

The envelope bearing Ricardo is almost eaten by a dog before it is delivered to the Pagana villa. Stella opens it while at her dressing table, and Ricardo rides aboard one of her earrings as she puts it on. The sound vibrations of her conversation with Saramela nearly shake him off his precarious perch on her outer ear, so he runs inside her head.

Ricardo steps through a rip in Stella's tympanic membrane, her eardrum, and begins a journey across the delicate bonework of the ear ossicals. The Eustachian tube yawns beneath him like a bottomless chasm. When Stella tilts her head, he is swung violently around. He seeks shelter in the little vestibule of the fenestra Ovale. Then he ventures down the coils of the Scala Vestibule, through the Ductis Cochlearis to the Internal Spiral Sulcus, following the bunched cables of spiral ganglion to the swamplike Subarachnoid space, which is ankle-deep in water and choked with seaweed-like filaments. As he picks his way along the labyrinth of the Sylvian Fissure, he damages a few neurons and is buffeted by electrical discharges. This causes Stella to experience sudden and unexplained memories of her mother, who died while foraging for food in the hill country after suffering mysterious pains in her head. Ricardo arrives at the Hippocampal Gyrus at the base of Stella's brain and sees the mammilary bodies, the "street sign" that leads him to his target, the Amygdaloid Nucleus. He thrusts his radioactive needle home in the area designated by Strab.

Stella screams and staggers about. DR. SOMON, her physician, attempts to help her, but when she regains her feet there is a curiously radiant expression on her face. When Mondo asks her what is wrong, she says, softly, "So much. In all the world there is so much wrong. Hunger there is, and beating, and such suffering as must make God cry." Sorrow overwhelms her. "We do not see that the stars are His tears, wept to remind us, and to light our long nights." With rising passion, now, she says, "We must, we must use the starlight, the tearlight, we must *see* by it. See the suffering, and end it. See the beatings, and stop them.

See the hungry, and feed them. Yes!" As she dashes up the stairs, Ricardo is knocked from one end of the Sylvian Fissure to the other, causing electrical explosions all the way. He is beginning to grow.

Stella madly sweeps all of her jewelry into a box. She plucks off her earrings last, unaware that Ricardo has made it out and is now visible clinging to one of them, and drops them in. Juan Prudencia is captured outside the villa gate, having been recognized as one of the Comitia, and is disarmed and dragged before Stella by the guards. "The day we were permitted to flee, you argued you wanted Ricardo Del Rio to kill me," Stella says. "You had no pity?"

"I had no room for it," says Juan. "My fear was too big." Stella hands him the box crammed with priceless jewels—and Ricardo. "The Comitia loves my people still? You will give this to them? Take [the jewels] back where they belong."

Juan leaves, bewildered but happy, momentarily forgetting what Dr. Strab had told Ricardo back at the lab: "If you are successful... if your people must have someone to worship and obey, they couldn't get anything closer to a saint than the woman Stella Pagana *will* be."

THE LINEMAN

Working title of a Leslie Stevens "bottle show" that was never needed. A telephone lineman dies by falling into the wire work on an electrical tower. His consciousness transfers into the endless network of wires, giving him a "body" that extends almost everywhere, and people start hearing him on their home phones. "It was just an outline," said Stevens. "It was ready to do if I *had* to."

UNTITLED

A story treatment by Joseph Stefano and Lou Morheim involving an astronaut who is lost in Earth orbit for ten days, then recovered. According to Leon Chooluck, either the man's brain is removed and replaced with a computer of alien origin, or an alien telemetry device is inserted into the astronaut's brain to relay Earth data back to the homeworld. In one scene, the astronaut's wife sees him remove a portion of his scalp to get at the device. ABC vetoed this episode on behalf of NASA, feeling that it would look bad for an astronaut to get lost "out there."

THE WATCHBIRD

A Francis Cockrell script developed for the second season, in which an alien empath, a "watchbird," monitors and compensates for the actions prompted by the more violent human emotions. It is ultimately killed because its benevolent influence is a curative for malign thoughts, and Earth people feel entitled to their primitivism.

UNTITLED

A Robert Dennis original written for the second season. The protagonist is a boy living on a farm in the rural Midwest. Outcast and ignored, his only friend, a little girl, moves with her family to California. He is alone until one night, he sees a shooting star crash down into a nearby field. He discovers the remains of an alien probe, sent to Earth on a trial basis with a cargo of various samples of animal life native to the other planet. The boy saves the bizarre-looking creatures, harboring and nourishing them. The animals reciprocate his affection and become his pets. The local hicks get wind of the boy's little zoo and vent their paranoia by killing all the creatures. A school teacher tries to comfort the boy by telling him, "At least this means we're not alone." The story was vetoed by Ben Brady because it depicted the farmers slaughtering the alien animals.

UNTITLED

B. Ritchie Payne recalled an idea submitted by Oliver Crawford for the second season: "It was just a beautiful thing, about the stars going out in heaven."

Appendix III

Production & Broadcast Schedules

FIRST SEASON

PRODUCTION

"Please Stand By"
3–14 December 1962

"The Borderland"
22–29 May 1963

"The Human Factor"
31 May–10 June 1963

"Tourist Attraction"
11–19 June 1963

"The Architects of Fear"
19–26 June 1963

"Controlled Experiment"
27 June–2 July 1963

"The Hundred Days of the Dragon"
3–11 July 1963

"The Man With the Power"
29 July–3 August 1963

"A Feasibility Study"
5–12 August 1963

"Specimen: Unknown"
12–20 August 1963

"The Sixth Finger"
20–27 August 1963

BROADCAST/SYNDICATION

"The Galaxy Being"
16 September 1963

"The Hundred Days of the Dragon"
23 September 1963

"The Architects of Fear"
30 September 1963

"The Man With the Power"
7 October 1963

"The Sixth Finger"
14 October 1963

"The Man Who Was Never Born"
28 October 1963

"O.B.I.T."
4 November 1963

"The Human Factor"
11 November 1963

"Corpus Earthling"
18 November 1963

"Nightmare"
2 December 1963

"It Crawled Out of the Woodwork"
9 December 1963

PRODUCTION	BROADCAST/SYNDICATION
"The Man Who Was Never Born" 27 Aug–4 Sept 1963	"The Borderland" 16 December 1963
"Moonstone" 5–12 September 1963	"Tourist Attraction" 23 December 1963
"O.B.I.T." 13–20 Sept 1963 (series premieres 16 Sept)	"The Zanti Misfits" 30 December 1963
"Nightmare" 23–30 Sept 1963	"The Mice" 6 January 1964
"Corpus Earthling" 1–8 October 1963	"Controlled Experiment" 13 January 1964
"The Zanti Misfits" 9–17 October 1963	"Don't Open Till Doomsday" 20 January 1964
"It Crawled Out of the Woodwork" 18–25 October 1963	"ZZZZZ" 27 January 1964
"The Mice" 28 Oct–5 Nov 1963	"The Invisibles" 3 February 1964
"The Invisibles" 6–14 November 1963	"The Bellero Shield" 10 February 1964
"ZZZZZ" 15 Nov–5 Dec 1963	"The Children of Spider County" 17 February 1964
"Don't Open Till Doomsday" 26 Nov–5 Dec 1963	"Specimen: Unknown" 24 February 1964
"The Bellero Shield" 6–16 December 1963	"Second Chance" 2 March 1964
"The Unknown" (pilot) 2–21 January 1964	"Moonstone" 9 March 1964
"The Children of Spider County" 6–13 January 1964	"The Mutant" 16 March 1964
"The Mutant" 15–21 January 1964	"The Guests" 23 March 1964

PRODUCTION	BROADCAST/SYNDICATION
"Second Chance" 22–28 January 1964	"Fun and Games" 30 March 1964
"Fun and Games" 30 Jan–6 Feb 1964	"The Special One" 6 April 1964
"The Guests" 6–13 February 1964	"A Feasibility Study" 13 April 1964
"The Production and Decay of Strange Particles" 19–25 February 1964	"The Production and Decay of Strange Particles" 20 April 1964
"The Special One" 26 Feb–4 March 1964	"The Chameleon" 27 April 1964
"The Chameleon" 5–11 March 1964	"The Forms of Things Unknown" 4 May 1964

SECOND SEASON

PRODUCTION	BROADCAST/SYNDICATION
"Cold Hands, Warm Heart" 25 June–2 July 1964	"Soldier" 19 September 1964
"Soldier" 3–10 July 1964	"Cold Hands, Warm Heart" 26 September 1964
"The Invisible Enemy" 13–20 July 1964	"Behold, Eck!" 3 October 1964
"Counterweight" 21–27 July 1964	"Expanding Human" 10 October 1964
"Behold, Eck!" 28 July–4 August 1964	"Demon With a Glass Hand" 17 October 1964
"Wolf 359" 5–12 August 1964	"Cry of Silence" 24 October 1964
"Keeper of the Purple Twilight" 13–20 August 1964	"The Invisible Enemy" 31 October 1964
"Expanding Human" 21–28 August 1964	"Wolf 359" 7 November 1964

PRODUCTION

"Demon With a Glass Hand"
31 August–7 Sept 1964

"Cry of Silence"
10–17 September 1964

"I, Robot"
18–25 September 1964
(series premieres 19 Sept)

"The Inheritors" (Two-part episode)
28 September–13 October 1964

"The Duplicate Man"
15–22 October 1964

"The Brain of Colonel Barham"
23–30 October 1964

"The Premonition"
2–9 November 1964

"The Probe"
10–16 November 1964

BROADCAST/SYNDICATION

"I, Robot"
14 November 1964

"The Inheritors" Part One
21 November 1964

"The Inheritors" Part Two
28 November 1964

"Keeper of the Purple Twilight"
5 December 1964

"The Duplicate Man"
19 December 1964

"Counterweight"
26 December 1964

"The Brain of Colonel Barham"
2 January 1965

"The Premonition"
9 January 1965

"The Probe"
16 January 1965

Appendix IV

End Credits

The executive staff at Daystar Productions was comprised of the following people.

TITLE	FIRST SEASON	SECOND SEASON
Executive Producer	Leslie Stevens	Leslie Stevens
Executive Vice-President	Dominic Frontiere	Dominic Frontiere
Business Operations Mgr; Vice-President/Treasurer	Jerry Fischer	Jerry Fischer
Production Coordinator	Elaine Michea	Elaine Michea
VP: Publicity	Allan Balter	*
VP: Administration	Ron Silverman	Ron Silverman
VP: New Projects; Production Executive	Ralph Riskin	Ralph Riskin
Assistant to Mr. Stevens	Lloyd Haines	*

ADDITIONAL DAYSTAR STAFF: Constantine Sinkevitch, Sudie DeSimone, Lynda Hamblin, Byron Meyers.

Mr. Stevens's Secretary	Mona Skager	Bonnie Bloom
Mr. Frontiere's Sec'y	Pamela Tarpey	Pamela Tarpey
Mr. Fischer's Sec'y	Ynez Rich	Ynez Rich
Producer	Joseph Stefano	Ben Brady

*Information not available

TITLE	FIRST SEASON	SECOND SEASON
Associate Producer/Story Editor	Louis Morheim	Seeleg Lester
Associate Producer/ Supervising Producer	Leon Chooluck	Sam White
Associate Editor	*	William Koenig
Production Supervisor	Lindsley Parsons, Jr.	Claude Binyon, Jr.
Art Director	Jack Poplin	Jack Poplin
Casting	John Erman/Meryl Abeles	Meryl Abeles/ Harvey Claremont
1st AD	Robert H. Justman/ Lee H. Katzin	Robert H. Justman/ William P. Owens
Alternate 1st AD	Gregg Peters/Wilson Shyer	Rusty Meek
2nd AD	Tom Schmidt	James Benjamin
Production Sec'y	Jeanne Lund	Jeanne Lund
Script Supervisor	Hope McLaughlin	Hope McLaughlin
Supervising Film Editor	Richard Brockway	Richard Brockway
Film Editors	Tony DiMarco/Fred Baretta	Tony DiMarco/Fred Baretta
Sound Effects Editor	Jack Cornall	Jack Cornall
Commercial Integration	Ed Knize	Ed Knize
Negative Cutter	Helen Wright	Helen Wright
Music Supervisor	Dominic Frontiere	Harry Lubin
Music Coordinator	John Elizalde	John Caper, Jr.
Music Copyist	Roger A. Ferris	*

*Information not available

TITLE	FIRST SEASON	SECOND SEASON
1st Cameraman	Conrad Hall/John Nickolaus/ Kenneth Peach, Sr.	Kenneth Peach, Sr.
1st Assistant Cameraman	Kenneth Peach, Jr.	Gerald W. Finnerman
Camera Operator	William Fraker	Seymour J. Hoffberg
2nd Ass't Cameraman	Tom Laughridge	Herb Pearl
Gaffer	Lloyd L. Garnell	Lloyd L. Garnell
Best Boy	Norman McClay	Norman McClay
Key Grip	Henry Maak	Henry Maak
2nd Co. Grip	*	Jack Boyd
Set Designer	Tracy R. Bousman	Tracy R. Bousman
Construction Foreman	Lowell Thomas	Lowell Thomas
Set Decorator	Chester Bayhi	Chester Bayhi
Lead Man	Gerald Kobold	Gerald Kobold
Property Master	Richard M. Rubin	Richard M. Rubin
2nd Prop Man	Ted Ross	Karl Brainard
Special Effects	Harry Redmond, Jr./ Thol Simonsen/ James Welcker	Pat Dinga
Special Photographic Effects	M. B. Paul/Larry Butler/Project Unlimited	Frank Van Der Veer/ Project Unlimited
Sound Mixer	Jay Ashworth	Jay Ashworth
Sound Recorder	Ray Barons	Richard D. Cook
Sound Boom Man	Don M. Valentine	Jerry Kosloff

*Information not available

TITLE	FIRST SEASON	SECOND SEASON
Sound Cable Man	Charles Knight	Charles Knight
Men's Costumer	Forrest T. Butler	Forrest T. Butler
Women's Costumer	Sabine Manela	Sabine Manela
Asst. Costumer	Michael Butler	Michael Butler
Makeup Artist	Fred B. Phillips	Fred B. Phillips
Hairdresser	Gertrude Reade	Gertrude Reade
Craft Serviceman	Frank Finochio	Frank Finochio
Transportation Captain	Dave Lesser	Dave Lesser
First Aid	John Ward	John Ward
Greensman	Harold Becker	Harold Becker
Painter	Robert Stephen	Robert Stephen

DAYSTAR OFFICE STAFF

Switchboard	Maryann Nadeau
Receptionist	Karen Warner
Messenger	Arthur Fisher

CASTING DEPARTMENT

Meryl Abeles was John Erman's assistant. When Erman left and Abeles was promoted, her assistant was Lee Wenner. In the second season, Harvey Claremont was assisted by his wife.

ACCOUNTING DEPARTMENT

Production Accountant: Robert C. Johnson
Elaine Michea's Secretary: Cathern Robinson
Staff: Robert Knoechel, Gertrude Pohle, Marge Townsend

OTHER FIRST SEASON CREW

Camera Assistant	John Harris
Draperies	Allen Price
Ass't Grips	Hilton Anderson Warren Ryan
Ass't Set Decoration	Warren Welch
Transportation Pool	Bob Alpert Jerry Cipperley Harold "Ham" Miller
Construction Crew	William H. Sheriff Peter Bal Hendrik Wyands Lonnie Stewart Chris Ebsen Hugh Langtry Richard Rankin George Puleo Walter Machado Origene Leduc
Electrical Department	James Barber Al Ronzo Richard Breitmeir George Breslaw Joseph Wharton Frank McKane Ralph McCarthy Robert McCarthy
Ass't Film Editors	Ray Daniels (stock shots) Robert Daniels (stock shots) William Keith

VILLA DI STEFANO

Assistant to the Producer	Tom Selden
Mr. Stefano's Secretary	Barbara Williams
Mr. Morheim's Secretary	Eleanor Tyrrell

The following credits were listed for the second season only.

Extra Talent-Casting	Hollywood Casting (Bob Cochrane)
Catering	Michaelson's
ABC-TV Representatives	David Heilweil, Mitch Gamson
ABC-TV Publicity Rep.	Fran McFall
UATV Representatives	Howard Gottfried, R. Don Guest, Dixon Dern
Mr. Lester's Assistant	Calvin Ward
Mr. Brady's Secretary	Carol Steffen
Assistant to the Producer	B. Ritchie Payne
Mr. White's Secretary	Colleen Dent
Mr. Lester's Secretary	Margaret Lutwen
Stereo/Process Projection (optical effects)	Bill Hansard
Board of Education	Florence Springer
American Humane Society	Harold Melniker

The Plant Manager at Paramount Sunset was Howard Davis. Consolidated Film Industries was the film processing lab used during both seasons. During the second season, two additional lab accounts were established at DuPont and Eastman. Script mimeographing services were the responsibility of Ed Leavitt throughout both seasons.

Index

Note: Italic-faced page listings refer to photographs.